WiX 3.6: A Developer's Guide to Windows Installer XML

An in-and-out, to-the-point introduction to Windows Installer XML

Nick Ramirez

BIRMINGHAM - MUMBAI

WiX 3.6: A Developer's Guide to Windows Installer XML

First published: October 2010

Second edition: December 2012

Production Reference: 1051212

Published by Packt Publishing Ltd.
Livery Place
35 Livery Street
Birmingham B3 2PB, UK.

ISBN 978-1-78216-042-7

www.packtpub.com

Cover Image by Abhishek Pandey (abhishek.pandey1210@gmail.com)

Credits

Author
Nick Ramirez

Reviewers
Neil Sleightholm
Martin Oberhammer
Paul Michniewicz
Roel van Bueren
ENG. Nir Bar

Acquisition Editor
Usha Iyer

Lead Technical Editor
Dayan Hyames

Technical Editor
Jalasha D'costa

Project Coordinator
Arshad Sopariwala

Proofreader
Maria Gould

Indexer
Rekha Nair

Production Coordinator
Arvindkumar Gupta

Cover Work
Arvindkumar Gupta

About the Author

Nick Ramirez is a software developer living in Columbus, Ohio. As a believer that deployment shouldn't be a moment of terror, he has become a big fan of technologies such as WiX. Other related interests include build automation, software architecture, and playing Portal 2. Nick lives with his wife and two cats.

I would like to thank the hard-working folks at Packt Publishing. Their organization and planning make all the difference! I would also like to thank the dedicated people of the WiX community, who tirelessly volunteer their time to answer questions. Finally, I would like to thank the developers who contribute source code to the WiX project. Their expertise and commitment have gone towards making the best Windows deployment tool on the market.

About the Reviewers

Neil Sleightholm is an IT consultant working in the UK. He has an engineering background with experience in software development, application architecture, electronics development, and mechanical engineering.

His current focus is on configuration management, build automation, installation development, and deployment.

Neil has worked with most of the Microsoft platform technologies and has programmed in C, C++, C#, Visual Basic, .NET, SQL, ASP.NET, and ASP. In the build and source control field he has experience with NAnt, MSBuild, TeamBuild, Subversion (SVN), TFS, VSS, Mercurial, and CVS. He has written installation systems using Windows Installer, Windows Installer XML (WiX), Windows Installer Custom Actions (using DTF), dotNetInstaller, InnoSetup, and Wise Installation System.

Neil has worked with open source projects and has been a contributor to Windows Installer XML (WiX), dotNetInstaller, and the AlienBBC plugin for Logitech Squeezebox.

In his spare time he is a petrol head and keen motorcyclist.

If you want to know more about him, you can check out his LinkedIn profile at: `http://www.linkedin.com/in/neilsleightholm`.

Martin Oberhammer currently works as a Software Engineer at Sophos in Vancouver, BC.

He studied computer science at the Johannes Kepler University in Linz, Austria, where he graduated in 2002. His first job in software deployment was at Utimaco Safeguard AG. In 2008, he moved to the USA and then to Canada, where he now resides. Nick and Martin where at one point colleagues and created a software installer using WiX technology.

Paul Michniewicz is a software developer and educational consultant with diverse experiences in academia, government, and industry.

As a developer, Paul has spent more than 12 years in software development and testing. Much of that time was spent in configuration management where he has managed source control systems, developed build and test automation strategies, and authored several installers in the enterprise space for companies such as JetForm and Adobe.

As an educational consultant, Paul has developed and delivered introductory Java courses to professionals and students. He currently runs a tutoring business where he teaches mathematics, physical sciences, and software development to students of all ages. Paul has a special interest in working with students who have developmental needs.

Paul lives in Ottawa, Canada with his wife Anne and two children Zygmunt and Moira. He is currently a stay-at-home dad and homeschools his son. To know more about Paul, you can check out his LinkedIn profile at `ca.linkedin.com/in/pmichnie`.

Roel van Bueren works as senior consultant, trainer, and developer for ROVABU NetWorks BV and ROVABU Software BV. Roel is specialized in Software Packaging using Windows Installer and Flexera AdminStudio, Application and Desktop Management by using Microsoft System Center Configuration Manager and Novell ZENworks Configuration Management, Desktop Deployment of Microsoft Windows XP, Windows 7, and Windows 8 by using Microsoft SCCM/MDT, Novell ZENworks Configuration Management, ENGL Imaging Toolkit, and also Microsoft .NET/C# development and application virtualization.

His latest projects involve "Bundle Commander" for Novell ZENworks Configuration Management and "Setup Commander" for Microsoft System Center Configuration Manager 2012, Microsoft Deployment Toolkit, and other deployment solutions such as Dell KACE and RES Automation Manager, for which customized transform files are needed to deploy MSI packages or silent switches to deploy legacy setups.

ENG. Nir Bar is a computer engineer, and graduate of Technion – Israel Institute of Technology.

Nir Bar has over 13 years experience in software and hardware development. He has worked with RAFAEL – Advanced Defense Systems, Marvell Technology Group, Agilent Technologies, Applied Materials, McKesson, and other leading high tech companies. He has worked in the Microsoft platform technologies and has programmed in C, C++, C# .NET, and SQL Server.

In the Linux platform, Nir Bar has programmed in C, C++, and PERL.

He is also experienced in pre-Silicon verification methodologies and tools. Currently, Nir is an independent software consultant, developer, and tutor. He consults and develops software products from the idea stage through analysis, design, development stages, and to ready-to-market products.

Nir Bar tutors Windows Installer technology to Israeli software companies.

To contact Nir Bar you can drop an e-mail to: `nir.bar@panel-sw.co.il`.

To my wife Sarit and to my sons Itay and Yehonathan for their love, support, and encouragement.

---

www.PacktPub.com

Support files, eBooks, discount offers and more

You might want to visit www.PacktPub.com for support files and downloads related to your book.

Did you know that Packt offers eBook versions of every book published, with PDF and ePub files available? You can upgrade to the eBook version at www.PacktPub.com and as a print book customer, you are entitled to a discount on the eBook copy. Get in touch with us at service@packtpub.com for more details.

At www.PacktPub.com, you can also read a collection of free technical articles, sign up for a range of free newsletters and receive exclusive discounts and offers on Packt books and eBooks.

http://PacktLib.PacktPub.com

Do you need instant solutions to your IT questions? PacktLib is Packt's online digital book library. Here, you can access, read and search across Packt's entire library of books.

Why Subscribe?

- Fully searchable across every book published by Packt
- Copy and paste, print and bookmark content
- On demand and accessible via web browser

Free Access for Packt account holders

If you have an account with Packt at www.PacktPub.com, you can use this to access PacktLib today and view nine entirely free books. Simply use your login credentials for immediate access.

To my wife, Heidi, for her patience while I disappeared into research and writing.

Table of Contents

Preface

Since *Rob Mensching* offered up the WiX toolset as the first open source project from Microsoft in 2004, it has been quietly gaining momentum and followers. Today, thousands use it to build Window Installer packages from simple XML elements. Gone are the days when you would have had to pay for software to build an installer for you. Now, you can do it yourself for cheap.

Not only that, but WiX has matured into a fairly slick product that's sufficiently easy to use. Best of all, it has the bells and whistles you want, including functionality to add user interface wizards, Start menu shortcuts, control Windows services, and read and write to the registry.

This new edition, *WiX 3.6: A Developer's Guide to Windows Installer XML*, brings you up-to-date on the latest changes to the toolset. Whether you're new to WiX or an established pro, you're likely to find new insights. Each chapter gets straight to the point, giving you hands-on experience, so you'll master the technology quickly.

What this book covers

Chapter 1, *Getting Started*, explains how after downloading and installing the WiX toolset, you'll start using it right away to create a simple installer. Then, you'll see how to add a basic user interface to it, install it with logging turned on, and view its internal database.

Chapter 2, *Creating Files and Directories*, gives you a deeper understanding of how files are installed and the best way to organize them in your project. You'll then use the tool Heat.exe to generate WiX markup. Last, you'll learn about copying and moving files, and installing special-case files.

Chapter 3, Putting Properties and AppSearch to Work, introduces you to Windows Installer properties, including those that are defined automatically and those that are invented by you. Afterwards, you'll check the end user's computer for specific files, directories, registry keys, and INI file settings using AppSearch.

Chapter 4, Improving Control with Launch Conditions and Installed States, teaches you to leverage conditional statements to set prerequisites for running your installer or to exclude particular features or components from the install. You'll also discover how to check the action state and installed state of your features and components.

Chapter 5, Understanding the Installation Sequence, gives you a clear picture of how the whole installation process works as you examine the order and meaning of installer actions. You will then create custom actions and add them to this built-in sequence. Then, you'll learn the basics of using the Deployment Tools Foundation library for writing custom action code in C#.

Chapter 6, Adding a User Interface, after giving you a quick introduction to the standard dialogue wizards that come with the WiX toolset, shows how to build your own from scratch. You'll learn all of the required elements for displaying dialogs and linking them together. You'll also see how to display common messages such as errors and cancellation confirmations.

Chapter 7, Using UI Controls, gives you hands-on experience with each type of UI control including buttons, textboxes, and progress bars.

Chapter 8, Tapping into Control Events, breathes life into your UI controls by having them publish and subscribe to events. We'll get details on what each event does and take a closer look at those you'll use on a routine basis.

Chapter 9, Working from the Command Line, emphasizes the fact that we don't particularly need Visual Studio to compile our projects. We'll cover the commands necessary to build an installer from the command line using Candle.exe, our compiler, and Light.exe, our linker/binder. We will also explore how to use preprocessor statements and how to create a custom preprocessor extension.

Chapter 10, Accessing the Windows Registry, illustrates how our installer may read and write to the Windows Registry. We'll add and remove keys, copy values, and set permissions.

Chapter 11, Controlling Windows Services, provides some solid examples for installing and interacting with Windows services. You'll see how to set the service's user account, add service dependencies, and set failure recovery.

Chapter 12, Localizing Your Installer, tackles how to render your UI for different languages and how Light.exe, the WiX linker, plays a role. You'll then get involved in making a single multi-language installer.

Chapter 13, Upgrading and Patching, covers the all-so-important topic of upgrading and patching. You'll get the low down on major upgrades, minor upgrades, and small updates.

Chapter 14, Extending WiX, jumps into adding new, custom XML elements for extending the core functionality of WiX. We'll write a library, using C#, that takes our installer to places it's never been.

Chapter 15, Bootstrapping Prerequisites with Burn, discusses the new bootstrapping functionality called Burn. We'll create a single executable that installs all necessary prerequisites for our software.

Chapter 16, Customizing the Burn UI, solves the problem of customizing our Burn user interface by crafting a new one using C# and WPF. We'll discover the places where we can hook into the bootstrapper engine and how best to pass information from the user to our installation packages.

What you need for this book

In order to both write and run the code demonstrated in this book, you will need the following:

- Visual Studio 2005 or newer (Standard Edition or higher)
- The WiX toolset, which can be downloaded from `http://wixtoolset.org/`

Who this book is for

If you are a developer and want to create installers for software targeting the Windows platform, then this book is for you. Those new to WiX and Windows Installer should feel right at home as we start with the basics and gradually work up to more complex subjects. Others with more experience will benefit as we catalog the new features in WiX 3.6. If you're coming from an earlier version of WiX, you'll be happy to know that for the most part, things that used to work will still work. However, several tasks, such as implementing a major upgrade, have been simplified. We'll highlight the big changes, but keep an eye on familiar elements as some subtle changes have been made.

Conventions

In this book, you will find a number of styles of text that distinguish between different kinds of information. Here are some examples of these styles, and an explanation of their meaning.

Code words in text are shown as follows: "If you would like conditions to be re-evaluated during a re-install, you should set the Transitive attribute on the parent component to yes."

A block of code is set as follows:

```
<Feature Id="MainFeature"
        Title="Main Feature"
        Level="1">
  <ComponentRef Id="CMP_InstallMeTXT" />

  <Condition Level="0">
    <![CDATA[NOT REMOVE = "ALL" AND MyProperty = "some value"]]>
  </Condition>
</Feature>
```

When we wish to draw your attention to a particular part of a code block, the relevant lines or items are set in bold:

```
<Property Id="MyProperty"
        Value="1" />
<Component Id="CMP_InstallMeTXT"
         Guid="7AB5216B-2DB5-4A8A-9293-F6711FFAAA83">
  <File Id="FILE_InstallMeTXT"
      Source="InstallMe.txt"
      KeyPath="yes" />
  <Condition>MyProperty = 1</Condition>
</Component>
```

Any command-line input or output is written as follows:

```
msiexec /i myInstaller.msi /l*v install.log
```

New terms and **important words** are shown in bold. Words that you see on the screen, in menus or dialog boxes for example, appear in the text like this: "using the **Add Reference** option in **Solution Explorer**".

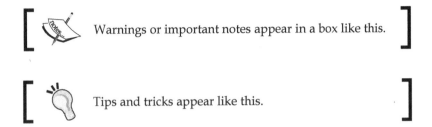

Warnings or important notes appear in a box like this.

Tips and tricks appear like this.

Reader feedback

Feedback from our readers is always welcome. Let us know what you think about this book—what you liked or may have disliked. Reader feedback is important for us to develop titles that you really get the most out of.

To send us general feedback, simply send an e-mail to feedback@packtpub.com, and mention the book title through the subject of your message.

If there is a topic that you have expertise in and you are interested in either writing or contributing to a book, see our author guide on www.packtpub.com/authors.

Customer support

Now that you are the proud owner of a Packt book, we have a number of things to help you to get the most from your purchase.

Downloading the example code

You can download the example code files for all Packt books you have purchased from your account at http://www.packtpub.com. If you purchased this book elsewhere, you can visit http://www.packtpub.com/support and register to have the files e-mailed directly to you.

Errata

Although we have taken every care to ensure the accuracy of our content, mistakes do happen. If you find a mistake in one of our books—maybe a mistake in the text or the code—we would be grateful if you would report this to us. By doing so, you can save other readers from frustration and help us improve subsequent versions of this book. If you find any errata, please report them by visiting http://www.packtpub. com/support, selecting your book, clicking on the **errata submission form** link, and entering the details of your errata. Once your errata are verified, your submission will be accepted and the errata will be uploaded to our website, or added to any list of existing errata, under the Errata section of that title.

Piracy

Piracy of copyright material on the Internet is an ongoing problem across all media. At Packt, we take the protection of our copyright and licenses very seriously. If you come across any illegal copies of our works, in any form, on the Internet, please provide us with the location address or website name immediately so that we can pursue a remedy.

Please contact us at copyright@packtpub.com with a link to the suspected pirated material.

We appreciate your help in protecting our authors, and our ability to bring you valuable content.

Questions

You can contact us at questions@packtpub.com if you are having a problem with any aspect of the book, and we will do our best to address it.

1
Getting Started

Windows Installer XML (WiX) is a free, open source XML markup that's used to author installation packages for Windows-based software. The underlying technology is called Windows Installer, which is the established standard for installing to any Windows operating system. Until recently, WiX was a Microsoft offering, but is now supported by the non-profit Outercurve Foundation. It is used by countless companies around the world. Microsoft uses it to deploy its own software including Microsoft Office and Visual Studio. In fact, Microsoft uses WiX for these products.

Windows Installer has many features, but how do you leverage them? How do you even know what they are? This book will help you by making you more familiar with the wide range of capabilities that are available. The good news is that WiX makes many of the arcane and difficult-to-understand aspects of the Windows Installer technology simple to use. This book will teach you the WiX syntax so that you can create a professional-grade installer that's right for you.

In this chapter, we will cover the following topics:

- Getting WiX and using it with Visual Studio
- Creating your first WiX installer
- Examining an installer database with Orca
- Logging an installation process
- Adding a simple user interface

Introducing Windows Installer XML

In this section, we'll dive right in and talk about what WiX is, where to get it, and why you'd want to use it when building an installation package for your software. We'll follow up with a quick description of the WiX tools and the new project types made available in Visual Studio.

What is WiX?

Creating a Windows Installer, or **MSI** package, has always been a challenging task. The package is actually a relational database that describes how the various components of an application should be unpacked and copied to the end user's computer.

In the past you had two options:

- You could try to author the database yourself — a path that requires a thorough knowledge of the Windows Installer API.

- You could buy a commercial product such as InstallShield to do it for you. These software products will take care of the details, but you'll forever be dependent on them. There will always be parts of the process that are hidden from you.

WiX offers a route that exists somewhere in the middle. Abstracting away the low-level function calls while still allowing you to write much of the code by hand, WiX is a framework for building an installer in ways that mere mortals can grasp. Best of all, it's free. As an open source product, it has quickly garnered a wide user base and a dedicated community of developers. Much of this has to do not only with its price tag but also with its simplicity. It can be authored in a simple text editor (such as Notepad) and compiled with the tools provided by WiX. As it's a flavor of XML, it can be read by humans, edited without expensive software, and lends itself to being stored in source control where it can be easily merged and compared.

The examples in this first chapter will show how to create a simple installer with WiX using Visual Studio. However, later chapters will show how you can build your project from the command line using the compiler and linker from the WiX toolset. The WiX source code is available for download, so you can be assured that nothing about the process will be hidden if you truly need to know more about it.

Is WiX for you?

It's fairly simple to copy files to an end user's computer. If that's all your product needs, then the Windows Installer technology might be overkill. However, there are many benefits to creating an installable package for your customers, some of which might be overlooked. The following is a list of features that you get when you author a Windows Installer package with WiX:

- All of your executable files can be packaged into one convenient bundle, simplifying deployment
- Your software is automatically registered with **Programs and Features**
- Windows takes care of uninstalling all of the components that make up your product when the user chooses to do so
- If files for your software are accidently removed, they can be replaced by right-clicking on the MSI file and selecting **Repair**
- You can create different versions of your installer and detect which version has been installed
- You can create patches to update only specific areas of your application
- If something goes wrong while installing your software, the end user's computer can be rolled back to a previous state
- You can create Wizard-style dialogs to guide the user through the installation

Many people today simply expect that your installer will have these features. Not having them could be seen as a real deficit. For example, what is a user supposed to do when they want to uninstall your product but can't find it in the **Programs and Features** list and there isn't an uninstall shortcut? They're likely to remove files in a haphazard manner and wonder why you didn't make things easy for them.

Maybe you've already figured that Windows Installer is the way to go, but why WiX? One of my favorite reasons is that it gives you greater control over how things work. You get a much finer level of control over the development process. Commercial software that does this for you also produces an MSI file but hides the details about how it was done. It's analogous to crafting a website. You get much more control when you write the HTML yourself as opposed to using a WYSIWYG software.

Even though WiX gives you more control, it doesn't make things overly complex. You'll find that making a simple installer is very straightforward. For more complicated projects, the parts can be split up into multiple XML source files to make it easier to work with. Going further, if your product is made up of multiple applications that will be installed together as a suite, you can compile the different chunks into libraries that can be merged together into a single MSI file. This allows each team to isolate and manage its part of the installation package.

WiX is a stable technology, having been first released to the public in 2004, so you don't have to worry about it disappearing. It's also had a steady progression of version releases. These are just some of the reasons why you might choose to use WiX.

Where can I get it?

You can find the latest version of WiX at http://wixtoolset.org/, which has both stable releases and weekly builds. The current release is Version 3.6. Once you've downloaded the WiX installer package, double-click on it to launch it. It relies on having an Internet connection to download the .NET 4.0 platform, if it's not already installed.

If you want to install on a computer that isn't connected to the Internet, first download the installer on a computer that is and then open a command prompt and run the WiX executable with the following command wix36.exe /layout LayoutDirectory. The layout option takes the name of a target directory where the WiX files will be downloaded to. You can then take these files (which include a new installer) to the computer that doesn't have an Internet connection and use them there.

This installs all of the necessary files needed to build WiX projects. You'll also get the WiX SDK documentation and the settings for Visual Studio IntelliSense and project templates. Version 3.6 supports Visual Studio versions 2005 through 2012, although not the Express editions.

WiX comes with the tools outlined in the following table:

Tool	What it does
Candle.exe	Compiles WiX source files (.wxs) into intermediate object files (.wixobj)
Light.exe	Links and binds .wixobj files to create a final .msi file. Also creates cabinet files and embeds streams in an MSI database
Lit.exe	Creates WiX libraries (.wixlib) that can be linked together by Light
Dark.exe	Decompiles an MSI file into WiX code
Heat.exe	Creates a WiX source file that specifies components from various inputs
Insignia.exe	Inscribes an MSI with the digital signatures that its external CAB files are signed with
Melt.exe	Converts a merge module (.msm) into a component group in a WiX source file
Torch.exe	Generates a transform file used to apply changes to an in-progress installation or to create a patch file
Shine	Creates a DGML diagram from an MSI
Smoke.exe	Runs validation checks on an MSI or MSM file
Pyro.exe	Creates a patch file (.msp) from .wixmsp and .wixmst files
WixCop.exe	Converts Version 2 WiX files to Version 3
WixUnit.exe	Validates WiX source files
Lux.exe and Nit.exe	Authors and runs unit tests on custom actions

In order to use some of the functionality in WiX, you may need to download a more recent version of Windows Installer. You can check your current version by viewing the help file for `msiexec.exe`, which is the Windows Installer service. Open a Windows command prompt and then type `msiexec /?` to bring up a window, as shown in the following screenshot:

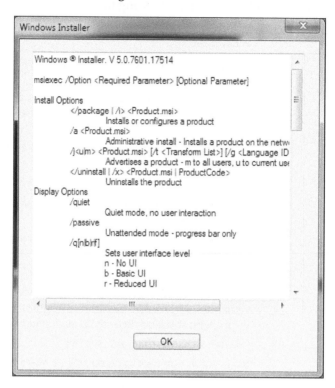

If you'd like to install a newer version of Windows Installer, you can get it from the Microsoft Download Center website. Go to:

`http://www.microsoft.com/downloads/en/default.aspx`

Search for **Windows Installer**. The current version for Windows XP, Vista, Server 2003, and Server 2008 is 4.5. Windows 7, Windows Server 2008 R2, and Windows 8 can support Version 5.0. Each new version is backwards compatible and includes the features from earlier editions.

Visual Studio package (Votive)

The WiX toolset provides files that update Visual Studio to provide new WiX IntelliSense and project templates. Together these features, which are installed for you along with the other WiX tools, are called **Votive**. You must have Visual Studio 2005 or newer. Votive won't work on the Express versions. Refer to the WiX site for more information:

```
http://wix.sourceforge.net/votive.html
```

After you've installed WiX, you should see a new category of project types in Visual Studio labeled under the title **Windows Installer XML**, as shown in the following screenshot:

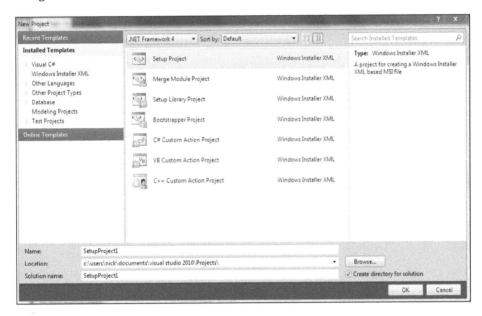

There are seven new project templates:

- **Setup Project**: Creates a Windows Installer package from one or more WiX source files
- **Merge Module Project**: Creates a merge module (MSM) file
- **Setup Library Project**: Creates a .wixlib library
- **Bootstrapper Project**: Creates a prerequisite bootstrapper
- **C# Custom Action Project**: Creates a .NET custom action in C#
- **C++ Custom Action Project**: Creates an unmanaged C++ custom action
- **VB Custom Action Project**: Creates a VB.NET custom action

Using these templates is certainly easier than creating the files on your own with a text editor. To start creating your own MSI installer, select the template **Setup Project**. This will create a new `.wxs` (WiX source file) for you to add XML markup to. Once we've added the necessary markup, you'll be able to build the solution by selecting **Build Solution** from the **Build** menu or by right-clicking on the project in the **Solution Explorer** and selecting **Build**. Visual Studio will take care of calling `candle.exe` and `light.exe` to compile and link your project files.

If you right-click on your WiX project in **Solution Explorer** and select **Properties**, you'll see several screens where you can tweak the build process. One thing you'll want to do is set the amount of information that you'd like to see when compiling and linking the project, and how non-critical messages are treated. Refer to the following screenshot:

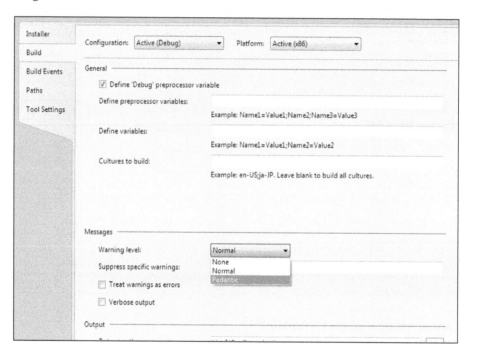

Here we're selecting the level of messages that we'd like to see. To see all warnings and messages, set **Warning Level** to **Pedantic**. You can also check the **Verbose output** checkbox to get even more information. Checking **Treat warnings as errors** will cause warning messages that normally would not stop the build to be treated as fatal errors.

You can also choose to suppress certain warnings. You'll need to know the specific warning message number though. If you get a build-time warning, you'll see the warning message, but not the number. One way to get it is to open the WiX source code (available at `http://wix.codeplex.com/releases/view/93929`) and view the `messages.xml` file in the `src\wix\Data` folder. Search the file for the warning and from there you'll see its number. Note that you can suppress warnings but not errors.

Another feature of WiX is its ability to run validity checks on the MSI package. Windows Installer uses a suite of tests called **Internal Consistency Evaluators (ICEs)** for this. These checks ensure that the database as a whole makes sense and that the keys on each table join correctly. Through Votive, you can choose to suppress specific ICE tests. Use the **Tools Setting** page of the project's properties as shown in the following screenshot:

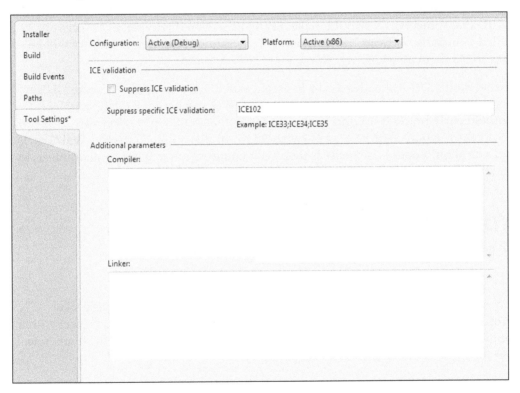

In this example, ICE test 102 is being suppressed. You can specify more than one test by separating them with semicolons. To find a full list of ICE tests, go to MSDN's **ICE Reference** web page at:

`http://msdn.microsoft.com/en-us/library/aa369206%28VS.85%29.aspx`

The **Tool Settings** screen also gives you the ability to add compiler or linker command-line flags. Simply add them to the textboxes at the bottom of the screen. We will discuss command-line arguments for Candle and Light later in the book.

A word about GUIDs

In various places throughout WiX, you'll be asked to provide a **GUID**, which is a **Globally Unique Identifier**. This is so that when your product is installed on the end user's computer, references to it can be stored in the Windows Registry without the chance of having name conflicts. By using GUIDs, Windows Installer can be sure that every software application, and even every component of that software, has a unique identity on the system.

Each GUID that you create on your computer is guaranteed to be different from a GUID that someone else would make. Using this, even if two pieces of software, both called "Amazing Software", are installed on the same computer, Windows will be able to tell them apart.

Visual Studio 2010 provides a way to create a GUID. Go to **Tools | Create GUID** and copy a new GUID using **Registry Format**. WiX can accept a GUID with or without curly brackets around it, as 01234567-89AB-CDEF-0123-456789ABCDEF or {01234567-89AB-CDEF-0123-456789ABCDEF}. In this book, I'll display real GUIDs, but you should not re-use them as then your components will not be guaranteed to be unique.

Your first WiX project

To get started, download the WiX toolset. It can be found at:

http://wixtoolset.org/

Once you've downloaded and installed it, open Visual Studio and select **New Project | Windows Installer XML | Setup Project**. This will create a project with a single .wxs (WiX source) file. Visual Studio will usually call this file Product.wxs, but the name could be anything as long as it ends with .wxs.

Even the most minimal installer must have the following XML elements:

- An XML declaration
- A Wix element that serves as the root element in your XML document
- A Product element that is a child to the Wix element, but all other elements are children to it
- A Package element

- A `Media` or `MediaTemplate` element
- At least one `Directory` element with at least one child `Component` element
- A `Feature` element

XML declaration and Wix element

Every WiX project begins with an XML declaration and a `Wix` element:

```
<?xml version="1.0" encoding="UTF-8"?>
<Wix xmlns="http://schemas.microsoft.com/wix/2006/wi">

</Wix>
```

Downloading the example code

You can download the example code files for all Packt books you have purchased from your account at http://www.packtpub.com. If you purchased this book elsewhere, you can visit http://www.packtpub.com/support and register to have the files e-mailed directly to you.

The **xmlns**, or XML namespace, just brings the core WiX elements into the local scope of your document. At the bottom of the file you'll have to close the `Wix` element, of course. Otherwise, it's not valid XML. The `Wix` element is the root element of the document. It comes first and last. All other elements will be nested inside of it.

For the most part, knowing only the basic rules of writing a well-formed XML document will be enough to get you up and running using WiX. The major points are as follows, as recommended by the W3C:

- The document must begin and end with the same root element
- All elements must have a matching closing tag or be closed themselves
- XML tags are case sensitive
- Elements must be properly nested, with inner elements not overlapping outer elements
- XML attributes should be quoted

At this point, you could also add the `RequiredVersion` attribute to the `Wix` element. Given a WiX toolset version number, such as "3.6.3303.0", it won't let anyone compile the `.wxs` file unless they have that version or higher installed. If, on the other hand, you're the only one compiling your project, then it's no big deal.

The Product element

Next, add a `Product` element.

```
<Wix ... >
  <Product Id="3E786878-358D-43AD-82D1-1435ADF9F6EA"
           Name="Awesome Software"
           Language="1033"
           Version="1.0.0.0"
           Manufacturer="Awesome Company"
           UpgradeCode="B414C827-8D81-4B4A-B3B6-338C06DE3A11">
  </Product>
</Wix>
```

This is where you define the characteristics of the software you're installing: its name, language, version, and manufacturer. The end user will be able to see these properties by right-clicking on your MSI file, selecting **Properties**, and viewing the **Summary** tab. Most of the time, these values will stay the same from one build of your project to the next. The exception is when you want to increment the software's version to indicate that it's an upgrade of a previous installation. In that case, you need to only change the `Version` attribute, and sometimes the `Id` attribute. We'll talk more about upgrading previous installations later on in the book.

The `Product` element's `Id` attribute represents the so-called **ProductCode** of your software. It's always a unique number — a GUID — that Windows will use to uniquely identify your software (and tell if it's already installed on the computer). You can either hardcode it, like here, or just put an asterisk. That way, WiX will pick a new GUID for you each time you compile the project.

```
<Wix ... >
  <Product Id="*"
           Name="Awesome Software"
           Language="1033"
           Version="1.0.0.0"
           Manufacturer="Awesome Company"
           UpgradeCode="B414C827-8D81-4B4A-B3B6-338C06DE3A11">
  </Product>
</Wix>
```

The `Name` attribute defines the name of the software. In addition to being displayed in the MSI file's **Properties** page, it will also be shown in various places throughout the user interface of your installer — that is, once you've added a user interface, which we'll touch on at the end of this chapter.

The Language attribute is used to display error messages and progress information in the specified language to the user. It's a decimal language ID (LCID). A full list can be found on Microsoft's LCID page at:

`http://msdn.microsoft.com/en-us/goglobal/bb964664.aspx`

The previous example used "1033", which stands for "English-United States". If your installer uses characters not found in the ASCII character set, you'll also need to add a Codepage attribute set to the code page that contains those characters. Don't worry too much about this now. We'll cover languages and code pages later in the book when we talk about localization.

The Version attribute is used to set the version number of your software. It can accept up to four numbers separated by periods. Typically, when you make a big enough change to the existing software, you'll increment the number. Companies often use the [MajorVersion].[MinorVersion].[Build].[Revision] format, but you're free to use any numbering system you like.

 During upgrade scenarios, the fourth digit in the Version attribute is ignored and won't make a difference when detecting previously installed software.

The Manufacturer attribute tells the user who this software is from and usually contains the name of your company. This is another bit of information that's available via the MSI file's **Properties** page.

The final attribute to consider is UpgradeCode. This should be set to a GUID and will identify your product across releases. It remains constant for a product line, even among different product versions. Think: Microsoft Office 2007 and Office 2010. Both would have the same UpgradeCode. Therefore, it should stay the same even when the ProductCode and Version change.

Windows will use this number in its efforts to keep track of all the software installed on the machine. WiX has the ability to search for previously installed versions of not only your own software, but also those created by others and it uses UpgradeCode to do it. Although, technically, this is an optional attribute, you should always supply it.

The Package element

Once you've defined your `Product` element, the next step is to nest a `Package` element inside. An example is shown as follows:

```
<Wix ... >
  <Product ... >
    <Package InstallerVersion="301"
             Compressed="yes"
             InstallScope="perMachine"
             Manufacturer="Awesome Company"
             Description="Installs Awesome Software"
             Keywords="Practice,Installer,MSI"
             Comments="(c) 2012 Awesome Company" />
  </Product>
</Wix>
```

Of the attributes shown in this example, only `Compressed` is really required. By setting `Compressed` to `yes`, you're telling the installer to package all of the MSI's resources into CAB files. Later, you'll define these CAB files with `Media` elements or a `MediaTemplate` element.

Technically, an `Id` attribute is also required, but by omitting it you're letting WiX create one for you. You'd have to create a new one anyway since every time you change your software or the installer in any way, the *package* (the MSI file) has changed and so the package's ID must change. This really, in itself, emphasizes what the `Package` element is. Unlike the `Product` element, which describes the software that's in the installer, the `Package` element describes the installer itself. Once you've built it, you'll be able to right-click on the MSI and select **Properties** to see the attributes you've set here.

The `InstallerVersion` attribute can be set to require a specific version of `msiexec.exe` (the Windows Installer service that installs the MSI when you double-click on it) to be installed on the end user's computer. If they have an older version, Windows Installer will display a dialog telling them that they need to upgrade. It will also prevent you from compiling the project unless you also have this version installed on your own computer. The value can be found by multiplying the major version by 100 and adding the minor version. So, for Version 4.5 of `msiexec.exe`, you'd set `InstallerVersion` to `405`.

The `InstallScope` attribute can be set to either `perMachine` or `perUser`. The former means that your software will be installed in the "All Users" context, meaning that all users will be able to access your application. As such, the person performing the install will need elevated privileges on a UAC enabled system such as Windows 7 to continue the installation. The latter means that it will be installed only for the current user. Behind the scenes this is setting a WiX property called `ALLUSERS` that we'll cover in more detail later when we discuss properties.

The rest of the attributes shown provide additional information for the MSI file's **Properties** window. `Manufacturer` is displayed in the **Author** text field, `Description` is shown as **Subject**, `Keywords` show up as **Keywords**, and `Comments` show as **Comments**. It's usually a good idea to provide at least some of this information, if just to help *you* distinguish one MSI package from another.

The MediaTemplate element

The files that you intend to install are compressed into **CAB** files and shipped along with the installer. You decide whether to embed them inside the MSI or provide them visibly alongside it. In WiX 3.6, a single `MediaTemplate` element handles all the details for you, intelligently splitting your files into the prescribed number of CAB files. Add it after the `Package` element, as shown in the following code snippet:

```
<Wix …>
  <Product … >
    <Package … />
    <MediaTemplate EmbedCab="yes" />
  </Product>
</Wix>
```

The `EmbedCab` attribute is optional and sets whether the CAB files will be embedded inside the MSI, the default being to not embed them. Either way, WiX will create up to 999 CAB files, each holding a maximum of 200 MB of data. You can change that limit with the `MaximumUncompressedMediaSize` attribute, set to a size in megabytes. If a single file is bigger than the maximum, it will be placed into its own CAB file with enough space to accommodate it.

If you want to split your installation up into several physical disks — conjure up images of "Please insert disk 2" — you want to use the `Media` element instead.

The Media element

The Media element is an older element that was replaced by MediaTemplate and if you use one you can't use the other. However, in some cases, the Media element is the only thing for the job. For each Media element that you add to your WiX markup, a new CAB file will be created.

```
<Wix ... >
  <Product ... >
    <Package ... />
    <Media Id="1"
           Cabinet="media1.cab"
           EmbedCab="yes" />
  </Product>
</Wix>
```

Each Media element gets a unique Id attribute to distinguish it in the MSI **Media** table. It must be a positive integer. If the files that you add to your installation package don't explicitly state which CAB file they wish to be packaged into, they'll default to using a Media element with an Id value of 1. Therefore, your first Media element should always use an Id value of 1.

The Cabinet attribute sets the name of the CAB file. You won't actually see this unless you set EmbedCab to no, in which case the file will be shipped alongside the MSI. This is atypical, but might be done to split the installation files onto several disks.

If you do choose to split the installation up into several physical disks (or even virtual ISO images), you'll want to add the DiskPrompt and VolumeLabel attributes. In the following example, I've added two Media elements instead of one. I've also added a Property element above them, which defines a variable called DiskPrompt with a value of Amazing Software - [1].

```
<Property Id="DiskPrompt"
          Value="Amazing Software - [1]" />

<Media Id="1"
       Cabinet="media1.cab"
       EmbedCab="no"
       DiskPrompt="Disk 1"
       VolumeLabel="Disk1" />

<Media Id="2"
       Cabinet="media2.cab"
       EmbedCab="no"
       DiskPrompt="Disk 2"
       VolumeLabel="Disk2" />
```

The `Property` element will be used as the text in the message box the end user sees, prompting them to insert the next disk. The text in the `DiskPrompt` attribute is combined with the text in the property's value, switched with [1], to change the message for each subsequent disk. Make sure you give this property an `Id` value of `DiskPrompt`.

So that Windows will know when the correct disk is inserted, the `VolumeLabel` attribute must match the "Volume Label" of the actual disk, which you'll set with whichever CD or DVD burning program you use. Once you've built your project, include the MSI file and the first CAB file on the first disk. The second CAB file should then be written to a second disk.

Although we haven't described the `File` element yet, it's used to add a file to the installation package. To include one in a *specific* CAB file, add the `DiskId` attribute, set to the `Id` attribute of the corresponding `Media` element. The following example includes a text file called `myFile.txt` in the `media2.cab` file:

```
<File Id="fileTXT"
      Name="myFile.txt"
      Source="myFile.txt"
      KeyPath="yes"
      DiskId="2" />
```

We'll discuss the `File` element in more detail later on in the chapter. If you're only using one `Media` element, you won't need to specify the `DiskId` attribute on your `File` elements.

The Directory element

So, now we've defined the identity of the product, set up its package properties, and told the installer to create a CAB file to package up the things that we'll eventually install. Then, how do you decide where your product will get installed *to* on the end user's computer? How do we set the default install path, for example, to some folder under `Program Files`?

When you want to install to `C:\Program Files`, you can use a sort of shorthand. There are several directory properties provided by Windows Installer that will be translated to their true paths at install time. For example, `ProgramFilesFolder` usually translates to `C:\Program Files`. The following is a list of these built-in directory properties:

Directory property	Actual path
AdminToolsFolder	Full path to directory containing administrative tools
AppDataFolder	Full path to roaming folder for current user
CommonAppDataFolder	Full path to application data for all users
CommonFiles64Folder	Full path to the 64-bit `Common Files` folder
CommonFilesFolder	Full path to the `Common Files` folder for current user
DesktopFolder	Full path to the `Desktop` folder
FavoritesFolder	Full path to the `Favorites` folder for current user
FontsFolder	Full path to the `Fonts` folder
LocalAppDataFolder	Full path to folder containing local (non-roaming) applications
MyPicturesFolder	Full path to the `Pictures` folder
NetHoodFolder	Full path to the `NetHood` folder
PersonalFolder	Full path to the `Documents` folder for current user
PrintHoodFolder	Full path to the `PrintHood` folder
ProgramFiles64Folder	Full path to the 64-bit `Program Files` folder
ProgramFilesFolder	Full path to 32-bit `Program Files` folder
ProgramMenuFolder	Full path to `Program Menu` folder
RecentFolder	Full path to `Recent` folder
SendToFolder	Full path to the `SendTo` folder for current user
StartMenuFolder	Full path to the `Start Menu` folder
StartupFolder	Full path to the `Startup` folder
System16Folder	Full path to the 16-bit system DLLs folder
System64Folder	Full path to the `System64` folder
SystemFolder	Full path to the `System` folder for current user
TempFolder	Full path to the `Temp` folder
TemplateFolder	Full path to the `Template` folder for current user
WindowsFolder	Full path to the `Windows` folder

This list can also be found at:
`http://msdn.microsoft.com/en-us/library/windows/desktop/aa370905(v=vs.85).aspx`

The easiest way to add your own directories is to nest them inside one of the predefined ones. For example, to create a new directory called `Install Practice` inside the `Program Files` folder, you could add it as a child to `ProgramFilesFolder`. To define your directory structure in WiX, use `Directory` elements:

```
<Wix ... >
  <Product ... >
    <Package ... />
    <MediaTemplate ... />

    <Directory Id="TARGETDIR"
               Name="SourceDir">
      <Directory Id="ProgramFilesFolder">
        <Directory Id="MyProgramDir"
                   Name="Install Practice" />
      </Directory>
    </Directory>

  </Product>
</Wix>
```

One thing to know is that you must start your `Directory` elements hierarchy with a `Directory` element with an `Id` attribute of `TARGETDIR` and a `Name` value of `SourceDir`. This sets up the "root" directory of your installation. Therefore, be sure to always create it first and nest all other `Directory` elements inside.

By default, Windows Installer sets `TARGETDIR` to the local hard drive with the most free space—in most cases, the `C:` drive. However, you can set `TARGETDIR` to another drive letter during installation. You might, for example, set it with a `VolumeSelectCombo` user interface control. We'll talk about setting properties and UI controls later in the book.

A `Directory` element always has an `Id` attribute that will serve as a primary key on the `Directory` table. If you're using a predefined name, such as `ProgramFilesFolder`, use that for `Id`. Otherwise, you can make one up yourself. The previous example creates a new directory called `Install Practice`, inside the `Program Files` folder. `Id`, `MyProgramDir`, is an arbitrary value.

When creating your own directory, you must provide the Name attribute. This sets the name of the new folder. Without it, the directory won't be created and any files that were meant to go inside it will instead be placed in the parent directory — in this case, Program Files. Note that you do not need to provide a Name attribute for predefined directories.

You can nest more subdirectories inside your folders by adding more Directory elements. The following is an example:

```
<Directory Id="TARGETDIR"
           Name="SourceDir">
  <Directory Id="ProgramFilesFolder">
    <Directory Id="MyProgramDir"
               Name="Install Practice">
      <Directory Id="MyFirstSubDir"
                 Name="Subdirectory 1">
        <Directory Id="MySecondSubDir"
                   Name="Subdirectory 2" />
      </Directory>
    </Directory>
  </Directory>
</Directory>
```

Here, a subdirectory called Subdirectory 1 is placed inside the Install Practice folder. A second subdirectory, called Subdirectory 2, is then placed inside Subdirectory 1, giving us two levels of nested directories under Install Practice.

If you've been following along using the Visual Studio Setup Project template, you'll notice that it places its boilerplate Directory elements inside of a Fragment element. We will discuss Fragment in the next chapter.

Before jumping into how to add files to your new directories, we should cover the elements that define the files themselves. The next section covers how to create **components**, which are the containers for the files you want to install.

The Component element

Once you've mapped out the directories that you want to target or create during the installation, the next step is to copy files into them. To really explain things, we'll need something to install. So let's create a simple text file and add it to our project's directory. We'll call it `InstallMe.txt`. For our purposes, it doesn't really matter what's in the text file. We just need something for testing.

Name	Date modified	Type
bin	7/15/2012 6:54 PM	File folder
AwesomeSoftware.wixproj	7/15/2012 6:54 PM	WiX Project File
InstallMe.txt	7/15/2012 6:58 PM	Text Document
Product.wxs	7/15/2012 6:57 PM	WiX Source File

Windows Installer expects every file to be wrapped up in a component before it's installed. It doesn't matter what type of file it is either. Each gets its own `Component` element.

Components, which always have a unique GUID, allow Windows to track every file that gets installed on the end user's computer. During an installation, this information is stored away in the registry. This lets Windows find every piece of your product during an uninstall so that your software can be completely removed. It also uses it to replace missing files during a **repair**, which you can trigger by right-clicking on an MSI file and selecting **Repair**.

Each `Component` element gets a unique GUID via its `Guid` attribute. To create a GUID in Visual Studio, go to **Tools | Create GUID** and copy a new GUID using the registry format. The component's `Id` attribute is up to you. It will serve as the primary key for the component in the MSI database, so each one must also be unique:

```
<Component Id="CMP_InstallMeTXT"
          Guid="E8A58B7B-F031-4548-9BDD-7A6796C8460D">

   <File Id="FILE_MyProgramDir_InstallMeTXT"
         Source="InstallMe.txt"
         KeyPath="yes" />
</Component>
```

In the preceding code snippet, I've created a new component called `CMP_InstallMeTXT`. I've started it with `CMP_` to label it as a component, which is just a convention that I like to use. Although it isn't required, it helps to prefix components in this way so that it's always clear what sort of element it refers to.

The `File` element inside the component references the file that's going to be installed. Here, it's the `InstallMe.txt` file located in the current directory (which is the same directory as your WiX source file). You can specify a relative or absolute path with the `Source` attribute.

You should always mark a `File` element as the **KeyPath** file and you should only ever include one `File` inside a component. A `KeyPath` file will be replaced if it's missing when the user triggers a repair (Windows Installer documentation calls this **resiliency**). Placing more than one `File` element inside a single `Component` element, at least in most cases, is not recommended. This is because only one file can be the `KeyPath` file, so the other files wouldn't be covered by a repair. You would really only ever place more than one `File` in a component if you *didn't* want the extra files to be resilient.

To add a component to a directory, you have several options. The first, which is the simplest, is to add your `Component` elements directly inside the target `Directory` element, as given in the following code snippet:

```
<Directory Id="TARGETDIR"
           Name="SourceDir">
  <Directory Id="ProgramFilesFolder">
    <Directory Id="MyProgramDir"
               Name="Install Practice">

      <Component Id="CMP_InstallMeTXT"
                 Guid="E8A58B7B-F031-4548-9BDD-7A6796C8460D">

        <File Id="FILE_MyProgramDir_InstallMeTXT"
              Source="InstallMe.txt"
              KeyPath="yes" />
      </Component>
    </Directory>
  </Directory>
</Directory>
```

In the previous code snippet, I've instructed the installer to copy the `InstallMe.txt` file to the `%ProgramFiles%\Install Practice` folder that we're creating on the end user's computer. Although this is the simplest solution, it isn't the cleanest. For one thing, if you're installing more than a handful of files, the XML file can begin to look tangled.

Another approach is to use a `DirectoryRef` element to reference your directories. This has the benefit of keeping the markup that defines your directories independent from the markup that adds files to those directories. The following is an example:

```
<Directory Id="TARGETDIR"
           Name="SourceDir">
  <Directory Id="ProgramFilesFolder">
    <Directory Id="MyProgramDir"
               Name="Install Practice" />
  </Directory>
</Directory>

<DirectoryRef Id="MyProgramDir">
  <Component ...>
    <File ... />
  </Component>
</DirectoryRef>
```

A third option is to group your components inside of a **ComponentGroup** and use its `Directory` attribute to set the target directory. We will cover component groups in more detail in the next chapter, but the following snippet will give you an idea:

```
<ComponentGroup Id="ProductComponents"
                Directory="MyProgramDir">
  <Component ...>
    <File ... />
  </Component>
</ComponentGroup>
```

The File element

As you've seen, the actual files inside components are declared with `File` elements. The `File` elements can represent everything from simple text files to complex DLLs and executables. Remember, you should only place one file into each component. The following example would add a file called `SomeAssembly.dll` to the installation package:

```
<Component ... >
  <File Id="FILE_MyProgramDir_SomeAssemblyDLL"
        Name="Some Assembly.dll"
        Source="SomeAssembly.dll"
        KeyPath="yes" />
</Component>
```

A `File` element should always get the `Source` attribute. `Source` defines the path to the file during compilation. I've listed a relative path here, but you could also specify an absolute path.

`Id`, `Name`, and `KeyPath` are optional. The `Id` attribute becomes the primary key for a row in the MSI database. It should be something unique, but you might consider starting it with `FILE` to make it clear that it refers to a `File` element. If not set, the `Id` value will match the filename. `Name` gives you a chance to change the name of the file once it's been copied to the end user's computer. By default, it will use the name in the `Source` attribute.

To mark a file as important (and that it should be replaced if it goes missing), set it as the `KeyPath` file for the component. Since you should only ever place one file inside a component, in almost all cases that file should be the `KeyPath` file. If not set, the first file in the component will be the `KeyPath` file automatically.

A few other optional but useful attributes for the `File` element include:

- `Hidden`: Set to `yes` to have the file's `Hidden` flag set. The file won't be visible unless the user sets the directory's options to show hidden files.

- `ReadOnly`: Set to `yes` to have the file's `Read-only` flag set. The user will be able to read the file, but not modify it unless they change the file's properties.

- `Vital`: Set to `no` to continue even if this file isn't installed successfully.

The Feature element

After you've defined your components and the directories that they'll be copied into, the next step is to define features. A **feature** is a group of components that the user can decide to install all at once. You'll often see these in an installation dialog as a list of modules, called a **feature tree**, where each is included or excluded from the installation. The following is an example of such a tree that has two features – **Main Product** and **Optional Tools**:

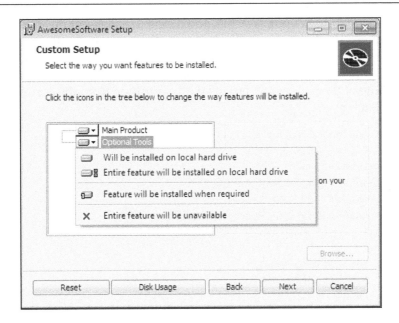

Every component must be included in a feature. Generally, you should group together components that rely on one another or that form a complete, self-sufficient unit. That way, if a feature is disabled, you won't have orphaned files (files that aren't being used) installed onto the computer. In many instances, if your product doesn't have any optional parts, you'll only want to create one feature.

If you've included a feature tree dialog (which we'll explain later in the book), such as the one shown, the user can simply click a feature to exclude it. However, even without this, they can select features from the command line. The following command only installs a feature called `MainProduct`:

```
msiexec /i myInstaller.msi ADDLOCAL=MainProduct
```

Here, we're using the `msiexec` program to launch an installer. The `/i` flag targets the MSI file to install. The `ADDLOCAL` property is set to the names of the features we want to include. If more than one, use commas to separate the names. To install all available features set `ADDLOCAL=ALL`, as shown:

```
msiexec /i myInstaller.msi ADDLOCAL=ALL
```

To create a new feature in your WiX file, add a `Feature` element inside the `Product` element. The following example installs three components under the feature `MainProduct`. Another feature called `OptionalTools` installs another component. Components are included in a feature with the `ComponentRef` element. The `Id` attribute of `ComponentRef` targets the `Id` attribute from the corresponding `Component` element:

```
<Feature Id="MainProduct"
         Title="Main Product"
         Level="1">
  <ComponentRef Id="CMP_MyAppEXE" />
  <ComponentRef Id="CMP_ReadMeTXT" />
  <ComponentRef Id="CMP_StartMenuShortcuts" />
</Feature>

<Feature Id="OptionalTools"
         Title="Optional Tools"
         Level="1">
  <ComponentRef Id="CMP_ToolsEXE" />
</Feature>
```

The `Feature` element's `Id` attribute uniquely identifies the feature and is what you'll reference when using the `ADDLOCAL` property on the command line. The `Title` attribute is used to set a user-friendly name that can be displayed on dialogs. Setting the `Feature` element's `Level` attribute to `1` means that that feature will be included in the installation by default. The end user will still be able to remove it through the user interface or via the command line. If, on the other hand, `Level` is set to `0`, that feature will be removed from the feature tree and the user won't be able to install it.

If you wanted to, you could create a more complex tree with features nested inside features. You could use this to create more categories for the elements in your product and give the user more options concerning what gets installed. You would want to make sure that all possible configurations function correctly. Windows Installer makes this somewhat manageable in that if a parent feature is excluded, its child features will be too. The following is an example of a more complex feature setup:

```
<Feature Id="MainProduct"
         Title="Main Product"
         Level="1">
  <ComponentRef Id="CMP_MyAppEXE" />
  <ComponentRef Id="CMP_StartMenuShortcuts" />

  <Feature Id="SubFeature1"
           Title="Documentation"
           Level="1">
```

```
      <ComponentRef Id="CMP_ReadMeTXT" />
   </Feature>
</Feature>

<Feature Id="OptionalTools"
         Title="Optional Tools"
         Level="1">
   <ComponentRef Id="CMP_ToolsEXE" />
</Feature>
```

In the preceding code snippet, I've moved the ReadMe.txt file used in the previous examples into its own feature called Documentation that's nested inside the MainProduct feature. Disabling its parent feature (MainProduct) will also disable it. However, you could enable MainProduct and disable Documentation.

You have the ability to prevent the user from excluding a particular feature. Just set the Absent attribute to disallow. You might do this for the main part of your product where excluding it wouldn't make sense.

You might also consider adding the Description attribute, which can be set to a string that describes the feature. This could be displayed in your dialog alongside the feature tree, if you decide to use one. We'll cover feature trees and adding a user interface later in the book.

Start menu shortcuts

Having a working installer is good, but wouldn't it be nice to add some shortcuts to the Windows Start menu? First, add another Directory element that references the Start menu via the built-in ProgramMenuFolder property:

```
<Directory Id="TARGETDIR"
           Name="SourceDir">
  <Directory Id="ProgramFilesFolder">
    <Directory Id="MyProgramDir"
               Name="Awesome Software" />
  </Directory>
  <Directory Id="ProgramMenuFolder">
    <Directory Id="MyShortcutsDir"
               Name="Awesome Software" />
  </Directory>
</Directory>
```

In the previous code snippet we're adding a new folder to the Start menu called `Awesome Software`. Now, we can use a `DirectoryRef` element to reference our new shortcuts folder, as in the following code snippet:

```
<DirectoryRef Id="MyShortcutsDir">
  <Component Id="CMP_DocumentationShortcut"
             Guid="33741C82-30BF-41AF-8246-44A5DCFCF953">

    <Shortcut Id="DocumentationStartMenuShortcut"
              Name="Awesome Software Documentation"
              Description="Read Awesome Software Documentation"
              Target="[MyProgramDir]InstallMe.txt" />
  </Component>
</DirectoryRef>
```

Each `Shortcut` element has a unique identifier set with the `Id` attribute. The `Name` attribute defines the user-friendly name that gets displayed. `Description` is set to a string that describes the shortcut and will appear when the user moves their mouse over the shortcut link.

The `Target` attribute defines the path on the end user's machine to the actual file being linked to. For that reason, you'll often want to use properties that update as they're changed, instead of hardcoded values. In the previous example, the main installation directory is referenced by placing the `Id` attribute of its corresponding `Directory` element in square brackets, which is then followed by the name of the file. Even if the path of `MyProgramDir` changes, it will still lead us to the `InstallMe.txt` file.

Two things that should accompany a shortcut are a `RemoveFolder` element and a `RegistryValue` element. `RemoveFolder` ensures that the new Start menu subdirectory will be removed during an uninstall. It uses an `Id` attribute to uniquely identify a row in the MSI `RemoveFile` table and an `On` attribute to specify when to remove the folder. You can set `On` to `install`, `uninstall`, or `both`. You can specify a `Directory` attribute as well to set to the `Id` attribute of a `Directory` element to remove. Without one, though, the element will remove the directory defined by the parent `DirectoryRef` or `ComponentGroup` element.

The `RegistryValue` element is needed simply because every component must have a `KeyPath` item. Shortcuts aren't allowed to be `KeyPath` items as they aren't technically files. By adding a `RegistryValue`, a new item is added to the registry and this is marked as `KeyPath`. The actual value itself serves no other purpose. We will cover writing to the registry in more detail later.

```
<DirectoryRef Id="MyShortcutsDir">
  <Component Id="CMP_DocumentationShortcut"
             Guid="33741C82-30BF-41AF-8246-44A5DCFCF953">

    <Shortcut Id="DocumentationStartMenuShortcut"
              Name="Awesome Software Documentation"
              Description="Read Awesome Software Documentation"
              Target="[MyProgramDir]InstallMe.txt" />

    <RemoveFolder Id="RemoveMyShortcutsDir"
                  On="uninstall" />

    <RegistryValue Root="HKCU"
                   Key="Software\Microsoft\AwesomeSoftware"
                   Name="installed"
                   Type="integer"
                   Value="1"
                   KeyPath="yes" />
  </Component>
</DirectoryRef>
```

There's actually another reason for using a `RegistryValue` element as `KeyPath`. The shortcut we're creating is being installed to a directory specific to the current user. Windows Installer requires that you always use a registry value as the `KeyPath` item when doing this in order to simplify uninstalling the product when multiple users have installed it.

Another type of shortcut to add is one that uninstalls the product. For this, add a second `Shortcut` element to the same component. This shortcut will be different in that it will have its `Target` set to the `msiexec.exe` program, which is located in the `System` folder. The following example uses the predefined `System64Folder` directory name because it will automatically map to either the 64-bit or 32-bit `System` folder, depending on the end user's operating system.

By setting `Target` to the path of an executable, you're telling Windows to launch that program when the user clicks the shortcut. The `msiexec` program can remove software by using the `/x` argument followed by the `ProductCode` attribute of the product you want to uninstall. The `ProductCode` attribute is the `Id` attribute specified in the `Product` element.

```
<DirectoryRef Id="ProgramMenuFolder">
  <Component Id="CMP_DocumentationShortcut"
            Guid="33741C82-30BF-41AF-8246-44A5DCFCF953">

    <Shortcut Id="DocumentationStartMenuShortcut"
            Name="Awesome Software Documentation"
            Description="Read Awesome Software Documentation"
            Target="[MyProgramDir]InstallMe.txt" />

    <Shortcut Id="UninstallShortcut"
            Name="Uninstall Awesome Software"
            Description=
            "Uninstalls Awesome Software and all of its components"
            Target="[System64Folder]msiexec.exe"
            Arguments="/x [ProductCode]" />

    <RemoveFolder Id="RemoveMyShortcutsDir"
              On="uninstall" />

    <RegistryValue Root="HKCU"
                Key="Software\Microsoft\AwesomeSoftware"
                Name="installed"
                Type="integer"
                Value="1"
                KeyPath="yes" />
  </Component>
</DirectoryRef>
```

Notice that we don't have to use the GUID from the `Product` element to get the `ProductCode` value. We can reference it using the built-in property called `ProductCode` surrounded by square brackets. If you'd like to add an icon to your shortcut, first add an `Icon` element as another child to the `Product` element. Then, reference that icon with the `Icon` attribute on the `Shortcut` element, as shown in the following code snippet:

```
<Icon Id="icon.ico" SourceFile="myIcon.ico"/>
<DirectoryRef ... >
  <Component ... >
    <Shortcut Id="DocumentationStartMenuShortcut"
```

```
                Name="Awesome Software Documentation"
                Description="Read Awesome Software Documentation"
                Target="[MyProgramDir]InstallMe.txt"
                Icon="icon.ico" />

      <RemoveFolder ... />
      <RegistryValue ... />
    </Component>
  </DirectoryRef>
```

Be sure to add the new component that contains the shortcuts to one of your features:

```
<Feature Id="ProductFeature"
         Title="Main Product"
         Level="1">
  <ComponentRef Id=" CMP_InstallMeTXT" />
  <ComponentRef Id="CMP_DocumentationShortcut" />
</Feature>
```

Putting it all together

Now that you've seen the different elements used to author an MSI package, the following is the entire .wxs file:

```
<?xml version="1.0" encoding="UTF-8"?>
<Wix xmlns="http://schemas.microsoft.com/wix/2006/wi">

  <Product Id="3E786878-358D-43AD-82D1-1435ADF9F6EA"
           Name="Awesome Software"
           Language="1033"
           Version="1.0.0.0"
           Manufacturer="Awesome Company"
           UpgradeCode="B414C827-8D81-4B4A-B3B6-338C06DE3A11">

    <Package InstallerVersion="301"
             Compressed="yes"
             InstallScope="perMachine"
             Manufacturer="Awesome Company"
             Description="Installs Awesome Software"
             Keywords="Practice,Installer,MSI"
             Comments="(c) 2012 Awesome Company" />

    <MediaTemplate EmbedCab="yes" />

    <!--Directory structure-->
```

```
<Directory Id="TARGETDIR"
           Name="SourceDir">
  <Directory Id="ProgramFilesFolder">
    <Directory Id="MyProgramDir"
               Name="Awesome Software" />
    <Directory Id="ProgramMenuFolder">
      <Directory Id="MyShortcutsDir"
                 Name="Awesome Software" />
    </Directory>
  </Directory>
</Directory>

<!--Components-->
<DirectoryRef Id="MyProgramDir">
  <Component Id="CMP_InstallMeTXT"
             Guid="E8A58B7B-F031-4548-9BDD-7A6796C8460D">
    <File Id="FILE_InstallMeTXT"
          Source="InstallMe.txt"
          KeyPath="yes" />
  </Component>
</DirectoryRef>

<!--Start Menu Shortcuts-->
<DirectoryRef Id="MyShortcutsDir">
  <Component Id="CMP_DocumentationShortcut"
             Guid="33741C82-30BF-41AF-8246-44A5DCFCF953">

    <Shortcut Id="DocumentationStartMenuShortcut"
              Name="Awesome Software Documentation"
              Description="Read Awesome Software Documentation"
              Target="[MyProgramDir]InstallMe.txt" />

    <Shortcut Id="UninstallShortcut"
              Name="Uninstall Awesome Software"
              Description="Uninstalls Awesome Software"
              Target="[System64Folder]msiexec.exe"
              Arguments="/x [ProductCode]" />

    <RemoveFolder Id="RemoveMyShortcutsDir"
                  On="uninstall" />

    <RegistryValue Root="HKCU"
                   Key="Software\Microsoft\AwesomeSoftware"
                   Name="installed"
```

```
                                   Type="integer"
                                   Value="1"
                                   KeyPath="yes" />
        </Component>
      </DirectoryRef>

      <!--Features-->
      <Feature Id="ProductFeature"
               Title="Main Product"
               Level="1">
        <ComponentRef Id="CMP_InstallMeTXT" />
        <ComponentRef Id="CMP_DocumentationShortcut" />
      </Feature>
    </Product>
</Wix>
```

Compile the project in Visual Studio and you should get a new MSI file:

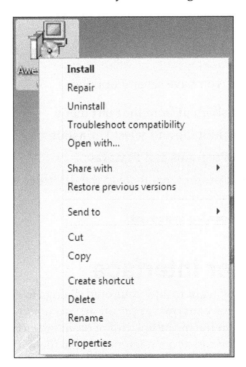

You can double-click on it or right-click and select **Install** to install the software. Doing so should create a subfolder for your program in the Start menu, as shown in the following screenshot:

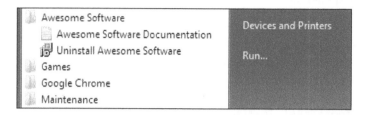

You should also find a new folder under **Program Files**:

Awesome Software	7/17/2012 10:27 PM	File folder
Common Files	7/13/2009 11:20 PM	File folder
Internet Explorer	7/5/2012 3:21 AM	File folder
Microsoft.NET	7/5/2012 3:01 AM	File folder
MSBuild	7/14/2009 1:32 AM	File folder
Reference Assemblies	7/14/2009 1:32 AM	File folder

To uninstall the software, you have several options:

- Use the uninstall shortcut from the Start menu
- Right-click on the MSI file and select **Uninstall**
- Uninstall it from **Programs** and **Features**
- From a command prompt, navigate to the directory where the MSI file is and use the following command:

```
msiexec /x AwesomeSoftware.msi
```

Adding a user interface

Although you'll eventually want to add your own dialogs to gather information from the user that's important for your own application, you may want to use one of WiX's built-in dialog sequences in the meantime. All of them are stored in an assembly called `WixUIExtension.dll`. You can add a reference to this file with Visual Studio's **Add a Reference** screen. The file exists in WiX's `Program Files` folder. You may have to navigate to `C:\Program Files (x86)\WiX Toolset v3.6\bin`.

Once you've added the new reference, add the following line to your WiX source file. It doesn't matter exactly where, as long as it's a child to the `Product` element:

```
<UIRef Id="WixUI_Minimal" />
```

This will insert the `Minimal` dialog set into your installation sequence. It shows a single dialog screen containing a license agreement and an **Install** button. Feel free to try any of the other dialog sets. Just replace `WixUI_Minimal`, with one of the other names in the `UIRef` element. `WixUI_Advanced` and `WixUI_InstallDir` require some further setup to really work properly. You can try out the following attributes:

- `WixUI_Advanced`
- `WixUI_FeatureTree`
- `WixUI_InstallDir`
- `WixUI_Mondo`

We will explore these standard dialogs in more detail later and also explain how to create your own.

Viewing the MSI database

I mentioned before that an MSI file is really a sort of relational database. WiX does all the work of creating tables, inserting rows, and matching up keys in this database. However, as we progress through the rest of the book, I encourage you to explore how it looks behind the scenes. For example, we discussed the `File` and `Component` elements. Sure enough, there are two tables called `File` and `Component` in the MSI package that contain the definitions you've set with your XML markup. To get inside the installer, you'll need a tool called **Orca**.

Orca.exe

Once you've compiled your project in Visual Studio, you'll have a working MSI package that can be installed by double-clicking on it. If you'd like to see the database inside, install the MSI viewer, `Orca.exe`. Orca is provided as part of the Windows SDK and despite the icon of a whale on the shortcut, it stands for **One Really Cool App.** You can find versions of the SDK at Microsoft's Windows Development Center website:

```
http://msdn.microsoft.com/en-us/windows/bb980924.aspx
```

After you've installed the SDK (specifically, the .NET tools that are included), you can find the installer for Orca — `Orca.msi` — in the `Microsoft SDKs` folder in `Program Files`. On my machine, it can be found in `C:\Program Files\Microsoft SDKs\ Windows\v7.0\Bin`.

Install Orca and then right-click on your MSI file and select **Edit with Orca**, as shown in the following screenshot:

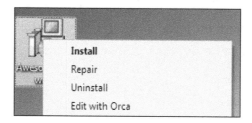

Orca lets you view the database structure of your installer. This can be a big help in troubleshooting problems or just to get a better idea about how different elements work together. The following is a screenshot of the `Component` database:

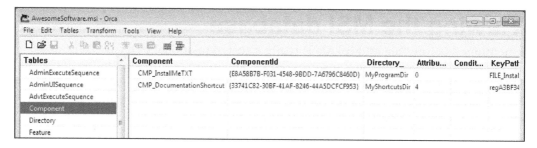

If you wanted to, you could edit your MSI package directly with Orca. This is helpful when learning or trying out different concepts. You'll need to know exactly which tables and rows to modify. Sometimes, though, you'll be able to just change a single value and check its effect.

Turning logging on during installation

If you get into trouble with your installer, it may help to run it with logging turned on. To do so, install your package from a command prompt using `msiexec` with the arguments `/l*v`, and the name of a file to write the log to. For example, if you had an installer called `myInstaller.msi`, you could use this command to write a log during the installation to a file called `myLog.txt`:

```
msiexec /i myInstaller.msi /l*v myLog.txt
```

Every event that occurs during installation will be recorded here. It works for uninstalls too. Simply use the /x argument instead of /i. The log can be pretty helpful, but also very verbose. If your installer fails midway through, you might try searching the log for the text return value 3. This indicates that an action returned a status of failure. Often, you'll also see a specific MSI error code. You can find its meaning by searching for that number in the **MSI SDK Documentation** help file that comes with WiX.

> You can also turn on logging for all MSI packages by editing the HKEY_LOCAL_MACHINE\Software\Policies\Microsoft\ Windows\Installer key in the Windows Registry. This should be used with care though so as not to use too much disk space. See http://support.microsoft.com/kb/223300 for more information.

Other resources

If you have specific questions about WiX, you'll find additional resources at the following websites:

- WiX users mailing list:

    http://sourceforge.net/mailarchive/forum.php?forum_name=wix-users

- Microsoft Windows Installer documentation:

    http://msdn.microsoft.com/en-us/library/cc185688(VS.85).aspx

Summary

In this chapter, we discussed downloading the WiX toolset and its various features. Creating a simple MSI package is relatively easy. There are only a handful of XML elements needed to get started. As we explore more complex setups, you'll be introduced to elements that are more specialized.

Throughout the rest of this book, I'll make references to the structure of the MSI database. Orca is an excellent tool for seeing this structure yourself. Although this book focuses on WiX and not the underlying Windows Installer technology, it helps sometimes to see how the mechanics of it work. You may find it useful to consult Microsoft's MSI documentation too, which can be found online or in a help file provided by WiX, to get a deeper understanding of the properties and constructs we will discuss.

2

Creating Files and Directories

In the previous chapter, we saw that creating a WiX installer isn't so tough. Less than seventy lines of code and you've got a professional-looking deployment solution. One of the things we covered was how to copy files and create directories on the end user's computer. We've covered the basics, but now it's time to dig deeper.

In this chapter you will learn how to:

- Organize your File and Directory elements using the DirectoryRef and ComponentGroup elements
- Split your WiX markup using Fragment elements to keep it manageable
- Use heat.exe to create the Component markup
- Install special case files such as installing to the GAC

The File element

The File element, as you've seen, is used to designate each file that you plan to copy to the end user's computer. At a minimum, it should contain a Source attribute that identifies the path to the file on your development machine, as shown:

```
<Component Id="CMP_MyProgramEXE"
           Guid="2C34F22F-1F48-4949-B68B-939F852F8B35">
  <File Source="MyProgram.exe" />
</Component>
```

There are a number of optional attributes available. The `Name` attribute tells the installer what the file will be called after it's installed. If omitted, the file will retain its original name as specified in the `Source` attribute. The `KeyPath` attribute explicitly marks the file as the keypath for the component, although if there is only one `File` element in `Component` it will, by default, be the keypath. The `Id` attribute uniquely identifies the file in the MSI database's `File` table. The following is an example that demonstrates these attributes:

```
<Component Id="CMP_MyProgramEXE"
           Guid="E8A58B7B-F031-4548-9BDD-7A6796C8460D">
  <File Id="FILE_MyProgramEXE"
        Source="MyProgram.exe"
        Name="NewName.exe"
        KeyPath="yes" />
</Component>

<Component Id="CMP_AnotherFileDLL"
           Guid="E9D74961-DF9B-4130-8FBC-1669A6DD288E">
  <File Id="FILE_AnotherFileDLL"
        Source="..\..\AnotherFile.dll"
        KeyPath="yes" />
</Component>
```

This example includes two files, `MyProgram.exe` and `AnotherFile.dll`, in the installation package. Both use relative paths for their `Source` attributes. The first file is located in the current directory while the second is two directories up. Another option is to use a **preprocessor variable** to store the location of your files.

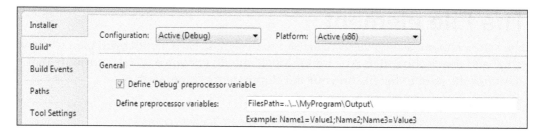

Preprocessor variables are evaluated at compile time and are replaced in the final MSI file with the strings that they've been set to. Here, I've added a variable called `FilesPath` on the **Build** page of my WiX project's **Properties** page, and set it to `..\..\myProgram\Output\`. In this case, the `Output` directory is where the files I plan to install are located on my computer. We can insert this variable in the markup by using `$(var.FilesPath)`, as in the following snippet:

```
<Component Id="CMP_MyProgramEXE"
           Guid="E8A58B7B-F031-4548-9BDD-7A6796C8460D">
  <File Id="FILE_MyProgramEXE"
        Source="$(var.FilesPath)MyProgram.exe"
        KeyPath="yes" />
</Component>
```

At compile time, the variable will be replaced with the path that we've defined. You can define more than one preprocessor variable on the **Build** page by separating them with semicolons.

You can also refer to other projects in your Visual Studio solution using preprocessor variables. For example, let's say you had a class library project in the same solution as your WiX setup. If you were to add that class library as a reference in the WiX project, you could then refer to its output directory using `$(var.`*ProjectName.*`TargetDir)`, as in the following example:

```
<Component Id="CMP_MyAssembly"
           Guid="{F53BAFE0-9BB1-44E6-BC93-D3BD0514BE14}">
  <File Source="$(var.MyAssembly.TargetDir)MyAssembly.dll" />
</Component>
```

Here, after we've added a project reference to the `MyAssembly` project, we are able to reference its output directory via the `$(var.MyAssembly.TargetDir)` variable. You can see other variables that are made available when adding a project reference in this way at:

http://wix.sourceforge.net/manual-wix3/votive_project_references.htm

A `File` element is always wrapped in its own `Component` element. Doing so will allow you to mark every file that you're installing as a `KeyPath` file. This allows them to be replaced if they're accidentally deleted. The process of replacing missing files is known as a **repair**. Repairs are triggered by right-clicking on an MSI file and selecting **Repair**. A component can have only one keypath file, but every component should have one. Although it's possible to put more than one file in the same component, it's considered bad practice.

Before moving on, two other helpful attributes on the `File` element are `Hidden` and `ReadOnly`. Setting the first to `yes` causes the installed file to be hidden from view. The second turns on the file's `read-only` flag.

The DirectoryRef element

In the previous chapter, you saw that to define which directories to copy your files into, you use `Directory` elements. These take an `Id` value and, if it's a new directory that you're creating, a `Name` attribute. You can use any of the built-in IDs to reference one of the common Windows directories. For example, suppose we wanted to add an XML configuration file for our software to the `%PROGRAMDATA%` folder. We'd add a reference to it using the built-in `CommonAppDataFolder` property as `Directory Id`:

```
<Directory Id="TARGETDIR" Name="SourceDir">
    <Directory Id="CommonAppDataFolder">
        <Directory Id="MyCommonAppDataFolder"
                   Name="Awesome Software" />
    </Directory>
</Directory>
```

Here we are placing a new folder called `Awesome Software` inside the `%PROGRAMDATA%` folder. The new folder gets a `Name` attribute to label it. The `Id` attribute is up to us and uniquely identifies the directory in the MSI database. To add a file to our directory we add a new `DirectoryRef`, as shown in the following code snippet:

```
<DirectoryRef Id="MyCommonAppDataFolder">
    <Component Id="CMP_SettingsXML"
               Guid="{F8901638-9E76-44F6-B755-155CBE135CF5}">
        <File Source="Settings.xml" />
    </Component>
</DirectoryRef>
```

The `DirectoryRef` element matches the `Directory` element that we used before. If you wanted to, you could use a new `DirectoryRef` element for each file. However, it's easier to use one `DirectoryRef` and place multiple `Component` elements inside of it:

```
<DirectoryRef Id="MyCommonAppDataFolder">
    <Component Id="CMP_GeneralSettingsXML"
               Guid="{971674AC-D9EB-4344-BA43-B685BA82EE56}">
        <File Source="GeneralSettings.xml" />
    </Component>

    <Component Id="CMP_DatabaseSettingsXML"
               Guid="{72D97E16-FA5E-4EAA-99DC-415BCBEED907}">
```

```
        <File Source="DatabaseSettings.xml" />
    </Component>
</DirectoryRef>
```

You could, for example, place hundreds of files inside the `MyCommonAppDataFolder` directory using only one `DirectoryRef` element.

The ComponentGroup element

The `ComponentGroup` element is used to group `Component` elements, which is helpful as it offers a way to reference all of your components with a single element. For example, when adding components to `Feature` (which you must always do), you *could* use `ComponentRef` elements directly. This is the technique we used in the previous chapter:

```
<Feature Id="ProductFeature"
        Title="Main Product"
        Level="1">
  <ComponentRef Id="CMP_MyProgramEXE" />
  <ComponentRef Id="CMP_AnotherFileDLL" />
</Feature>
```

However, by creating `ComponentGroup`, you can reference multiple components with a single `ComponentGroupRef` element. This is shown in the following snippet:

```
<Feature Id="ProductFeature"
        Title="Main Product"
        Level="1">
  <ComponentGroupRef Id="MyComponentGroup" />
</Feature>
```

Try it out by adding a new `CompontGroup` element to your `.wxs` file. It can go anywhere inside the `Product` element. Then, you have a choice. You can either nest `Component` elements inside it or use `ComponentRefs` to reference your components indirectly. For example, here we use `Component` elements inside `ComponentGroup`:

```
<ComponentGroup Id="MyComponentGroup">
  <Component Id="CMP_MyProgramEXE"
          Guid="E8A58B7B-F031-4548-9BDD-7A6796C8460D"
          Directory="INSTALLLOCATION">
    <File Id="FILE_MyProgramEXE"
          Source="MyProgram.exe"
          KeyPath="yes" />
```

```
    </Component>

    <Component Id="CMP_AnotherFileDLL"
               Guid="E9D74961-DF9B-4130-8FBC-1669A6DD288E"
               Directory="INSTALLLOCATION">
      <File Id="FILE_AnotherFileDLL"
            Source="AnotherFile.dll"
            KeyPath="yes" />
    </Component>
  </ComponentGroup>
```

Since the components aren't wrapped in a `DirectoryRef` element anymore, we're adding `Directory` attributes to the `Component` elements to set the target directory. This has the same effect though. It will tell the installer where to copy these files to. You can also put a `Directory` attribute on the `ComponentGroup` element itself, setting the target directory for all child components:

```
<ComponentGroup Id="MyComponentGroup"
                Directory="INSTALLLOCATION">
  <Component ... />
  <Component ... />
</ComponentGroup>
```

The other option is to continue to nest `Component` elements inside the `DirectoryRef` elements and then use the `ComponentRef` elements to include them in a group:

```
<DirectoryRef Id="INSTALLLOCATION">
  <Component Id="CMP_MyProgramEXE"
             Guid="E8A58B7B-F031-4548-9BDD-7A6796C8460D">
    <File Id="FILE_MyProgramEXE"
          Source="MyProgram.exe"
          KeyPath="yes" />
  </Component>

  <Component Id="CMP_AnotherFileDLL"
             Guid="E9D74961-DF9B-4130-8FBC-1669A6DD288E">
    <File Id="FILE_AnotherFileDLL"
          Source="AnotherFile.dll"
          KeyPath="yes" />
  </Component>
</DirectoryRef>

<ComponentGroup Id="MyComponentGroup">
  <ComponentRef Id="CMP_MyProgramEXE" />
  <ComponentRef Id="CMP_AnotherFileDLL" />
</ComponentGroup>
```

The usefulness of ComponentGroup becomes more obvious when your program needs to copy more than a few files to the end user's machine. You'll be able to include, remove, or move entire sets of components from a feature simply by moving the ComponentGroupRef element.

The Fragment element

Up to this point, we've been adding all of our WiX elements to the Product.wxs file. When your installer packages hundreds of files, you'll find that having all of your code in one place makes reading it difficult. You can split your elements up into multiple .wxs files for better organization and readability. Whereas your main source file, Product.wxs, nests everything inside a Product element, your additional .wxs files will use Fragment elements as their roots.

The Fragment element doesn't need any attributes. It's simply a container. You can place just about anything inside of it, such as all of your Directory elements or all of your Component elements. For the next example, add a new WiX source file to your project and place the following markup inside it. Here, we're using the same ComponentGroup that we discussed earlier. You can call the file Components.wxs, and it should look something like the following code snippet:

```xml
<?xml version="1.0" encoding="UTF-8"?>
<Wix xmlns="http://schemas.microsoft.com/wix/2006/wi">
  <Fragment>
    <ComponentGroup Id="MyComponentGroup"
                    Directory="INSTALLLOCATION">
      <Component Id="CMP_MyProgramEXE"
                 Guid="E8A58B7B-F031-4548-9BDD-7A6796C8460D">
        <File Id="FILE_MyProgramEXE"
              Source="MyProgram.exe"
              KeyPath="yes" />
      </Component>

      <Component Id="CMP_AnotherFileDLL"
                 Guid="E9D74961-DF9B-4130-8FBC-1669A6DD288E">
        <File Id="FILE_AnotherFileDLL"
              Source="AnotherFile.dll"
              KeyPath="yes" />
      </Component>
    </ComponentGroup>
  </Fragment>
</Wix>
```

Now, the markup for the components is contained within a separate file. We've used `ComponentGroup` to group them, but of course, that's optional. To include this group in `Product.wxs`, reference it with a `ComponentGroupRef` element in one of your `Feature` elements, as shown:

```
<Feature Id="ProductFeature"
         Title="Main Product"
         Level="1">
  <ComponentGroupRef Id="MyComponentGroup" />
</Feature>
```

Although the `ComponentGroup` element is optional, it allows us to reference our fragment back in our main source file. Referencing any single element from a fragment like this will pull all of the elements in the fragment into the scope of your project. For components, this doesn't make much difference since you still have to reference all of them—or at least a `ComponentGroup` element of them—inside a `Feature` element. However, it makes more of a difference for other elements.

For example, **properties**, which are variables that you can use to store data, are represented by `Property` elements and could be stored in a separate file within a `Fragment` element. Then, by referencing just one of them in your main source file with a `PropertyRef` element, you'd pull all of them into your project. With fragments, it's all or nothing. Referencing one element in the fragment references them all.

Other elements that don't have a corresponding *Ref* counterpart need a little more help. For example, there's no reference element for the `Media` element. There's no such thing as a "MediaRef". However, if you included a `Property` element in the same fragment as your `Media` elements, you could pull them in too by referencing that property with `PropertyRef`. The `Media.wxs` file would look like the following code snippet:

```
<?xml version="1.0" encoding="UTF-8"?>
<Wix xmlns="http://schemas.microsoft.com/wix/2006/wi">
  <Fragment>
    <Property Id="MediaProperty"
              Value="1" />
    <Media Id="1" Cabinet="media1.cab" EmbedCab="yes" />
    <Media Id="2" Cabinet="media2.cab" EmbedCab="yes" />
    <Media Id="3" Cabinet="media3.cab" EmbedCab="yes" />
  </Fragment>
</Wix>
```

To reference the `Media` elements in your project, reference the property that's with them. This is done by adding the following code to `Product.wxs`:

```xml
<?xml version="1.0" encoding="UTF-8"?>
<Wix xmlns="http://schemas.microsoft.com/wix/2006/wi">
  <Product Id="3E786878-358D-43AD-82D1-1435ADF9F6EA"
           Name="Awesome Software"
           Language="1033"
           Version="1.0.0.0"
           Manufacturer="Awesome Company"
           UpgradeCode="B414C827-8D81-4B4A-B3B6-338C06DE3A11">
    <Package InstallerVersion="301"
             Compressed="yes" />

    <PropertyRef Id="MediaProperty" />

    <Directory Id="TARGETDIR"
               Name="SourceDir">
      <Directory Id="ProgramFilesFolder">
        <Directory Id="MyProgramDir"
                   Name="Awesome Software" />
      </Directory>
    </Directory>

    <DirectoryRef Id="MyProgramDir">
      <Component Id="CMP_InstallMeTXT"
                 Guid="E8A58B7B-F031-4548-9BDD-7A6796C8460D">
        <File Id="FILE_InstallMeTXT"
              Source="InstallMe.txt"
              KeyPath="yes" />
      </Component>
    </DirectoryRef>

    <Feature Id="ProductFeature"
             Title="Main Product"
             Level="1">
      <ComponentRef Id="CMP_InstallMeTXT" />
    </Feature>
  </Product>
</Wix>
```

Fragments are a great way of splitting up your code to make it more manageable. As we've seen, it's easy to pull them into the scope of your project. You could even pull one fragment into another and then pull that one into your main source file. WiX will take care of running the validity checks to make sure that everything links together properly.

Note that it's possible to have more than one `Fragment` element in the same source file. In that case, you must use a reference element for each one. They're sort of like islands. They're isolated from one another. However, it's often simpler to stick to one fragment per file. The following file defines two fragments:

```xml
<?xml version="1.0" encoding="UTF-8"?>
<Wix xmlns="http://schemas.microsoft.com/wix/2006/wi">
  <Fragment>
    <Property Id="MediaProperty"
              Value="1" />
    <Media Id="1"
           Cabinet="media1.cab"
           EmbedCab="yes" />
  </Fragment>

  <Fragment>
    <Property Id="MediaProperty2"
              Value="1" />
    <Media Id="2"
           Cabinet="media2.cab"
           EmbedCab="yes" />
  </Fragment>
</Wix>
```

Referencing the `MediaProperty` property with `PropertyRef` will only pull in the elements in the first fragment. To get those in the second fragment, you'd have to also reference the `MediaProperty2` property.

The `Fragment` element is so helpful that the WiX team has employed its use for an even bigger type of project organization: `.wixlib` files. These are separate projects that by default contain a single fragment and compile into a **WiX library** (`.wixlib`) that can be added as a reference in your main WiX project. This allows other teams to handle their own WiX code and send it to you already compiled. To try it out, create a new project in your solution using the **Setup Library Project** template.

Setup Project		Windows Installer XML	**Type:** Windows Installer XML
Merge Module Project		Windows Installer XML	A project for creating a wixlib library
Setup Library Project		Windows Installer XML	
Bootstrapper Project		Windows Installer XML	

The contents of this type of project aren't anything you haven't seen before. It's simply a fragment. You'll start off with the following markup:

```xml
<?xml version="1.0" encoding="UTF-8"?>
<Wix xmlns="http://schemas.microsoft.com/wix/2006/wi">
  <Fragment>
    <!-- TODO: Put your code here. -->
  </Fragment>
</Wix>
```

You can add properties, components, and anything else you'd ordinarily be able to add to a fragment. When it's compiled, you'll have a `.wixlib` file that can be added as a reference in your main WiX project. Use the **Add Reference** option in your **Solution Explorer** window. Like other fragments, you'll be able to reference the `.wixlib` file's contents by using a reference element such as `PropertyRef`. This is a great tool that allows multiple teams to work on the installer without stepping on one another's toes.

In the past, installation developers often used **merge modules** (`.msm`) to separate installation code. Merge modules, much like WiX libraries, contain compiled installer code and offer a way of splitting up large projects. WiX libraries, which are easier to author, can serve as a replacement for merge modules.

WiX does provide an XML element called `Merge` for importing a merge module into your project. You'd probably only need to use this to install a third-party component. However, even for dependencies such as Microsoft's Visual C++ Runtime, you may be able to avoid using a merge module and use an executable installer instead. An installer for the Visual C++ Runtime is available and by using WiX's new bootstrapper technology, **Burn**, it can be installed as a prerequisite before your own software is installed. We'll cover Burn later in the book.

Harvesting files with heat.exe

When your project contains many files to install, it can be a chore to create `File` and `Component` elements for all of them. Instead, WiX can do it for you. One of the tools that ships with the toolset is called **heat.exe**. You can find it in the `bin` directory of the WiX program files. Navigate to WiX's `bin` directory from a command prompt and type `heat.exe -?` to see information about its usage.

To make things easy, consider adding the path to the WiX `bin` directory to your computer's `PATH` environment variable so that you won't have to reference the full path to the executable each time you use it. You can do this on Windows 7 by right-clicking on **My Computer** in your Start Menu and then going to **Properties | Advanced system settings | Environment Variables**. From there, you can add the WiX `bin` path, `C:\Program Files (x86)\WiX Toolset v3.6\bin`, to **PATH** by finding **PATH** in the list of system variables and clicking on **Edit**.

 Note that WiX, during its installation, adds an environment variable called `WIX`, but this references the `bin` folder's parent directory. You could add `%WIX%bin` to `PATH`.

The following is the general syntax for Heat:

```
heat.exe harvestType harvestSource <harvester arguments>
 -o[ut] sourceFile.wxs
```

Heat can look at a directory, evaluate all of the files in it, and create a `.wxs` file defining the components you'd need to install all of those files. First, let's create a new directory and then add some empty text files in it. You can create it anywhere you like.

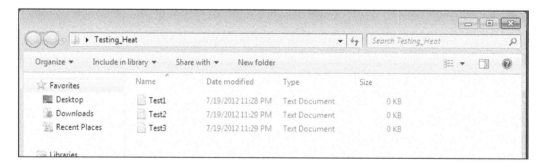

Open a command prompt and navigate to this directory. I'll assume that the WiX `bin` directory has been added to your `PATH` environment variable and won't reference the full path to `heat.exe`. The first argument that you have to give to Heat is a `harvestType`, which can be one of the following:

- `dir`: This type harvests a directory
- `file`: This type harvests a file
- `payload`: This type harvests a bundle payload as `RemotePayload`
- `perf`: This type harvests performance counters

- `project`: This type harvests output of a VS project
- `reg`: This type harvest a `.reg` file
- `website`: This type harvests an IIS website

We'll be harvesting all the files from the directory we've created, so we'll use `dir`. The second argument is the path to the directory. It can be a relative or absolute path and should not end in a backslash. I'll truncate it in this example for the sake of clarity. The last argument, which is preceded by the `-out` flag, is the name of a source file that Heat will create. So, our Heat command looks like this so far:

```
heat.exe dir "C:\Testing_Heat" -out ".\HeatFile.wxs"
```

We've asked it to create a file called `HeatFile.wxs` in the current directory. The following is what it would contain:

```xml
<?xml version="1.0" encoding="utf-8"?>
<Wix xmlns="http://schemas.microsoft.com/wix/2006/wi">
  <Fragment>
    <DirectoryRef Id="TARGETDIR">
      <Directory Id="dirB81CE037F36D241058F8A43AAFDFE612"
                 Name="Testing_Heat" />
    </DirectoryRef>
  </Fragment>

  <Fragment>
    <DirectoryRef Id="dirB81CE037F36D241058F8A43AAFDFE612">
      <Component Id="cmp154B5D55534D51EA6679BF67168C1D72"
                 Guid="PUT-GUID-HERE">
        <File Id="filB2F0330A7280060ACCD0CFAF56B40DA8"
              KeyPath="yes"
              Source="SourceDir\Test1.txt" />
      </Component>
    </DirectoryRef>
  </Fragment>

  <Fragment>
    <DirectoryRef Id="dirB81CE037F36D241058F8A43AAFDFE612">
      <Component Id="cmp735C6BDA70156318193CB4A6C649FC6A"
                 Guid="PUT-GUID-HERE">
        <File Id="fil0719BEF9518EFD5FC8C9C75E5A670F00"
              KeyPath="yes"
              Source="SourceDir\Test2.txt" />
      </Component>
    </DirectoryRef>
```

```
      </Fragment>

      <Fragment>
        <DirectoryRef Id="dirB81CE037F36D241058F8A43AAFDFE612">
          <Component Id="cmpC9439409E8A1642355A4FDF410CC7EFD"
                     Guid="PUT-GUID-HERE">
            <File Id="filE46FE85CD981AEB0AD645246FCB018B3"
                  KeyPath="yes"
                  Source="SourceDir\Test3.txt" />
          </Component>
        </DirectoryRef>
      </Fragment>
    </Wix>
```

It created WiX markup for us. However, things aren't quite as good as they could be. For one thing, it has created a `Directory` element with a `Name` attribute of `Testing_Heat`, the same as my impromptu folder. This will create a directory called `Testing_Heat` on the end user's computer. That's not what I wanted. Also, it has set the `Guid` attribute on each `Component` to `PUT-GUID-HERE`. Although this could be useful in some circumstances, I'd much rather it created the GUIDs for me.

It has also set the `Source` attribute on each `File` element to `SourceDir\FILENAME`. This means that when we build the project, the compiler will expect to find the text files in the same directory where the `HeatFile.wxs` file is. Finally, it hasn't made it easy for us to reference the components that it created. It would have been nice to see all of these components grouped into a `ComponentGroup` element.

To fix these problems, we'll just add some more arguments to our call to Heat, as outlined in the following table:

Argument	What it does
-cg <ComponentGroup>	Add the -cg flag with a name to use for a new ComponentGroup element. Heat will then group the components.
-dr <DirectoryName>	Use the -dr flag with the name of one of the directories you actually wanted to create. That way, the components will be copied into that directory during the installation.
-gg	To have Heat create GUIDs for us, add the -gg flag.
-g1	To have the GUIDs not have curly brackets, use the -g1 flag. This is just a preference.
-sfrag	By default, Heat puts each component and your directory structure in separate Fragment elements. Adding -sfrag puts these elements into the same Fragment element.

Argument	What it does
-srd	There's not really any reason to harvest the folder where the files are, so add the -srd flag.
-var <VarName>	We can use the -var flag with the name of a preprocessor variable (preceded by var) to insert in place of SourceDir. Later on, we can set the variable from within the project's **Properties** settings or on the command line.

Now, our call to Heat will look something like the following command:

```
heat.exe dir "C:\New Folder" -dr MyProgramDir -cg NewFilesGroup
-gg -gl -sf -srd -var "var.MyDir" -out ".\HeatFile.wxs"
```

The new HeatFile.wxs looks like the following code snippet:

```xml
<?xml version="1.0" encoding="utf-8"?>
<Wix xmlns="http://schemas.microsoft.com/wix/2006/wi">
  <Fragment>
    <DirectoryRef Id="MyProgramDir" />
  </Fragment>
  <Fragment>
    <ComponentGroup Id="NewFilesGroup">
      <Component Id="cmp6E6E0088162FB06CBCEA9A4AA7CBC603"
                 Directory="MyProgramDir"
                 Guid="94CB90AB-C291-4D2D-B9B1-DED3FA5DB93A">
        <File Id="filCA67D5B125E878518FEA8F7FB62EF550"
              KeyPath="yes"
              Source="$(var.MyDir)\Test1.txt" />
      </Component>
      <Component Id="cmpC3D97EF2ADF77EB61AEF04285A25C2D2"
                 Directory="MyProgramDir"
                 Guid="9D73E105-CF60-4665-9CA4-7682859E6034">
        <File Id="filA2FD0B78B439D62B0C28A829A9508C01"
              KeyPath="yes"
              Source="$(var.MyDir)\Test2.txt" />
      </Component>
      <Component Id="cmp5B1A530DE50F4D3437F2171E2CAB91A6"
                 Directory="MyProgramDir"
                 Guid="1949BEDC-8B91-424A-8977-A5C8F85FAE92">
        <File Id="fil3C980C5A1D26D4B12D481104B14E98D2"
              KeyPath="yes"
              Source="$(var.MyDir)\Test3.txt" />
      </Component>
    </ComponentGroup>
  </Fragment>
</Wix>
```

This looks a lot better. Now, the components are grouped, each `Component` has a GUID and is being installed into the `MyProgramDir` folder that I'm creating, and the `File` elements are using the `$(var.MyDir)` variable in their `Source` attributes. To include these new components in `Product.wxs`, add a reference to `ComponentGroup` with a `ComponentGroupRef` element inside one of the features:

```
<Feature Id="ProductFeature"
         Title="Main Product"
         Level="1">
  <ComponentRef Id="CMP_InstallMeTXT" />
  <ComponentGroupRef Id="NewFilesGroup" />
</Feature>
```

Also, be sure to add a value for the `MyDir` variable. Here, we set it to a folder named **SomeFolder** in our project's directory (assuming we move our text files there before compiling the project):

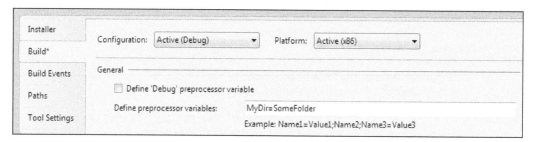

After you've compiled the project, you can use Orca to look at the MSI data that this produces. The **Component** table will show the new components and the **File** table will show the new files:

Tables	Component	ComponentId	Directory_
AdminExecuteSequence	cmp6E6E0088162FB06CBCEA9A4AA7CBC603	{94CB90AB-C291-4D2...	MyProgramDir
AdminUISequence	cmpC3D97EF2ADF77EB61AEF04285A25C2D2	{9D73E105-CF60-4665-...	MyProgramDir
AdvtExecuteSequence	cmp5B1A530DE50F4D3437F2171E2CAB91A6	{1949BEDC-8B91-424A...	MyProgramDir
Component			
Directory			

Remember that every time you run Heat on a directory, and you've set the `-gg` flag, it will create new GUIDs for your components. If you've already shipped a version of your software to customers, then these GUIDs should not be changed. To do so would prevent Windows from accurately keeping track of them. Heat will also create new `Id` attributes for `File` and `Component` elements each time you use it. This is just something to keep in mind, especially if other parts of your installer expect the `Id` attribute to stay the same from one day to the next.

Copying and moving files

`File` and `Component` elements allow you to add new files to the end user's computer. However, WiX also provides ways to copy and move files. For these tasks, you'll use the `CopyFile` element. We'll discuss how to use it in the following sections.

Copying files you install

The `CopyFile` element can copy a file that you're installing and place it in another directory. You'll nest it inside the `File` element of the file you want to duplicate. First, we'll add a subdirectory to the `MyProgramDir` folder that we're already creating under `Program Files`. The new directory will be called `Copied Files`.

```
<Directory Id="TARGETDIR"
           Name="SourceDir">
  <Directory Id="ProgramFilesFolder">
    <Directory Id="MyProgramDir"
               Name="Awesome Software">
      <Directory Id="CopiedFiles"
                 Name="Copied Files" />
    </Directory>
  </Directory>
</Directory>
```

Now, we can nest a `CopyFile` element inside the `File` element of the file we want to copy. Here, we're copying the `InstallMe.txt` file to the `Copied Files` folder and renaming it to `InstallMeCOPY.txt`. Notice that we use the `DestinationDirectory` attribute to specify the `Id` attribute of the `Copied Files` directory. We use the `DestinationName` attribute to specify the new filename. Every `CopyFile` element has to have a unique ID, so we set that too:

```
<!--Components-->
<DirectoryRef Id="MyProgramDir">
  <Component Id="CMP_InstallMeTXT"
             Guid="E8A58B7B-F031-4548-9BDD-7A6796C8460D">
    <File Id="FILE_InstallMeTXT"
          Source="InstallMe.txt"
          KeyPath="yes">
      <CopyFile Id="Copy_InstallMeTXT"
                DestinationDirectory="CopiedFiles"
                DestinationName="InstallMeCOPY.txt" />
    </File>
  </Component>
</DirectoryRef>
```

That's all you need. During installation, the `InstallMe.txt` file will be copied to the `Copied Files` folder and named `InstallMeCOPY.txt`. If you wanted to, you could nest multiple `CopyFile` elements under the same `File` element and copy that file to several places. Just be sure to give each `CopyFile` element a unique ID.

If you don't want to hardcode the destination directory, you can use the `DestinationProperty` attribute instead of `DestinationDirectory` to reference a directory at install time. `DestinationProperty` accepts the name of a property that's set to a directory path. The following is an example:

```
<Property Id="CopiedFilesFolder"
          Value="C:\CopiedFiles" />
<DirectoryRef Id="MyProgramDir">
  <Component Id="CMP_InstallMeTXT"
             Guid="E8A58B7B-F031-4548-9BDD-7A6796C8460D">
    <File Id="FILE_InstallMeTXT"
          Source="InstallMe.txt"
          KeyPath="yes">
      <CopyFile Id="Copy_InstallMeTXT"
                DestinationProperty="CopiedFilesFolder"
                DestinationName="InstallMeCOPY.txt" />
    </File>
  </Component>
</DirectoryRef>
```

So here we've hardcoded the path again. It's just that this time we used a property to do it instead of a `Directory` element. The `DestinationProperty` attribute is most useful when you can set the property dynamically. There are various ways that you can do this:

- Ask the user for it on a UI dialog and then set the property with the result. We'll talk about setting properties from dialogs later in the book.

- Set the property from a custom action. This is something else we'll cover later. The action that you create must be executed before the `DuplicateFiles` action in `InstallExecuteSequence`.

- Set the property from the command line. We'll cover this in the next chapter.

- Use **AppSearch**, which we'll cover, to find the directory you want and set the property with it.

Copying existing files

In addition to being able to copy files that you're installing, you can also copy files that already exist on the end user's computer. For this, you'll nest the CopyFile element inside its own Component element and not inside a File element. The following is an example that copies a file called TEST.txt that's on the desktop to a folder called Copied Files:

```
<!--Directory structure-->
<Directory Id="TARGETDIR"
           Name="SourceDir">
  <Directory Id="ProgramFilesFolder">
    <Directory Id="MyProgramDir"
               Name="Awesome Software">
      <Directory Id="CopiedFiles"
                 Name="Copied Files" />
    </Directory>
  </Directory>
  <Directory Id="DesktopFolder" />
</Directory>

<!--Components-->
<DirectoryRef Id="MyProgramDir">
  <Component Id="CMP_CopyTestTXT"
             Guid="E25E8584-D009-43bE-99E9-A46D58105DD0"
             KeyPath="yes">
    <CopyFile Id="CopyTest"
              DestinationDirectory="CopiedFiles"
              DestinationName="TESTCopy.txt"
              SourceDirectory="DesktopFolder"
              SourceName="TEST.txt" />
  </Component>
</DirectoryRef>
```

We've added a Directory element to reference the Desktop folder so that we can reference it later in the CopyFile element. The Component element that holds the CopyFile has its KeyPath attribute set to yes. We did this because we're not installing anything with this component and *something* has to be the keypath. In cases such as this, when there's nothing else to serve the purpose, it's fine to mark the component itself as the KeyPath file.

The `CopyFile` element here has the `DestinationDirectory` and `DestinationName` attributes like before, but it also has the `SourceDirectory` and `SourceName` attributes. `SourceDirectory` is set to the `Id` attribute of a `Directory` element where the file you want to copy is. `SourceName` is the name of the file you want to copy. If you wanted to, you could use the `DestinationProperty` attribute instead of `DestinationDirectory`, and `SourceProperty` instead of `SourceDirectory`. These are used to set the directory paths at installation time, as discussed before.

Moving existing files

Suppose you didn't want to copy a file that already existed, but rather move it to some other folder. All you need to do is add the `Delete` attribute to your `CopyFile` element. This will delete the file from its current location and copy it to the new location. So, that's another way of saying "move". The following is an example:

```
<DirectoryRef Id="MyProgramDir">
  <Component Id="CMP_MoveTestTXT"
             Guid="E25E8584-D009-43bE-99E9-A46D58105DD0"
             KeyPath="yes">
    <CopyFile Id="MoveTest"
              DestinationDirectory="CopiedFiles"
              DestinationName="TESTCopy.txt"
              SourceDirectory="DesktopFolder"
              SourceName="TEST.txt"
              Delete="yes" />
  </Component>
</DirectoryRef>
```

Unfortunately, when you uninstall the software, it doesn't move the file back. It just removes it completely from its current location.

Installing special-case files

In the following sections, we'll take a look at installing files that are different from other types that we've talked about so far. Specifically, we'll cover how to install an assembly file (`.dll`) to the Global Assembly Cache and how to install a TrueType font file.

Adding assembly files to the GAC

The **Global Assembly Cache (GAC)** is a central repository in Windows where you can store .NET assembly files so that they can be shared by multiple applications. You can add a .NET assembly to it with WiX by setting the `File` element's `Assembly` attribute to `.net`. The following example installs an assembly file to the GAC:

```
<DirectoryRef Id="MyProgramDir">
  <Component Id="CMP_MyAssembly"
             Guid="4D98D593-F4E0-479B-A7DA-80BBB78B54CB">
    <File Id="File_MyAssembly"
          Assembly=".net"
          Source="MyAssembly.dll"
          KeyPath="yes" />
  </Component>
</DirectoryRef>
```

Even though we've placed this component inside a `DirectoryRef` element, that references the `MyProgramDir` directory, it won't really be copied there since we're installing it to the GAC. Another approach is to create a dummy folder called `GAC` that's used solely for this purpose. In that case, you wouldn't give that `Directory` a `Name` attribute, which would prevent it from truly being created.

I'm using an assembly called `MyAssembly.dll` in this example, that I created with a separate Visual Studio project. Any DLL that you want to install to the GAC must be strongly signed. You can do this by opening the **Properties** page for that project in Visual Studio, viewing the **Signing** page, checking the box that says **Sign the assembly**, and creating a new `.snk` file, as shown in the following screenshot:

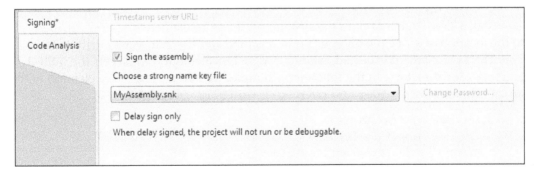

Once you've installed the package that now contains the strongly-signed assembly, you'll be able to check if the DLL file actually made it into the GAC. Navigate to the GAC `assembly` folder to see a list of installed assemblies:

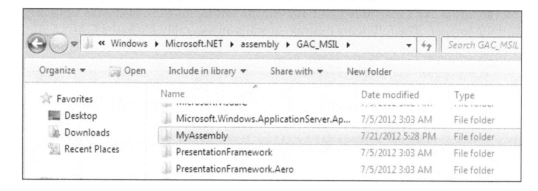

 Assemblies that target the .NET 4 Framework will use the new GAC folders under `C:\Windows\Microsoft.NET\assembly`. Assemblies targeting an earlier framework will be placed in `C:\Windows\assembly`.

The nice thing is that when the user uninstalls the software the assembly will be removed from the GAC—that is, unless another software product is still using it. Windows keeps a count of products using each assembly and deletes your `.dll` only when the count reaches zero.

Installing a TrueType font

To install a TrueType font onto the system, set the `File` element's `Source` attribute to the location of a TTF file on your build machine and the `TrueType` attribute to yes. The `File` element is nested inside a `Component` element that targets the built-in `FontsFolder` directory. In the following example, we add a `Directory` element with an `Id` value of `FontsFolder` and reference it with `DirectoryRef`:

```
<Directory Id="TARGETDIR"
           Name="SourceDir">
  <Directory Id="ProgramFilesFolder">
    <Directory Id="MyProgramDir"
               Name="Awesome Software" />
  </Directory>
  <Directory Id="FontsFolder" />
```

```xml
</Directory>

<DirectoryRef Id="FontsFolder">
  <Component Id="CMP_MyFont"
            Guid="CFF27814-D7A8-4054-B3B1-F5DB44CD5AB9">
    <File Id="myFontFile"
          Source="myFont.TTF"
          TrueType="yes"
          KeyPath="yes" />
  </Component>
</DirectoryRef>
```

In the preceding code snippet, the File element is using the TrueType attribute to signify that this file is a font file. It will include myFont.TTF from the current build directory, in the install package and copy it to the end user's C:\WINDOWS\Fonts folder.

Installing 64-bit files

Let's say that you have a .NET assembly that's targeting the x64 platform and you want the installer for it to place that file into the 64-bit Program Files folder (available on 64-bit Windows operating systems). For the uninitiated: you can set the platform for the assembly using Visual Studio's **Configuration Manager**, as shown in the following screenshot:

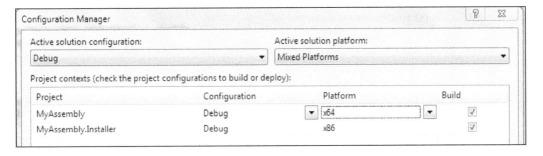

The first thing to do is to open **Properties** for the WiX project and, on the **Tools Settings** tab, add `-arch x64` to the **Compiler** parameters, as shown in the following screenshot:

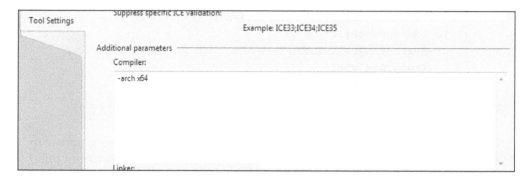

Next, change the `Directory` element that is referencing `ProgramFilesFolder` to instead reference `ProgramFiles64Folder`, given as follows:

```
<Directory Id="TARGETDIR" Name="SourceDir">
  <Directory Id="ProgramFiles64Folder">
    <Directory Id="INSTALLFOLDER" Name="My Software" />
  </Directory>
</Directory>
```

Now your 64-bit assembly can be put into this directory. WiX detects the architecture of the .NET assemblies for you. You'll get a compile-time error if you try to put a 64-bit file into a 32-bit folder, or vice versa.

Creating an empty folder

Ordinarily, Windows Installer won't let you create empty folders. However, there is a way: Use the `CreateFolder` element inside an otherwise empty `Component` element. First, you'll define the name of your empty directory with a `Directory` element. Follow this example:

```
<Directory Id="TARGETDIR"
           Name="SourceDir">
  <Directory Id="ProgramFilesFolder">
    <Directory Id="MyProgramDir"
               Name="Awesome Software">
      <Directory Id="MyEmptyDir"
                 Name="Empty Directory" />
    </Directory>
  </Directory>
</Directory>
```

In the example, we've added a new `Directory` element named `Empty Directory` inside our main application folder. The next step is to add a component to this directory by using a `DirectoryRef` element. Notice that we've set the `KeyPath` attribute on the component to `yes`, as there will be no file to serve this purpose:

```
<DirectoryRef Id="MyEmptyDir">
  <Component Id="CMP_MyEmptyDir"
             Guid="85DAD4AE-6404-4A40-B713-43538091B9D3"
             KeyPath="yes">
    <CreateFolder />
  </Component>
</DirectoryRef>
```

The only thing inside the component is a `CreateFolder` element. This tells Windows Installer that the folder will be empty, but that it should still create it during the install. As always, be sure to add this new component to a feature, as given in the following code snippet:

```
<Feature Id="ProductFeature"
         Title="Main Product"
         Level="1">
  <ComponentRef Id="CMP_InstallMeTXT" />
  <ComponentRef Id="CMP_MyEmptyDir" />
</Feature>
```

Setting file permissions

WiX allows you to set the permissions that Windows users and groups have to the files that you install. You can see these permissions by right-clicking on a file and selecting the **Security** tab. On Windows XP, you may have to configure your system so that this tab is visible. In Windows Explorer, open the folder that you want to configure and go to **Tools | Folder Options | View**. Then, uncheck the box that says **Use simple file sharing**. The following is an example of the **Security** tab on a file:

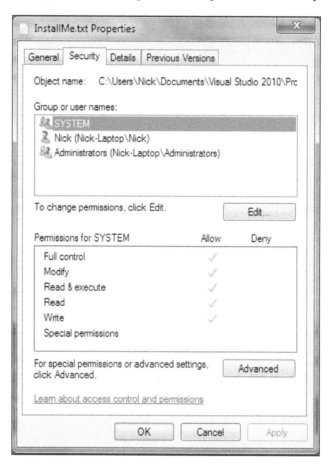

To set the permissions for a file that you're installing, nest a `PermissionEx` element inside the corresponding `File` element. This element, which is available from `WixUtilExtension`, has various attributes that can be used to define file permissions. Before you can use it, you'll need to add a reference to `WixUtilExtension.dll` in your project. Go to **Add Reference** in **Solution Explorer** and select the `WiXUtilExtension` assembly. Next, add the following namespace to your `Wix` element:

```
<Wix xmlns="http://schemas.microsoft.com/wix/2006/wi"
     xmlns:util="http://schemas.microsoft.com/wix/UtilExtension">
```

The following attributes are available to the `PermissionEx` element. Each can be set to either `yes` or `no`:

Attribute	What it does
GenericAll	Gives the user all permissions.
GenericRead	Must have at least one other permission specified. Grants all Read privileges: "Read Data", "Read Attributes", "Read Extended Attributes", and "Read Permissions".
GenericWrite	Grants "Write Data, "Append Data", "Write Attributes", and "Read Permissions".
GenericExecute	Grants "Execute File", "Read Attributes", and "Read Permissions".
Read	Grants "Read Data".
Write	Grants "Write Data".
Execute	Grants "Execute File" permission.
Append	Grants "Append Data".
Delete	Grants "Delete".
ChangePermission	Grants "Change Permissions".
ReadPermission	Grants "Read Permissions".
TakeOwnership	Grants "Take Ownership".
Synchronize	If "yes", then threads must wait their turn before accessing the file.

The following example references the **util** namespace from the `Wix` element and uses its `PermissionEx` element to set file permissions on the `InstallMe.txt` file. Notice that I'm also using another element from `WixUtilExtension` called **User**. This can be used to create a new Windows user on the target computer. The `Product.wxs` file would look something like the following code content:

```
<?xml version="1.0" encoding="UTF-8"?>
<Wix xmlns="http://schemas.microsoft.com/wix/2006/wi"
     xmlns:util="http://schemas.microsoft.com/wix/UtilExtension">

  <Product Id="3E786878-358D-43AD-82D1-1435ADF9F6EA"
```

```
            Name="Awesome Software"
            Language="1033"
            Version="1.0.0.0"
            Manufacturer="Awesome Company"
            UpgradeCode="B414C827-8D81-4B4A-B3B6-338C06DE3A11">

      <Package InstallerVersion="301"
            Compressed="yes"
            InstallScope="perMachine" />

   <MediaTemplate EmbedCab="yes" />

      <!--Directory structure-->
      <Directory Id="TARGETDIR"
               Name="SourceDir">
        <Directory Id="ProgramFilesFolder">
          <Directory Id="MyProgramDir"
                   Name="Awesome Software" />
        </Directory>
      </Directory>

      <!--Components-->
      <DirectoryRef Id="MyProgramDir">
        <Component Id="CMP_InstallMeTXT"
                 Guid="E8A58B7B-F031-4548-9BDD-7A6796C8460D">

          <!--Creates new user-->
          <util:User Id="MyNewUser"
                   CreateUser="yes"
                   Name="nickramirez"
                   Password="password"
                   PasswordNeverExpires="yes"
                   RemoveOnUninstall="yes"
                   UpdateIfExists="yes" />
          <File Id="FILE_InstallMeTXT"
              Source="InstallMe.txt" KeyPath="yes">

            <!--Sets file permissions for user-->
            <util:PermissionEx User="nickramirez"
                             GenericAll="yes" />
          </File>
        </Component>
```

```
      </DirectoryRef>

      <!--Features-->
      <Feature Id="ProductFeature"
               Title="Main Product"
               Level="1">
        <ComponentRef Id="CMP_InstallMeTXT" />
      </Feature>
    </Product>
  </Wix>
```

In this example, we've given all privileges to the user we just created, nickramirez. You can see all of the users for a computer by going to your Start Menu, right-clicking on **Computer**, selecting **Manage**, and viewing the **Local Users and Groups** node. The PermissionEx element's GenericAll attribute gives the user all possible privileges. Just so you know, any users that you create during an installation will be removed during an uninstallation if you set the User element's RemoveOnUninstall attribute to yes.

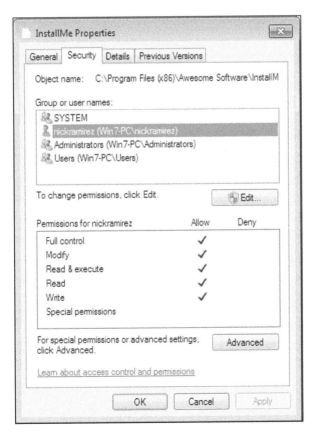

Speeding up file installations

We haven't talked too much about how the files and directories that you author in your WiX source files are stored in the MSI database's tables. The files are stored in a table called **File**, the directories in a table called **Directory**, and the components in a table called **Component**. You can see this by opening the MSI package with Orca.exe.

In the following example, I have four files that are being installed. I've used the convention of prefixing my file IDs with FILE_, giving me FILE_InstallMeTXT, for example:

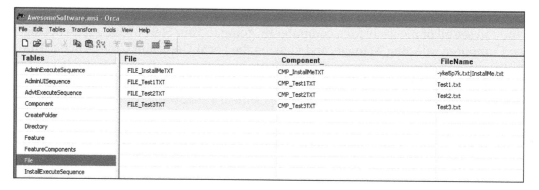

Each file in the **File** table is sorted alphabetically by the Id value you gave to it via the File element. This is the order in which the files are copied to the end user's computer. So, how can you make things faster? You can give your files IDs that will cause WiX to sort them more efficiently.

The file copy process takes longer when Windows has to write to one directory and then switch to another and then another and so on. If it could copy all of the files that belong to a certain directory at the same time and then move to another location, the process would be more efficient. As it is, Windows may leave and return to the same directory several times as it goes through the alphabetical list.

To speed things up, we should add the name of the directory where the file is set to go to the Id attribute of the file. To be effective, this should come at the beginning of Id. That way, files going to the same place will appear next to each other in the list. So, in addition to prefixing our file IDs with FILE_, we could also indicate the directory that each is being copied to. For example, FILE_MyProgramDir_InstallMeTXT signifies that this file is being copied to the MyProgramDir directory. Any other files being copied to the same place should also get MyProgramDir in their IDs.

The following example displays a list that is better organized. It uses the name of the destination directory as part of the files' IDs. Files going to the same place will be grouped together in the alphabetical list, as shown in the following screenshot:

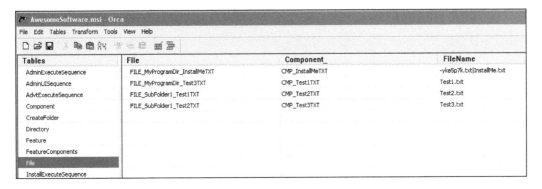

I've used underscores to separate the prefixes, but it's also common to use periods. So, I could have named the first file `FILE.MyProgramDir.InstallMe.Txt` instead of `FILE_MyProgramDir_InstallMeTXT`. It's really just a matter of preference.

Summary

In this chapter, we discussed the elements used to install files and create directories. The `File`, `Directory`, and `Component` elements play vital roles here, but you may also benefit from using `ComponentGroup` to group your components. This allows you to better organize your markup and even to separate it into multiple WiX source files.

The `heat.exe` tool can create `Component` elements for you. You simply need to point it at a certain directory. However, it's best to fine-tune its arguments so that the output that you get is optimal. We discussed a few other topics such as how to copy a file, how to set file permissions, and how to organize your `File` element `Id` attributes for maximum installation speed.

In the next chapter, we'll move on to discuss WiX properties and the various ways of searching the end user's system for files, directories, and settings.

3

Putting Properties and AppSearch to Work

When using WiX, **properties** are the variables that store any temporary data during an install. As such, they provide definitions for various predefined and custom-made installer settings, store input from the user, and provide a means of transferring information from one task to another. Additionally, they can store the results of searching the user's computer for files, directories, registry keys, and settings.

In this chapter, you will learn:

- The syntax for declaring and setting properties
- How to reference properties in other parts of your markup
- The built-in properties that Windows Installer sets for you
- What AppSearch is and how to use it to search the end user's computer for installed components, registry keys, and so on

Custom properties

You'll often need to define and set custom properties to hold your install time data. In the following sections, we will explore the meaning of WiX properties and how best to use them. I should say that properties are not just a feature of WiX, but are innate to Windows Installer itself. So, additional information about them can be found in the Windows Installer documentation.

Declaring and setting properties

To declare a property, add a `Property` element to your WiX markup. A `Property` element only needs two attributes: `Id` and `Value`. The `Id` attribute sets the name of the property, and the `Value` attribute sets the data contained inside. The following example creates a new property called `myProperty` and sets its value to the string `my value`. Note that this can go anywhere inside the `Product` element.

```
<Property Id="myProperty"
          Value="my value" />
```

`Id` should begin with either a letter or underscore and consist of only lower and uppercase letters, numbers, underscores, and periods. When referencing it, it's case sensitive. So, `MyPropertyId` is not the same as `MyPropertyID`.

The data in `Value` can be almost any string. If you need to use double quotes in the value, you can either surround it with single quotes, as in the following example:

```
<Property Id="myProperty"
          Value='Do you see the "quotes"?' />
```

Or you can use the XML entity `&quot;` in place of the double quotes:

```
<Property Id="myProperty"
          Value="Do you see the &quot;quotes&quot;?" />
```

If you omit the `Value` attribute, the property will be set to `null`. During compilation, properties with null values are left out of the MSI package. It will be as if you hadn't declared them at all.

You can also set the value of a `Property` element by adding inner text to it, as in the following example:

```
<Property Id="myProperty">my value</Property>
```

Properties can also be set from the command line. If you do, you're not required to declare the property in your WiX markup first. Declaring them on the command line creates them dynamically. When defining properties on the command line, their IDs must be uppercase. This is to make them "public", which we'll discuss later in the chapter. To add a property in this way, add the name and value of your property, separated by an equals sign, after the `msiexec` command.

```
msiexec /i myInstaller.msi PROPERTY1=100 PROPERTY2="my value"
```

Here we're declaring two properties at install time, PROPERTY1 and PROPERTY2, and setting their respective values. You can add more than one property by separating them with spaces, as we've done here. Literal string values that have spaces in them should be surrounded by double quotes. If the value itself has double quotes in it, you can escape them by using two double quotes instead of one:

```
msiexec /i myInstaller.msi PROPERTY1="Game title: ""Starcraft""."
```

You can clear a property by setting its value to an empty string, such as:

```
msiexec /i myInstaller.msi PROPERTY1=""
```

Properties declared on the command line override those set in your WiX markup. So, you could declare a WiX `Property` element in your XML to give it a default value, and then override that value from the command line.

Referencing properties

One of the common uses of properties is to reference them in another WiX element. There is a limited list of elements that can reference a property, including the following:

- `Control`: This references a `Text` attribute
- `ListItem`: This references a `Text` attribute
- `Dialog`: This references a `Title` attribute
- `Shortcut`: This references `Target`, `Arguments`, and `Description` attributes
- `Condition`: This references `Message` attribute
- `RegistryValue`: This references `Name` and `Value` attributes

Generally, any attribute on an element that becomes something the end user will see in the UI (text on dialogs, labels on buttons, items in lists, and so on) or the names of shortcuts and registry keys will have the ability to interpret it. In the element's attribute, add the `Id` attribute of the property with square brackets around it. For example, to refer to a property called USERNAME, you'd use [USERNAME]. You'll run across more elements like this throughout the rest of the book.

In the next example, we'll create a property called myProperty that has a value of 0. A `Condition` element that follows checks the value to see if it's equal to 1. Notice that I'm using the square bracket notation in the `Message` attribute to reference myProperty:

```
<Property Id="myProperty"
          Value="0" />

<Condition Message=
```

```
"Value of myProperty is [myProperty]. Should be 1">

    <![CDATA[Installed OR myProperty = "1"]]>
</Condition>
```

The `Message` attribute is used to show a modal window to the user. In this case, they'll see **Value of myProperty is 0. Should be 1**.

Conversely, when you use a property in the *inner text* of an element, you don't need the square brackets. Conditional statements, such as those found inside the `Condition` element, are a good example. Look back at the previous example to see that `myProperty` is referenced in the inner text of the `Condition` element without using square brackets.

```
<![CDATA[Installed OR myProperty = "1"]]>
```

> The **Installed** keyword is a built-in property set by WiX that signifies that the product is already installed. By checking it, we ensure that the second half of our condition will only be evaluated if the product is not currently installed.

Declaring properties in your main `.wxs` file is fine if you only have a few. Once you've got a good number it's easier to move them into their own source file and nest them inside a `Fragment` element. To access these in your main `.wxs` file, add a `PropertyRef` element with the `Id` attribute of one of the properties. A `PropertyRef` element brings that property, and all others defined in the fragment, into the scope of your project.

```
<Product ... >
  ...
  <PropertyRef Id="myProperty" />
</Product>

<Fragment>
  <Property Id="myProperty" Value="my value" />
</Fragment>
```

Property visibility and scope

Two things to consider when working with properties are **visibility** and **scope**. With regards to visibility, consider that when you install an MSI package it's simple to get a log of the process. You can see this log by installing from the command line with logging turned on.

You can also turn on logging by changing keys in the registry or through Group Policy. Refer to the following web page for more information: http://support.microsoft.com/kb/223300.

The following command installs a package called myInstaller.msi and writes a verbose log using the /l*v flag:

```
msiexec /i myInstaller.msi /l*v log.log
```

When you submit this command, it will log every event that happens during the install to a text file called log.log. At the end of the log, all properties with their values will be listed in plain text. This isn't a good thing if one of your properties contains a password or other sensitive data. To prevent a specific property from showing in the install log, mark it as Hidden:

```
<Property Id="MY_PASSWORD"
          Value="some value"
          Hidden="yes" />
```

Set the Hidden attribute to yes if you don't want to show the property as an entry in the log. Marking a property as hidden does not, however, prevent it from displaying its value in the MSI database's Property table. Therefore, you probably shouldn't set the literal value of a password directly in a property, as in the previous example. Instead, set the value from the command line or collect it from the user via the UI. That way, it is defined dynamically and the user cannot see it by opening the MSI package with Orca.exe.

Scope is another consideration. By default, properties are not public, meaning that they are not available when the installer runs through its execution phase (when changes are made to the end user's system). We'll talk more about this phase later on. For now, just know that if you plan on using your properties when writing to the registry, laying down files, or during any other act that changes the user's computer, then those properties must be made public.

Making a property public is just a matter of making its Id value all uppercase. The property MY_PASSWORD is public, while my_Password is not. One example of when to do this is when you collect information from the user with a dialog and then want to take some action on it during the execution phase, such as store it in the registry.

The following property, because it's uppercase, will persist throughout the entire installation.

```
<Property Id="MY_PROPERTY"
          Value="my string" />
```

However, this will not:

```
<Property Id="My_Property"
        Value="my string" />
```

You could consider this a **private property**. It will only last during the current session. We will discuss the install phases in detail in *Chapter 5, Understanding the Installation Sequence*.

Secure properties

Ordinarily, an installer will prompt a non-admin user to elevate their privileges, or in other words enter the password of an administrator account, before performing tasks that change directories and registry keys outside their permissions zone. However, administrators can, through various means discussed shortly, allow non-admin users to install approved software without being asked to elevate their privileges.

This has the benefit of simplifying distribution of software on a company network, for example, but comes at a price. Windows Installer may mark the installation as **restricted**. This means that the properties you set could be ignored. The following scenarios may set this in motion:

- The user performing the install is not an administrator
- The install is marked as per-machine instead of per-user, meaning the ALLUSERS property is set to 1 in your markup or the Package element's InstallScope attribute is set to perMachine
- Through various means, discussed shortly, the user does not need to enter an administrator's password to elevate their permissions like they normally would to complete the install

There are several ways to allow a non-administrator to continue an installation without elevating. The first is when an administrator *publishes* the MSI to all computers in an Active Directory domain using Group Policy. This allows non-admin users to go to **Programs and Features** and install the MSI from the network without the need to enter an administrator's password. More information can be found at http://support. microsoft.com/kb/816102. The user would see packages available for install, as in the following example:

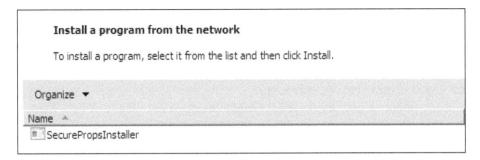

Install a program from the network

To install a program, select it from the list and then click Install.

Organize ▼

Name ▲

SecurePropsInstaller

Another scenario is when an administrator has *advertised* the MSI for non-admin users to install on that same computer. This is done by using the `/jm` command-line option to advertise the package for all users. An admin calls:

```
msiexec /jm \\PCName\MyShare\AwesomeInstaller.msi
```

This advertises the installer. A user can then install the MSI without needing to elevate their privileges.

A third scenario is when the `AlwaysInstallElevated` value has been set to `1` in the following registry keys:

- `HKEY_CURRENT_USER\Software\Policies\Microsoft\Windows\Installer`
- `HKEY_LOCAL_MACHINE\Software\Policies\Microsoft\Windows\Installer`

This lets non-admin users install any MSI without using an administrator's password.

When one of these scenarios happens, the installer, marking that actions are being done by a non-administrator, labels the whole process as restricted. In that case, only a small list of approved properties is allowed to be passed to the Execute sequence, which is the phase during which changes are made to the computer. To add more properties to that list, you'll need to mark them as `Secure`, as shown in the following code snippet:

```
<Property Id="MY_PROPERTY"
          Value="my string"
          Secure="yes" />
```

 You can find a list of the default secure properties at `http://msdn.microsoft.com/en-us/library/windows/desktop/aa371243(v=vs.85).aspx`.

You can tell when you need to use the `Secure` attribute if, in the install log, you see that the `RestrictedUserControl` property has been set automatically. You'll also see some of your properties, if they're used in the execute sequence, being ignored. The following is a sample log of that happening:

```
MSI (s) (C8:BC) [23:49:58:906]:
          Machine policy value 'EnableUserControl' is 0
MSI (s) (C8:BC) [23:49:58:906]: PROPERTY CHANGE:
          Adding RestrictedUserControl property. Its value is '1'.
MSI (s) (C8:BC) [23:49:58:906]:
          Ignoring disallowed property MYPROPERTY
```

Notice that there's another property called `EnableUserControl`. If you set it to `1` in your markup, all properties will be marked as `Secure`.

Property data types

The properties in WiX are not strongly typed, meaning that you don't need to specify whether a property is an integer or a string. Most of the time, you'll be setting properties by using the WiX `Property` element. The alternative is to set them from the command line or set them dynamically with a UI control or custom action. Using a `Property` element always implicitly casts the property as a string. Therefore, you can always treat these properties as string values. However, depending on how you reference it, it's possible for WiX to interpret your property as an integer.

If, in a conditional statement, you compare your property to an integer (a whole number without quotes around it), WiX will assume that your property is an integer too. For example, here I compare a property to the number 3 without quotes around it. WiX will cast my property to an integer and then perform the comparison:

```
<Property Id="MyProperty"
          Value="5" />

<Condition Message="Some message if condition is false." >
  <![CDATA[MyProperty > 3]]>
</Condition>
```

The same is true when comparing a property to a string. WiX will assume your property is a string and perform the comparison:

```
<Property Id="MyProperty"
          Value="5" />

<Condition Message="Some message if condition is false.">
  <![CDATA[MyProperty = "5"]]>
</Condition>
```

The following table shows the comparison operators and examples for integers and strings that evaluate to true:

Operator	Meaning	Integer example	String example
<	Less than	`1 < 2`	`"abc" < "def"`
>	Greater than	`2 > 1`	`"b" > "a"`
<=	Less than or equal to	`2 <= 3`	`"a" <= "b"`
>=	Greater than or equal to	`3 >= 2`	`"b" >= "a"`
=	Equal to	`2 = 2`	`"a" = "a"`
<>	Not equal to	`2 <> 1`	`"a" <> "b"`
><	Left string contains right string (strings only)	n/a	`"abc" >< "b"`
<<	Left string starts with right string (strings only)	n/a	`"abcde" << "ab"`
>>	Left string ends with right string (strings only)	n/a	`"abcde" >> "de"`

With the "greater than" and "less than" signs, a string is considered less than another if, from left to right, one of its characters comes before the character in the other string. For example, the string "abc" is less than "abd" because "c" comes before "d".

Note that if the property is a decimal, such as 2.0, then you can't compare it to a numeric value unless you put quotes around that value. This is because WiX has no concept of decimals and so must evaluate them as strings. For example, the following statement, unexpectedly, evaluates to `false`:

```
<Property Id="myNum"
          Value="2.0" />

<Condition Message="myNum must be > 1.">
  <![CDATA[myNum > 1]]>
</Condition>
```

However, by putting quotes around 1, it evaluates to `true` as it should:

```
<Property Id="myNum"
          Value="2.0" />

<Condition Message="myNum must be > 1.">
  <![CDATA[myNum > "1"]]>
</Condition>
```

Normally, when you compare two string values, the case counts. However, if you prefix the comparison operator with a tilde (~), the case will be ignored. The following condition evaluates to `true`:

```
<Property Id="MyProperty"
          Value="sample string" />

<Condition Message="Some message if condition is false.">
  <![CDATA[MyProperty ~= "SAMPLE STRING"]]>
</Condition>
```

Something else you can do is check if a property is defined at all. Evaluating a property by itself checks that it has been set, as in the following example:

```
<Condition Message="Some message if condition is false">
  <![CDATA[MY_PROPERTY]]>
</Condition>
```

Placing the NOT keyword in front of the property checks that the property is *not* set:

```
<Condition Message="Some message if condition is false">
  <![CDATA[NOT MY_PROPERTY]]>
</Condition>
```

WiX data types are very simplistic. After all, if you were to look at the MSI's `Property` table, you'd see only two columns: `property` and `value`. There's no extra column to tell what type of data it is. Take this into account when planning the conditional statements that you write.

Predefined Windows Installer properties

You've seen that you can define your own properties, but there are also a number that come predefined for you. Quite a few are created automatically as part of the install process. For example, there's the property called `Installed` that's set if the product is already installed locally. Looking through the install log will uncover many more.

In this section, you'll be introduced to some of these automatic properties. You'll also see that some properties, although their `Id` attributes are defined for you, only come to life when you instantiate them with `Property` elements.

Implied properties

There are certain properties that don't need to be set with a `Property` element. They're implied. They're set for you. First, there are those that are created when you set attributes on the `Product` element. So, for example, the following code snippet:

```
<Product Id="3E786878-358D-43AD-82D1-1435ADF9F6EA"
         Name="Awesome Software"
         Language="1033"
         Version="1.0.0.0"
         Manufacturer="Awesome Company"
         UpgradeCode="B414C827-8D81-4B4A-B3B6-338C06DE3A11">
```

This creates the following properties:

- `ProductCode`
- `ProductName`
- `ProductLanguage`
- `ProductVersion`
- `Manufacturer`
- `UpgradeCode`

You can use these properties just as you would those you create yourself. They're available to you in all phases of the install. They can be accessed in the attributes and inner text of other elements just like normal.

Another set of implied properties are **directories**. We discussed the built-in directory properties in *Chapter 1, Getting Started*. They're given names such as `ProgramFilesFolder`. In addition to using them in your `Directory` elements, you can use these names anywhere that other properties are used. Also, any directories that you create with `Directory` elements are also available as properties. The directory's `Id` attribute becomes the ID of the property.

Another set of implied properties are those that guide how Windows Installer does its job. For example, there's the `Installed` property, which tells you that the product is already installed. You'll usually see it during an uninstall or if the product is in maintenance mode. Another is the `Privileged` property, which is set when the install is performed by an administrator. Another example is the `REMOVE` property, which is only set during an uninstall. Taking a look at the install log will reveal many of these.

Cited properties

Most of the properties that are built into Windows Installer *aren't* implied. You have to set them explicitly with a `Property` element. They're different from the properties that you'll create yourself, in that the `Id` attribute must match the predefined name and they're generally used to toggle various Windows Installer settings. There is a fairly long list of these available. Check the *Property Reference* in the *MSI SDK* help file that comes with WiX by searching in it for the phrase "Property Reference". You can also find them at:

`http://msdn.microsoft.com/en-us/library/aa370905%28v=VS.85%29.aspx`

I won't list them all here, but to give you an idea, here are properties that affect what gets shown in **Programs and Features** once your product has been installed. Your product will automatically show up in the list without the use of properties, but these provide extra information or disable the default functionality:

Property	Description
ARPAUTHORIZEDCDPREFIX	URL of the update channel for the application
ARPCOMMENTS	Provides comments for **Add/Remove Programs**
ARPCONTACT	Provides the contact for **Add/Remove Programs**
ARPINSTALLLOCATION	Fully qualified path to the application's primary folder
ARPHELPLINK	URL for technical support
ARPHELPTELEPHONE	Technical support phone numbers
ARPNOMODIFY	Prevents displaying a **Change** button for the product in **Add/Remove Programs**
ARPNOREMOVE	Prevents displaying a **Remove** button for the product in **Add/Remove Programs**
ARPNOREPAIR	Disables the **Repair** button in **Add/Remove Programs**
ARPPRODUCTICON	Identifies the icon to display for the product in **Add/Remove Programs**
ARPREADME	Provides the ReadMe for **Add/Remove Programs**
ARPSIZE	Estimated size of the application in kilobytes
ARPSYSTEMCOMPONENT	Prevents the application from displaying at all in **Add/Remove Programs**
ARPURLINFOABOUT	URL for the application's home page
ARPURLUPDATEINFO	URL for the application's update information

The following are a few examples of how these properties would be set:

```
<Icon Id="myIcon"
      SourceFile="..\myIcon.ico" />


<Property Id="ARPPRODUCTICON"
          Value="myIcon" />
<Property Id="ARPCOMMENTS"
          Value="(c) Amazing Software" />
<Property Id="ARPNOREPAIR"
          Value="1" />
<Property Id="ARPCONTACT"
          Value="Nick Ramirez" />
<Property Id="ARPHELPLINK"        Value="http://www.MYURL.com/
AmazingSoftware/support.html"/>
<Property Id="ARPREADME"          Value="http://www.MYURL.com/
AmazingSoftware/readme.html" />
```

As you can see, setting a built-in property is just like setting your own custom properties except that the Id value must use the predefined name.

One other built-in property that you should know about is ALLUSERS. You can set it to a 1, 2, or an empty string (""). A 1 means that the install will be performed in the per-machine context. This means that its components will be installed to folders accessible to anyone that uses the system. Setting ALLUSERS to an empty string tells the installer to use the per-user context, meaning that its components will be installed only for the current user. A value of 2 means that the installer will sometimes be in the user context and sometimes in the machine context, depending on whether or not the user who initiated it has administrator rights. However, even this rule varies based upon the operating system.

In general, you should set ALLUSERS to 1, the per-machine context. Setting it to the per-user context can only be done if you're certain that no registry keys or files will be installed to machine-level locations. This is rarely the case. A value of 2 usually causes scenarios that are too complex to plan for. So, it's best to avoid it. The following example sets the ALLUSERS property to 1:

```
<Property Id="ALLUSERS"
          Value="1" />
```

The reason that this property is important is that during an upgrade, you'll want to find out if a previous version of the software is already installed. For that, the ALLUSERS property must be set to the same value as it was originally. Otherwise, the installer may look in the wrong place and fail to detect the software, even if it's there. So, keep it consistent. Always set it to the same value, preferably 1.

One thing to note is that you can also set the `InstallScope` attribute on the `Package` element to either `perMachine` or `perUser`. This will have the same effect as setting the `ALLUSERS` property directly. If you do, you should remove any `Property` element that sets it.

AppSearch

Windows Installer lets you search the computer during an install for specific files, directories, and settings. Collectively, these fall under the category of **AppSearch**, which is the name of the MSI database table where search tasks are stored.

There are five types of searches:

- **DirectorySearch**: This searches for the existence or path of a directory
- **FileSearch**: This searches for a specific file
- **ComponentSearch**: This searches for a file by its component GUID
- **RegistrySearch**: This searches the Windows Registry for a key
- **IniFileSearch**: This searches inside INI files for configuration settings

Each of these types refers to the WiX element that you'd use to perform the search. Each is the child element of a `Property` element. So, you'll start off with a `Property` element whose value will be set to the result of the search.

There's an attribute of the `Property` element, `ComplianceCheck`, that can be used when doing an AppSearch. When set to `yes`, an error dialog will be shown if the search isn't successful. It will then end the installation.

The error message you get is very generic though. You're better off detecting whether or not a certain file exists, setting a property based on the result, and crafting a targeted message if it isn't found (using a launch condition, discussed later). That way, users will know *what* wasn't found. Although there's nothing stopping you from creating a custom launch condition and setting `ComplianceCheck` to `yes`, it isn't necessary since the install will end if the launch condition fails and launch conditions always come before the compliance check is performed.

DirectorySearch

You may want to check if a directory exists on a computer and, if it does, get its path. You can do this by using a `DirectorySearch` element. A `DirectorySearch` element is nested inside of a `Property` element, as shown in the following code snippet:

```
<Property Id="NPP_PATH">
  <DirectorySearch Path=" C:\Program Files (x86)\Notepad++"
                   Depth="0"
                   AssignToProperty="yes"
                   Id="NppFolderSearch"/>
</Property>
```

In this example, we're seeing if the popular text editor Notepad++ has been installed by checking for a directory called `Notepad++` in the `Program Files` folder. We start by declaring a `Property` and giving it an `Id` attribute of our choosing. If the search finds a directory that matches, based on the `Path` attribute, it will set this property's value to the path. Otherwise, the property will be null.

The `AssignToProperty` attribute tells the installer to use this `DirectorySearch` element to set the property. This becomes more valuable when you've got `DirectorySearch` elements nested inside other `DirectorySearch` elements, as you'll see.

Notice that this search is pretty specific about where this directory should be: we've given an *absolute* path to the directory we're looking for. The `Depth` attribute is set to zero to signify that there's no need to drill down into any subfolders.

What if I didn't know exactly where this directory was, though? For example, suppose we didn't want to assume that the user has a C:? We could be more generic with the search criteria. We could, for example, just give the name of the folder we're looking for:

```
<Property Id="NPP_PATH">
  <DirectorySearch Path="Notepad++"
                   Depth="5"
                   AssignToProperty="yes"
                   Id="NppFolderSearch" />
</Property>
```

Here we've set the `Path` attribute to just `Notepad++` and the `Depth` attribute to 5. Now we're telling the installer to search for a folder called `Notepad++` and that we're willing to go five directories deep to find it. Because we haven't explicitly told it where to start the search from it will search all attached drives starting at their root directories (such as `C:\`, `D:\`, and others).

Because our search is so generic, you might be in for a wait. Worse, on Vista or Windows 7, you'll probably get an error as the installer tries to search through the hidden, restricted junction point C:\Documents and Settings.

In cases such as this, you should tell Windows Installer where to start searching by nesting the DirectorySearch elements inside one another. Then, the outer-most DirectorySearch becomes the starting point and the child becomes the directory you're searching for. As in the following example:

```
<Property Id="NPP_PATH">
    <DirectorySearch Path="[ProgramFilesFolder]"
                     Depth="0"
                     AssignToProperty="no"
                     Id="ProgramFilesFolderSearch">
        <DirectorySearch Path="Notepad++"
                         Depth="0"
                         AssignToProperty="yes"
                         Id="NppFolderSearch"/>
    </DirectorySearch>
</Property>
```

Now we're searching inside the Program Files folder for the Notepad++ folder. Note that the first DirectorySearch element has its AssignToProperty attribute set to no. We want the inner DirectorySearch element to be the only one to set the property. Also note that we could have set the Depth attribute of the inner DirectorySearch element to a number greater than zero. It would then search that many folders deep inside Program Files until it either found what it was looking for or ran out of folders to look through.

The following is another example that uses three DirectorySearch elements to find the Notepad++ plugins folder:

```
<Property Id="NPP_PATH">
    <DirectorySearch Path="[ProgramFilesFolder]"
                     Depth="0"
                     AssignToProperty="no"
                     Id="ProgramFilesFolderSearch">
        <DirectorySearch Path="Notepad++"
                         Depth="0"
                         AssignToProperty="no"
                         Id="NppFolderSearch">
            <DirectorySearch Path="plugins"
                             Depth="0"
                             AssignToProperty="yes"
                             Id="pluginsSearch" />
```

```
            </DirectorySearch>
          </DirectorySearch>
        </Property>
```

The `Path` attribute actually gives you quite a few options. It can accept any of the following:

- A WiX property
- A Windows share, such as `\\myshare\myFolder`
- A path relative to the top-level directory for any attached drives, such as `\temp`
- An absolute path, such as `C:\temp`
- The name of a folder, such as `temp`
- An environment variable (using WiX preprocessor syntax), such as `$(env.ALLUSERSPROFILE)`

You should know that if the installer can't find the path you set in the parent element, it will skip it and use its default—every attached drive's root directory.

Although it seems superfluous, each `DirectorySearch` element must get its own ID. Windows Installer uses these `Id` attributes to tie all of the elements together into one cohesive search. It's interesting to look inside the MSI package and see how all of this is stored. Directory searches are found in the `DrLocator` table. The following is what you'd find for the previous search:

Signature	Parent	Path	Depth
pluginsSearch	NppFolderSearch	plugins	0
NppFolderSearch	ProgramFiles FolderSearch	Notepad++	0
ProgramFiles FolderSearch		[ProgramFilesFolder]	0

The table structure mirrors the parent-child relationship seen in WiX. In the `AppSearch` table, you'd see a row with the property `NPP_PATH` mapped to the signature `pluginsSearch`.

FileSearch

There may be times when you want to find a specific file instead of just a directory. For this, you'll still use a DirectorySearch element, but you'll nest a FileSearch element inside it. This tells the installer that you're looking for a file inside that directory:

```
<Property Id="README_FILE">
  <DirectorySearch Path="C:\Program Files (x86)\Notepad++"
                   Depth="0"
                   AssignToProperty="no"
                   Id="NppSearch">

    <FileSearch Name="readme.txt"
                Id="readmeFileSearch" />
  </DirectorySearch>
</Property>
```

The FileSearch element names the file you're looking for with its Name attribute. If it's found, the property will be populated with the absolute path to the file. In this case, it will be set to C:\Program Files (x86)\Notepad++\readme.txt. You can use any of the various definitions for the DirectorySearch element's Path attribute discussed in the last section as well as nesting DirectorySearch elements. Or if you omit the Path attribute altogether, you'll be telling the installer to look at all attached drives for the file you specify. Set the AssignToProperty attribute to no on the DirectorySearch elements.

> Be wary of accidentally putting a space in front of the value in Path, such as Path=" C:\". The search will fail and you'll be hard pressed to find out why.

The FileSearch element can't do recursive searches through subfolders. So, its parent DirectorySearch element must name the exact folder where the file is supposed to be, if it specifies a path with the Path attribute.

You can add other attributes to the FileSearch element to refine your search, such as the MinSize and MaxSize attributes for a range of file sizes (in bytes), MinDate and MaxDate for range of modification dates, and MinVersion and MaxVersion for a range of file versions. This is shown in the following snippet:

```
<FileSearch Name="readme.txt"
            Id="readmeFileSearch"
            MinSize="100"
            MaxSize="200"
            MinVersion="1.5.0.0"
```

```
        MaxVersion="2.0.0.0"
        MinDate="2009-12-20T12:30:00"
        MaxDate="2009-12-25T12:30:00" />
```

Note that `MinDate` and `MaxDate` must use the format, "YYYY-MM-DDTHH:mm:ss", where "YYYY" is the year, "MM" the month, "DD" the day, "HH" the hour, "mm" the minute, and "ss" the second. "T" is actually the letter "T". You can also add a `Language` attribute to limit the search to files with a specific language ID. For example, "1033" is "English, United States". To specify more than one language, separate them by commas.

You can see the searches you've set up in the MSI database under the `Signature` table. There, the filename, version, size, date, and language are listed. An `Id` value on that table is joined to the `DrLocator` table where the directory structure is defined. The entire search is referenced on the `AppSearch` table, where it is linked with a property. You can probably see how defining the structure and data of the MSI is greatly simplified by using WiX's declarative markup.

ComponentSearch

A second way to search for files installed on the end user's computer is to use a `ComponentSearch` element. Like other search elements, `ComponentSearch` is nested inside a `Property` element. If the file you're looking for is found, the path of its folder will be saved to the property. Note that it won't be the full path to the file itself, but close enough.

To understand `ComponentSearch`, you have to remember that Windows Installer uses components with unique GUIDs as containers for the files that get copied to a computer. `ComponentSearch` looks for the GUID that was set on a component or more specifically, the file that was marked as the keypath in that component. So, as long as you know the GUID, you can find the file. In fact, you can even look for files installed by other programs, as long as you know the GUID.

Use `Orca.exe` to open an MSI installer and check the `Component` table for a file's GUID. It's marked as `ComponentId`. The actual filename is available on the `File` table and is mapped to the `Component` table via the `Component` column. To set the GUID in the `ComponentSearch` element, use the `Guid` attribute. The following is an example that, as a very simple case, searches for the path to the `Orca.exe` tool itself:

```
<Property Id="ORCA_PATH">
   <ComponentSearch Id="orcaSearch"
                    Guid="{BE928E10-272A-11D2-B2E4-006097C99860}" />
</Property>
```

Here, we are looking for the `orca.exe` file. The MSI for it can be found after installing the Windows SDK. If you've installed Orca, this search should return a path to the executable, something like `C:\Program Files (x86)\Orca\`.

`ComponentSearch` has several uses. You might use it to find out where the user installed your software, as it returns the absolute path to the directory where the specified file is. You could also use it to check if someone else's software is installed. To make such a check reliable, be sure to look for a file that's definitely going to be there. The downside to `ComponentSearch` is that you're relying on the GUIDs staying the same. This is pretty safe when it's your own software, but can be risky with anyone else's.

There's one other optional attribute of the `ComponentSearch` element: `Type`. The `Type` attribute can be set to either `file`, its default, or `directory`. Setting it to file causes it to do what it normally does—look for the `KeyPath` file of the component and return its parent directory. You would set `Type` to `directory` only when your search involves a component that did not specify a file as its `KeyPath`. Take the following example:

```
<DirectoryRef Id="INSTALLLOCATION">
  <Directory Id="newDir" Name="New Directory">
    <Component Id="newDirComp"
               Guid="EA8062E0-E9C2-49E7-B76D-32161923F9F9"
               KeyPath="yes">

      <CreateFolder />
    </Component>
  </Directory>
</DirectoryRef>
```

Here, we've created a component that is tasked with creating an empty folder called `New Directory` in the install directory. There are no files in the component to make a keypath out of. So, we've set the `KeyPath` attribute to yes on the `Component` element itself. If we don't specify a `KeyPath` value at all, the component will be assumed to be the keypath by default.

When there's no file specified as the keypath, you can set the `ComponentSearch` element's `Type` attribute to `directory` and it will return the path to the component's parent directory—just like normal. Otherwise, we get the strange behavior of `ComponentSearch` returning the directory above the parent directory. For example, if we set the `Type` to `file` (or leave it out), we get the install directory, `INSTALLLOCATION`, back. If we set `Type` to `directory`, we get the component's parent directory, `newDir`. So, it's basically something you have to do just to get the expected behavior.

```
<!--Returns INSTALLLOCATION: C:\Program Files\mySoftware\-->
<Property Id="MY_DIRECTORY_PATH ">
  <ComponentSearch Id="myCompSearch"
                   Guid="{EA8062E0-E9C2-49E7-B76D-32161923F9F9}"
                   Type="file" />
</Property>

<!--Returns newDir: C:\Program Files\mySoftware\New Directory-->
<Property Id="MY_DIRECTORY_PATH ">
  <ComponentSearch Id="myCompSearch"
                   Guid="{EA8062E0-E9C2-49E7-B76D-32161923F9F9}"
                   Type="directory" />
</Property>
```

Of course, if there *is* a `KeyPath` file, setting the `ComponentSearch` element's `Type` attribute to `directory` will cause the search to return `null`. In general, the applications for this confusing logic are so few that you'll rarely have to worry about using the `Type` attribute.

RegistrySearch

WiX lets you read values from the Windows Registry with its `RegistrySearch` element. Like the previous search types, `RegistrySearch` has a `Property` element as its parent. If the registry value you're looking for is found, its value will be saved to the property. The following is an example:

```
<Property Id="DIRECTX_VERSION">
  <RegistrySearch Id="DirectX_Version"
                  Root="HKLM"
                  Key="SOFTWARE\Microsoft\DirectX"
                  Name="Version"
                  Type="raw" />
</Property>
```

This searches for the version of DirectX installed on the user's computer. The version number is located in the registry as a value called Version in the HKEY_LOCAL_ MACHINE\SOFTWARE\Microsoft\DirectX key. If the search finds it, it saves the value to the property DIRECTX_VERSION, which is an arbitrary name.

To get there with RegistrySearch, set the Root attribute to the abbreviated version of HKEY_LOCAL_MACHINE, which is HKLM. Your possible values for Root are:

- HKLM: For HKEY_LOCAL_MACHINE
- HKCR: For HKEY_CLASSES_ROOT
- HKCU: For HKEY_CURRENT_USER
- HKU: For HKEY_USERS

The Key attribute is the registry path beneath Root to the item you're looking for. In this example, it's set to SOFTWARE\Microsoft\DirectX. This path is not case sensitive. The Name attribute is the value in the key that you want to read. This is also not case sensitive.

The Type attribute tells the installer what sort of data it can expect to find in this registry item. You have three options here: directory, file, or raw. Using directory or file lets you combine RegistrySearch with either FileSearch or DirectorySearch. It's used as a way to search the computer's directory structure for a file or directory after it gets the location of it from the registry.

Suppose you want to read a value from the registry and that value is the path to a file. You then want to check that the file is truly where it says it is on the filesystem. As an example, assume that there's a registry item HKLM\SOFTWARE\WIXTEST\ PathToFile that's set to the value C:\Program Files\mySoftware\myFile.txt. You can get this value from the registry by using the RegistrySearch element, as in the following example:

```
<Property Id="MY_PROPERTY">
  <RegistrySearch Id="myRegSearch"
                  Root="HKLM"
                  Key="SOFTWARE\WIXTEST"
                  Name="PathToFile"
                  Type="file">

    <FileSearch Id="myFileSearch" Name="[MY_PROPERTY]" />
  </RegistrySearch>
</Property>
```

Here, the `RegistrySearch` element finds the item in the registry and sets the value of `MY_PROPERTY`. Next, the nested `FileSearch` element can now read that property and use it to find the file on the computer. If it finds it, it replaces the value of `MY_PROPERTY` with the location of the file—which should be the same. If it doesn't find it, it sets the value to `null`.

In order for this to work, you have to set the `RegistrySearch` element's `Type` attribute to `file`. This tells the installer that it should expect to find the path to a file in the registry and that you intend to nest a `FileSearch` element inside the `RegistrySearch` element.

You can do something similar with `DirectorySearch`. Take this example, assuming there is another registry item called `PathToDirectory` where the value is the path to the directory `C:\Program Files\mySoftware\myDirectory\`:

```
<Property Id="MY_PROPERTY">
  <RegistrySearch Id="myRegSearch"
                  Root="HKLM"
                  Key="SOFTWARE\WIXTEST"
                  Name="PathToDirectory"
                  Type="directory">

    <DirectorySearch Id="myDirSearch"
                     Path="[MY_PROPERTY]" />
  </RegistrySearch>
</Property>
```

Here, `Type` is set to `directory` allowing you to nest a `DirectorySearch` element inside `RegistrySearch`. This type also tells the installer that it should expect the registry value to hold the path to a directory. Like the `FileSearch` example, this one uses the `RegistrySearch` result to set a property and then uses that property to search the filesystem. This time, it's looking for a directory instead of a file. If it finds it, it will set the property to the path. If not, the property will be set to `null`.

Setting `Type` to `raw` lets you read the registry value and set a property, but nothing more. In many cases, this will be all you want. Be aware that Windows Installer will add special characters to the value to distinguish different data types. The following table explains what it will add to different kinds of values. This only applies when `Type` is set to `raw`:

Type of data	Characters added
DWORD	Starts with "#" optionally followed by "+" or "-"
REG_BINARY	Starts with "#x" and the installer converts and saves each hexadecimal digit as an ASCII character prefixed by "#x"

Type of data	Characters added
REG_EXPAND_SZ	Starts with "#%"
REG_MULTI_SZ	Starts with "[~]" and ends with "[~]"
REG_SZ	No prefix, but if the first character of the registry value is "#", the installer escapes the character by prefixing it with another "#"

All of the attributes mentioned so far — Id, Key, Root, Name, and Type — are required. There is one optional attribute though called **Win64**. When set to yes, it will search the 64-bit portion of the registry instead of the 32-bit one. Of course, this only applies to 64-bit operating systems. The following is an example:

```
<Property Id="MY_PROPERTY">
  <RegistrySearch Id="myRegSearch"
                  Root="HKLM"
                  Key="SOFTWARE\WIXTEST"
                  Name="myRegistryItem"
                  Type="raw"
                  Win64="yes" />
</Property>
```

Registry searches are represented in the MSI database on the RegLocator table. There you'll find a column for the Root, Key, Name, and Type attributes. The Id attribute is listed under the Signature column and is referenced by various other tables including AppSearch, DrLocator, and Signature. For complex searches where FileSearch or DirectorySearch elements are nested inside RegistrySearch, these tables are joined together by this Id.

IniFileSearch

The last type of search in the WiX arsenal is IniFileSearch, which lets you search INI configuration files for settings. An **INI** file is a text file with an .ini extension that uses a simple syntax to list configuration settings. The following is a sample INI file:

```
; Test INI file
[section1]
name=Nick Ramirez
occupation=software developer

[section2]
car=Mazda3
miles=70000

[section3]
breakfast=yogurt
```

WiX always searches the `%windir%` directory, which is usually `C:\Windows` for INI files. So, save this code as `myConfigFile.ini` in that directory.

In an INI file, you can comment out text by putting a semicolon at the beginning of the line. Mark different sections by putting brackets around the name. In each section, create key-value pairs separated by equal signs. And there you have it, pretty simple stuff.

An `IniFileSearch` uses four attributes: `Id`, `Name`, `Section`, and `Key`. Let's look at an example:

```
<Property Id="MY_PROPERTY">
  <IniFileSearch Id="myIniSearch"
                 Name="myConfigFile.ini"
                 Section="section1"
                 Key="name"
                 Type="raw" />
</Property>
```

The `Id` attribute specifies the primary key of the item in the MSI database `IniLocator` table. It's also referenced on the `AppSearch` table where it's tied to the `MY_PROPERTY` property. The `Name` attribute is the name of the INI file. `Section` refers to the bracketed section name and `Key` is the left-hand side of one of the key-value pairs under that section. This particular search will set the property to "Nick Ramirez". That's the value of the `name` key in the `section1` section.

The `Type` attribute can be `file`, `directory`, or `raw`. **Raw** is the simplest as it just returns the literal value of the key. Unlike `RegistrySearch`, there won't be any special characters added to it. This is what you'll use in most cases.

If you set `Type` to `file`, Windows Installer will expect the INI value to be the path to a file. Once it finds this value, it will use it to set the parent property. After that, you're free to use that property in a nested `FileSearch` element to confirm that the file exists. If it doesn't, the property will be set to `null`.

```
[section1]
filePath=C:\Program Files\mySoftware\myFile.txt
```

Product.wxs

```
<Property Id="MY_PROPERTY">
  <IniFileSearch Id="myIniSearch"
                 Name="myConfigFile.ini"
                 Section="section1"
                 Key="filePath"
```

```
                  Type="file">

    <FileSearch Id="myFileSearch"
                Name="[MY_PROPERTY]" />
  </IniFileSearch>
</Property>
```

Here, the installer searches for the INI file, finds it, and uses the specified key to set the value of the property. It then uses that property in the `FileSearch` element's `Name` attribute to check if the file is where `MY_PROPERTY` says it is.

Setting the `Type` attribute to `directory` works the same way except that you nest a `DirectorySearch` element instead. In this case, the `DirectorySearch` element checks that the directory in the property exists.

`myConfigFile.ini`

```
[section1]
directoryPath=C:\Program Files\mySoftware\
```

`Product.wxs`

```
<Property Id="MY_PROPERTY">
  <IniFileSearch Id="myIniSearch"
                 Name="myConfigFile.ini"
                 Section="section1"
                 Key="dirPath"
                 Type="directory">

    <DirectorySearch Id="myDirSearch"
                     Path="[MY_PROPERTY]" />
  </IniFileSearch>
</Property>
```

In this example, the `directoryPath` key in the INI file is set to `C:\Program Files\mySoftware\`. The `DirectorySearch` element checks that this directory really exists once it has been set as the property value. If it does, the property will keep the path as its value. Otherwise, it will be set to `null`.

Summary

In this chapter, we discussed Windows Installer properties and the AppSearch feature. Properties allow you to store information during the course of the installation. Properties are referenced with square brackets when used in the attribute of another element. Be sure to look up whether or not a particular element attribute can interpret the square bracket notation. When used in the inner text of another element, the square brackets aren't needed.

We talked about some of the built-in Windows Installer properties. There are actually quite a few of these and we'll probably cover many more as we continue on. You've seen some that affect things such as the **Add/Remove Programs** list, but there are also less flashy ones that Windows Installer uses just to do its job. However, knowing about them can be to your advantage when it comes to debugging or even creating conditional statements based upon them.

Windows Installer can do a variety of searches with its AppSearch feature: file, directory, registry, component, and INI file searches. These go hand-in-hand with properties as the result of the searches are saved to properties. Probably one of the handiest uses for AppSearch is to find out if a particular bit of software is installed. You can use this as part of a prerequisite check before installing your own software. You can also use them to find if directories or files exist, and if so, where they are. In the next chapter, we'll cover conditional statements and how to read the install state of features and components.

4

Improving Control with Launch Conditions and Installed States

We've covered how to store data in properties and how to search the target computer for files, directories, and settings using AppSearch. All by itself that makes WiX an attractive solution for deploying software. However, things are about to get more interesting. We're going to discuss how to use the information you've collected to control *what* gets installed and *if* the installer will continue past its initial startup.

WiX gives you a powerful tool that allows you to make these decisions — conditions. In this chapter, you will learn to:

- Set launch conditions to require prerequisites for your install
- Utilize feature and component conditions to prevent a portion of your software from being installed
- Read the action state and installed state of your features and components

The syntax of conditions

There are several types of conditions examined in this chapter and all use the Condition element to house their logic. The meaning of this element changes depending on where it's placed relative to other elements and which attributes it uses. We'll discuss three types: **launch conditions**, **feature conditions**, and **component conditions**.

Launch conditions check for prerequisites at the beginning of the installation and prevent it from continuing if their requirements aren't met. They're placed anywhere inside either the `Product` element in your main.wxs file, or a `Fragment` element in a separate file.**Feature conditions** and **component conditions** are child elements to `Feature` and `Component` elements, respectively. Both prevent a specific feature or component from being installed if a condition isn't satisfied.

First, we'll take a look at the generic syntax of conditional statements and then move on to discussing each of the three types.

Condition syntax

Conditions contain statements that evaluate to either true or false. In most cases you'll be comparing a property to some value. We discussed the logical operators that you can use for comparisons in the previous chapter. The following is a table that summarizes each one:

Operator	Meaning
<	Less than
>	Greater than
<=	Less than or equal to
>=	Greater than or equal to
=	Equal to
<>	Not equal to
><	Left string contains right string (strings only)
<<	Left string starts with right string (strings only)
>>	Left string ends with right string (strings only)
OR	Combines two conditions; if either is true, the condition passes

You can use a single property as a condition to check that that property has been defined. Use the NOT keyword before it to check that it has *not* been defined. Or, getting more complex, you can use the AND and OR operators to string several conditional statements together. The following examples should give you an idea about the different statements you can make:

- `PropertyA`: This returns `true` if `PropertyA` has been set to *any* value including 0 or false

- `NOT PropertyA`: This returns `true` if `PropertyA` has not been set

- `PropertyA < PropertyB`: This returns `true` if `PropertyA` is less than `PropertyB`

- `PropertyA <> "1"`: This returns `true` if `PropertyA` is not equal to 1, which is also the case if `PropertyA` is not set

- `PropertyA = "1" AND PropertyB = "2"`: This returns `true` if `PropertyA` equals 1 and `PropertyB` equals 2

- `PropertyA = "1" OR PropertyB = "2"`: This returns `true` if `PropertyA` equals 1 or `PropertyB` equals 2

These statements are the inner text of the `Condition` element. It's a good idea to always place them inside `CDATA` tags so that the XML parser won't mistake them for XML elements. The following is an example that uses `CDATA` tags:

```
<Condition ... >
<![CDATA[PropertyA < PropertyB]]>
</Condition>
```

As you can see, the conditional statement is placed inside a `Condition` element. As we cover different types of conditions, we'll look at the attributes that are used in each case.

Launch conditions

The MSI database for an installer has a table called `LaunchCondition` that lists rules that the end user must comply with in order to install the software. Each rule is called a **launch condition**. To add one, place a `Condition` element inside your `Product` element. You'll find that this table is evaluated early on, right after AppSearch is performed. This makes it the second thing to happen during the installation process. This is good in two ways. It lets you inform the user that they're missing something before they get too far along and it allows you to use the results from AppSearch in your conditions.

Examples of launch conditions include requiring that a version of .NET is installed, that the computer has a certain operating system, or that the user is an administrator. You should know that although WiX allows you to create a long list of conditions, you cannot control the order in which they're evaluated. Therefore, you should try to think of each one as having equal weight. If any one of them fails, the installation will abort. The order should be thought of as inconsequential. You can add more conditions by adding more `Condition` elements.

The following example shows a launch condition that checks the value of a property. In a real-world scenario this property would contain something useful such as the result of a component or file search. It shows the basic structure though:

```xml
<?xml version="1.0" encoding="UTF-8"?>
<Wix ... >
  <Product ... >
    <Package ... />
    <MediaTemplate ... />
    <Property Id="MyProperty"
              Value="3" />

    <Condition Message="MyProperty must be set to 2">
      <![CDATA[Installed OR MyProperty = 2]]>
    </Condition>

  </Product>
</Wix>
```

In the preceding example, we're setting a property called `MyProperty` to a value of 3. The condition checks that the variable is set to 2. When it evaluates to `false`, a message box will pop up and display the text we've set in the `Condition` element's `Message` attribute.

Notice that we've used the predefined `Installed` property to say that we only want to evaluate this condition if the software has not already been installed. Otherwise, it will be evaluated during both install and uninstall. The last thing you want is to prevent the user from uninstalling the software because they're missing a prerequisite. The following screenshot is what the user will see when the condition fails:

In real-world conditional statements, you'll use properties that were set during the course of the installation, such as during AppSearch or by a custom action. We'll talk about using custom actions in the next chapter.

A great thing about WiX is that there are already a lot of properties defined for you that you could use in your launch conditions. Some of these, as you've seen, are available from the get-go. Others become available after you've added a reference to one of the WiX extensions, such as **WixNetFxExtension**.

Throughout the book we'll make use of the **extensions** that come with the WiX toolset. These add various bits of functionality that aren't found in the core XML elements or, as with `WixNetFxExtension`, define additional properties. Extensions are packaged as .NET class libraries (`.dll`) and can be added as references in your **Setup** project. Once added, you'll be able to immediately use the new functionality. In some cases, you'll need to add a new namespace to the root `Wix` element first, but I'll mention it if that's the case. Later in the book, you'll see how to create your own extension.

The next example checks that .NET 4.0 has been installed by using the `NETFRAMEWORK40FULL` property from `WixNetFxExtension`. Begin by adding a reference in your project to `WixNetFxExtension.dll`, found in the WiX `bin` directory. The Votive plugin has gotten pretty slick in that, by default, the **Add Reference** window starts off in the WiX `bin` directory. Then add the following markup to check that the `NETFRAMEWORK40FULL` property has been set:

```
<PropertyRef Id="NETFRAMEWORK40FULL"/>

<Condition Message=
"You must install Microsoft .NET Framework 4.0 or higher.">

<![CDATA[Installed OR NETFRAMEWORK40FULL]]>
</Condition>
```

Since the property is only set when that version of the .NET Framework is installed, we only need to check for its existence. Notice that we pull the property into the scope of our project by using a `PropertyRef` element. This is because in `WixNetFxExtension`, the property is defined within a `Fragment` element. `WixNetFxExtension` defines other properties for checking other versions of .NET, as shown in the following table:

Property name	Meaning
NETFRAMEWORK10	.NET Framework 1.0 is installed
NETFRAMEWORK20	.NET Framework 2.0 is installed
NETFRAMEWORK20INSTALLROOTDIR	Location of the .NET 2.0 install root directory
NETFRAMEWORK20INSTALLROOTDIR64	Location of the x64 .NET 2.0 install root directory
NETFRAMEWORK30	.NET Framework 3.0 is installed
NETFRAMEWORK35	.NET Framework 3.5 is installed
NETFRAMEWORK40FULL	.NET Framework 4.0 is installed
NETFRAMEWORK40CLIENT	.NET Framework 4.0 client profile is installed
NETFRAMEWORK40FULLINSTALLROOTDIR	Location of the .NET 4.0 Full install root directory
NETFRAMEWORK40FULLINSTALLROOTDIR64	Location of the x64 .NET 4.0 Full install root directory
NETFRAMEWORK45	.NET Framework 4.5 is installed
WINDOWSSDKCURRENTVERSION	The Windows SDK current active version

There's also `WixPSExtension` that defines the `POWERSHELLVERSION` property. You can use it to check the version of Windows PowerShell that's installed. Add a reference in your project to `WixPSExtension` and then use the following snippet:

```
<PropertyRef Id="POWERSHELLVERSION" />

<Condition Message="You must have PowerShell 1.0 or higher.">
<![CDATA[Installed OR POWERSHELLVERSION >= "1.0"]]>
</Condition>
```

Notice here that I had to put quotes around 1.0 in the condition because `POWERSHELLVERSION` returns a decimal number. In that case, you must quote the value you compare it to.

In addition to the WiX extension files, such as `WixNetFxExtension` and `WixPSExtension`, Windows Installer also provides many built-in properties. For these, you don't have to reference any additional files or use `PropertyRefs` to gain access to them. A useful one is `VersionNT`, which can be used to check the operating system. Its value is an integer that corresponds to a particular OS. Refer to the following table:

Operating system	VersionNT value
Windows 2000	500
Windows XP	501
Windows Server 2003	502
Windows Vista	600
Windows Server 2008	600
Windows Server 2008 R2	601
Windows 7	601
Windows 8	602

With `VersionNT`, the numbers get higher with each new OS, so you can use "greater than or equal to" comparisons to make sure that an OS is greater than or equal to a certain product. The following is an example that checks if the system is running Windows Vista or newer:

```
<Condition Message=
"OS must be Windows Vista, Server 2008, or higher.">
<![CDATA[Installed OR VersionNT >= 600]]>
</Condition>
```

You might also use the `VersionNT64` property to check if the OS is 64-bit and if so, get its version number. There's also the `ServicePackLevel` property for detecting which service pack for that OS is installed. The next example checks that the operating system is Windows XP with Service Pack 2:

```
<Condition Message=
        "This install requires Windows XP Service Pack 2.">
<![CDATA[
        Installed OR
        VersionNT = 501 AND
        ServicePackLevel >= 2
    ]]>
</Condition>
```

Two more useful ones are `MsiNTProductType` and `Privileged`, as shown in this table:

Property name	Meaning
MsiNTProductType	Tells you if the end user's computer is a workstation (value of 1), domain controller (2), or server that isn't a domain controller (3)
Privileged	If set, installation is being performed with elevated privileges, such as by an administrator

Other Windows Installer properties can be seen at the MSDN site:

http://msdn.microsoft.com/en-us/library/aa370905(VS.85).aspx

You can also use environment variables in conditional statements. Prefix the variable with a percent sign (%) to reference it. The following example shows this:

```
<Condition Message=
"You need at least two processors. You have [%NUMBER_OF_PROCESSORS]">
<![CDATA[Installed OR %NUMBER_OF_PROCESSORS >= 2]]>
</Condition>
```

This condition checks that at least two processors exist on the computer. Notice how the greater-than-or-equal-to operator is used. This may be counterintuitive since we're trying to find out if the computer has less than two, not more than. With launch conditions, though, you only want to show the error message when the condition evaluates to `false`. Sometimes, this means thinking backwards.

Ordinarily, you place `Condition` elements for launch conditions inside the `Product` element in your main `.wxs` file. However, if you'd rather be more modular you can separate your launch conditions into their own `.wxs` file. There you can nest the `Condition` elements inside a `Fragment` element; the `LaunchConditions.wxs` file would look like the following code snippet:

```
<?xml version="1.0" encoding="UTF-8"?>
<Wix xmlns="http://schemas.microsoft.com/wix/2006/wi">
  <Fragment>
    <Property Id="LaunchConditionsFile"
              Value="1" />

    <Condition Message=
        "OS must be Windows Vista, Server 2008, or higher.">
      <![CDATA[Installed OR VersionNT >= 600]]>
    </Condition>
  </Fragment>
</Wix>
```

Before these launch conditions can be included in the MSI database they have to be referenced in your main WiX file. You can add a property, as in the previous example, that can be referenced in the main file with a `PropertyRef` element. The `LaunchConditionsFile` property we have here can be referenced with a `PropertyRef` element to pull in the `Condition` statement; the `Product.wxs` file would include the following line:

```
<PropertyRef Id="LaunchConditionsFile" />
```

This one line will bring all of the launch conditions in the separate `Fragment` element into the scope of your project. It's not a bad idea to use different source files to better organize your code, especially for large projects.

Feature conditions

A **feature condition** is where a `Condition` element is placed inside a `Feature` element. There, it can change whether or not that feature gets installed depending on if the statement evaluates to `true`.

Recall that features contain `ComponentRef` or `ComponentGroupRef` elements and are used to group a set of related files that the end user may install independently. For example, you may have a feature called "Documentation" that installs documentation files for your product. The user can choose to turn this feature off and not copy those files to their computer through the user interface or from the command line.

Feature conditions take this decision somewhat out of the end user's hands, allowing you as the developer to have the final say in whether it is appropriate to install a particular feature. In most cases, you'll evaluate properties in these statements, maybe those set from AppSearch or from a custom action.

Feature conditions work by changing the `Level` attribute of the parent `Feature` element. Every feature has a level. It's a number that tells the installer whether or not this feature should be "on". In a simple setup, having a level of `1` would include the feature in the install, a `0` would exclude it. So, if our condition sets the level to `0`, the feature will *not* be installed. The following is an example:

```
<Feature Id="MainFeature"
         Title="Main Feature"
         Level="1">
<ComponentRef Id="CMP_InstallMeTXT" />

<Condition Level="0">
<![CDATA[NOT REMOVE = "ALL" AND MyProperty = "some value"]]>
</Condition>
</Feature>
```

This feature starts off with a level set to 1, meaning that by default the components that it contains will be copied to the computer. However, our condition checks that the property MyProperty equals some value. If it does, meaning the condition evaluates to true, the feature's level will be changed to 0. This is specified by the Condition element's Level attribute. Notice that we also check the **REMOVE** property so that our feature will be enabled during an uninstall so that it can be properly removed no matter what.

When you change a feature's level with a feature condition, it doesn't just disable that feature. It removes it completely from the list shown in the user interface. To see this in action, add the WixUI_FeatureTree dialog set from WixUIExtension. It has a dialog with a feature tree, showing which features are available. You'll need to add a project reference to WixUIExtension.dll using the **Add Reference** option in **Solution Explorer**.

```xml
<?xml version="1.0" encoding="UTF-8"?>
<Wix xmlns="http://schemas.microsoft.com/wix/2006/wi">
  <Product Id="B55596A8-93E3-47EB-84C4-D7FE07D0CAF4"
           Name="Awesome Software"
           Language="1033"
           Version="2.0.0.0"
           Manufacturer="Awesome Company"
           UpgradeCode="B414C827-8D81-4B4A-B3B6-338C06DE3A11">
    <Package InstallerVersion="301" Compressed="yes" />
    <Media Id="1" Cabinet="media1.cab" EmbedCab="yes" />
    <!--Directory structure-->
    <Directory Id="TARGETDIR"
               Name="SourceDir">
      <Directory Id="ProgramFilesFolder">
        <Directory Id="INSTALLLOCATION"
                   Name="Awesome Software" />
      </Directory>
    </Directory>

    <!--Components-->
    <DirectoryRef Id="INSTALLLOCATION">
      <Component Id="CMP_InstallMeTXT"
                 Guid="E8A58B7B-F031-4548-9BDD-7A6796C8460D">
        <File Id="FILE_InstallMeTXT"
              Source="InstallMe.txt"
              KeyPath="yes" />
      </Component>
```

```
      </DirectoryRef>

      <Property Id="MyProperty" Value="some value" />
      <Feature Id="MainFeature"
               Title="Main Feature"
               Level="1">
        <ComponentRef Id="CMP_InstallMeTXT" />
        <Condition Level="0">
          <![CDATA[NOT REMOVE = "ALL" AND MyProperty = "some value"]]>
        </Condition>
      </Feature>

      <!--UI-->
      <UIRef Id="WixUI_FeatureTree" />
    </Product>
  </Wix>
```

Here, the condition is checking the `MyProperty` property for a specific value. You can change this property's value in your markup to see different results in the UI. If the condition evaluates to `true`, then the `MainFeature` feature will disappear from the feature tree.

The reason for this is that the installer evaluates feature conditions early in the installation process, before any dialogs are shown. Specifically, they're evaluated during the **FileCost** action, during which the installer checks how much disk space is going to be needed to copy your files to the system. It only makes sense for it to factor in features that won't be installed at this time. So, by the time the user sees your feature tree in a dialog, the excluded features have been removed from the list.

If you only want to show the feature as disabled but still visible, set the `ADDLOCAL` property to a comma-delimited list of the `Feature` element ID's to enable, as shown:

```
<Property Id="ADDLOCAL"
          Value="MainFeature,SecondFeature" />
```

Here, two features are enabled by default: `MainFeature` and `SecondFeature`. Any others will still be visible in the feature tree, but disabled. The user will be able to turn them back on if they want to. Be warned that setting `ADDLOCAL` will give you a compile-time warning due to the ICE87 validation check that prefers `ADDLOCAL` to only be set from the command line.

An alternative way to deactivate a feature is to set its Level value to a number higher than the built-in INSTALLLEVEL property—whose default value is 1. This will deactivate the feature but not remove it. The following is an example that deactivates the feature without using ADDLOCAL by using a Condition element to set the feature's level to 2 (1 higher than INSTALLLEVEL):

```
<Property Id="MyProperty" Value="some value" />

<Feature Id="MainFeature"
        Title="Main Feature"
        Level="1">
<ComponentRef Id="CMP_InstallMeTXT" />

<Condition Level="2">
<![CDATA[MyProperty = "some value"]]>
</Condition>
</Feature>
```

The INSTALLLEVEL property serves an important function. Every feature's level is compared to this number. We've said that you can change a Feature element's Level attribute, but be aware that it can accept an integer value anywhere between 0 and 32767. If the level is less than or equal to INSTALLLEVEL, but greater than zero, it will be enabled. If it's enabled, it gets installed. You can change INSTALLLEVEL yourself with a Property element to give it a different default value or change it dynamically with a custom action or from the command line.

You could use this to create a dialog with a button that says **Typical Install** and another one that says **Full Install**. "Full" might set INSTALLLEVEL to 100 when clicked on and consequently install all of the features with a level of 100 or less. "Typical", on the other hand, might set INSTALLLEVEL to 50 and only install *some* of the features. This assumes you're not showing a feature tree where the user could reactivate each individual feature themselves. That is, unless you provide a **Custom Install** button that allows the user to do just that.

Component conditions

Component conditions are a lot like feature conditions except that they affect whether or not a single component gets installed. In this case, you add a Condition element inside a Component element. You don't need to specify a Level attribute. In fact, these conditions don't expect any attributes. The following example only installs the CMP_InstallMeTXT component if the property MyProperty equals 1:

```
<Property Id="MyProperty"
        Value="1" />
```

```
<Component Id="CMP_InstallMeTXT"
        Guid="7AB5216B-2DB5-4A8A-9293-F6711FFAAA83">
<File Id="FILE_InstallMeTXT"
      Source="InstallMe.txt"
      KeyPath="yes" />
<Condition>MyProperty = 1</Condition>
</Component>
```

Again, I've hardcoded the property's value but in practice you'd set it dynamically. The benefit of component conditions is that they are much more granular than feature conditions. You're able to target a single file, folder, or registry key. For example, if the user does not have Windows PowerShell installed you could disable a component that installs a PowerShell script and instead enable one that installs a CMD shell script. The following code is how it would look:

```
<PropertyRef Id="POWERSHELLVERSION" />
<DirectoryRef Id="INSTALLLOCATION">
  <Component Id="CMP_psShellScript"
          Guid="7E348141-0005-4203-A1FE-D9264EBA7E50">
    <File Id="psScript" Source="script.ps1" KeyPath="yes" />
    <Condition>POWERSHELLVERSION</Condition>
  </Component>

  <Component Id="CMP_cmdShellScript"
          Guid="C1CE3886-2081-4F62-9E58-0B1E8080143D">
    <File Id="cmdScript"
          Source="script.cmd"
          KeyPath="yes" />
    <Condition>NOT POWERSHELLVERSION</Condition>
  </Component>
</DirectoryRef>
```

The first thing we have to do to use this example is add a reference in our project to the WiX extension `WixPSExtension`. We're then able to pull in the `POWERSHELLVERSION` property with `PropertyRef`. This contains the version number of PowerShell that's installed. In the `CMP_psShellScript` component, the `Condition` element checks simply if `POWERSHELLVERSION` exists. If it does then the PowerShell component is installed. Otherwise, `CMP_cmdShellScript` is chosen. Notice that I've used the opposite condition there, so there's no ambiguity about which should be used. It's always either one or the other.

Ordinarily, component conditions are only evaluated during an installation and not during a re-install. To re-install an MSI package, completely replacing all features, install from the command line and set the REINSTALL property to ALL.

msiexec /i myInstaller.msi REINSTALL=ALL

If you would like conditions to be re-evaluated during a re-install, you should set the Transitive attribute on the parent component to yes. In the following example, the Component elements are marked as transitive, causing their conditions to be re-evaluated during a re-install:

```
<Component Id="CMP_vistaDLL"
        Guid="7E348141-0005-4203-A1FE-D9264EBA7E50"
        Transitive="true">
  <File Id="vistaDll"
        Source="library_vista.dll"
        Name="library.dll"
        KeyPath="yes" />
  <Condition>VersionNT = 600</Condition>
</Component>

<Component Id="CMP_win7DLL"
        Guid="C1CE3886-2081-4F62-9E58-0B1E8080143D"
        Transitive="true">
  <File Id="win7Dll"
        Source="library_win7.dll"
        Name="library.dll"
        KeyPath="yes" />
  <Condition>VersionNT = 601</Condition>
</Component>
```

Here there are two components. The first has a condition to only install itself if the operating system is Windows Vista (VersionNT=600) and the other only if it's Windows 7 (VersionNT=601). Only one of the components will be true and be allowed to copy its file to the system. However, since we've added the Transitive attribute, these conditions will be checked again during a re-install. So, if the Vista file had originally been installed and the end user has since upgraded to Windows 7, the CMP_Win7DLL component will replace the CMP_VistaDLL one.

Action state

We talked about the `Level` attribute on `Feature` elements and how it's used to enable or disable features. Behind the scenes, what you're doing is setting the action state of the feature. The **action state** is the thing that stores whether or not the end user has requested that the feature be installed. The same exists for components since we can enable and disable them too. It can have any of the following values:

- **Unknown**: This indicates that the state is not known, usually because costing has not taken place. No action will be taken on the component or feature.

- **Advertised**: This indicates that the feature will be installed as advertised, meaning install on demand. This doesn't exist for components.

- **Absent**: This indicates that the feature or component will not be installed.

- **Local**: This indicates that the feature or component will be installed to the local hard disk.

- **Source**: This indicates that the feature or component will be run from source, such as from a network share.

Action state is initially unknown until **costing** has taken place. Costing is the process of finding out how much space for your software will be required on the hard drive. Action state is set during costing, specifically during a step called **CostFinalize**. We'll talk about many of the install steps in detail in the next chapter.

Once it's available after costing, you can get the action state for your features and components by using a special syntax. To get the action state of a feature, place an ampersand (`&`) in front of its name. For components, use a dollar sign (`$`). For example, the following statement checks if the feature that has an ID of `MainFeature` is set to be installed locally:

```
&MainFeature = 3
```

To check a component's action state, use a dollar sign:

```
$ComponentA = 3
```

You might be tempted to use this in your feature and component conditions. It won't work though. The reason is that component and feature conditions are evaluated during the `FileCost` action but action state isn't available until after the `CostFinalize` action has run. If you attempt to access it in one of these conditions, you'll always get a value of "Unknown".

So where can you use it? You can use it anywhere after `CostFinalize`, such as, in custom actions that you schedule later in the installation process. You can also use them in conditional statements that affect UI controls, which we'll cover later in the book. You can pair these statements with "NOT Installed" to have Windows Installer evaluate them only during installation.

Earlier, I checked the action state against the number three. The five possible action states each correspond to a number, as listed in the following table:

Action state	Meaning
-1	Unknown
1	Advertised
2	Absent
3	Local
4	Source

Note that you don't have to use the equals sign. You can use any of the conditional operators that can be used with launch conditions. For example, you might use the "greater than" operator, as in:

```
&MainFeature > 2
```

This checks if a feature is set to be installed locally or to source. During an install, you can see the action state being written to the install log. Use the `l*v` flag to record to a logfile, as shown:

```
msiexec /i myInstaller.msi /l*v install.log
```

The following snippet from the log shows a feature called `ProductFeature` with a `Request:Local`. That's its action state. The component, similarly, has `Request:Local`. The Action is what ultimately happened during the install such as `Action:Local`.

```
Action ended 0:25:17: CostFinalize. Return value 1.
MSI (s) (C0:F0) [00:25:17:452]: Doing action: InstallValidate
MSI (s) (C0:F0) [00:25:17:452]: Note: 1: 2205 2:  3: ActionText
Action 0:25:17: InstallValidate. Validating install
Action start 0:25:17: InstallValidate.
MSI (s) (C0:F0) [00:25:17:452]: Feature: ProductFeature;
Installed: Absent;   Request: Local;   Action: Local
MSI (s) (C0:F0) [00:25:17:452]: Component: CMP_InstallMeTXT;
Installed: Absent;   Request: Local;   Action: Local
```

Checking the log can help out when it's unclear why a certain feature or component isn't getting installed.

Installed state

While Windows Installer uses action state to determine if a feature or component should be installed, it uses the **installed state** to see if a feature or component has already been installed by a previous installation. In other words, does it currently exist on the computer?

Unlike the action state, the value of installed state can be used in feature and component conditions. For features, you'll prefix the feature's Id attribute with an exclamation mark (!), as shown:

```
!MainFeature = 3
```

For components, you'll use a question mark (?):

```
?ComponentA = 3
```

This allows you to include features and components based on whether they were installed before. You can also use them in custom actions and UI control conditions, such as to change which dialogs are displayed. Windows Installer uses this functionality itself, at least in regards to features, when you use the feature tree control. During a re-install, it will show the features as enabled that have been selected before and disables those that haven't. This makes for a better user experience.

The same values apply for installed state as for action state. For example, 3 refers to a component or feature that was installed to the local hard disk. The following table gives you the installed state and its corresponding meaning:

Installed state	Meaning
-1	Unknown
1	Feature was installed as Advertised
2	Feature or component was Absent (not installed)
3	Feature or component was installed Local, to the hard disk
4	Feature or component was installed to Source

Often, you will pair the action state with the installed state in a condition. Although we haven't discussed custom actions yet, you should know that you can place a conditional statement inside of the Custom element to control whether a custom action gets executed. You might check that a component has been installed to the local hard disk, but is now being uninstalled, as a condition of running the action:

```
<Custom Action="MyCustomAction" ...>
<![CDATA[$ComponentA = 2 AND ?ComponentA = 3]]>
</Custom>
```

Summary

In this chapter, we talked about the meaning of launch conditions and how they can be used to prevent an install on a system that doesn't meet the minimum requirements you've set. When paired with AppSearch or the built-in Windows Installer properties, launch conditions are able to detect the operating system, .NET version, and whether or not required software is installed.

We touched on feature and component conditions and how they allow you to exclude a specific feature or component from the install. These conditions take the decision out of the hands of the end user and lets you have the final say. You saw that using feature conditions to set Level to 0 will completely remove a feature from a feature tree list. You may prefer to use the ADDLOCAL property instead or change the feature's level to a number higher than INSTALLLEVEL to disable it without hiding it.

Towards the end, we discussed what action and installed state is. An action state can't be used in feature and component conditions like installed state can, but it can still come in handy in other types of conditions such as those used in custom actions. In the next chapter, we'll discuss custom actions and learn how they allow you to extend the behavior of WiX.

5

Understanding the Installation Sequence

In order to coordinate the use of the WiX elements that we've seen and the jobs that they do, there are two tables in the MSI database, **InstallUISequence** and **InstallExecuteSequence**, that contain the order in which installation events should occur. For example, AppSearch always happens before launch conditions.

In this chapter, we'll talk about how these tables work. Specifically, we'll cover:

- The events that happen during the UI sequence and how to access them
- The events that happened during the Execute sequence and how to access them
- How to author and schedule your own custom actions
- Some tips on writing C# custom actions via the Deployment Tools Foundation (DTF) library

InstallUISequence

The **InstallUISequence** is both the name of a database table in the MSI package and a way of referring to the first half of the installation. During this time, we can show a graphical user interface and execute tasks that don't alter the user's computer, such as using AppSearch and evaluating launch conditions.

If you use Orca to look inside your MSI package, as described in *Chapter 1, Getting Started*, you'll find a table called `InstallUISequence`. This is where the actions that happen during the first half of the installation are defined. The following screenshot shows what it will look like:

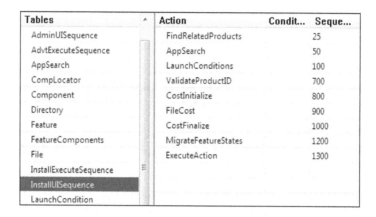

Tables	Action	Condit...	Seque...
AdminUISequence	FindRelatedProducts		25
AdvtExecuteSequence	AppSearch		50
AppSearch	LaunchConditions		100
CompLocator	ValidateProductID		700
Component	CostInitialize		800
Directory	FileCost		900
Feature	CostFinalize		1000
FeatureComponents	MigrateFeatureStates		1200
File	ExecuteAction		1300
InstallExecuteSequence			
InstallUISequence			
LaunchCondition			

The table contains three columns: **Action**, **Condition**, and **Sequence**. For now, we're just interested in **Action** and **Sequence**. **Action** is the name of the **standard action** to run. A standard action is a task that's already defined by Windows Installer. **Sequence** is the order in which it happens in relation to other actions. You can sort the **Sequence** column from lowest to highest by clicking on the column header. This is the order as it happens.

You're likely to see the following standard actions in your list:

- **FindRelatedProducts**
- **AppSearch**
- **LaunchConditions**
- **ValidateProductID**
- **CostInitialize**
- **FileCost**
- **CostFinalize**
- **MigrateFeatureStates**
- **ExecuteAction**

You've already seen some of these, but we'll go over each in the next section.

UI standard actions

We'll take a moment here to describe each of the standard actions we've listed in the order in which they'd be executed.

FindRelatedProducts

The `FindRelatedProducts` action looks through a table in the MSI called `Upgrade`. This table lists upgrade codes, version numbers, and languages that the installer uses as criteria when searching for prior versions of your software. If it finds a match, Windows Installer properties specified in that table are set to the product codes of the found software. These properties can then be checked to discover whether the current install is an upgrade or a downgrade.

AppSearch

The `AppSearch` action reads the `AppSearch` table, which holds the signatures of the searches you've authored in your WiX markup. During this phase, you could look for files and directories on the end user's system, read registry values, or peek inside INI configuration files. The `AppSearch` table utilizes various other tables for this including (and in this order) `CompLocator`, `RegLocator`, `IniLocator`, and `DrLocator`.

LaunchConditions

The `LaunchConditions` action references the table called `LaunchCondition` that lists conditional statements that must be true before the installer can continue. This is how prerequisites are defined, such as requiring the .NET Framework.

ValidateProductID

You can collect a software registration key from the end user and store it in a property called `PIDKEY`. During the `ValidateProductID` action, this property is compared to another property you've set called `PIDTemplate`, that defines a pattern `PIDKEY` must match. If everything checks out, a third property called `ProductID` is set for you. After `ValidateProductID` has run, you may check for the existence of `ProductID` to see if the key that was entered is in the valid format.

CostInitialize

The `CostInitialize` action starts the "costing" process wherein the disk space needed for your product is calculated. At this point, the `Component` and `Feature` tables are loaded into memory, which sets the stage for the installer to check which components and features will be installed.

FileCost

During the `FileCost` action, the installer starts the cost calculation. The rows in the `File` table are examined to see how much hard drive space they require. If one of the files already exists on the end user's system due to a prior installation of the same parent `Component`, it will only be replaced if the file's version is newer. In that case, the size of the file will be added to the disk space needed.

CostFinalize

During the `CostFinalize` action, the costing calculation takes into consideration the components and features that shouldn't be installed because of a component or feature-level condition. It then verifies that all target directories are writable. This phase ends the costing process.

MigrateFeatureStates

If a previous version of your software was installed, the `MigrateFeatureStates` action checks which features were installed last time and then sets the action state of those features to the same state in the current installer. That way, the new installer will show a feature tree with the corresponding features enabled or disabled.

ExecuteAction

The last standard action in the UI sequence is called `ExecuteAction`. It looks at a property called `EXECUTEACTION` to see which table to pass control to. As this is a normal installation that started off by reading `InstallUISequence`, the property will be set to `INSTALL` and this action will pass control to the `InstallExecuteSequence` table. For other scenarios, `EXECUTEACTION` may be set to `ADMIN` or `ADVERTISE`.

InstallExecuteSequence

After `ExecuteAction` has fired in `InstallUISequence`, the installation continues into `InstallExecuteSequence`. During this phase, changes are made to the computer such as laying down files, updating the registry, and adding a new entry in **Programs and Features**. This part of the installation is called the "server side" and the `InstallUISequence` table is called the "client side", which is a way of conceptualizing that the two are run in different sessions and with different privileges. The client side runs as the user who launched the MSI while the server side is run as the `LocalSystem` user.

If you install with logging turned on you can see the split between the client and server. Actions that occur during the first half start with MSI (c), as shown in the following example:

```
MSI (c) (64:80) [13:41:32:203]: Switching to server:
```

That's the last entry from the client before switching to the server. Then you'll see log entries begin with MSI (s).

```
MSI (s) (D0:4C) [13:41:32:218]: Grabbed execution mutex.
```

By taking ownership of the execution mutex, the server side is saying that no other MSI package can be run while the execution phase is in progress. The following actions are scheduled here:

- AppSearch
- LaunchConditions
- ValidateProductId
- CostInitialize
- FileCost
- CostFinalize
- InstallValidate
- InstallInitialize
- ProcessComponents
- UnpublishFeatures
- RemoveRegistryValues
- RemoveShortcuts
- RemoveFiles
- InstallFiles
- CreateShortcuts
- WriteRegistryValues
- RegisterUser
- RegisterProduct
- PublishFeatures
- PublishProduct
- InstallFinalize

The first six are repeats from the UI phase and will be skipped if they've already run. Note that you can skip the UI portion and go straight to execute by setting the `quiet` flag on the command line. People sometimes do this for unattended installs.

```
msiexec /i myInstaller.msi /quiet
```

In the next section, we'll discuss the standard actions that are new.

Execute standard actions

Now, let's look at each of the standard actions that are unique to the Execute sequence.

InstallValidate

The `InstallValidate` action uses the total calculated by the costing phase to verify that there's enough disk space available, and whether any running processes have a lock on files needed by the MSI.

InstallInitialize

The `InstallInitialize` action marks the beginning of the "deferred" stage of the Execute sequence. Any actions between it and `InstallFinalize` are included in a transaction, and can be rolled back if an error occurs. This prevents leaving the user's computer in a half-finished state.

ProcessComponents

The `ProcessComponents` action makes note of the components that are in your installer and stores their GUIDs in the registry. It tracks which file is the keypath for each component.

UnpublishFeatures

During uninstallation, `UnpublishFeatures` removes component-to-feature mappings in the registry and discards information about which features were selected.

RemoveRegistryValues

The `RemoveRegistryValues` action looks at the MSI's `Registry` and `RemoveRegistry` tables to find registry items to remove during an uninstall.

RemoveShortcuts

The RemoveShortcuts action removes any shortcuts during uninstallation that your installer created.

RemoveFiles

During uninstallation, the RemoveFiles action deletes files and folders that were copied to the system. You can add files and folders for it to remove by using the RemoveFolder and RemoveFile elements. These elements may also delete files during install by setting their On attributes to install or both.

InstallFiles

The InstallFiles action uses information from the Directory and File tables to copy files and folders into their appropriate locations. It's smart enough to know that if a file already exists from a previous install and its component GUID and version haven't changed to leave the file as is.

CreateShortcuts

During installation, CreateShortcuts adds shortcuts as specified in the Shortcut table. Refer back to *Chapter 1, Getting Started*, for a discussion on how to author shortcuts into the Windows Start menu.

WriteRegistryValues

You can use the WiX elements RegistryKey and RegistryValue to write to the registry. The WriteRegistryValues action does the work.

RegisterUser

The RegisterUser action records to the registry who the user was who initiated the installation.

RegisterProduct

The RegisterProduct action registers your product with **Programs and Features** and stores a copy of the MSI package in the Windows Installer Cache, found at %WINDIR%\Installer.

PublishFeatures

During the `PublishFeatures` action, the installed state (installed, advertised, or absent) is written to the registry and components are mapped to features.

PublishProduct

Used only by an advertised installation, the `PublishProduct` action "publishes" the product to a computer, or in other words makes it available to be installed on-demand by non-administrator users.

InstallFinalize

The `InstallFinalize` action marks the end of the rollback-protected stage called the **deferred** phase. If your installation gets this far it means that it was successful.

Immediate versus deferred

There are reasons for separating the installation into two parts. The biggest is to have an obvious time during which the end user should expect changes to be made to the system. During the UI phase, they can safely fill information into the UI's dialogs without the fear that their computer will be altered. Typically, it isn't until they click a button labeled **Install** that changes begin to take effect. Therefore, the standard actions only make system changes during the second half, during the Execute sequence.

By keeping all system changes in one area, Windows Installer is able to offer something else: rollback protection if an error occurs. It works in the following way: no changes to the system are made when the Execute phase starts. At first, the installer reads what actions are in the `InstallExecuteSequence` table and prepares itself by storing a script of what's to be done. All actions *between* `InstallInitialize` and `InstallFinalize` are included. This initial phase, when the script is prepared but the rollback protection hasn't started yet, is called the Execute sequence's **immediate** phase.

Once things actually start happening, it's called the **deferred** stage. If an error occurs, the installer will use the script it created to roll back the actions that had taken place up to that point. Only the deferred stage has rollback protection. The UI sequence does not have this feature and so actions that alter the system should never take place there.

In the next section, you'll learn about creating custom actions that you can add to either the UI or the Execute phase. Take special care to mark those actions that make system changes as "deferred" and schedule them to run somewhere after the `InstallInitialize` action and before `InstallFinalize` in the Execute phase. As you'll see, you'll need to create your own rollback actions to complement your deferred custom actions.

Custom actions

Knowing what the standard actions do and when prepares you for what's next: making your own actions, called **custom actions**, and scheduling them appropriately.

Any custom action that changes the system, whether it involves changing files, setting up databases, or adjusting user rights, should happen during the deferred stage of the Execute sequence. Otherwise, you're free to place them where you like during either the UI or the Execute sequence.

Custom actions are declared with the **CustomAction** element. Use its `Execute` attribute to define how it should run, and its `Return` attribute to tell how its return status should be treated. For example, this would declare a custom action called `MyAction` that runs during the deferred stage and is checked for success upon completion:

```
<CustomAction Id="MyAction" Execute="deferred"
    Return="check" ... />
```

That's the basics, although there are seven specific types of custom actions that add their own necessary attributes. We'll cover each of the following types:

- Setting a Windows Installer property
- Setting the location of a directory
- Running embedded VBScript or JScript code
- Calling an external VBScript or JScript file
- Calling a method from a dynamic-link library
- Running an executable
- Sending an error that stops the installation

To add our custom action to the Execute sequence, we'll use the `InstallExecuteSequence` element and the `Custom` element.

```
<?xml version="1.0" encoding="UTF-8"?>
<Wix xmlns="http://schemas.microsoft.com/wix/2006/wi">
    <Product ... >
```

```
            <Package ... />
        <Media ... />

        <CustomAction Id="MyAction" Execute="deferred"
            Return="check" ... />

        <InstallExecuteSequence>
            <Custom Action="MyAction" After="InstallInitialize" />
        </InstallExecuteSequence>
    </Product>
</Wix>
```

The `Custom` element's `Action` attribute refers to the `Id` attribute of the `CustomAction` element we want to run. We can use its `After` attribute to schedule the action to run after `InstallInitialize` in the Execute sequence. You can also use the `Before` attribute to schedule it before some action, or the `Sequence` attribute, which sets a specific number to use in the `InstallExecuteSequence` table's `Sequence` column. You can even schedule your custom actions based on other custom actions, as in the next example:

```
<InstallExecuteSequence>
    <Custom Action="MyAction" After="InstallInitialize" />
    <Custom Action="Action2" After="MyAction" />
</InstallExecuteSequence>
```

To schedule actions during the UI sequence use the `InstallUISequence` element instead. It works in the same way:

```
<CustomAction Id="MyUIAction" Execute="immediate" Return="ignore" ...
/>

<InstallUISequence>
  <Custom Action="MyUIAction" After="CostFinalize" />
</InstallUISequence>
```

The `CustomAction` element gives you control over when it is executed through its `Execute` attribute, which you'll usually set to "immediate", "deferred", "rollback", or "commit". The last three only apply to the Execute sequence. Setting `Execute` to "commit" schedules the action to be run once the installation has completed. We'll cover rollback actions in detail later in the chapter.

Note that you can run the same custom action in both sequences if needed. You might do that to accommodate silent installs, in which the UI sequence is skipped. If you set the `Execute` attribute to `firstSequence`, the action will only be run once — the first time it's encountered. Setting it to `secondSequence` will cause it to be run during the Execute sequence only if it has already been run in the UI sequence.

The Return attribute tells the installer whether it should wait for the custom action to complete its processing before continuing, and whether the return code should be evaluated. These values are available for the Return attribute:

Return value	Meaning
asyncNoWait	The custom action will run asynchronously and execution may continue after the installer terminates.
asyncWait	The custom action will run asynchronously but the installer will wait for the return code at sequence end.
check	The custom action will run synchronously and the return code will be checked for success. This is the default.
ignore	The custom action will run synchronously and the return code will not be checked.

During the deferred stage, if a custom action returns failure and the Return attribute is check or asyncWait, a rollback will occur, reverting any changes made up to that point. During the immediate phase, failure will end the installation on the spot.

For the rest of this section, we'll look at the different types of custom actions.

Setting a Windows Installer property

You aren't limited to setting a property with a Property element or from the command line. You can, through the use of a **Type 51** custom action, set one at any point during the installation. These "Type" numbers come from the Type column in the CustomAction table. To set a property, use the CustomAction element's Property and Value attributes.

```
<CustomAction
    Id="rememberInstallDir"
    Property="ARPINSTALLLOCATION"
    Value="[INSTALLLOCATION]" />
```

This is a useful example that uses the built-in ARPINSTALLLOCATION property to save the install directory. Any directory property you save to it will be stored for you in the registry and can be recalled later during uninstallation or repair. By using square brackets around the ID of my install directory, here called INSTALLLOCATION, I'm referencing that directory's path. That's a special case using a built-in property, but you can set the value of any of your custom properties using the same type of custom action.

Next, schedule the custom action so that it happens after `InstallValidate` in the Execute sequence — that's when directories are checked for write access and truly set.

```
<InstallExecuteSequence>
    <Custom Action="rememberInstallDir"
            After="InstallValidate" />
</InstallExecuteSequence>
```

You can, during uninstallation for example, access this property using another type of custom action — one in a C# assembly, which we'll discuss later — by using the `ProductInstallation` class in your C# code, as shown in the following code snippet:

```
ProductInstallation install =
    new ProductInstallation(session["ProductCode"]);
string installDir = install.InstallLocation;
```

When it comes to writing C# that can interact with your installer, there's a lot to cover. We'll hit some of the major points when we talk about the Deployment Tools Foundation library at the end of this chapter. It's what provides access to the underlying installer functionality.

There's a second, short-hand way of declaring a Type 51 custom action: use the **SetProperty** element. In the following example, we will set a property called `MyProperty` to the value `123` after the `InstallInitialize` action in the Execute sequence:

```
<SetProperty Id="MyProperty"
             Value="123"
             After="InstallInitialize"
             Sequence="execute" />
```

Behind the scenes, a custom action will be created called `SetMyProperty`. You can use a different name by adding the `Action` attribute set to the name you want the custom action to have.

Setting the location of an installed directory

A **Type 35** custom action sets the path of a `Directory` element. Use the `CustomAction` element's `Directory` and `Value` attributes, as shown in the following code snippet:

```
<CustomAction Id="SetAppDataDir"
              Directory="DataDir"
              Value="[CommonAppDataFolder]MyProduct" />
```

Assuming we've already defined a `Directory` element with an `Id` of `DataDir`, this action will change its location to a folder called `MyProduct` in the `C:\Documents and Settings\All Users\Application Data` folder on Windows XP or `C:\ProgramData` on Windows 7. To test this out, you'll need to add a `Directory` element with an `Id` of `DataDir` and place at least one component inside it.

You should schedule this type of custom action to run during the Execute sequence before `InstallFiles` or, if you're installing empty folders using the `CreateFolder` element, before the `CreateFolders` action.

```
<InstallExecuteSequence>
   <Custom Action="SetAppDataDir" Before="InstallFiles" />
</InstallExecuteSequence>
```

You may also change a directory by using the **SetDirectory** element as shown in the following code snippet:

```
<SetDirectory Id="DataDir"
              Value="[CommonAppDataFolder]MyProduct"
              Sequence="execute" />
```

Its `Id` attribute points to the `Id` attribute of a `Directory` element. `Value` sets the path to the new folder and `Sequence` controls whether the action will be run during the Execute or UI sequence. It can be set to one of the following values: `execute`, `ui`, `both`, or `first`. Using `both` will run the action in both sequences and `first` will execute it during the UI sequence ordinarily, but during the Execute sequence if the UI sequence is skipped.

Running embedded VBScript or JScript

A **Type 37** (JScript) or **Type 38** (VBScript) custom action executes embedded script. You'll define the script as the inner text of the `CustomAction` element and declare its type with the `Script` attribute set to either `vbscript` or `jscript`. The following is an example that displays two message boxes and returns success:

```
<CustomAction Id="testVBScript" Script="vbscript"
Execute="immediate" >
   <![CDATA[
     msgbox "this is embedded code..."
      msgbox "MyProperty: " & Session.Property("MyProperty")
   ]]>
</CustomAction>
```

Note that you can access existing WiX properties using `Session.Property`. Then, we just need to schedule it to run. For this example, we'll display the message boxes during the UI sequence after `LaunchConditions`:

```
<InstallUISequence>
   <Custom Action="testVBScript" After="LaunchConditions" />
</InstallUISequence>
```

Accessing installer data always starts with the `Session` object. You can learn more at:

```
http://msdn.microsoft.com/en-us/library/windows/desktop/
aa371675(v=vs.85).aspx
```

The following are a few example usages:

```
<CustomAction Id="testVBScript" Script="vbscript"
Execute="immediate" >
   <![CDATA[
     ' Write a message to the install log
     Dim rec
     Set rec = Session.Installer.CreateRecord(0)
     rec.StringData(0) = "My log message"
     Session.Message &H04000000, rec

     ' Change the install level
     Session.SetInstallLevel(1000)

     ' Get properties set by the Product element
     Dim productName
     productName = Session.ProductProperty("ProductName")

     ' Get the target path of a Directory element
     Dim installFolder
     installFolder = Session.TargetPath("INSTALLFOLDER")
   ]]>
</CustomAction>
```

There have been a number of voices in the Windows Installer community, including Rob Mensching the project lead of the WiX toolset, warning against the use of VBScript and JScript custom actions. Reasons for this include the lack of debugging support and better tooling for other languages such as C++ and C#.

Calling an external VBScript or JScript file

A **Type 5** (JScript) or **Type 6** (VBScript) custom action calls a subroutine or function from an external script file. Let's say we have a file called `myScript.vbs` that contains a function called `myFunction`:

```
Function myFunction()
  If Session.Property("MY_PROPERTY") = "1" Then
    msgbox "Property is 1. Returning success!"
    myFunction = 1
    Exit Function
  End If

  msgbox "Property not 1. Returning failure."
  myFunction = 3
  Exit Function
End Function
```

Note that returning 1 from the function indicates success, while returning 3 indicates failure, and will abort the install. In our WiX markup, we must reference this file with a `Binary` element. This will store the file inside the MSI.

```
<Binary Id="myScriptVBS" SourceFile=".\myScript.vbs" />
```

Then, our `CustomAction` element uses the `BinaryKey` and `VBScriptCall`, or `JScriptCall` if this had been a JScript file, attributes to access the function:

```
<CustomAction
    Id="myScript_CA"
    BinaryKey="myScriptVBS"
    VBScriptCall="myFunction"
    Execute="immediate"
    Return="check" />
```

Be sure to schedule it during one of the sequences. Remember, any code that alters the system should be marked with an `Execute` attribute of `deferred`, and scheduled during `InstallExecuteSequence`.

If you are creating your JScript or VBScript files in Visual Studio, beware that by default it encodes text files as UTF-8. However, Windows Installer won't be able to interpret this encoding. An easy way to correct this is to open the file with Notepad, choose **Save As**, and then change **Encoding** to `ANSI`. Otherwise, you may get an error at install time regarding unexpected characters found at the beginning of the file.

Calling a function from a dynamic-link library

A **Type 1** custom action calls a method from a dynamic-link library (.dll). The Votive plugin for Visual Studio provides a template you can use.

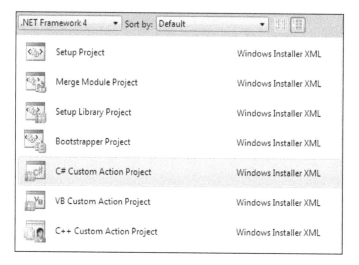

We will be writing our custom action using .NET code in C#. Technically, a Type 1 custom action means authoring an unmanaged C/C++ DLL. Windows Installer cannot natively support a .NET custom action. The template we're using allows us to write a managed code that will build the C/C++ DLL for us when we compile. This unmanaged library will wrap our .NET code. In the end, that is what our installer will reference. Be aware that the end user will need to have the targeted version of the .NET Framework installed. If that's not an option for you, WiX also provides a template for a C++ custom action.

Create a new **C# Custom Action Project** and you'll get a source file that references the Microsoft.Deployment.WindowsInstaller namespace. This contains helpful classes like Session that allow you to access the properties, features, and components of your installer.

myCustomActions.cs

```
using System;
using Microsoft.Deployment.WindowsInstaller;

namespace myLibrary
{
    public class CustomActions
    {
        [CustomAction]
```

```
public static ActionResult MyFunction(Session session)
{
    string myProperty = session["myProperty"];
    return ActionResult.Success;
}
    }
}
```

The signature for the method has a return value of type `ActionResult`. Use this to notify the installer that the custom action succeeded or failed. The method is decorated with the `CustomAction` attribute and has a `Session` object as its parameter. You're free to name the method, class, and namespace whatever you like.

There's a cap on the number of custom actions you can define in a single .NET assembly. It used to be 16, as defined by the WiX source code in the `src\DTF\Tools\SfxCA\EntryPoints.h` file, but in WiX 3.6 it has been raised to 128. If you do exceed the limit, you can add another custom action project and keep on going.

All of this comes from a framework called the **Deployment Tools Foundation** (**DTF**). DTF is a library that allows you to write .NET code that can interact with the lower-level Windows Installer technology. It provides a number of useful classes under the `Microsoft.Deployment.WindowsInstaller` namespace. We'll cover some basics at the end of the chapter.

When you compile this project you'll end up with two files: one that ends in `.dll` and one that ends `.CA.dll`. It's the second that you'll reference in your WiX project as it has the unmanaged code that can be understood by the MSI.

There are two ways to reference this DLL. The first is to not use the **Add a Reference** screen, but simply copy the file to your WiX project and reference it with a `Binary` element. Use a relative path to the `.CA.dll` file. Back in our WiX markup, we'd add the following to `Product.wxs`:

```
<Binary Id="myCustomActionsDLL"
        SourceFile=".\myCustomActions.CA.dll" />
```

As you can see, once the DLL has been copied to our WiX project's folder, it can be referenced with a relative path.

A second way is to use the **Add a Reference** screen to reference the C# project in your WiX project and then use the `$(var.ProjectName.TargetDir)` preprocessor variable to point to the referenced project's output directory:

```
<Binary Id="myCustomActionsDLL"
        SourceFile=
"$(var.myCustomActions.TargetDir)myCustomActions.CA.dll" />
```

You'll then use the `CustomAction` element's `BinaryKey` and `DllEntry` attributes to specify the C# method to call.

```xml
<CustomAction
    Id="CA_myCustomAction"
    BinaryKey="myCustomActionsDLL"
    DllEntry="MyFunction"
    Execute="immediate"
    Return="check" />
```

Then, schedule it to run:

```xml
<InstallUISequence>
  <Custom Action="CA_myCustomAction" After="CostFinalize" />
</InstallUISequence>
```

Any of these script files, DLLs, or executables that we're using to define custom actions will not be installed to the end user's computer. They perform their action during the install, but stay packaged inside the MSI.

Triggering an executable

There are three ways to run an executable file (`.exe`) from a custom action. The first, a **Type 2**, uses the `Binary` element to store the file inside the MSI and calls it from there. That way, it doesn't need to be copied to the end user's computer.

Here we're referencing a file called `MyProgram.exe`. `$(sys.SOURCEFILEDIR)` is a system variable defined by WiX that points to your project's directory. For a change, we'll be running this custom action during the `deferred` phase of `InstallExecuteSequence`:

```xml
<Binary
    Id="myProgramEXE"
    SourceFile="$(sys.SOURCEFILEDIR)myProgram.exe" />

<CustomAction
    Id="myProgramEXE_CA"
    BinaryKey="myProgramEXE"
    Impersonate="yes"
    Execute="deferred"
    ExeCommand=""
    Return="check" />
```

The CustomAction element's Impersonate attribute tells the installer whether to impersonate the user who launched the installer. The default is no, meaning that the custom action, when launched during the Execute sequence, should run as the *LocalSystem* user — an all-powerful, built-in account that has the privileges needed to make changes to the user's computer. If you don't need that, set it to yes to run the custom action in the context of the current user. You'll only ever use this flag for a deferred custom action. Immediate custom actions don't run as LocalSystem and you'll get an ICE68 warning if you set Impersonate to no on one.

The ExeCommand attribute takes any command-line arguments you'd want to pass to the executable. You should always specify this, even if it's set to an empty string. It's a required attribute.

We can schedule this to run during the Execute sequence:

```
<InstallExecuteSequence>
    <Custom Action="myProgramEXE_CA"
            Before="InstallFinalize" />
</InstallExecuteSequence>
```

The second way of calling an executable, called a **Type 18** custom action, is by copying it to the end user's computer first. Let's say that we're going to copy a file called MainApp.exe to the INSTALLLOCATION folder, as shown here:

```
<DirectoryRef Id="INSTALLLOCATION">
    <Component Id="CMP_MainAppEXE"
        Guid="7AB5216B-2DB5-4A8A-9293-F6711FFAAA83">

        <File Id="mainAppEXE"
              Source="MainApp.exe"
              KeyPath="yes" />
    </Component>
</DirectoryRef>
```

Our CustomAction element can then use the FileKey attribute to specify the ID of our File element, thereby executing it.

```
<CustomAction
    Id="RunMainApp"
    FileKey="mainAppEXE"
    ExeCommand=""
    Execute="commit"
    Return="ignore" />
```

For illustration purposes, I've decided not to run this during the `deferred` stage. By marking it as `commit`, it will only run if the install is successful. Also, by setting the `Return` attribute to `ignore` we're saying that we don't care if the job succeeds or fails.

 If you want to run an executable, but prevent it from displaying, such as for a command window, consider using the **QtExec** action from `WixUtilExtension`. More information can be found at `http://wix.sourceforge.net/manual-wix3/qtexec.htm`.

The last way, called a **Type 34** custom action, is to use the `Directory` attribute, targeting the directory where the executable is on the end user's computer. The `ExeCommand` attribute should also reference this directory and the name of the `.exe` file including any command-line arguments.

```
<CustomAction
    Id="RunMainApp"
    Directory="INSTALLLOCATION"
    ExeCommand="[INSTALLLOCATION]Main_App.exe -myArg 123"
    Execute="commit"
    Return="ignore" />
```

Sending an error that stops the installation

A **Type 19** custom action sends an error to the installer and ends it. It uses the `Error` attribute and looks like the following code snippet:

```
<Property Id="myProperty" Value="0" />

<CustomAction Id="ErrorCA" Error="Ends the installation!" />

<InstallUISequence>
    <Custom Action="ErrorCA" Before="ExecuteAction">
        <![CDATA[
            myProperty <> 1
        ]]>
    </Custom>
</InstallUISequence>
```

I've placed a conditional statement inside the `Custom` element so that this error will only be triggered if `myProperty` is not equal to 1. Note that these types of custom actions can only be run during the `immediate` phase. So, the `Execute` attribute is unnecessary.

You can add a conditional statement inside any of your Custom elements. For example, you might check the Installed property to only run your action when the product hasn't been installed yet.

Rollback custom actions

Custom actions that are scheduled as "deferred" execute during the Execute sequence's rollback-protected phase. To give those actions rollback capabilities, you'll need to author separate custom actions that undo the work. These are scheduled as "rollback". Rollback custom actions are scheduled before the action they're meant to revert to in case of an error. The following is an example:

```
<CustomAction Id="systemChangingCA" Execute="deferred"
Script="vbscript">
    msgbox "Imagine this changes the system in some way"
</CustomAction>

<CustomAction Id="myRollbackCA" Execute="rollback"
Script="vbscript">
    msgbox "Imagine this undoes the changes"
</CustomAction>

<CustomAction Id="causeError" Execute="deferred"
   Script="vbscript">
      Err.Raise 507
</CustomAction>
```

We'll schedule these during the Execute sequence:

```
<InstallExecuteSequence>
    <Custom Action="myRollbackCA" Before="systemChangingCA" />
    <Custom Action="systemChangingCA" After="InstallInitialize" />
    <Custom Action="causeError" After="systemChangingCA" />
</InstallExecuteSequence>
```

Now, systemChangingCA will run during the deferred phase of InstallExecuteSequence. When the causeError action runs afterwards it causes an exception to be thrown, which triggers a rollback. Then, myRollbackCA runs. Deferred and rollback actions are always scheduled somewhere between InstallInitalize and InstallFinalize.

The WiX toolset provides its own custom action for stimulating a rollback called `WixFailWhenDeferred`. It's available as part of the `WixUtilExtension` and you can find more information at `http://wix.sourceforge.net/manual-wix3/wixfailwhendeferred.htm`. You could use it to test your rollback methods.

Having a rollback action for every deferred one that alters the user's system is a good idea. It covers you in case of an error. Of course, you'll need to author the code of your rollback action so that it really does revert what you've done.

Accessing properties in a deferred action

If you try to access a property from a custom action during the Execute sequence's deferred stage, you'll find that you get an error. This is because only a finite number of properties are available here. As a workaround, you can store the values of your properties in another property called `CustomActionData` and pass that to the deferred custom action.

There are two ways to do this: from your WiX code, or from inside another C# custom action. For the first, use a `Type 51` custom action to set the value of the `CustomActionData` property.

In the next example, we want to pass a property called `MYPROPERTY` to a custom action called `myDeferredCA`. So, we create another action called `SetProperty` that sets a property also called `myDeferredCA` to the value of `MYPROPERTY`. It's important that the name of the property you're setting matches the name of the deferred custom action.

```
<Property Id="MYPROPERTY" Value="my value" />

<CustomAction Id="SetProperty"
              Property="myDeferredCA"
              Value="[MYPROPERTY]" />

<InstallExecuteSequence>
  <Custom Action="SetProperty" Before="myDeferredCA" />
  <Custom Action="myDeferredCA" After="InstallInitialize" />
</InstallExecuteSequence>
```

Now, myDeferredCA will have access to our MYPROPERTY property, indirectly, through the Session object's CustomActionData.

```
[CustomAction]
public static ActionResult myDeferredCA(Session session)
{
    string myProperty = session.CustomActionData;
    return ActionResult.Success;
}
```

You can also store several properties in CustomActionData by separating them with semi-colons.

```
<Property Id="PROP1" Value="abc123" />
<Property Id="PROP2" Value="def567" />
<Property Id="PROP3" Value="ghi890" />


<CustomAction
    Id="SetProperty"
    Property="myDeferredCA"
    Value="Prop1=[PROP1];Prop2=[PROP2];Prop3=[PROP3]" />
```

We have changed our SetProperty custom action so that its Value is set to a list of key-value pairs separated by semi-colons. You can then access each value in CustomActionData in the following way:

```
[CustomAction]
public static ActionResult myDeferredCA(Session session)
{
    ICollection<string> values =
        session.CustomActionData.Values;

    foreach (string value in values)
    {
        // shows 3 message boxes:
        // abc123, def567 and ghi890
        MessageBox.Show(value);
    }

    return ActionResult.Success;
}
```

Notice that we are accessing the `Values` property on `CustomActionData`. You could also access the key-value pairs we've set using hash table syntax:

```
MessageBox.Show(session.CustomActionData["Prop1"]);
MessageBox.Show(session.CustomActionData["Prop2"]);
MessageBox.Show(session.CustomActionData["Prop3"]);
```

It's also possible to set the data directly in an immediate C# custom action. So, instead of setting a property using a `CustomAction` element, you could set the `CustomActionData` value from code:

```
[CustomAction]
public static ActionResult myImmediateCA(Session session)
{
  CustomActionData data = new CustomActionData();
  data["property1"] = "abc";
  data["property2"] = "def";
  data["property3"] = "ghi";

  session["myDeferredCA"] = data.ToString();

  return ActionResult.Success;
}
```

You can then access the data from within your deferred custom action as follows:

```
[CustomAction]
public static ActionResult myDeferredCA(Session session)
{
  CustomActionData data = session.CustomActionData;
  string property1 = data["property1"];

  return ActionResult.Success;
}
```

Adding conditions to custom actions

After you've defined your custom actions and scheduled them into either `InstallUISequence` or `InstallExecuteSequence`, you have the option of adding conditions to them. These are added as the inner text of the `Custom` element and prevent the action from running if the condition is false. A common use for this is to only run the action during installation by using the `NOT Installed` condition.

```
<InstallExecuteSequence>
  <Custom Action="myCustomAction" After="InstallInitialize">
```

```
        NOT Installed
    </Custom>
</InstallExecuteSequence>
```

Other common conditions are `Installed`, which is true if the software is already installed, and `REMOVE="ALL"`, which is true if the product is being uninstalled.

You can also use the action state and installed state of features and components or check the values of your custom properties. Look back to *Chapter 4, Improving Control with Launch Conditions and Installed States*, to review the discussion about these types of conditional statements. It's a good idea to try out an installation and uninstallation of your product just to make sure your custom actions are running only when you expect them to. You can see this in the install log by looking for the words "Doing action".

Deployment Tools Foundation

Writing custom actions with .NET code means making use of the **Deployment Tools Foundation (DTF)**. Here, we'll touch on some of the more common parts of the DTF library. However, you should also take a look at the DTF documentation that comes with WiX if you'd like to explore some of its other features. For example, although we won't cover it here, DTF has support for LINQ and CAB file compression. The examples in this section draw from DTF's `Microsoft.Deployment.WindowsInstaller` namespace.

The session object

When the `InstallUISequence` and `InstallExecuteSequence` tables run through their lists of actions, they're doing so in their own memory space—called a **session**. You've seen how this requires you to mark WiX properties as public (uppercase) to get them from one session to the other. In DTF, the `Session` object is your pipeline into each sequence's running state. Every .NET custom action method receives `session` in its parameter list. If you recall, the generic signature of one of these custom actions is this:

```
[CustomAction]
public static ActionResult CustomAction1(Session session)
```

You'll use `Session` as the starting place for almost everything you do when working with the `WindowsInstaller` namespace. Its methods and properties return the various other objects that DTF provides. The following sections each use this object in some way to accomplish a task.

Getting and setting properties

To access a WiX property, such as those set with the `Property` element, use the `Session` object's indexer. The following is an example:

```
[CustomAction]
public static ActionResult CustomAction1(Session session)
{
  string myProperty = session["MY_PROPERTY"];
  return ActionResult.Success;
}
```

Setting properties is just as easy. You'll set the value by referencing the key with the name of your property. Here's an example:

```
[CustomAction]
public static ActionResult CustomAction1(Session session)
{
  session["MY_PROPERTY"] = "abc";
  return ActionResult.Success;
}
```

If the property doesn't exist when you set it, it will be created. Similarly, you can clear a property by settings its value to null. Creating or changing property values from a custom action doesn't stop the installer from displaying those properties in the install log. So, if a property holds information that has to be hidden, you're better off declaring it in your WiX markup first and setting its `Hidden` attribute to `yes`:

```
<Property Id="MY_PROPERTY" Hidden="yes" />
```

Logging

You can add your own messages to the install log by using the `Session` object's `Log` method. The simplest way is to just pass it a string, as shown in the following code snippet:

```
session.Log("This will show up in the log.");
```

You can also pass it a formatted string, as in the next example:

```
string currentTime =
  System.DateTime.Now.ToString("HH:mm:ss",
    CultureInfo.CurrentCulture);
string functionName = "CustomAction1";
string message = "This will show up in the log.";

  session.Log("{0} : Method = {1}: {2}", currentTime,
    functionName, message);
```

This will produce the following message in the log:

18:05:19 : Method = CustomAction1: This will show up in the log.

You can also use the `Message` method for the same effect. You'll need to create a `Record` object that contains your text and pass it, along with `InstallMessage.Info`, to the method. Here's an example:

```
Record record = new Record(0);
record[0] = "This will show up in the log";
session.Message(InstallMessage.Info, record);
```

Be aware that the `Log` and `Message` methods don't work when the custom action is called from a UI control such as a button click. You'll learn about calling custom actions from UI controls using the `DoAction` event in *Chapter 8, Tapping into Control Events*.

Showing a message box

The `Message` method can also be used to display a message box to the user. All you need to do is change the first parameter to `InstallMessage.Warning` or `InstallMessage.Error`. Either will show a message box, although the icon used may differ, depending on the operating system.

The following example displays a warning message to the user:

```
[CustomAction]
public static ActionResult CustomAction1(Session session)
{
    Record record = new Record(0);
    record[0] = "This is a warning!";
    session.Message(InstallMessage.Warning, record);

    return ActionResult.Success;
}
```

The following is the result:

To show an error message box, use `InstallMessage.Error` instead:

```
[CustomAction]
public static ActionResult CustomAction1(Session session)
{
    Record record = new Record(0);
    record[0] = "This is an error!";
    session.Message(InstallMessage.Error, record);

    return ActionResult.Success;
}
```

Note that these only provide an **OK** button. If you need more than that, you'll need to use something like a Windows Forms dialog, which you can do by adding the appropriate .NET assembly reference. Something else to consider is that, as we did when logging, we're using the `Message` method here. So, it will not work if called from a UI control.

Accessing feature and component states

To access a feature's action or installed state, use the **Features** collection. You can look up a feature by name.

```
FeatureInfo productFeature =
    session.Features["ProductFeature"];

//will return "Absent" during an installation
InstallState installedState = productFeature.CurrentState;

//will return "Local" during an installation
InstallState actionState = productFeature.RequestState;
```

Here, we're using the `FeatureInfo` object's `CurrentState` for installed state and `RequestState` for action state. You can do the same thing for components by using the `Components` collection, as shown in the following code snippet:

```
ComponentInfo cmpInfo = session.Components["cmp_myFile"];
InstallState cmpCurrentState = cmpInfo.CurrentState;
InstallState cmpRequestState = cmpInfo.RequestState;
```

Querying the MSI database

You can read any of the data that's in the MSI database. First, get a reference to the MSI database with the `Session` object's `Database` property. Be aware that you cannot access the `Database` property during a deferred custom action. In that case, you may set up `CustomActionData`, as described earlier, during an immediate custom action and pass the information to the deferred phase that way. In the following example, we access the `Session` object's `Database` property:

```
Database db = session.Database;
```

Next, if you just want to get one value from a table, use the `ExecuteScalar` method. This will return the value from the column in your SQL query. Here's an example:

```
string property = "ProductName";

string value = (string)db.ExecuteScalar(
    "SELECT `Value` FROM `Property` WHERE `Property` = '{0}'",
    property);

db.Close();
```

Notice that I cast the result to a string. This works in this example because the `Value` column on the `Property` table contains strings. If, on the other hand, the column had contained integers I would have had to cast the result to an integer.

If you'd like to get multiple rows back from your query, use the `ExecuteQuery` method. It returns a collection of type `System.Collections.IList`.

```
string query =
    "SELECT `Property` FROM `Property` ORDER BY `Property`";
System.Collections.IList result = db.ExecuteQuery(query);
db.Close();
```

Inserting rows into the MSI database

You can't insert new data into the MSI database while it's installing and unfortunately, that's often exactly when you want to! To get around this, you can make *temporary* inserts using the `View` object's `InsertTemporary` method. You can get a `View` by calling the `OpenView` method on the `Database` object, passing in a `SELECT` statement of the data you want to work with. Here's an example that adds a new property, called `NEW_PROPERTY`, to the `Property` table:

```
Database db = session.Database;
View view = db.OpenView("SELECT * FROM `Property`");
Record rec = new Record("NEW_PROPERTY", "new_value");
view.InsertTemporary(rec);
db.Close();
```

The first thing we did here was use the `Database` object's `OpenView` method to get a `View`. We selected all of the existing rows from the `Property` table and then inserted a new row with `InsertTemporary`. It's perfectly acceptable to get a smaller view by adding a `WHERE` clause to the SQL query.

You'll need to know the number and order of the columns in the table you're working with before you start inserting new rows. When you create your `Record` object, you have to place the values in the same order as the columns. You can omit columns you don't use as long as they come at the end.

Another example is to add a new control to a dialog during the course of the install. Just be sure to add it *before* `CostInitialize` in the UI phase or your change will go unnoticed. In the following example, we'll add a Text control to the `ProgressDlg` dialog. This is assuming you're using one of WiX's built-in dialog sets and that `ProgressDlg` exists.

```
[CustomAction]
public static ActionResult AddControl(Session session)
{
    Database db = null;

    try
    {
        db = session.Database;

        //create control on ProgressDlg:
        View view = db.OpenView("SELECT * FROM `Control`");

        Record record = new Record(
            "ProgressDlg",
            "MyText",
            "Text",
            "20",
            "150",
            "150",
            "15",
            "1");

        view.InsertTemporary(record);

        //subscribe that control to the ActionData event:
        View view2 =
            db.OpenView("SELECT * FROM `EventMapping`");

        Record record2 = new Record("ProgressDlg",
```

```
            "MyText", "ActionData", "Text");

        view2.InsertTemporary(record2);
    }
    catch (Exception err)
    {
        session.Log(err.Message + ": " + err.StackTrace);
        return ActionResult.Failure;
    }
    finally
    {
        if (db != null)
        {
            db.Close();
        }
    }

    return ActionResult.Success;
}
```

First, we get a handle to the MSI database by using `session.Database`. Next, we insert a new temporary record into the `Control` table. That will be our Text control. To make things interesting, we've also added a record to the `EventMapping` table, subscribing our Text control to the `ActionData` event. We'll discuss control events in more detail later. For now, know that this will cause the Text control to automatically update itself with any status messages of actions that occur during the installation.

It's a good idea to catch any exceptions that might happen and return `ActionResult.Failure` after we've logged the error. This is better than allowing uncaught exceptions to bubble up and kill the installation. This also allows us to log exactly what went wrong.

Summary

In this chapter, we began by discussing standard actions, which are actions that are built into Windows Installer. Knowing the order and function of these events can be a big help in understanding and debugging the installer. We saw that there are two sequences, `InstallUISequence` and `InstallExecuteSequence`, and how we can access them from our WiX markup. We explored how to create custom actions and schedule them into a sequence. We also covered the major points of the Deployment Tools Foundation library.

In the next chapter, we will cover the fundamentals of adding a user interface to help guide users through the install process. We will start by using the dialogs that come with WiX and then branch out to creating our own.

6

Adding a User Interface

The WiX toolset ships with several user interface wizards that are ready to use out of the box. You can drop one into your installer by first adding a reference to `WixUIExtension.dll` and then adding a `UIRef` element with the name of the wizard. We'll briefly discuss each of the available dialog sets and then move on to learning how to create your own from scratch. In this chapter, you'll learn about:

- Adding dialogs into `InstallUISequence`
- Linking one dialog to another to form a complete wizard
- Getting basic text and window styling working
- Including necessary dialogs such as those needed to display errors

WiX standard dialog sets

The wizards that come prebuilt with WiX won't fit every need, but they're a good place to get your feet wet. To begin with, use the **Add a Reference** screen in Visual Studio to add a reference to `WixUIExtension.dll`. It can be found in the `bin` directory of the WiX program files.

Adding this reference is like adding a new WiX source file. This one contains dialogs. To use one you'll need to use a `UIRef` element to pull the dialog into the scope of your project. For example, this line, anywhere inside the `Product` element, will add the "Minimal" wizard to your installer:

```
<UIRef Id="WixUI_Minimal" />
```

It's definitely minimal, containing just one screen.

It gives you a license agreement, which you can change by adding a `WixVariable` element with an `Id` value of `WixUILicenseRtf` and a `Value` attribute that points to a Rich Text Format (`.rtf`) file containing your new license agreement:

```
<WixVariable Id="WixUILicenseRtf"
             Value="newLicense.rtf" />
```

You can also override the background image (red CD on the left, white box on the right) by setting another `WixVariable` called `WixUIDialogBmp` to a new image. The dimensions used are 493 x 312. The other available wizards offer more and we'll cover them in the following sections.

WixUI_Advanced

The "Advanced" wizard adds a few more dialogs to the mix, in addition to the EULA. The user can choose to install right away or to configure the advanced options. You'll need to change your `UIRef` element to use `WixUI_Advanced`, as shown here:

```
<UIRef Id="WixUI_Advanced" />
```

You'll also have to make sure that your install directory has an `Id` attribute of `APPLICATIONFOLDER`, as in this example:

```
<Directory Id="TARGETDIR"
           Name="SourceDir">
```

```
<Directory Id="ProgramFilesFolder">
  <Directory Id="APPLICATIONFOLDER"
            Name="My Program" />
  </Directory>
</Directory>
```

Next, set two properties: `ApplicationFolderName` and `WixAppFolder`. The first sets the name of the install directory as it will be displayed in the UI. The second sets whether this install should default to being per user or per machine. It can be set to either `WixPerMachineFolder` or `WixPerUserFolder`.

```
<Property Id="ApplicationFolderName"
         Value="My Program" />
<Property Id="WixAppFolder"
         Value="WixPerMachineFolder" />
```

The new screens include the **Installation Scope** screen, where the user can choose to install for all users or just for him or herself. The default will be set by the `WixPerMachineFolder` property, as shown in the following screenshot:

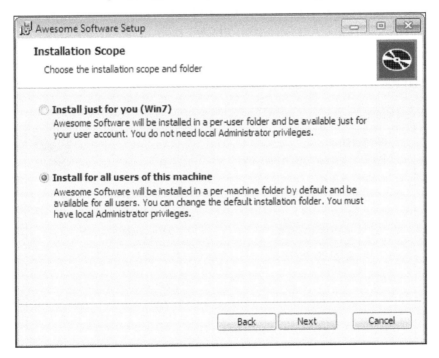

There's also a screen for changing the install directory's path and another for changing which features will get installed. You'll notice that many of these screens have a banner at the top (white background with the familiar red CD to the right).

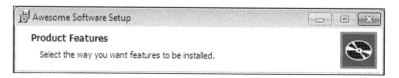

You can replace it with your own image by setting the `WixUIBannerBmp` variable. Its dimensions are 493 x 58. You can set it in the following way:

```
<WixVariable Id="WixUIBannerBmp"
             Value="myBanner.bmp" />
```

WixUI_FeatureTree

The `WixUI_FeatureTree` wizard shows a feature tree same as the Advanced wizard, but it doesn't have the **Install Scope** or **Install Path** dialogs. To use it, you only need to set the `UIRef` to `WixUI_FeatureTree`, like so:

```
<UIRef Id="WixUI_FeatureTree" />
```

Here's what the feature tree dialog looks like:

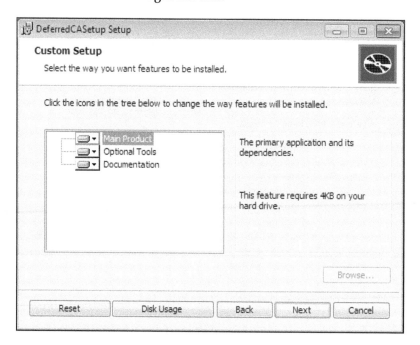

Notice that in the image, the **Browse** button is disabled. If any of your Feature elements have the ConfigurableDirectory attribute set to the ID of a Directory element then this button will allow you to change where that particular feature gets installed to. The Directory element's Id attribute must be all uppercase.

WixUI_InstallDir

WixUI_InstallDir shows a dialog where the user can change the installation path. Change the UIRef to WixUI_InstallDir, like so:

```
<UIRef Id="WixUI_InstallDir" />
```

Here, the user can choose the installation path. This is seen in the following screenshot:

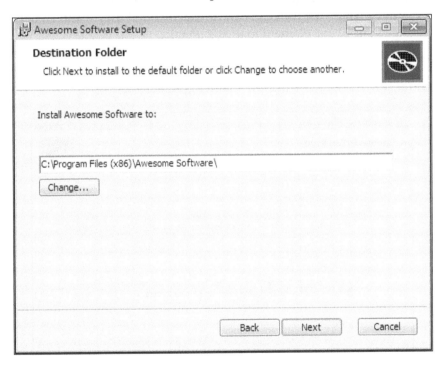

You'll have to set a property called WIXUI_INSTALLDIR to the Id attribute you gave your install directory. So, if your directory structure used INSTALLLDIR for the Id attribute of the main install folder, use that as the value of the property, as given in the following code snippet:

```
<Directory Id="TARGETDIR"
            Name="SourceDir">
  <Directory Id="ProgramFilesFolder">
    <Directory Id="INSTALLDIR"
```

```
                    Name="My Program" />
    </Directory>
  </Directory>

  <Property Id="WIXUI_INSTALLDIR"
            Value="INSTALLDIR" />
```

WixUI_Mondo

The `WixUI_Mondo` wizard gives the user the option of installing a **Typical**, **Complete**, or **Custom** install. **Typical** sets the `INSTALLLEVEL` property to 3 while **Complete** sets it to 1000. You can set the `Level` attribute of your `Feature` elements accordingly to include them in one group or the other. Selecting a **Custom** install will display a feature tree dialog where the user can choose exactly what they want. To use this wizard, change your `UIRef` element to `WixUI_Mondo`:

```
<UIRef Id="WixUI_Mondo" />
```

This would result in a window like the following screenshot:

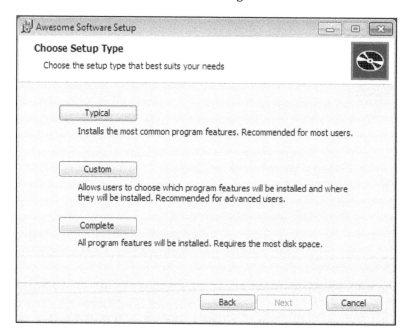

Recall that features that have a `Level` value less than or equal to `INSTALLLEVEL` will be installed.

Customizing a standard dialog set

Each of the dialog sets shown can be customized by adding screens, removing some, or changing the look and text. Usually, this means downloading the WiX source code from `wix.codeplex.com` and changing the markup in the dialogs. You can find them under the `src\ext\UIExtension\wixlib` folder of the source code.

The general procedure is to copy the `.wxs` file that has the name of the wizard, such as `WixUI_Minimal.wxs`, to your project with a different name such as `Custom_Minimal.wxs`. Then, add or remove `DialogRef` elements from that file to add or remove dialogs. `DialogRefs` are the references to the dialogs in the other files. Files such as `WixUI_Minimal.wxs` just tie them all together into a wizard. For example, here's part of what you'd find in the Minimal wizard's main source file:

```
<DialogRef Id="ErrorDlg" />
<DialogRef Id="FatalError" />
<DialogRef Id="FilesInUse" />
<DialogRef Id="MsiRMFilesInUse" />
<DialogRef Id="PrepareDlg" />
<DialogRef Id="ProgressDlg" />
<DialogRef Id="ResumeDlg" />
<DialogRef Id="UserExit" />
<DialogRef Id="WelcomeEulaDlg" />
```

Here, you could remove the welcome dialog from the wizard by removing the `WelcomeEulaDlg` line. The Minimal wizard is pretty small to begin with so you're probably better off customizing a set such as Mondo.

Scanning through the rest of the file, you'll find that it uses the `Publish` elements to define where the **Next** button on each dialog takes you to. You can, in your custom file, change that. Here's what you'd find in `WixUI_Mondo.wxs`:

```
<Publish Dialog="WelcomeDlg"
        Control="Next"
        Event="NewDialog"
        Value="LicenseAgreementDlg">1</Publish>

<Publish Dialog="LicenseAgreementDlg"
        Control="Back"
        Event="NewDialog"
        Value="WelcomeDlg">1</Publish>

<Publish Dialog="LicenseAgreementDlg"
```

```
               Control="Next"
               Event="NewDialog"
               Value="SetupTypeDlg"
               Order="2">LicenseAccepted = "1"</Publish>
```

This is all unfamiliar still and we'll go over the `Publish` element in more detail when we talk about creating our own dialogs. For now, notice that we pair `Dialog` and `Control` attributes to find a particular UI control, such as a button, on a specific dialog. The first `Publish` element, for example, finds the **Next** button on the `WelcomeDlg` dialog. Use the `Event` attribute to add an event such as `NewDialog` to the button.

Here, we're saying we want the **Next** button to fire the `NewDialog` event with `Value` of `LicenseAgreementDlg`. This means that when the button is clicked, `WelcomeDlg` will be replaced with `LicenseAgreementDlg`. You can customize any control on any dialog from here, usually to change where the **Next** and **Back** buttons take you. This allows you to insert new dialogs or skip one you don't want.

Here's an example that inserts a custom dialog called `MyDialog` between `WelcomeDlg` and `LicenseAgreementDlg`. Add this to your `Custom_Mondo.wxs` file:

```
<Publish Dialog="WelcomeDlg"
         Control="Next"
         Event="NewDialog"
         Value="MyDialog">1</Publish>

<Publish Dialog="MyDialog"
         Control="Back"
         Event="NewDialog"
         Value="WelcomeDlg">1</Publish>

<Publish Dialog="MyDialog"
         Control="Next"
         Event="NewDialog"
         Value="LicenseAgreementDlg">1</Publish>

<Publish Dialog="LicenseAgreementDlg"
         Control="Back"
         Event="NewDialog"
         Value="MyDialog">1</Publish>
```

Remember, you'd need to get the original `WixUI_Mondo.wxs` file from the WiX source and rename it to something like `Custom_Mondo.wxs` before adding it to your project. You'll then reference the custom file with `UIRef`.

```
<UIRef Id="Custom_Mondo" />
```

Be sure to change the UI element in the `Custom_Mondo.wxs` file to match.

```
<Wix xmlns="http://schemas.microsoft.com/wix/2006/wi">
    <Fragment>
        <UI Id="Custom_Mondo">
```

We'll explain more about referencing dialog sets when we discuss creating dialogs from scratch.

Creating your own dialogs

In this section, we'll discard the premade dialogs and create our own. This should give you a much deeper understanding of how things work.

ICE20 errors

For these first exercises, you'll have to ignore some of WiX's warnings. Go to the **Properties** page for the project, select **Tools Settings** and add a rule to ignore the validation test **ICE20**. This test checks that you've added the `FilesInUse`, `Error`, `FatalError`, `UserExit`, and `Exit` dialogs. That's a lot to start out with, so for now just ignore those rules.

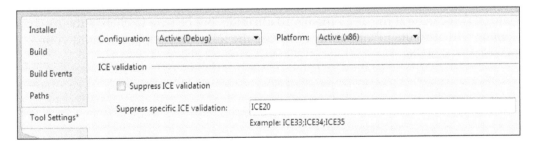

What are these dialogs? They are all windows that show an error message or indicate that the install has been completed successfully. They show up automatically when they're needed. Later in the chapter, I'll show how you can create these dialogs to meet the requirements of ICE20.

Adding dialog files

Let's remove the reference to `WixUIExtension.dll` and `UIRef` that points to a standard dialog. We'll be creating everything ourselves now to get the best working knowledge. Each dialog window that you create should be placed into its own WiX source file (`.wxs`). In Visual Studio, you can right-click on your project and select **Add | New Item | WiX File**.

This will create an XML file containing a `Wix` root element and a `Fragment` element. Fragments can be used to split your code into separate files and as such can be used for many different purposes. To create a dialog out of one, you'll need to add two more elements: `UI` and `Dialog`. In this example, I've added a `UI` element and given it an `Id` value of `CustomWizard`. Inside that, I've nested a `Dialog` element, which I've called `InstallDlg`. You could name this file `InstallDlg.wxs` and it should now look like the following snippet:

```
<Wix xmlns="http://schemas.microsoft.com/wix/2006/wi">
  <Fragment>
    <UI Id="CustomWizard">
      <Dialog Id="InstallDlg">
        <!--Controls like buttons and text go here-->
      </Dialog>
    </UI>
  </Fragment>
</Wix>
```

This is the basic structure that you'll use for each new dialog. The first dialog that you create can serve as the entry point for the others. If, for example, we created a second dialog called `SecondDlg`, we could set it up in the same way. On additional dialogs, you can omit the `UI` element's `Id` attribute, but be sure to change the `Dialog` element's `Id` attribute to something new. Use the following snippet to build your `SecondDlg.wxs` file:

```
<Wix xmlns="http://schemas.microsoft.com/wix/2006/wi">
  <Fragment>
    <UI>
      <Dialog Id="SecondDlg">
        <!--Controls like buttons and text go here-->
      </Dialog>
    </UI>
  </Fragment>
</Wix>
```

Then, to reference `SecondDlg` in our first dialog, add a `DialogRef` element to our `InstallDlg.wxs` file:

```
<Wix xmlns="http://schemas.microsoft.com/wix/2006/wi">
  <Fragment>
    <UI Id="CustomWizard">
      <DialogRef Id="SecondDlg"/>

      <Dialog Id="InstallDlg">
      </Dialog>
    </UI>
  </Fragment>
</Wix>
```

To add both dialogs to our project, use a `UIRef` element in your main source file. Its `Id` attribute should match the `Id` attribute value you gave to your `UI` element in `InstallDlg`. Add the following line to `Product.wxs`:

```
<UIRef Id="CustomWizard"/>
```

The Dialog element

Our `InstallDlg` won't work properly yet. We still need to add more attributes to the `Dialog` element to set its size, title, and whether or not it can be minimized:

```
<Dialog Id="InstallDlg"
        Width="370"
        Height="270"
        Title="Amazing Software"
        NoMinimize="no">
```

You can set `Width` and `Height` larger or smaller, but 370 and 270 are the dimensions used by the WiX dialog sets. Together, these define the size of the window. The `Title` attribute sets the text that will be displayed at the top of the window. Setting `NoMinimize` to no means that the user will be able to minimize the dialog. This is the default so specifying it isn't strictly necessary. There's one other attribute that you're likely to use early on and that's `Modeless`, which can be set to yes. This will make the dialog not wait for user input and is often used for progress bar dialogs. We'll cover it later in the chapter.

Scheduling dialogs

For now, we only need to schedule one of our dialogs in the UI sequence. To do that, place a `Show` element inside an `InstallUISequence` element with a `Dialog` attribute set to the `Id` attribute of the `InstallDlg` file's `Dialog` element. Then add a `Before` attribute and schedule it before `ExecuteAction`. The following snippet shows this, which we can place inside the `InstallDlg.wxs` file, inside the `Fragment` element:

```
<InstallUISequence>
  <Show Dialog="InstallDlg"
        Before="ExecuteAction" />
</InstallUISequence>
```

Now, when the installer is launched our first dialog will be shown. To get from our first dialog to our second one, we'll add a **Next** button that takes us there. We'll cover buttons in detail in the next chapter, but basically, you'll add a `Control` element of `Type = "PushButton"` inside the `InstallDlg` file's `Dialog` element. It will, in turn, contain another element called `Publish` that closes the current dialog and opens the second. The `InstallDlg.wxs` file will contain this code:

```
<Dialog ...>
  <Control Id="Next"
           Type="PushButton"
           X="245"
           Y="243"
           Width="100"
           Height="17"
           Text="Next">
    <Publish Event="NewDialog"
             Value="SecondDlg" />
  </Control>
</Dialog>
```

This technique can be used to navigate from one dialog to another, or even to go back via **Back** buttons. You only need to change the value of the `Publish` element's `Value` attribute to the `Id` attribute of a different `Dialog` element. We could add a **Back** button on our `SecondDlg` file that takes us back to `InstallDlg`:

```
<Dialog ...>
  <Control Id="Back"
           Type="PushButton"
           X="180"
           Y="243"
           Width="100"
           Height="17"
           Text="Back">
```

```
        <Publish Event="NewDialog"
                Value="InstallDlg" />
    </Control>
</Dialog>
```

If you add more than one button to the same dialog, you'll also need to change the Id attribute of the Control element and change its X and Y attributes. Otherwise, all of your buttons would sit on top of one another and have the same key in MSI's Control table. The following is a screenshot of a dialog that has both **Back** and **Next** buttons:

Adding TextStyle elements

Our dialog isn't useable yet. It needs at least one TextStyle element to set the default font for the text on the window. You'll only need to do this for the first dialog you create. The other dialogs can re-use the styles you set there. A TextStyle element uses the FaceName, Size, Bold, Italic, and Underline attributes to set a font. The following example creates a vanilla 8pt Tahoma font to be used as our default:

```
<TextStyle Id="Tahoma_Regular"
            FaceName="Tahoma"
            Size="8" />
<Property Id="DefaultUIFont"
            Value="Tahoma_Regular" />
```

Since this will be our default font, we have to add a Property element with an Id attribute set to DefaultUIFont and a Value attribute set to the ID of our TextStyle element. These will go inside our UI element as siblings to our Dialog element. You can add more TextStyle elements for titles, fine print, and so on.

```
<Wix xmlns="http://schemas.microsoft.com/wix/2006/wi">
  <Fragment>
    <UI Id=»InstallDlg_UI»>
      <TextStyle Id="Tahoma_Regular"
                  FaceName="Tahoma"
                  Size="8" />
      <Property Id="DefaultUIFont"
```

```
                    Value="Tahoma_Regular" />

        <TextStyle Id="Tahoma_Bold"
                   FaceName="Tahoma"
                   Size="8"
                   Bold="yes" />
        <TextStyle Id="Tahoma_Italic"
                   FaceName="Tahoma"
                   Size="8"
                   Italic="yes" />
        <TextStyle Id="Tahoma_Title"
                   FaceName="Tahoma"
                   Size="12"
                   Underline="yes" />

        <Dialog Id="InstallDlg"
                Width="370"
                Height="270"
                Title="Amazing Software"
                NoMinimize=»no»>
        </Dialog>
      </UI>
    </Fragment>
  </Wix>
```

You can use these styles on, for example, a `Control` element of `Type = "Text"`, which displays a label, by adding the `TextStyle` element's `Id` attribute in curly brackets to the `Control` element's `Text` attribute. Prefix it with a backslash as shown:

```
<Control  Id="myText"
          Type="Text"
          X="10" Y="10"
          Width="200"
          Height="17"
          Text="{\Tahoma_Bold}Here is some text" />
```

The following table lists the possible attributes for your `TextStyle` elements:

Attribute	Meaning
Blue	Set to a number between 0 and 255 of how blue the text should be.
Green	Set to a number between 0 and 255 of how green the text should be.
Red	Set to a number between 0 and 255 of how red the text should be.
Italic	If yes, the text will be italic.

Attribute	Meaning
Bold	If yes, the text will be bold.
Size	Sets the numeric size of the text.
Strike	If yes, the text will have a line through it.
Underline	If yes, the text will be underlined.
FaceName	The font face of the text.

Here is an example that uses several TextStyle elements in Text controls:

Adding a tabbable control

Our InstallDlg still isn't ready. We need to add at least one control that can be tabbed to inside our Dialog element. For a simple, one screen wizard, we can just add a button that, when clicked, continues the installation. It could say **Install** on it. For that, we'll create a button that publishes the EndDialog event with a Value attribute of Return. This is illustrated in the following code snippet:

```
<Control Id="InstallButton"
         Type="PushButton"
         Text="Install"
         Height="17"
         Width="56"
         X="245"
         Y="243">
  <Publish Event="EndDialog"
           Value="Return" />
</Control>
```

We can also add a button that says **Cancel**. It will also publish the `EndDialog` event, but with a `Value` attribute of `Exit`. If we add the `Cancel` attribute to it, this button will be triggered if the user clicks the **X** button on the window or presses *Esc*.

```
<Control Id="CancelButton"
         Type="PushButton"
         Text="Cancel"
         Height="17"
         Width="56"
         X="180"
         Y="243"
         Cancel="yes">
    <Publish Event="EndDialog"
             Value="Exit" />
</Control>
```

Here's our `InstallDlg` now, ready for use:

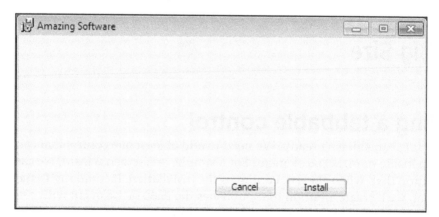

The following is the entire markup:

```
<?xml version=»1.0» encoding=»UTF-8»?>
<Wix xmlns=»http://schemas.microsoft.com/wix/2006/wi»>
  <Fragment>
    <UI Id="CustomWizard">
      <TextStyle Id="Tahoma_Regular"
                 FaceName="Tahoma"
                 Size="8" />
      <Property Id="DefaultUIFont"
                Value="Tahoma_Regular" />

      <Dialog Id="InstallDlg"
              Width="370"
```

```
                    Height="270"
                    Title="Amazing Software"
                    NoMinimize="no">

            <Control Id="InstallButton"
                    Type="PushButton"
                    Text="Install"
                    Height="17"
                    Width="56"
                    X="245"
                    Y="243">
              <Publish Event="EndDialog"
                    Value="Return" />
            </Control>

            <Control Id="CancelButton"
                    Type="PushButton"
                    Text="Cancel"
                    Height="17"
                    Width="56"
                    X="180"
                    Y="243"
                    Cancel="yes">
              <Publish Event="EndDialog"
                    Value="Exit" />
            </Control>
          </Dialog>

          <InstallUISequence>
            <Show Dialog="InstallDlg"
                    Before="ExecuteAction" />
          </InstallUISequence>
        </UI>
      </Fragment>
    </Wix>
```

Don't forget to add a `UIRef` element to your `Product.wxs` file to reference your wizard:

```
<Product ...>
  <Package ... />
  <MediaTemplate ... />
  ...
  <UIRef Id="CustomWizard" />
</Product>
```

When adding controls it's important to know that the order in which they appear in your XML markup (from top to bottom) will be their tab order on the window. So, you should place the button you'd want to receive the focus first at the top of your markup, followed by the control that you'd want to receive the focus next, down the line. In our example, the **Install** button would be focused when the window first loads and pressing **Tab** would take you to the **Cancel** button.

You can prevent a control from being the default focused control by setting its `TabSkip` attribute to `yes`. In that case, the next control in line will be focused when the screen is first displayed.

> Note that `TabSkip` only prevents a control from having the focus when the dialog is first shown. The user will still be able to tab to that control.

Adding a progress dialog

So what happens when we click the **Install** button? It installs but there's no indication that anything has happened. We need a dialog that shows a progress bar to inform the user that the install is happening. Add a new WiX source file to your project and call it `ProgressDlg.wxs`. Add a `UI` element, like before, and then a `Dialog` element with the `Id` attribute set to `"ProgressDlg"` to differentiate it in the MSI database. The `ProgressDlg.wxs` file will look like the following code:

```
<Wix xmlns="http://schemas.microsoft.com/wix/2006/wi">
  <Fragment>
    <UI>
      <Dialog Id="ProgressDlg"></Dialog>
    </UI>
  </Fragment>
</Wix>
```

Back in `InstallDlg.wxs`, add a `DialogRef` element inside the `UI` element to reference this new file:

```
<Fragment>
  <UI Id="CustomWizard">
    <DialogRef Id="ProgressDlg" />
```

The `Dialog` element in `ProgressDlg.wxs` will use the `Modeless` attribute to signify that it shouldn't wait for user interaction. The installation process will continue, but it will allow this dialog to remain up for the remainder of the installation. This allows the dialog to respond to events that fire during the Execute sequence, which will enable the dialog's progress bar to increment itself.

```
<Dialog Id="ProgressDlg"
        Width="370"
        Height="270"
        Title="Amazing Software"
        Modeless="yes">
```

If you like, you can add a **Cancel** button to this dialog, just in case the user decides to cancel at this point. Refer back to `InstallDlg` for the markup. We'll also add a `Control` element of type `ProgressBar` that uses the `Subscribe` element to receive progress updates:

```
<Control Id="MyProgressBar"
         Type="ProgressBar"
         X="70"
         Y="150"
         Width="200"
         Height="20"
         ProgressBlocks="yes">

  <Subscribe Event="SetProgress"
             Attribute="Progress" />
</Control>
```

By subscribing to the `SetProgress` event, the progress bar is able to increment itself as actions occur. The following screenshot is what it will look like:

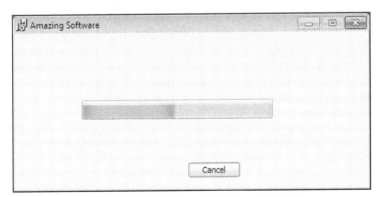

Before, when we talked about adding a **Next** button to take us to a second dialog, there would have been no need to explicitly add that dialog to the UI sequence. The button takes us to it. It would have been up to that second dialog to then have an **Install** button that ended the dialog wizard and allowed the rest of the install to continue. In other words, we must always end with a button that publishes the EndDialog event with a Value of Return. Usually, that button is marked **Install**.

Our ProgressDlg, however, will remain up as the rest of the install continues. It's "modeless". Therefore, we should schedule it to run after InstallDlg and before ExecuteAction. This is shown in the following code:

```
<InstallUISequence>
  <Show Dialog="ProgressDlg"
        After="InstallDlg" />
</InstallUISequence>
```

If you look at the InstallUISequence table in Orca, you can see how things look:

Action	Condit...	Seque...
FindRelatedProducts		25
LaunchConditions		100
ValidateProductID		700
CostInitialize		800
FileCost		900
CostFinalize		1000
MigrateFeatureStates		1200
InstallDlg		1298
ProgressDlg		1299
ExecuteAction		1300

Even if we'd had a second, third, and fourth dialog, each arrived at by clicking a **Next** button on the dialog before, we wouldn't see any of them in this table. The InstallDlg is our entry point. When it closes, via the EndDialog event, ProgressDlg pops up. Since ProgressDlg is Modeless, ExecuteAction fires immediately and takes us into the Execute sequence. The following is a complete sample for the progress dialog:

```
<?xml version=»1.0» encoding=»UTF-8»?>
<Wix xmlns=»http://schemas.microsoft.com/wix/2006/wi»>
  <Fragment>
    <UI>
      <Dialog Id="ProgressDlg"
              Width="370"
              Height="270"
```

```
                Title="Amazing Software"
                Modeless="yes">

        <Control Id="CancelButton"
                Type="PushButton"
                TabSkip="no"
                Text="Cancel"
                Height="17"
                Width="56"
                X="180"
                Y="243"
                Cancel="yes">
          <Publish Event="EndDialog"
                Value="Exit" />
        </Control>

        <Control Id="MyProgressBar"
                Type="ProgressBar"
                X="70"
                Y="150"
                Width="200"
                Height="20"
                ProgressBlocks="yes">
          <Subscribe Event="SetProgress"
                Attribute=»Progress» />
        </Control>
      </Dialog>

      <InstallUISequence>
        <Show Dialog="ProgressDlg"
                After="InstallDlg" />
      </InstallUISequence>
    </UI>
  </Fragment>
</Wix>
```

Modal windows

Up to this point, closing one dialog opened another in its place. You can also create "modal" windows that pop up on top of the current window. Instead of publishing the NewDialog event inside a button, such as with our **Next** button, we can publish the SpawnDialog event.

Modal windows are usually a little bit smaller in size than normal windows so that the parent window can be seen in the background. Suppose we had a dialog called PopupDlg, such as in the following snippet:

```xml
<?xml version="1.0" encoding="UTF-8"?>
<Wix xmlns="http://schemas.microsoft.com/wix/2006/wi">
  <Fragment>
    <UI>
      <Dialog Id="PopupDlg"
              Width="300"
              Height="200"
              Title="Amazing Software">

        <Control Id="OkButton"
                 Type="PushButton"
                 Text="OK"
                 Height="17"
                 Width="56"
                 X="200"
                 Y="175">
          <Publish Event="EndDialog"
                   Value="Return" />
        </Control>
      </Dialog>
    </UI>
  </Fragment>
</Wix>
```

We could use the SpawnDialog event to open it modally. Typically, modal windows have an **OK** button that publishes the EndDialog event with a Value attribute of Return. This allows them to be closed and have focus return to the parent window.

The following is what a button on InstallDlg would look like if it were set to open PopupDlg modally:

```xml
<Control Id="PopupButton"
         Type="PushButton"
         Text="Show Popup"
         Height="17"
         Width="56"
         X="100"
         Y="243"
         Default="yes">
  <Publish Event="SpawnDialog"
           Value="PopupDlg" />
</Control>
```

Here's what the result looks like:

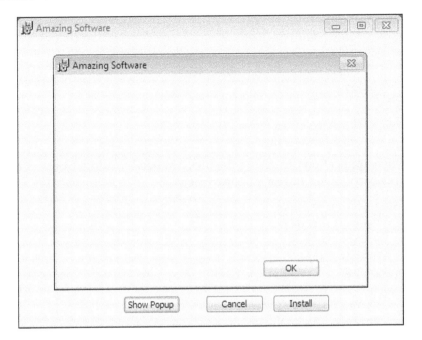

ICE20 revisited

ICE20 is the validation check that makes sure you have the necessary dialogs defined to handle things such as showing a friendly message when the user cancels the install. We initially suppressed this check in the project's properties. Now, let's remove that suppression and add these dialogs. Note that all are defined in the WiX source files and you may find it easier to simply copy them to your project.

We need to define five dialogs: `FilesInUse`, `Error`, `FatalError`, `UserExit`, and `Exit`.

FilesInUse

The `FilesInUse` dialog allows the user to shut down applications that are accessing files the installer needs to update or delete. The MSI finds this dialog by looking in the MSI `Dialog` table for a dialog with an `Id` attribute of `FilesInUse`. So, in our new WiX source file, the `Dialog` element's `Id` attribute must match this name. The `FilesInUseDlg.wxs` file will look like the following snippet:

```
<?xml version=»1.0» encoding=»UTF-8»?>
<Wix xmlns=»http://schemas.microsoft.com/wix/2006/wi»>
```

```
<Fragment>
  <UI>
    <Dialog Id="FilesInUse"
            Width="370"
            Height="270"
            Title="Amazing Software">
    </Dialog>
  </UI>
</Fragment>
</Wix>
```

To show which applications are using the files, we need to add a ListBox control that uses a property called FilesInUseProcess.

```
<Control Id="InUseFiles"
         Type="ListBox"
         Width="300"
         Height="150"
         X="30"
         Y="60"
         Property="FileInUseProcess"
         Sorted="yes" />
```

We also need to add three buttons, **Ignore**, **Retry**, and **Exit**. Set the EndDialog event to these values:

```
<Control Id="Retry"
         Type="PushButton"
         X="304"
         Y="243"
         Width="56"
         Height="17"
         Default="yes"
         Cancel="yes"
         Text="Retry">
  <Publish Event="EndDialog"
           Value="Retry">1</Publish>
</Control>

<Control Id="Ignore"
         Type="PushButton"
         X="235"
         Y="243"
         Width="56"
         Height="17"
```

```
            Text="Ignore">
  <Publish Event="EndDialog"
          Value="Ignore">1</Publish>
</Control>

<Control Id="Exit"
         Type="PushButton"
         X="166"
         Y="243"
         Width="56"
         Height="17"
         Text="Cancel">
  <Publish Event="EndDialog"
          Value="Exit">1</Publish>
</Control>
```

Remember to add a `DialogRef` element to this dialog in your `InstallDlg.wxs` file:

```
<DialogRef Id="FilesInUseDlg" />
```

Error

An installer uses the **Error** dialog to display error messages. Create a new source file and call it `ErrorDlg.wxs`. This file should set a property called `ErrorDialog` to the value you've set the `Dialog` element's `Id` attribute to. In addition, the `Dialog` element should set the `ErrorDialog` attribute to `yes`. The file should contain the following snippet:

```
<?xml version="1.0" encoding="UTF-8"?>
<Wix xmlns="http://schemas.microsoft.com/wix/2006/wi">
  <Fragment>
    <UI>
      <Property Id="ErrorDialog"
                Value="ErrorDlg" />

      <Dialog Id="ErrorDlg"
              Width="370"
              Height="270"
              Title="Amazing Software"
              ErrorDialog="yes">
      </Dialog>
    </UI>
  </Fragment>
</Wix>
```

You'll also need to add a Text control inside the Dialog element and set its Id attribute to ErrorText. This will be used to display the error message:

```
<Control  Id="ErrorText"
          Type="Text"
          X="50"
          Y="15"
          Width="200"
          Height="60" />
```

Next, add seven new buttons. Each will publish the EndDialog event with one of the following values:

- ErrorAbort

- ErrorCancel

- ErrorIgnore

- ErrorNo

- ErrorOk

- ErrorRetry

- ErrorYes

For example, here's the first that sets the ErrorAbort button:

```
<Control  Id="A"
          Type="PushButton"
          X="100"
          Y="80"
          Width="56"
          Height="17"
          TabSkip="yes"
          Text="Cancel">
   <Publish Event="EndDialog"
          Value="ErrorAbort">1</Publish>
</Control>
```

You can change the Text attribute of each button so that it matches the type, such as Yes for ErrorYes and No for ErrorNo. The X and Y attributes can remain the same. Remember to reference this new dialog with a DialogRef element in your InstallDlg file.

FatalError

The **FatalError** dialog is shown when an unrecoverable error is encountered
during the install, causing a premature end. Add a new WiX source file and call it
FatalErrorDlg.wxs. The message will always be the same so you can add a Text
control that displays a static message, as in the following example:

```
<?xml version=»1.0» encoding=»UTF-8»?>
<Wix xmlns=»http://schemas.microsoft.com/wix/2006/wi»>
  <Fragment>
    <UI>
      <Dialog Id="FatalErrorDlg"
              Width="370"
              Height="270"
              Title="Amazing Software">

        <Control Id="Description"
                 Type="Text"
                 X="50"
                 Y="70"
                 Width="220"
                 Height="80"
                 Text="[ProductName] Setup Wizard ended prematurely
because of an error. Your system has not been modified. To install
this program at a later time, run Setup Wizard again." />
        <Control Id="Finish"
                 Type="PushButton"
                 X="180"
                 Y="243"
                 Width="56"
                 Height="17"
                 Default="yes"
                 Cancel="yes"
                 Text="Finish">
          <Publish Event="EndDialog"
                   Value="Exit" />
        </Control>
      </Dialog>
    </UI>

    <InstallUISequence>
      <Show Dialog="FatalErrorDlg"
            OnExit="error" />
```

```
        </InstallUISequence>

        <AdminUISequence>
          <Show Dialog="FatalErrorDlg"
                OnExit="error" />
        </AdminUISequence>
      </Fragment>
    </Wix>
```

The Text control uses the Text attribute to set the message to display. You may notice that I'm using [ProductName] to reference a WiX property. The syntax, when referencing a property in an attribute, is to surround the property's name with square brackets. You should also add a button that publishes the EndDialog event with a Value attribute of Exit to allow the user to quit the install.

We've added this dialog into two sequences: InstallUISequence and AdminUISequence. This is required even if you aren't supporting administrative installs. In both cases, set the Show element's OnExit attribute to error. This will schedule the dialog in the appropriate place in those sequences.

UserExit

The **UserExit** dialog appears when the user cancels the install. Typically, it contains some text and a Finish button that publishes the EndDialog event with a Value attribute of Exit. Like the FatalError dialog, it must appear in both InstallUISequence and AdminUISequence. This time, we'll set the Show element's OnExit attribute to cancel.

The following is an example:

```
    <?xml version=»1.0» encoding=»UTF-8»?>
    <Wix xmlns=»http://schemas.microsoft.com/wix/2006/wi»>
      <Fragment>
        <UI>
          <Dialog Id="UserExitDlg"
                  Width="370"
                  Height="270"
                  Title="Amazing Software">

            <Control Id="Description"
                     Type="Text"
                     X="50"
                     Y="70"
                     Width="220"
                     Height="80"
```

```
                    Text="[ProductName] setup was interrupted. Your
system has not been modified. To install this program at a later time,
please run the installation again." />

            <Control Id="Finish"
                    Type="PushButton"
                    X="180"
                    Y="243"
                    Width="56"
                    Height="17"
                    Default="yes"
                    Cancel="yes"
                    Text="Finish">
              <Publish Event="EndDialog"
                    Value="Exit" />
            </Control>
          </Dialog>
        </UI>

        <InstallUISequence>
          <Show Dialog="UserExitDlg"
              OnExit="cancel" />
        </InstallUISequence>

        <AdminUISequence>
          <Show Dialog="UserExitDlg"
              OnExit="cancel" />
        </AdminUISequence>
      </Fragment>
    </Wix>
```

Exit

The **Exit** dialog is shown at the end of a successful installation. Typically, it contains some text and a **Finish** button. It must also be added to both `InstallUISequence` and `AdminUISequence`. Here, set the `Show` element's `OnExit` attribute to `success` as in the following example:

```
<?xml version=»1.0» encoding=»UTF-8»?>
<Wix xmlns=»http://schemas.microsoft.com/wix/2006/wi»>
  <Fragment>
    <UI>
      <Dialog Id="ExitDlg"
              Width="370"
```

```
            Height="270"
            Title="Amazing Software">

    <Control Id="Description"
            Type="Text"
            X="50"
            Y="70"
            Width="220"
            Height="80"
            Text="[ProductName] setup has completed
                successfully. Click 'Finish' to exit the
                Setup Wizard." />

    <Control Id="Finish"
            Type="PushButton"
            X="180"
            Y="243"
            Width="56"
            Height="17"
            Default="yes"
            Cancel="yes"
            Text="Finish">
        <Publish Event="EndDialog"
                Value="Exit" />
    </Control>
  </Dialog>
</UI>

<InstallUISequence>
  <Show Dialog="ExitDlg"
        OnExit="success" />
</InstallUISequence>

<AdminUISequence>
  <Show Dialog="ExitDlg" OnExit="success" />
</AdminUISequence>
</Fragment>
</Wix>
```

Summary

In this chapter, we covered the basics of making simple dialogs. There are a few required dialogs, as enforced by the ICE20 validation check, but for the most part you're free to create as many of your own customized dialogs as you want.

In the next chapter, we'll explore UI controls such as buttons, text, and lists. This should give you plenty of options when designing your install wizard.

7
Using UI Controls

Now that you've seen how to create windows for your user interface, it's time to explore the controls you can use on them. Controls are the buttons, textboxes, lists, and images that we've all interacted with before and that make up any graphical UI. In this chapter, we'll discuss the following topics:

- The Control element and its basic attributes
- The various types of controls and their unique features

Attributes common to all controls

Placing a Control element inside a Dialog element adds a new control to that window. You'll use its Type attribute to specify which kind of control it is: PushButton, Text, and so on. Beware that these names are case sensitive. "Pushbutton" isn't the same as "PushButton" and will give you an install time error.

Positioning and sizing are always the same: Use the X and Y attributes to place your control at a specific coordinate on the window and the Width and Height attributes to size it. You must also always give it an Id attribute that uniquely identifies it on that dialog. So, you can have two buttons with the same ID if they're on two different dialogs, but not if they're on the same dialog.

Disabling or hiding a control is straightforward. Set the Disabled attribute to yes to prevent the user from interacting with it. Similarly, set Hidden to yes to hide the control. You can also toggle these values at install time. Place a Condition element inside the Control element. This uses an Action attribute to enable/disable or hide/show your control, depending upon the state of some property.

To give you an idea, the following example disables a button if a property called MyProperty is set to abc. Otherwise, it's enabled. To set this property at install time, we'll add a checkbox that when checked, sets MyProperty to abc. When unchecked, the property's value is cleared. That way, by checking and unchecking the box, you'll see the button enabled and disabled.

```xml
<!--Checkbox that enables the button-->
<Control Id="myCheckbox"
        Type="CheckBox"
        Property="MyProperty"
        CheckBoxValue="abc"
        Text="Enable the button!"
        X="50"
        Y="25"
        Height="10"
        Width="150" />

<!--The button that is enabled/disabled-->
<Control Id="myButton"
        Type="PushButton"
        Text="A buton to enable"
        Height="17"
        Width="100"
        X="50"
        Y="50">

   <Condition Action="enable">
     <![CDATA[MyProperty = "abc"]]>
   </Condition>

   <Condition Action="disable">
     <![CDATA[MyProperty <> "abc"]]>
   </Condition>

   <Publish Event="EndDialog" Value="Exit" />
</Control>
```

The following screenshot displays the result:

The interesting parts are where we set `MyProperty` with the checkbox, using its `Property` attribute. Then, within the second control, which is our button, we nest two `Condition` elements. The first checks whether `MyProperty` is equal to "abc". If it is, its `Action` tells the control to enable itself. The other condition does the opposite.

I could also set `Action` attributes to `hide` and `show` to toggle the button's visibility. This sort of thing is used in the WiX dialog sets to enable the **Next** button when the end user license agreement is accepted.

Specific control syntax

In the following sections, we will explore each type of control. We'll begin with the simpler types such as `PushButton` and `Text`, and then move on to complex controls such as `SelectionTree` and `ProgressBar`.

PushButton

A button is one of the most basic types of controls and the one you'll probably use the most. In WiX, it's created by setting the `Control` element's `Type` attribute to `PushButton`. Use the `Text` attribute to set its label:

```
<Control
    Id="MyButton"
    Type="PushButton"
    Text="Click Me!"
    X="50"
    Y="50"
    Height="17"
    Width="75">

    <Publish Event="EndDialog" Value="Exit" />
</Control>
```

The following screenshot is what it looks like:

You always need to add a **Publish** element inside it or else the button won't do anything. The Publish element executes an action, called a **control event**, when the button is clicked. In the last example, I'm calling the EndDialog event with a value of Exit to quit the install. A value of Return would have continued the install. There are many control events available and we will explore them in the next chapter.

As far as styling your buttons, reference a text style in the Text attribute to use a particular font:

```
<Control
    Id="MyButton"
    Type="PushButton"
    Text="{\Tahoma_Bold}Click me!"
    ... >
```

You can also use an icon instead of text. In that case, set the Text attribute to the ID of a Binary element that uses its SourceFile attribute to point to an .ico file. Also, set the Control element's Icon attribute to yes and its IconSize to the size of your icon: 16, 32, or 48:

```
<Binary Id="myIcon" SourceFile="iconFile.ico" />

<Dialog ...>
    <Control
        Id="myButton"
        Type="PushButton"
        Text="myIcon"
        Icon="yes"
        IconSize="48"
        Height="50"
        Width="50"
        X="50"
        Y="50">

        <Publish Event="EndDialog"
                 Value="Exit" />
    </Control>
</Dialog>
```

Here's the result:

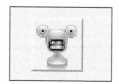

Something else to consider is whether to add a keyboard shortcut for your button. To do so, add an ampersand (&) in front of one of the letters in the `Text` attribute. Then, pressing *Alt* and that letter will trigger the button. You'll want to use the `Text` element inside your control instead of the `Text` attribute, so that you can surround the text with CDATA tags.

```
<Control
    Id="InstallButton"
    Type="PushButton"
    ... >

    <Text><![CDATA[&Install]]></Text>
    <Publish Event="EndDialog" Value="Return" />
</Control>
```

One last attribute for the `PushButton` control is called **ElevationShield**:

```
<Control Id="Install"
        ElevationShield="yes"
        Type="PushButton"
        Text="Install"
        Height="20"
        Width="70"
        ... >
```

If you set `ElevationShield` to `yes` then on systems that have UAC, such as Windows Vista and newer, if the user doesn't have elevated privileges a shield icon will be added to the button, as shown in the following screenshot:

The shield will not be shown if the user has elevated privileges, such as from being an administrator.

Text

A `Text` control places a block of text on the dialog. The following code snippet is an example:

```
<Control
    Id="SampleText"
    Type="Text"
    Text="This text comes from a Text control"
    Height="17"
    Width="200"
    X="50"
    Y="50" />
```

This is what it will look like:

```
                This text comes from a Text control
```

Be sure to make it wide enough so that the text isn't clipped. Another option is to make the height bigger and then set the `NoWrap` attribute to `no` so that the text wraps to a new line when it runs out of width space. If the text runs out of height space it gets clipped and will be replaced with an ellipsis (...).

Recall from the last chapter that you can use the `TextStyle` elements to format the text. The following example creates a new style and applies it to the control:

```
<TextStyle Id="TahomaBold"
           FaceName="Tahoma"
           Size="12"
           Bold="yes"/>

    <Dialog ... >
       <Control Id="SampleText"
                Type="Text"
                Text="{\TahomaBold}Isn't this bold?"
                Height="17"
                Width="200"
                X="50"
                Y="50" />
```

This produces the following stylized result:

> **Isn't this bold?**

Two other useful attributes are `Transparent` and `RightAligned`. The `Transparent` attribute allows any background behind the control, such as a bitmap image, to show through. `RightAligned` right justifies the text.

ScrollableText

The `ScrollableText` control is used to display large amounts of text that wouldn't fit on the dialog window otherwise. It creates a read-only textbox with a scroll bar and is often used to show a license agreement. To set the text, you can use a `Text` element that points to a Rich Text Format (`.rtf`) file:

```
<Control
    Id="myScrollableText"
    Type="ScrollableText"
    Height="150"
    Width="300"
    X="50"
    Y="50"
    Sunken="yes">

    <Text SourceFile="Document.rtf" />
</Control>
```

Or you can add the RTF text directly inside the `Text` element:

```
<Control
    Id="myScrollableText"
    Type="ScrollableText"
    Height="150"
    Width="300"
    X="50"
    Y="50"
    Sunken="yes">

<Text><![CDATA[{\rtf1\ansi\ansicpg1252\deff0\deflang1033{\fonttbl{\f0\
fswiss\fcharset0 Arial;}}
{\*\generator Msftedit5.41.21.2500;}\viewkind4\uc1\pard\f0\fs20 This
is a bunch of text...\par
}]]>
</Text>
</Control>
```

The RTF text created by Microsoft's WordPad tends to work better than that created by Microsoft Word. The following screenshot is what it might look like:

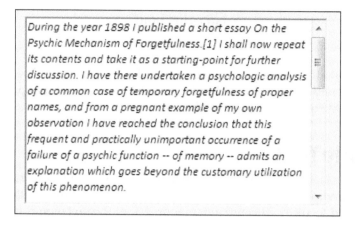

If you'd rather see the scroll bar on the left, set the `LeftScroll` attribute to `yes`.

Line

A `Line` control is definitely the simplest of all. It creates a visible horizontal line starting at the point specified by `X` and `Y`, and stretching the length specified by `Width`. You can set `Height` to 0, as the attribute is ignored.

```
<Control Id="sampleLine" Type="Line" Height="0" Width="370"
    X="2" Y="50" />
```

It looks like this:

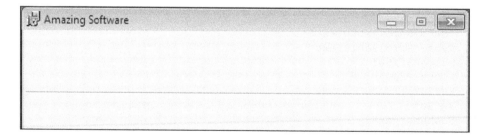

You might use this to separate bold title text on your dialogs from other content such as text fields and buttons.

GroupBox

A close relative to the `Line` control is the `GroupBox` control. It creates a rectangle that you can use to visually group other controls. You have the option of displaying a caption at the top by setting the `Text` attribute. The following is an example:

```
<Control
    Id="myGroupBox"
    Type="GroupBox"
    Text="My GroupBox"
    X="10"
    Y="10"
    Height="100"
    Width="200" />
```

To have controls appear inside the box, you'll have to position them there manually using the `X` and `Y` attributes of each one. The `GroupBox` control doesn't offer any true functionality. You can, however, stylize its caption by referencing a text style in its `Text` attribute. The following is what a basic `GroupBox` looks like:

Bitmap

`Bitmap` controls show images on your dialog. You could use this to show a picture on only a portion of the window or to skin the entire area. First, you must use a `Binary` element to point to an image file. Then, reference that element's ID in your control's `Text` attribute. Note that the image must be a raster graphics image, so BMP and JPEG files will work but not vector graphics images such as PNGs.

```
<UI>
    <Binary Id="myPic" SourceFile="gradientBackground.jpg" />

    <Dialog ... >
        <Control
            Id="myBitmap"
```

```
Type="Bitmap"
Text="myPic"
Height="270"
Width="370"
X="0"
Y="0"
TabSkip="no" />
```

Here, we're using an image that will cover the entire window. So, we set X and Y to 0 so that it will line up with the top-left corner. The image that you use will scale up or down to the size you've set with `Width` and `Height`. Content that overflows the window's bounds will be clipped.

If you add `Text` controls positioned over an image, set their `Transparent` attributes to `yes` so that the background can be seen behind them. Things also tend to work out better when you place the `Bitmap` control first in the markup and set its `TabSkip` attribute to `no`. The following screenshot is what it might look like, with several other elements on top:

Icon

The Icon control is used to display an .ico image on your dialog. Like the Bitmap control, you'll need to first reference the .ico file with a Binary element as shown:

```
<Binary Id="myIcon" SourceFile="myIcon.ico" />
```

Then, add a Control element of type Icon and reference the Binary element's ID in the Text attribute. Use the IconSize attribute to specify the size of the icon: 16, 32, or 48:

```
<Control
    Id="myIcon"
    Type="Icon"
    Text="myIcon"
    X="50"
    Y="50"
    Height="48"
    Width="48"
    IconSize="48" />
```

The following screenshot is what it might look like:

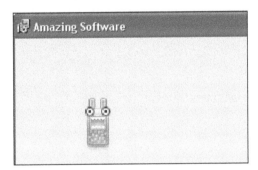

Edit

An Edit control creates a textbox that the user can type into. You'll use its Property attribute to set the value of a property to what the user types. It isn't necessary to declare this property beforehand, as it will be created on the fly. The following is an example that sets a property called USER_NAME. Make the property public, so that it will be available during the Execute sequence, by using uppercase letters:

```
<Control
    Id="myEdit"
    Type="Edit"
    Property="USER_NAME"
```

```
Height="17"
Width="100"
X="50"
Y="50" />
```

It looks like the following screenshot:

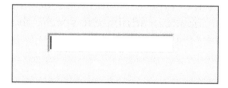

You can see this property being created by keeping a log of the install and then searching it for the name of the property. Here's the entry:

```
MSI (c) (54:98) [13:33:25:734]: PROPERTY CHANGE: Adding USER_NAME
property. Its value is 'Nick'.
```

If you're collecting a password or other sensitive data, you can hide the user's input by setting the `Control` element's `Password` attribute to `yes`. This will only show asterisks (*) as the user types. To be even more secure, you can declare the property before and set its `Hidden` attribute to `yes`. That way, the value won't be visible in the install log either:

```
<Control
    Id="myPassword"
    Type="Edit"
    Property="USER_PASSWORD"
    Password="yes"
    Height="17"
    Width="100"
    X="50"
    Y="50" />
```

You can also limit the number of characters that the user can enter by adding the maximum number in curly brackets to the `Text` attribute. This could even be combined with a text style, as in the next example:

```
<Control
    Id="myEdit"
    Type="Edit"
    Text="{\Tahoma_Bold}{50}"
    Height="17"
    Width="100"
    X="50"
    Y="50"
    Property="MY_PROPERTY" />
```

The Edit control has another attribute called Multiline that when set to yes should, according to the Windows Installer documentation, create a multi-line edit control with a vertical scroll bar. It's best avoided, however, because of its unconventional operation. What you'll actually get is a textbox that adds a new line if you press *Ctrl + Enter*, and adds a scroll bar if you run out of vertical space. It won't be what users are expecting.

MaskedEdit

The MaskedEdit control is used with the ValidateProductID standard action to validate a product serial number. To use it you'll first need to define a **mask**, which is the pattern that the user's input must match. You'll define this with a property named PIDTemplate. Be sure to mark it as Hidden so that the user can't see the mask in the install log.

The following is a mask that says the user must enter three numbers; a dash, three numbers, another dash, and then four numbers. The pound signs (#) stand for numbers and the dashes are literal characters.

```
<Property Id="PIDTemplate" Hidden="yes">
<![CDATA[<###-###-####>]]>
</Property>
```

The following table explains the characters that have special meaning in a mask:

Symbol	Meaning
#	It can be any number.
&	It can be any letter.
?	It can be a number or letter.
^	It can be any letter, but it will always be converted to uppercase.
@	It creates a random number. This is only used in the "hidden" part of the mask.
<	It marks the beginning of the visible textbox (visible part of the mask).
>	It marks the end of the visible textbox.

In the previous example, our mask began with the less-than sign (<) and ended with the greater-than sign (>). These mark the beginning and end of the part of the mask that the user must match. You can also add characters before and after this part, and these extra characters will be added to what the user enters. For example, the next mask prepends "12345" to the beginning of the user's input and five random numbers to the end.

```
12345<###-###-####>@@@@@
```

To use this in a `MaskedEdit` control, set the `Control` element's `Text` attribute to the ID of the property. Surround it with square brackets as shown:

```
<Control
    Id="myMaskedEdit"
    Type="MaskedEdit"
    Text="[PIDTemplate]"
    Property="PIDKEY"
    Height="17"
    Width="150"
    X="50"
    Y="50" />
```

Here's what it looks like:

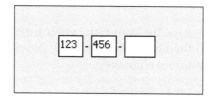

As we're using a property called `PIDKEY` and a mask called `PIDTemplate`, the `ValidateProductID` action will run and check the value. If it's a match, a new property called `ProductID` will be set that combines the user's input with the hidden characters in the mask. If not, that property won't be set. Either way, you'll know if the user's input was valid. You would expect to see this in the log:

```
Property(C): PIDKEY = 123-456-7890
Property(C): ProductID = 12345-123-456-7890-64010
```

From here, you could execute a custom action that truly checks the serial number. For example, you could write a C# method that calls a web service, passing it the serial number, to evaluate its validity. You'd likely add a conditional statement to this custom action so that it only runs if `ProductID` has been set. Be aware that because you're collecting the number during the UI, `ValidateProductID` won't have a chance to validate it until it runs in the Execute sequence. So, your custom action should run after that. That's not to say that you couldn't forgo the `ValidateProductID` action altogether and roll your own validation to be run during the UI sequence.

PathEdit

A `PathEdit` control is used to change the path that one of your `Directory` elements points to. To use it, the `Directory` element must have an ID that's a public property, meaning it must be uppercase. Suppose that this was our directory structure:

```
<Directory Id="TARGETDIR" Name="SourceDir">
    <Directory Id="ProgramFilesFolder">
        <Directory Id="INSTALLLOCATION"
                   Name="Amazing Software" />
    </Directory>
</Directory>
```

Here, our main install directory has an ID of `INSTALLLOCATION`. Now, we can reference this directory in the `Property` attribute of our control:

```
<Control
    Id="myPathEdit"
    Type="PathEdit"
    Property="INSTALLLOCATION"
    Height="17"
    Width="200"
    X="50"
    Y="50" />
```

Here's what it looks like:

The user can edit this and when they do the installation path will be changed. There's just one thing: The installer won't know that it's changed. To alert it, we need to fire the `SetTargetPath` event and pass it our new path. This is best called by a `PushButton` control so let's add one:

```
<Control  Id="OKButton"
          Type="PushButton"
          Height="17"
          Width="56"
          X="50"
          Y="70"
```

```
                Text="OK">

        <Publish Event="SetTargetPath"
                Value="INSTALLLOCATION"
                Order="1">1</Publish>

        <!--Other Publish element to go to next dialog-->

    </Control>
```

The `PushButton` control publishes the `SetTargetPath` event with `Value` set to the ID of our directory. When the user clicks it, the new path will be set. This event does some basic validation on the path such as checking that the drive letter exists or, if it's a UNC path, the remote location can be reached.

CheckBox

A `CheckBox` control is a checkbox that the user can click to set a property. You'll specify which property to set with the `Property` attribute and what to set it *to* with the `CheckBoxValue` attribute. If you want to stress that this value is meant to be a number, set the `Integer` attribute to `yes`. Here's an example:

```
<Control
    Id="myCheckbox"
    Type="CheckBox"
    Property="myCheckboxResult"
    CheckBoxValue="my value"
    Text="Check the box please."
    X="50"
    Y="50"
    Height="10"
    Width="150" />
```

The `Text` attribute is the text that appears to the right of the checkbox and explains what the box is for. Be sure to make the control wide enough to fit all of this text in. Here's what it looks like:

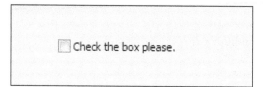

When the user checks the box, the property `myCheckboxResult` will be set to `my value`. Deselecting the box will delete the property. If you declare the property beforehand with a `Property` element, the box will be checked by default:

```
<Property Id="myCheckboxResult" Value="my value" />
```

RadioButtonGroup

A `RadioButtonGroup` control creates a list of radio buttons, only one of which can be selected at a time. As one of the buttons has to be selected by default, you must create a `Property` element first and reference it on the control. In the following, a `Property` element is created with a value of `1`. The radio button with that value will be selected as the default.

```
<Property Id="buttonGroup" Value="1" />
```

To reference this property, set the `Control` element's `Property` attribute to its ID:

```
<Control
    Id="myRadioGroup"
    Type="RadioButtonGroup"
    Property="buttonGroup"
    Height="100"
    Width="100"
    X="50"
    Y="50">
</Control>
```

Now to add our radio buttons. Although you can define them outside of the `Control` element—placing them inside the `UI` element instead—it's more common to add them as children to the control. Each button is created by a `RadioButton` element whose `Text` attribute sets its label. The property will be changed by each button's `Value` attribute. All of the radio buttons are held inside a `RadioButtonGroup` element that, such as the `Control` element, references our property.

Here's our control with three radio buttons nested inside:

```
<Control
    Id="myRadioGroup"
    Type="RadioButtonGroup"
    Property="buttonGroup"
    Width="100"
    Height="100"
    X="50"
```

```
            Y="50">

    <RadioButtonGroup Property="buttonGroup">
        <RadioButton Value="1"
                        Text="One"
                        Height="17"
                        Width="50"
                        X="0"
                        Y="0" />

        <RadioButton Value="2"
                        Text="Two"
                        Height="17"
                        Width="50"
                        X="0"
                        Y="20" />

        <RadioButton Value="3"
                        Text="Three"
                        Height="17"
                        Width="50"
                        X="0"
                        Y="40" />
    </RadioButtonGroup>
  </Control>
```

The following is what it looks like:

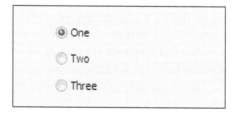

Selecting a different radio button will set the buttonGroup property to that button's value.

You can change the look of the buttons with the Control element's HasBorder, Sunken, and RightAligned attributes. HasBorder will put a GroupBox control around the buttons, although you should then change the X and Y attributes of the RadioButton elements so that they have some padding. Sunken will place a sunken border edge around the buttons. RightAligned will place the labels (One, Two, Three) on the left-hand side of the buttons.

You also have the option of displaying icons next to your radio buttons instead of text. For that, replace the Text attribute on the RadioButton control with an Icon attribute set to the ID of a Binary element pointing to an .ico file.

ComboBox

A ComboBox control creates a drop-down list of selectable items. First, create a Control element of type ComboBox and set its Property attribute to the name of a property that will store the item the user selects from the list. If you want your items to be sorted alphabetically, set the Sorted attribute to yes. Also, be sure to always set the ComboList attribute to yes. Here's an example where the option the user selects will be stored in a property called selectedItem:

```
<Control
    Id="myComboBox"
    Type="ComboBox"
    Width="100"
    Height="50"
    X="50"
    Y="50"
    Property="selectedItem"
    ComboList="yes"
    Sorted="yes">

</Control>
```

The items in your list are defined with the ListItem elements nested inside a ComboBox element. Although you can place this outside of the Control element, it's clearer to place it directly inside. The ComboBox element uses its Property attribute to tie it to the control. Each ListItem sets a Text attribute, which is what gets displayed, and a Value attribute that sets the value of the item. Let's add three items to our list:

```
<Control ... >

    <ComboBox Property="selectedItem">
        <ListItem Text="One" Value="1" />
        <ListItem Text="Two" Value="2" />
        <ListItem Text="Three" Value="3" />
    </ComboBox>

</Control>
```

If you want to set one of the items as the default, set a `Property` element with an ID that matches the property name we're using in our control and a `Value` attribute that matches the value of `ListItem`. This, for example, would set the default item selected to `ListItem` that has a `Value` attribute of 2:

```
<Property Id="selectedItem" Value="2" />
```

This is what it will look like:

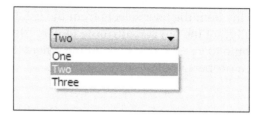

ListBox

A `ListBox` control is similar to a `ComboBox` control except that the options are all displayed at once. Create a `Control` element and set its `Type` attribute to `ListBox`. This control also uses the `Property` and `Sorted` attributes such as a `ComboBox`. You can add list items in the same way as before, using `ListItem` elements, except that this time they'll be contained inside a `ListBox` element:

```
<Control
    Id="myListBox"
    Type="ListBox"
    Width="100"
    Height="45"
    X="50"
    Y="50"
    Property="selectedItem"
    Sorted="yes">

    <ListBox Property="selectedItem">
        <ListItem Text="One" Value="1" />
        <ListItem Text="Two" Value="2" />
        <ListItem Text="Three" Value="3" />
    </ListBox>
</Control>
```

If you want to set a default selected item, create a `Property` element with an ID that matches your `ListBox` element's property and a `Value` attribute that's the same as the value of a `ListItem`.

```
<Property Id="SelectedItem" Value="2" />
```

It looks like the following screenshot:

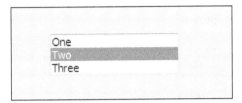

You can also add the `Sunken` attribute, set to `yes`, to give your list box a sunken border.

ListView

A `ListView` control is like a `ListBox` control except that it displays an icon *and* text for each selectable option. For each item, you'll need to define a `Binary` element that points to an icon file.

```
<Fragment>
    <UI>
        <Binary Id="face1" SourceFile="icons/alien1.ico" />
        <Binary Id="face2" SourceFile="icons/alien2.ico" />
        <Binary Id="face3" SourceFile="icons/alien3.ico" />
```

The next step is to create a `Control` element of type `ListView` and set the `IconSize` attribute to the size of your icons: `16`, `32`, or `48`. Also, set its `Property` attribute to store the option the user selects:

```
<Control
    Id="myComboBox"
    Type="ListView"
    Width="200"
    Height="150"
    X="10"
    Y="10"
    Property="selectedItem"
    IconSize="32">

    <ListView Property="selectedItem">
        <ListItem Text="Alien 1" Icon="face1" Value="1" />
```

```
        <ListItem Text="Alien 2" Icon="face2" Value="2" />
        <ListItem Text="Alien 3" Icon="face3" Value="3" />
    </ListView>
</Control>
```

Here, we've added a `ListView` element inside the control with `ListItem` for each option. Each one gets a `Text` attribute for the label, an `Icon` attribute that references one of the `Binary` elements, and a `Value` attribute to hold the value of the item. The following is what it looks like:

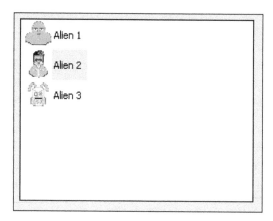

To set a default selected item, set a `Property` element with an ID that matches your control's `Property` attribute to the value of one of your `ListItems`. As you can see from this example, the image quality is usually poor, even if your `.ico` files are good.

DirectoryList

A `DirectoryList` control displays a directory and the folders that are in it. It can be used to set the path of one of your `Directory` elements. Here's one that sets a `Directory` element with an ID of `INSTALLLOCATION`:

```
<Control
    Id="myDirectoryList"
    Type="DirectoryList"
    Property="INSTALLLOCATION"
    Height="150"
    Width="320"
    X="10"
    Y="30" />
```

If you add this to one of your dialogs, you won't be very impressed with the result. All you'll see is a blank box. That's because you're looking inside the `INSTALLLOCATION` directory—a directory that hasn't been installed yet and no folders exist inside it.

To get some benefit from this, we need to add some more controls around it to alert the user to where they are in the folder hierarchy. At the very least, you should add a `PathEdit` control that displays the current directory. For example, this could be something like the following code snippet:

```
<Control
    Id="myPath"
    Type="PathEdit"
    Height="17"
    Width="320"
    X="10"
    Y="10"
    Property="INSTALLLOCATION" />
```

The following screenshot shows a dialog with even more bells and whistles:

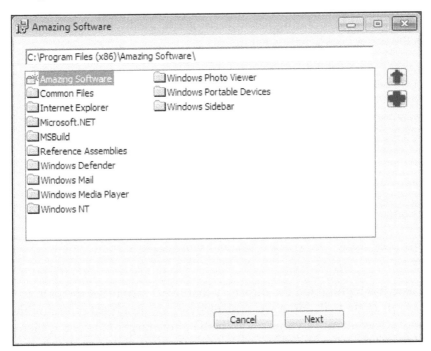

Here, the giant directory list in the middle of the dialog is showing the **Program Files** folder after we navigated out of INSTALLLOCATION (whose friendly name is **Amazing Software**). Creating a button that navigates up one directory is done by adding a PushButton control to the same dialog as your directory list and having it publish the DirectoryListUp event with a value of 0. In this example, it uses an icon that looks like an arrow pointing up:

```
<Control
    Id="DirUpButton"
    Type="PushButton"
    Height="17"
    Width="20"
    X="340"
    Y="30"
    Icon="yes"
    Text="upIcon"
    IconSize="16">

    <Publish Event="DirectoryListUp" Value="0" />
</Control>
```

There's also a button for creating new directories (labeled with a plus sign). It publishes the DirectoryListNew event:

```
<Control
    Id="NewDirButton"
    Type="PushButton"
    Height="17"
    Width="20"
    X="340"
    Y="50"
    Icon="yes"
    Text="addIcon"
    IconSize="16">

    <Publish Event="DirectoryListNew" Value="0" />
</Control>
```

Once the user has highlighted the directory that they want to set the path to, you'll need to save it. To do that, add a Publish element inside a **Next** button with a SetTargetPath event and a value set to the ID of the target Directory element. Here, I add such a button and also have it open the next dialog as shown in the following code snippet:

```
<Control Id="NextButton"
```

```
            Type="PushButton"
            Text="Next"
            Height="17"
            Width="56"
            X="245"
            Y="243">

    <Publish Event="SetTargetPath"
            Value="INSTALLLOCATION"
            Order="1">1</Publish>

    <Publish Event="NewDialog"
            Value="SecondDlg"
            Order="2">1</Publish>
</Control>
```

DirectoryCombo

A `DirectoryCombo` control displays a drop-down list of directories and drives. You can use it to show the install directory and other drives it can be changed to. The next example shows the `INSTALLLOCATION` directory and any remote and fixed drives that are accessible:

```
<Control
    Id="myDirectoryCombo"
    Type="DirectoryCombo"
    Property="INSTALLLOCATION"
    Fixed="yes"
    Remote="yes"
    X="10"
    Y="10"
    Width="200"
    Height="100" />
```

Here's the result:

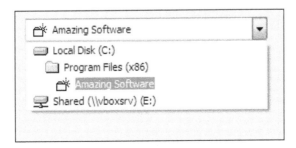

This example displays the available fixed (otherwise known as internal) and remote drives. The following table explains all of your options:

Attribute	Description
Fixed	Lists the fixed internal hard drives.
Remote	Lists the remote volumes.
Removable	Lists the removable drives.
CDROM	Lists the CD-ROM volumes.
Floppy	Lists the floppy drives.
RAMDisk	Lists the RAM disks.

A DirectoryCombo control by itself cannot drill down into drives and their directories. Therefore, it works best when paired with another control that can, such as a DirectoryList.

SelectionTree

A SelectionTree displays a tree of the features defined in your installer. The user can use this to include or exclude certain features at install time. Be sure to add the Property attribute to the Control element, specifying your main install directory.

```
<Control
    Id="MySelectionTree"
    Type="SelectionTree"
    Property="INSTALLLOCATION"
    X="10"
    Y="30"
    Width="200"
    Height="120" />
```

Here is what it looks like:

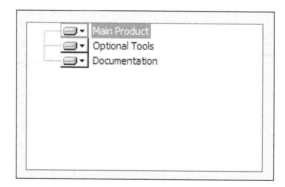

When you click on one of the features you're given the option to install it locally, install it as an advertised feature, or to not install it. The text for these options has to be defined by the UIText elements inside the UI element. Define the following elements: MenuLocal, MenuAllLocal, MenuAdvertise, and MenuAbsent:

```
<UIText Id="MenuLocal">The feature will be installed locally.</UIText>

<UIText Id="MenuAllLocal">The feature and all of its subfeatures will
be installed locally.</UIText>

<UIText Id="MenuAdvertise">The feature will be installed when
needed.</UIText>

<UIText Id="MenuAbsent">The feature will not be installed.</UIText>
```

When you click on a feature you'll see these options, as shown in the following screenshot:

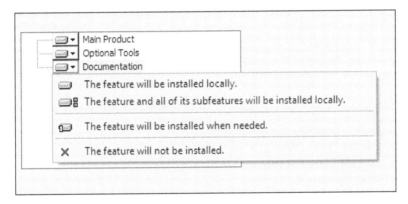

Your Feature elements, defined in your main .wxs file, can use the Description attribute to show information about what they contain, as in this example:

```
<Feature Id="ProductFeature"
        Title="Main Product"
        Level="1"
        Description="The main feature for the product">

    <ComponentRef Id="cmp_myFile" />
</Feature>
```

To show this on the dialog that has your `SelectionTree`, add a `Text` control
that subscribes to the `SelectionDescription` event. The `Subscribe` element's
`Attribute` must be set to `Text`. You can also show the size of the feature by
subscribing another `Text` control to the `SelectionSize` event.

```
<Control Id="MySelectionDescription"
         Type="Text"
         X="220"
         Y="30"
         Width="100"
         Height="30">
    <Subscribe Event="SelectionDescription" Attribute="Text" />
</Control>

<Control Id="MySelectionSize"
         Type="Text"
         X="220"
         Y="70"
         Width="100"
         Height="50">
    <Subscribe Event="SelectionSize" Attribute="Text" />
</Control>
```

When you use `SelectionSize`, you have to define a few more `UIText` elements:

```
<UIText Id="Bytes">Bytes</UIText>
<UIText Id="KB">KB</UIText>
<UIText Id="MB">MB</UIText>
<UIText Id="GB">GB</UIText>

<UIText Id="SelChildCostPos">Feature will use [1] on your hard
    drive.</UIText>

<UIText Id="SelChildCostNeg">Feature will free [1] on your
    hard drive.</UIText>

<UIText Id="SelChildCostPending">Figuring space needed for
    this feature...</UIText>
```

The format for these messages is defined by Windows Installer, which will insert the applicable value where you've placed [1]. Here's the final result:

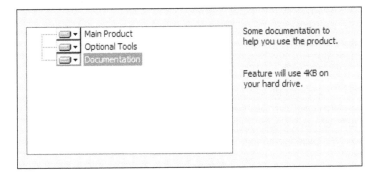

VolumeCostList

A VolumeCostList control displays available hard drives and the amount of disk space your installation will require on them.

```
<Control
    Id="myVolumeCostList"
    Type="VolumeCostList"
    Fixed="yes"
    Text="{50}{50}{70}{50}{50}"
    X="10"
    Y="10"
    Width="300"
    Height="100" />
```

In this example, we're only showing the space required on the fixed drives. Any of the attributes available to the DirectoryCombo control are also available to VolumeCostList. The Text attribute sets the widths of each column in VolumeCostList. Here's what it looks like:

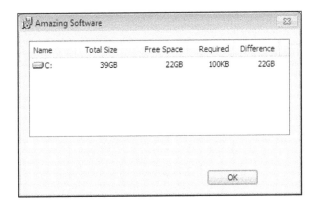

You'll need to define the following UIText elements inside the UI element, some of which are repeats from the SelectionTree control:

```
<UIText Id="Bytes">Bytes</UIText>
<UIText Id="KB">KB</UIText>
<UIText Id="MB">MB</UIText>
<UIText Id="GB">GB</UIText>

<UIText Id="VolumeCostAvailable">Free Space</UIText>
<UIText Id="VolumeCostDifference">Difference</UIText>
<UIText Id="VolumeCostRequired">Required</UIText>
<UIText Id="VolumeCostSize">Total Size</UIText>
<UIText Id="VolumeCostVolume">Name</UIText>
```

Typically, this control is shown on a modal window during the installation. The user may click a button that says something like "Disk Cost" on the main window and the modal window will be displayed over the top. There's a practical reason for doing this. If you try to show VolumeCostList too soon, such as on the very first dialog, the numbers won't be calculated yet. You'd likely see a column of zeroes in the **Required** column. This is because these numbers aren't available until several properties, including CostingComplete, have been set. This happens during the costing phase at the beginning of the install.

VolumeSelectCombo

A VolumeSelectCombo control is a drop-down list that shows available drives. Using the TARGETDIR property, you might use this to change the drive that your files are installed to. In the following example, I display all fixed drives in the list:

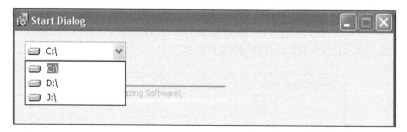

You might pair it with a `PathEdit` control that shows the user what the install path is currently set to. If you don't want to let the user edit the `PathEdit` control, set its `Disabled` attribute to `yes`:

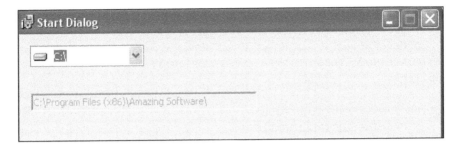

When the user selects a new option, the install path will be changed to use that drive as shown:

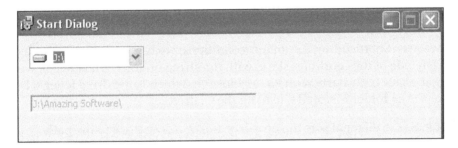

Notice that if they select **D:** or **J:** in this example, we don't target the `Program Files` folder as that only exists on the `C:\`. Instead, we just install to the root folder of that drive. Here's the control's markup:

```
<Control
    Id="myVolumeSelectCombo"
    Type="VolumeSelectCombo"
    Property="TARGETDIR"
    Fixed="yes"
    Remote="yes"
    X="10"
    Y="10"
    Width="100"
    Height="17">

<Publish
      Property="INSTALLLOCATION"
      Value="[ProgramFilesFolder]Amazing Software\"
      Order="1">
```

```
     <![CDATA[TARGETDIR << %SYSTEMDRIVE]]>
</Publish>

<Publish
     Property="INSTALLLOCATION"
     Value="[TARGETDIR]Amazing Software\"
     Order="2">
  <![CDATA[NOT (TARGETDIR << %SYSTEMDRIVE)]]>
</Publish>

<Publish Event="SetTargetPath"
         Value="INSTALLLOCATION"
         Order="3">1</Publish>
</Control>
```

In the `Control` element we've set the `Type` attribute to `VolumeSelectCombo`, and the `Property` to `TARGETDIR`. By using the `Fixed` attribute, we're saying we only want to see that type of drive in the list.

So that we aren't hardcoding `C:\` in our conditions, we use the `<<` operator to check that the left side of the condition starts with the string on the right side. So, we'll be checking if `TARGETDIR` starts with `%SYSTEMDRIVE`, which is the drive letter where the `Program Files` folder is stored — usually the C: drive.

The first `Publish` element sets the property `INSTALLLOCATION` to the path `[ProgramFilesFolder]Amazing Software\`, but only if the user has selected the `%SYSTEMDRIVE`, a.k.a. `C:\`. The second `Publish` element is only used if the user has *not* chosen the `C:\`. In that case, we set `INSTALLLOCATION` to `[TARGETDIR]Amazing Software\`, which would be `J:\Amazing Software`, for example.

The last `Publish` element calls the `SetTargetPath` event to save the new install path to the installation session. Without that, the change wouldn't really be noticed by the installer.

Billboard

A `Billboard` control displays a slideshow to entertain the user while the installation is in progress. Unlike the other controls we've seen, which are shown during the UI sequence, a `Billboard` control can only be used during the deferred stage of the Execute sequence. Therefore, you'll need to place it on a "Modeless" dialog shown at the end of your wizard, just like the progress dialog we saw in the last chapter.

Remember, to create this type of dialog, set the `Dialog` element's `Modeless` attribute to yes:

```
<Wixxmlns="http://schemas.microsoft.com/wix/2006/wi">
   <Fragment>
      <UI>
         <Dialog Id="BillboardDlg"
                 Width="370"
                 Height="270"
                 Title="Amazing Software"
                 NoMinimize="no"
                 Modeless="yes">

<!--Our Billboard will go here-->

         </Dialog>

         <InstallUISequence>
            <Show Dialog="BillboardDlg" After="InstallDlg" />
         </InstallUISequence>
      </UI>
   </Fragment>
</Wix>
```

We've set up a new dialog called `BillboardDlg` and set it to be shown after `InstallDlg`. This will allow it to stay up as the installer enters the Execute phase. Remember to add a `DialogRef` element to this dialog in `InstallDlg`:

```
<DialogRef Id="BillboardDlg" />
```

Now to add our `Billboard` control: Add a `Control` element of `Type` set to `Billboard` inside your new dialog and have it subscribe to the `SetProgress` event. This allows it to change its picture as the install progresses. Make sure that the `Control` element's `Width` and `Height` attributes are big enough for your images to fit into. In this example, the image will fill the entire space of the dialog:

```
<Dialog Id="BillboardDlg"...>

   <Control Id="MyBillboard"
            Type="Billboard"
            X="0"
            Y="0"
            Height="270"
            Width="370">
      <Subscribe Event="SetProgress" Attribute="Progress" />
   </Control>
</Dialog>
```

To set the images to display on the billboard, add `Binary` elements that point to your image files:

```
<Binary Id="Billboard1" SourceFile="BillboardImage1.jpg" />
<Binary Id="Billboard2" SourceFile="BillboardImage2.jpg" />
<Binary Id="Billboard3" SourceFile="BillboardImage3.jpg" />
```

Next, add a `BillboardAction` element inside the `UI` element. Its `Id` attribute will determine during which Execute standard action the billboards will be shown. For example, `BillboardAction` will be displayed during the `InstallFiles` action. Here, we've scheduled two billboards to be displayed while `InstallFiles` is happening. However, we can add more within that same `BillboardAction` and they will be shown in sequence:

```
<BillboardAction Id="InstallFiles">
    <Billboard Id="BB1" Feature="ProductFeature">
        <Control Id="InstallFilesBillboard1"
                Type="Bitmap"
                X="0"
                Y="0"
                Height="270"
                Width="370"
                Text="Billboard1" />
    </Billboard>

    <Billboard Id="BB2" Feature="ProductFeature">
        <Control Id="InstallFilesBillboard2"
                Type="Bitmap"
                X="0"
                Y="0"
                Height="270"
                Width="370"
                Text="Billboard2" />
    </Billboard>
</BillboardAction>
```

The `Billboard` element inside `BillboardAction` contains a `Bitmap` control that points to the image to display. You can think of this as being one slide in the slideshow. By adding more `Billboard` elements, we get more slides—but only during the `InstallFiles` action in this case. To cover other actions, you'll need to add more `BillboardAction` elements. The result is shown in the following screenshot:

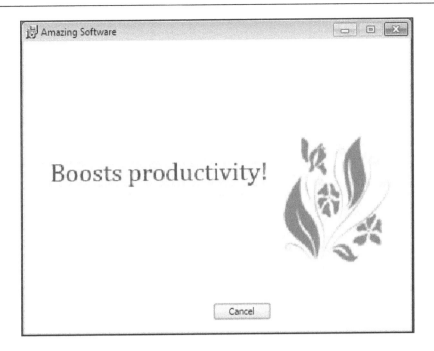

The `Billboard` element's `Feature` attribute tells the installer to only show this set of slides if that feature is being installed. The `Bitmap` control inside sets its `X` and `Y` attributes to `0` to line it up with the top-left corner of the `Billboard` control. It's possible to have one `Billboard` element contain multiple controls, such as `Text` controls positioned over `Bitmap` controls. This would give you a layered effect of text and images.

Often, it takes a moment for anything in your billboard to be displayed because the Execute sequence first runs through its **immediate** phase, gathering information before proceeding to the **deferred** stage. During this immediate phase, your billboard won't be displayed. For that reason, you may decide to add a `Bitmap` control or some text that is displayed from the very start. This will be replaced by the billboard when it's ready. The `Bitmap` control can be positioned in the same spot as where your `Billboard` will go:

```
<Dialog Id="BillboardDlg" ...>

    <Control Id="StartingBillboard"
             Type="Bitmap"
             X="0"
             Y="0"
             Height="200"
             Width="300"
             Text="Billboard1" />
```

ProgressBar

A ProgressBar control is a bar that incrementally fills with tick marks to illustrate the installation's progress. Like the Billboard control, a ProgressBar control should appear on a modeless dialog that's sequenced as the last dialog during the UI phase. That way, it can remain up during the Execute sequence and show the progress of the deferred stage. The markup looks like the following code snippet:

```
<Control  Id="MyProgressBar"
          Type="ProgressBar"
          X="50"
          Y="150"
          Width="250"
          Height="20">
    <Subscribe Event="SetProgress" Attribute="Progress" />
</Control>
```

This control should subscribe to the SetProgress event so that it can update itself as the install continues. It looks like the following screenshot:

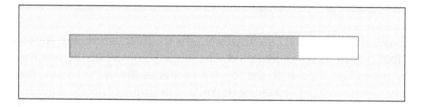

If you set the ProgressBlocks attribute to yes the look changes, as shown in the following screenshot:

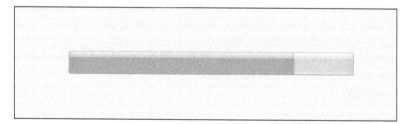

It's possible to reset and increment a `ProgressBar` control from a C# custom action. This is done by using the `Session` object's `Message` method. This method can accept a variety of message types, including a progress message. We'll use a `Record` object, which is a type of collection, to set our message. You can find documentation about setting `Record` objects at `http://msdn.microsoft.com/en-us/library/aa370354%28VS.85%29.aspx`. The following code, where the first value in the record is 0, resets the `ProgressBar` control:

```
private static void ResetProgress(Session session)
{
    Record record = new Record(4);
    record[1] = "0"; // "Reset" message
    record[2] = "1000"; // total ticks
    record[3] = "0"; // forward motion
    record[4] = "0"; // execution is in progress

    session.Message(InstallMessage.Progress, record);
}
```

The `Message` method sets its type through the `InstallMessage` enumeration, which we've set to `Progress`. To increment the bar a certain number of ticks, set the record's first value to 2, and its second to the number of ticks to add:

```
private static void IncrementProgress(
    Session session, int ticks)
{
    Record record = new Record(2);
    record[1] = "2"; // "Increment" message
    record[2] = ticks.ToString(); // ticks to increment

    session.Message(InstallMessage.Progress, record);
}
```

You could then call these methods in your custom action:

```
[CustomAction]
public static ActionResultMyCustomAction(Session session)
{
    // reset bar
    ResetProgress(session);

    //do some stuff for the custom action...

    //add 100 tick marks
```

```
    IncrementProgress(session, 100);

    returnActionResult.Success;
}
```

If you'd rather have things happen more or less on their own without you having to specify each time how many tick marks to add, then we'll need to do things differently. This other way goes hand-in-hand with displaying info about what's happening in a `Text` control above the `ProgressBar` control.

First, add a `Text` control to your dialog that subscribes to the `ActionData` event:

```
<Control Id="InfoText"
         Type="Text"
         X="50"
         Y="130"
         Width="250"
         Height="17">
    <Subscribe Event="ActionData" Attribute="Text" />
</Control>

<Control Id="MyProgressBar"
         Type="ProgressBar"
         X="50"
         Y="50"
         Width="250"
         Height="20">
    <Subscribe Event="SetProgress" Attribute="Progress" />
</Control>
```

This new control will display messages about what's going on at any point during the install. To get a message about your custom actions to show up, add a `ProgressText` element to your dialog, inside the `UI` element:

```
<ProgressText Action="MyCustomAction"
              Template="Doing Stuff: [1]" />
```

Its `Action` attribute tells the installer when to show this message (during which action) and `Template` is what to display. The `[1]` in the template is where your messages will fill in as your custom action executes.

Now, at the beginning of your custom action, set up how many tick marks to add for each update you send. The following is a method that does that:

```
private static void NumberOfTicksPerActionData(
    Session session, int ticks)
```

```
{
    Record record = new Record(3);
    record[1] = "1"; // Bind progress bar to progress messages
    record[2] = ticks.ToString(); // ticks to add each time
    record[3] = "1"; // enable

    session.Message(InstallMessage.Progress, record);
}
```

The next method we create will do two things: display a message in the Text control and increment the ProgressBar control:

```
private static void DisplayActionData(
    Session session, string message)
{
    Record record = new Record(1);
    record[1] = message;

    session.Message(InstallMessage.ActionData, record);
}
```

Here's a custom action that illustrates how they're used. So that you have time to see the messages get displayed, we'll have the code sleep for two seconds between each update:

```
[CustomAction]
public static ActionResultMyCustomAction(Session session)
{
    ResetProgress(session);
    NumberOfTicksPerActionData(session, 100);

    DisplayActionData(session, "Sleeping for two seconds...");
    System.Threading.Thread.Sleep(2000);

    DisplayActionData(session, "Sleeping two more seconds...");
    System.Threading.Thread.Sleep(2000);

    DisplayActionData(session, "This is my third message");
    System.Threading.Thread.Sleep(2000);

    returnActionResult.Success;
}
```

Here's the result:

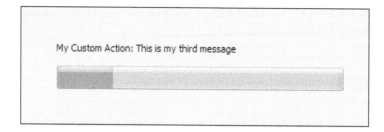

Summary

In this chapter, we discussed all of the available controls that you can use on your WiX dialogs. They range from simple lines and buttons to progress bars and billboards. With this knowledge, you can either create your own dialogs from scratch or add new controls to the dialogs that come with the WiX toolset's WixUIExtension library.

In the next chapter, we'll dig into the meaning of control events. These are used to subscribe a control to a particular Windows Installer event or to have a control publish one itself.

8

Tapping into Control Events

Windows Installer defines a limited number of events that your UI controls can listen out for or trigger. For example, a progress bar can listen for actions that say progress has taken place, and then react by showing more ticks. Or, a button can trigger an action that closes the current window. Listening for an event is known as **subscribing** and triggering one is known as **publishing**.

Because these events happen within the `Control` elements they're known as **Control Events**. We've covered several examples of control events already in *Chapter 7, Using UI Controls*, but we'll cover others that you haven't seen and show how the whole process works. In this chapter, we will:

- Use the `Publish` and `Subscribe` elements to connect to events
- Get some hands-on experience with both types

Publishing control events

To trigger an event, nests a `Publish` element inside a `Control` element. The **Event** attribute identifies the action that you want to publish and the **Value** attribute sets the required argument for that action. For example, to cause a `PushButton` control to open a new modal window, add a `Publish` element inside it that specifies the `SpawnDialog` event with `Value` set to the name of the dialog to open, as in the following snippet:

```
<Control  Id="ShowPopupButton"
          Type="PushButton"
          Text="Show Popup"
          Height="17"
          Width="56"
          X="245"
          Y="243"
```

```
              Default="yes">
    <Publish Event="SpawnDialog"
            Value="PopupDlg" />
    </Control>
```

You'll find that different events require different arguments in the `Value` attribute. Here, `Value` takes the ID of the `Dialog` element you want to open. Also, only certain events can be published by certain controls. The following table lists the events that can be published and which controls can use them:

Event	Used by	What it does
AddLocal	PushButton CheckBox SelectionTree	Sets which features to install locally.
AddSource	PushButton CheckBox SelectionTree	Sets which features to install and run from source.
CheckExistingTargetPath	PushButton SelectionTree	Checks if an existing path, given in `Value`, can be written to.
CheckTargetPath	PushButton SelectionTree	Given a file path via the `Value` attribute, checks if it's a valid path.
DirectoryListNew	PushButton	Creates a new folder in a `DirectoryList` control. `Value` set to 0.
DirectoryListOpen	PushButton	Selects a folder in a `DirectoryList` control. `Value` set to 0.
DirectoryListUp	PushButton	Moves up one directory in a `DirectoryList` control. `Value` set to 0.
DoAction	PushButton CheckBox SelectionTree	Executes the custom action specified by `Value`.
EnableRollback	PushButton SelectionTree	Turns rollback on or off, depending on if `Value` is `True` or `False`.
EndDialog	PushButton SelectionTree	Closes the current dialog window. `Value` can be exit, retry, ignore, or return.

Event	Used by	What it does
NewDialog	PushButton SelectionTree	Closes current dialog and shows dialog specified by Value.
Reinstall	PushButton SelectionTree	Sets which features to re-install.
ReinstallMode	PushButton SelectionTree	Specifies a string defining the type of re-install to do.
Remove	PushButton CheckBox SelectionTree	Sets which features to remove.
Reset	PushButton SelectionTree	Undoes any changes on controls on the current window. Value set to 0.
SelectionBrowse	PushButton	Spawns a Browse dialog.
SetInstallLevel	PushButton SelectionTree	Sets an integer that defines the install level for features.
SetTargetPath	PushButton SelectionTree	Sets the selected path. Value set to the Directory element's Id attribute.
SpawnDialog	PushButton SelectionTree	Displays the modal dialog window specified by Value.
SpawnWaitDialog	PushButton SelectionTree	Displays a dialog while a condition is false.
ValidateProductID	PushButton SelectionTree	Validates the ProductID property.

It's possible to stack several Publish elements inside a single control. This, of course, will cause several events to fire. As a contrived example, let's say that when we clicked a button we wanted to fire a custom action before moving to the next dialog. We could publish the DoAction event to execute the custom action and then publish NewDialog to navigate to the next dialog. Use the Order attribute to set which event occurs first.

Something else to watch out for: if you have more than one `Publish` event, they must have conditional statements as their inner text. Otherwise, all of the events simply won't be published. In the next example, our condition is simply `1`, which will always be true. The inner text is the place to perform real conditional rules though, such as checking that a property has been set. If the rule evaluates to false, the event won't be published:

```
<Control Id="Next"
        Type="PushButton"
        Text="Next"
        Height="17"
        Width="56"
        X="245"
        Y="243"
        Default="yes">

<Publish Event="DoAction"
        Value="MyCustomAction"
        Order="1">1</Publish>

<Publish Event="NewDialog"
        Value="AnotherDlg"
        Order="2">1</Publish>
</Control>
```

If the `MyCustomAction` custom action had set a property, we could have evaluated it in the inner text of the `NewDialog` event. If the conditional statement then evaluated to false, the `NewDialog` event wouldn't be called.

```
<Control Id="Next"
        Type="PushButton"
        Text="Next"
        Height="17"
        Width="56"
        X="245"
        Y="243"
        Default="yes">

<!--Assume MyCustomAction sets SomeProperty-->
<Publish Event="DoAction"
        Value="MyCustomAction"
        Order="1">1</Publish>

<!--Go to next dialog if SomeProperty equals "abc"-->
```

```
    <Publish Event="NewDialog"
            Value="AnotherDlg"
            Order="2">SomeProperty = "abc"</Publish>
</Control>
```

Notice that both `Publish` elements in this example use an `Order` attribute, causing the `DoAction` event to be called first.

Subscribing to control events

Some events can't be published, only listened for. In that case, you'll use a `Subscribe` element inside a `Control` element. Like we did when publishing an event, use its `Event` attribute to specify the event to listen for, but this time use `Attribute` to set the required argument.

The next example shows a `ProgressBar` control that subscribes to the `SetProgress` event. Whenever a standard or custom action notifies the installer that progress has been made, the `ProgressBar` control will know about it and add more ticks:

```
<Control Id="MyProgressBar"
        Type="ProgressBar"
        X="50"
        Y="50"
        Width="200"
        Height="20"
        ProgressBlocks="yes">
<Subscribe Event="SetProgress"
          Attribute="Progress" />
</Control>
```

Unlike the `Publish` element, the `Subscribe` element can't have a conditional statement as its inner text. A single control can, however, subscribe to more than one event. One example is to subscribe a `Text` control to both the `ScriptInProgress` and `TimeRemaining` events. The first will display a message while the Execute sequence is being loaded and the second will show the time left until completion.

The following table lists the events that can be subscribed to and their required arguments:

Event	Used by	Attribute argument
ActionData	The Text control to show info about latest action.	Text
ActionText	The Text control to show name of latest action.	Text

Event	Used by	Attribute argument
IgnoreChange	DirectoryCombo to not update itself if folder is highlighted but not opened in the neighboring DirectoryList.	IgnoreChange
ScriptInProgress	The Text control to show a message while the Execute sequence loads up.	Visible
SelectionAction	The Text control to describe the highlighted item in a neighboring SelectionTree.	Text
SelectionDescription	The Text control to display the description of a highlighted feature in a neighboring SelectionTree.	Text
SelectionNoItems	PushButton to disable itself if no items are present in a neighboring SelectionTree (Personally, I've found that this event has no effect).	Enabled
SelectionPath	The Text control to display the path of the highlighted item in a neighboring SelectionTree. Works if the item is set to be run from source.	Text
SelectionPathOn	The Text control to display whether or not there's a path for the highlighted item in a neighboring SelectionTree.	Visible
SelectionSize	The Text control to display the size of the highlighted item in a neighboring SelectionTree.	Text
SetProgress	ProgressBar to increment ticks.	Progress
TimeRemaining	The Text control to display time remaining for installation.	TimeRemaining

Publish events

In the following sections, we'll take a look at several events that you can publish. This should give you a good idea about how the Publish element works.

DoAction

The **DoAction** event calls a custom action that you've declared elsewhere in your markup. For example, suppose we'd defined a custom action called CA_ShowMessage that simply displays a message box with the text **You clicked?**:

```
<CustomAction Id="CA_ShowMessage"
              Script="vbscript"
              Execute="immediate">
    <![CDATA[msgbox "You clicked?"]]>
</CustomAction>
```

We could then trigger this action with a PushButton by publishing the DoAction event with a value of CA_ShowMessage.

```
<Control Id="DoActionButton"
         Type="PushButton"
         X="120"
         Y="100"
         Width="56"
         Height="17"
         Text="Click Me!">
    <Publish Event="DoAction"
             Value="CA_ShowMessage" />
</Control>
```

Clicking on the button will show the following message:

Often, you'll use this technique to validate a property or set one before other events are triggered. Recall that if you use more than one Publish element inside of a control, you must add an Order attribute and nest a condition statement inside each one.

EndDialog

The **EndDialog** event, which is used on a PushButton control, is used to close the current dialog window and can accept one of four values: Exit, Retry, Ignore, or Return.

In practice, you'll only ever use Exit or Return. The other two are used by the FilesInUse dialog and don't have much application elsewhere. Exit closes the current dialog and ends the installation. It's usually used on a **Cancel** button, as in this example:

```
<Control Id="CancelButton"
         Type="PushButton"
         Text="Exit"
         Height="17"
         Width="56"
         X="180"
         Y="243"
         Cancel="yes">
    <Publish Event="EndDialog"
           Value="Exit" />
</Control>
```

A Value of Return closes the current window, but continues the installation. It's usually used on an **Install** button on the last dialog in your UI. You'll also use it to close modal dialog windows and return control to the parent window. Here's an example **Install** button:

```
<Control Id="InstallButton"
         Type="PushButton"
         Text="Install"
         Height="17"
         Width="56"
         X="245"
         Y="243"
         Default="yes">
    <Publish Event="EndDialog"
           Value="Return" />
</Control>
```

NewDialog

The **NewDialog** event closes the current window and opens the one specified by the `Value` attribute. Typically, you'll use this for **Next** and **Back** buttons that move you from one dialog to another. For example, the following `PushButton` control opens a dialog called `NextDlg`:

```
<Control Id="NextButton"
        Type="PushButton"
        Text="Next"
        Height="17"
        Width="56"
        X="180"
        Y="243">
    <Publish Event="NewDialog"
            Value="NextDlg" />
</Control>
```

This is the perfect place to add a conditional statement so that the user may see one dialog instead of another depending on the state of some property. In the next example, if the property USE_SQLSERVER is set, then the dialog SetSqlCredentialsDlg is shown; otherwise, we show the NoSqlDlg dialog:

```
<Control Id="NextButton"
        Type="PushButton"
        Text="Next"
        Height="17"
        Width="56"
        X="180"
        Y="243">

    <Publish Event="NewDialog"
            Value="SetSqlCredentialsDlg"
            Order="1">
        USE_SQLSERVER
    </Publish>

    <Publish Event="NewDialog"
            Value="NoSqlDlg"
            Order="2">
        NOT USE_SQLSERVER
    </Publish>
</Control>
```

Here, I use a different conditional statement for each `Publish` element. The first evaluates to true only if the USE_SQLSERVER property has been set and the second only if it hasn't.

AddLocal

The `SelectionTree` control can be used to show the available features in your install package, and give the user the ability to select which ones they want. Windows Installer keeps track of which features to install through the ADDLOCAL property, which is a comma-delimited list of features to install locally. When it comes to the `SelectionTree` control, all of the logic of setting the ADDLOCAL property is handled for you behind the scenes. However, if you wanted to, you could do away with `SelectionTree` and create your own device for including features. For that, you'd publish the `AddLocal` control event.

`AddLocal`, like the property by the same name, can be used to set which features get installed. You'll set the `Publish` element's `Value` attribute to either the `Id` attribute of a single `Feature` element, or the string ALL, which will include all features. You can publish the event more than once to include additional features.

The next example puts this into action. Two `CheckBox` controls set properties indicating a certain feature to be installed. Later, we'll evaluate whether or not these checkboxes were checked via these properties, and set the value of the `AddLocal` event accordingly:

```
<Control  Id="Feat1Box"
          Type="CheckBox"
          X="20"
          Y="120"
          Width="75"
          Height="10"
          Text="Main Product"
          Property="MainProductFeatureChecked"
          CheckBoxValue="on" />

<Control  Id="Feat2Box"
          Type="CheckBox"
          X="20"
          Y="140"
          Width="75"
```

```
              Height="10"
              Text="Optional Tools"
              Property="OptionalToolsFeatureChecked"
              CheckBoxValue="on" />
```

Now, use a `PushButton` control to trigger the `AddLocal` event to include only the features in the install for which a box was checked. We use conditional statements inside the `Publish` elements for this:

```
<Control Id="OKButton"
         Type="PushButton"
         Text="OK"
         Height="17"
         Width="56"
         X="220"
         Y="173">

    <Publish Event="Remove"
             Value="ALL"
             Order="1">1</Publish>

    <Publish Event="AddLocal"
             Value="ProductFeature"
             Order="2">
        MainProductFeatureChecked
    </Publish>

    <Publish Event="AddLocal"
             Value="OptionalTools"
             Order="3">
        OptionalToolsFeatureChecked
    </Publish>

    <Publish Event="EndDialog"
             Value="Return"
             Order="4">1</Publish>
</Control>
```

If we add these controls to a modal dialog window, with a `SelectionTree` control so that we can see the changes, it would look like the following screenshot:

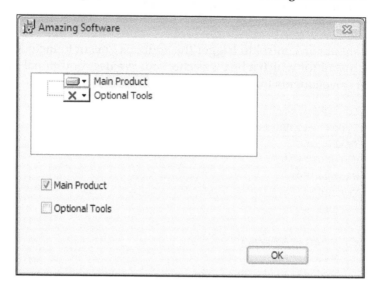

When you click on the **OK** button, the checkboxes will be evaluated, the `AddLocal` event called, features set, and the window will close. You must re-open the modal window to see the changes in the `SelectionTree` control since dialog windows aren't smart enough to redraw themselves dynamically.

So, what happened? Here's the process in detail:

- The first `Publish` element triggers an event called `Remove` to remove all features from the install. This gets us to a clean state:

```
<Publish Event="Remove"
         Value="ALL"
         Order="1">1</Publish>
```

- The second `Publish` element checks if the `MainProductFeatureChecked` property has been set and if it has, calls the `AddLocal` event for the `ProductFeature` feature. This adds that feature to the list to install:

```
<Publish Event="AddLocal"
         Value="ProductFeature"
         Order="2">
   MainProductFeatureChecked
</Publish>
```

- The third `Publish` element does the same for the `OptionalTools` feature:

```
<Publish Event="AddLocal"
        Value="OptionalTools"
        Order="3">
   OptionalToolsFeatureChecked
</Publish>
```

- The last `Publish` element calls the `EndDialog` event with a value of `Return`, which closes the modal window:

```
<Publish Event="EndDialog"
        Value="Return"
        Order="4">1</Publish>
```

Publishing a property

There's another event that you can publish, called `SetProperty`, that's used to assign a property's value. However, in WiX you won't set it in the normal way, but rather use the `Publish` element's `Property` and `Value` attributes. For example, the following is a button that sets the value of a property called `MYPROPERTY` to `123`:

```
<Control Id="MyButton"
        Type="PushButton"
        Text="Click me!"
        Height="17"
        Width="56"
        X="50"
        Y="50">
   <Publish Property="MYPROPERTY"
           Value="123">1</Publish>
</Control>
```

Many of the controls such as `Edit`, `PathEdit`, `CheckBox`, and `RadioButton` already have a mechanism for setting a property. However, if you need to set more than one or set a property with a button, the `Publish` element provides that capability.

Subscribe events

In the following sections, we'll look at the `Subscribe` element. We covered several subscribable control events in the last chapter, including those used by the `SelectionTree` and `ProgressBar`. We'll take a look at some others that we missed.

ScriptInProgress

You can subscribe a Text control to the ScriptInProgress event so that its text is only shown during the "immediate" phase of InstallExecuteSequence. This is when that sequence prepares itself for its "deferred" stage by creating a rollback script containing all of the actions it will need to perform.

You'd use this technique on a progress bar dialog. As you can see in the following example, all it does is show some text telling the user that things are gearing up:

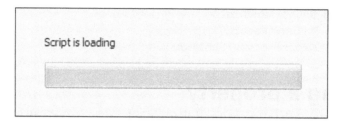

Here, we have a dialog called ProgressDlg that is shown during InstallExecuteSequence. It contains the following markup:

```xml
<?xml version="1.0" encoding="UTF-8"?>
<Wix xmlns="http://schemas.microsoft.com/wix/2006/wi">
  <Fragment>
    <UI>
      <Dialog Id=»ProgressDlg»
              Width="370"
              Height="270"
              Title="Awesome Software"
              Modeless="yes">
        <Control Id="CancelButton"
                 Type="PushButton"
                 TabSkip="no"
                 Text="Cancel"
                 Height="17"
                 Width="56"
                 X="180"
                 Y="243"
                 Cancel="yes">
          <Publish Event="EndDialog" Value="Exit" />
```

```
            </Control>


            <Control Id="MyProgressBar"
                    Type="ProgressBar"
                    X="70"
                    Y="150"
                    Width="200"
                    Height="20"
                    ProgressBlocks="yes">
              <Subscribe Event="SetProgress"
                    Attribute="Progress" />
            </Control>

            <Control Id="InfoText"
                    Type="Text"
                    X="70"
                    Y="130"
                    Width="200"
                    Height="17"
                    Text="Script is loading">
              <Subscribe Event="ScriptInProgress"
                    Attribute="Visible" />
            </Control>
          </Dialog>

          <InstallUISequence>
            <Show Dialog="ProgressDlg"
                    Before="ExecuteAction" />
          </InstallUISequence>
        </UI>
      </Fragment>
    </Wix>
```

The control named InfoText on ProgressDlg subscribes to the ScriptInProgress event. Attribute is set to Visible. Even though we're using a Text control to subscribe to this event, it only works if there's a ProgressBar control nearby. This is often the case with the Subscribe element. There must be a neighboring control that gives the event its meaning.

SelectionAction

The `SelectionAction` event is used by a `Text` control to display the current action state of the highlighted feature in a neighboring `SelectionTree`. In the following example, a feature called **Main Product** has been set to be installed locally. A `Text` control to the right displays the message **Feature will be installed locally**. It subscribes to `SelectionAction`:

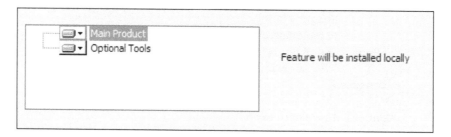

The first thing to do is add three new `UIText` elements inside the `UI` element on your dialog. These should have the following `Id` values:

- `SelAbsentLocal`
- `SelAbsentAdvertise`
- `SelAbsentAbsent`

These will contain the generic text to display as the user changes the action state of a feature. We can set them as follows:

```
<UIText Id="SelAbsentLocal">
  Feature will be installed locally
</UIText>

<UIText Id="SelAbsentAdvertise">
  Feature will be installed as advertised
</UIText>

<UIText Id="SelAbsentAbsent">
  Feature will not be installed
</UIText>
```

Our `Text` control, which must be on the same dialog as `SelectionTree`, subscribes to `SelectionAction`, and sets the `Subscribe` element's `Attribute` to `Text`, as in the following code:

```
<Control Id="SelectionAction"
        Type="Text"
```

```
                X="210"
                Y="40"
                Height="50"
                Width="150">
   <Subscribe Event="SelectionAction"
                Attribute="Text" />
   </Control>
```

As the user changes a feature's inclusion in the `SelectionTree` control, the text will change to reflect the new status.

TimeRemaining

The `TimeRemaining` event allows you to display the time left before the installation is complete. It looks like the following screenshot:

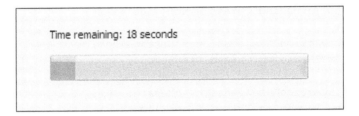

You'll need to add a `UIText` element with an `Id` attribute of `TimeRemaining` and inner text defining the text to show. It should follow this format:

```
<UIText Id="TimeRemaining">
   <![CDATA[Time remaining: {{[1] minutes }{[2] seconds}]]>
</UIText>
```

The inner text defines a template in which the minutes and seconds of the remaining time are shown. As you can see, if there is less than a minute of time left, only the seconds will be shown. Next, add a `Text` control that subscribes to the `TimeRemaining` event. Its `Publish` element should set `Attribute` to `TimeRemaining` too:

```
<Control Id="TimeRemaining"
         Type="Text"
         X="70"
         Y="130"
         Width="200"
         Height="17">
   <Subscribe Event="TimeRemaining"
              Attribute="TimeRemaining" />
</Control>
```

The standard actions in InstallExecuteSequence don't publish any TimeRemaining data. So, to see the effect, you'll have to publish it yourself from a custom action. Add a new C# custom action project to your solution and add the following code to it:

```
namespace CustomAction1
{
  usingMicrosoft.Deployment.WindowsInstaller;

  public class CustomActions
  {
    [CustomAction]
    public static ActionResult ShowTime(Session session)
    {
      ResetProgress(session);
      NumberOfTicksPerActionData(session, 100);
      DisplayActionData(session, "Message 1");
      System.Threading.Thread.Sleep(2000);

      DisplayActionData(session, "Message 2");
      System.Threading.Thread.Sleep(2000);

      DisplayActionData(session, "Message 3");
      System.Threading.Thread.Sleep(2000);

      returnActionResult.Success;
    }

    private static void ResetProgress(Session session)
    {
      Record record = new Record(4);
      record[1] = "0";
      record[2] = "1000";
      record[3] = "0";
      record[4] = "0";
      session.Message(InstallMessage.Progress, record);
    }

    private static void NumberOfTicksPerActionData(
      Session session, int ticks)
      {
      Record record = new Record(3);
      record[1] = "1";
      record[2] = ticks.ToString();
      record[3] = "1";
```

```
        session.Message(InstallMessage.Progress, record);
    }

    private static void DisplayActionData(
        Session session, string message)
    {
        Record record = new Record(1);
        record[1] = message;
        session.Message(InstallMessage.ActionData, record);
    }
  }
}
```

This sets up a custom action called `ShowTime` and three methods to support it. The first, `ResetProgressBar`, resets the ticks in the `ProgressBar` control to zero and sets up how many tick marks there should be in total. The second, `NumberOfTicksPerActionData`, sets up how many ticks to add for each action performed. The third, `DisplayActionData`, shows a message that any controls subscribing to the `ActionData` event will pick up. The `TimeRemaining` event uses all of this information to gauge how much time it should allot for this custom action.

When you add this custom action to the deferred stage of `InstallExecuteSequence`, you'll see that our `Text` control that's monitoring the `TimeRemaining` event will update itself with the approximate time left. Here's the markup to add to your main `.wxs` file to include this new custom action, assuming the C# project is named `CustomAction1`:

```
<Binary Id="CA_DLL"
        SourceFile="CustomAction1.CA.dll" />

<CustomAction Id="CA_ShowTime"
              BinaryKey="CA_DLL"
              DllEntry="ShowTime"
              Execute="deferred"
              Return="check" />

<InstallExecuteSequence>
  <Custom Action="CA_ShowTime"
          After="InstallInitialize">NOT Installed</Custom>
</InstallExecuteSequence>
```

Summary

In this chapter, we looked at the Publish and Subscribe elements that are used to trigger and listen for control events. Knowing the exact arguments to use for each event can be tricky, so be sure to consult the Windows Installer SDK to get specifics. Probably one of the most powerful events is DoAction, which lets you publish your own custom action. Pairing this with the ability to stack several events inside one control and to set the order in which they're called gives you quite a bit of power.

In the next chapter, we will explore the WiX command line. This will give you the knowledge to compile and link your project even without Visual Studio.

9
Working from the
Command Line

Creating an MSI file with WiX takes two steps: compiling your source files and then linking and binding them into a single package. A tool called **Candle** handles the compiling, transforming your .wxs files into .wixobj files. The linking and binding phases are handled by a tool called **Light**.

In this chapter, we'll discuss the following topics:

- The arguments to use when calling Candle and Light from the command line
- Compile-time and link-time variables
- How to build an MSI without using Visual Studio

Candle.exe

Candle, the WiX compiler, can be run from the command line to build your WiX source files (.wxs). Behind the scenes, Visual Studio is really just calling this tool for you. Compiling a WiX source file creates a WiX object file (.wixobj). These are later processed by Light, the WiX linker/binder, to create the final MSI. A simple example of using Candle would be where we simply pass it the path to a .wxs file:

```
"%WIX%bin\candle" Product.wxs
```

This will compile the Product.wxs file that's in the current directory and create an object file called Product.wixobj. I've used the %WIX% environment variable that expands to C:\Program Files (x86)\WiX Toolset v3.6\. This variable is available after you've installed WiX. The candle.exe file is located in the WiX bin directory, though, so we need to include that folder in the path.

To make accessing the WiX command-line tools easy, you should consider adding %WIX%bin to your PATH environment variable. Right-click on **Computer** in your **Start** menu, select **Properties**, and then the **Advanced system settings** link. Click on **Environment Variables** and from there, you can edit the Path variable and append %WIX%bin. From then on, you will be able to use Candle, Light, or any of the other WiX tools without specifying the path to the bin directory.

You can see more information about Candle by opening a command prompt and typing candle -?. From here on out, I won't specify the path to Candle, but will assume that you're either including the path or have added %WIX%bin to the PATH environment variable. Using the -? argument brings up the documentation and you'll see that the general syntax is as follows:

```
candle.exe [-?] [-nologo] [-out outputFile] sourceFile [sourceFile ...]
[@responseFile]
```

As indicated, you could specify an output file, via the -out flag, to give a name to the .wixobj file that's created. By default, the .wixobj file will have the same name as the .wxs. Yet if we wanted to change the name of the output file, we could do so, in the following manner:

```
candle Product.wxs -out AnotherName.wixobj
```

The sourceFile argument refers to the name of the .wxs file that we're compiling. You may give more than one, separated by spaces:

```
candle Product.wxs Directories.wxs Components.wxs
```

You could also use a wildcard (*) to compile all .wxs files in a directory and then output the .wixobj files to another directory. Here's an example that sends the compiled output to a directory called "wixobj":

```
candle *.wxs -out wixobj\
```

Notice that we must end the "wixobj" directory with a trailing backslash or Candle will think we're using the -out argument to rename a file rather than name a directory.

You could also provide the -arch flag, set to x64 or x86, to set the target architecture of your software, although it defaults to x86. This is essential if you're installing files to the 64-bit Program Files folder, for example. Also, if you've used any WiX extensions, such as the WixUIExtension, you should add them with the -ext flag. Here's a simple example that includes an extension and explicitly sets the target architecture:

```
candle Product.wxs -arch x86 -out wixobj\ -ext WixUIExtension
```

If you are using more than one extension, pass an -ext flag for each one.

Response files

Sometimes, your calls to Candle will be simple and it won't be much trouble entering them on the command line. However, as you start adding more optional arguments you could easily see them span several rows of the console window. In that case, you may find it easier to store your arguments in a **response file**, which can be a simple text file. The following is an example called MyCommands.txt that contains several compiler arguments:

```
-out wixobj\
-dConfig=Release
-trace
-arch x86
-ext WixUtilExtension
-ext WixUIExtension
```

You reference a response file by prefixing its name with the @ symbol. Here's an example:

```
candle.exe Product.wxs @MyCommands.txt
```

It is permissible to override the arguments in the response file by passing them on the command line:

```
candle.exe Product.wxs @MyCommands.txt -dConfig=Debug
```

We will explore the meaning of the arguments we haven't discussed yet later in the chapter.

.wixobj files

The compilation process ultimately produces a `.wixobj` file for every `.wxs` file. The linking phase will later combine all of the `.wixobj` files into a single MSI package. A `.wixobj` file consists of XML code with mainly table, row, and field elements. Together, these elements describe the rows in each table of the MSI database. The top-level element of a `.wixobj` file is `wixObject`.

```
<?xml version="1.0" encoding="utf-8"?>
<wixObject version="3.0.2002.0"
    xmlns="http://schemas.microsoft.com/wix/2006/objects">
```

Nested inside of the `wixObject` element are references to various MSI tables. The following is a section describing the `File` table with a single row for a text file called `ReadMe.txt`. The `sourceLineNumber` attribute of the row element has been truncated for space:

```
<table name="File">
<row sourceLineNumber="C:\InstallPractice\Product.wxs*21">
<field>file_readmeTXT</field>
<field>cmp_readmeTXT</field>
<field>ReadMe.txt</field>
<field>0</field>
<field />
<field />
<field>512</field>
<field />
</row>
</table>
```

You should never need to alter these files directly, but knowing how they work should help you to understand what the compiling stage does.

Command-line arguments (compiling)

In this section, we'll cover all of the optional arguments that you're likely to use with Candle. In addition to setting them on the command line, you may also set them within Visual Studio via your project's **Properties** page via the **Tool Settings** tab. There you'll find a textbox for Candle arguments, labeled **Compiler**, and another for Light, labeled **Linker**.

The following are quick descriptions of Candle's arguments:

-arch

The -arch flag sets the architecture for the build. This is important because certain elements in the MSI package, such as components, need to be marked as 64-bit if they are to be installed in a computer's 64-bit directories. This flag, if set to x64, also causes the compiler to check that you've specified an installer version of 2.0.0 or higher, as this is the minimum version needed for a 64-bit package.

-d

This -d flag, which stands for "define", allows you to set compile-time variables. These are replaced with the values that they've been set to when Candle creates the .wixobj file. We'll discuss this in more detail later in the chapter. The basic syntax is, with no space between the -d flag and the name of the variable:

```
-dVariableName=VariableValue
```

-ext

This flag is used to include a WiX extension, such as WixUIExtension or WixUtilExtension. Include it when your source file depends on a WiX extension.

-fips

Enabling the FIPS compliant algorithms with the -fips flag causes the installer to switch its hashing algorithm from MD5 to SHA1. **FIPS**, which stands for **Federal Information Processing Standards Publications**, is a governmental standard for ensuring security and interoperability when hashing data.

-I

A WiX **include file** (.wxi) contains preprocessor variables and conditional statements. There's a Visual Studio template for creating one. Although you can add each include file explicitly to your WiX project, a more dynamic way is to add the -I flag on the command line, set to the path of a directory that contains .wxi files. Candle will search that directory during compilation.

Let's say that one of your WiX source files references an include file via the include tags:

```
<?xml version="1.0" encoding="UTF-8"?>
<Wix xmlns="http://schemas.microsoft.com/wix/2006/wi">
    <?include SomeIncludeFile.wxi ?>
...
```

We'll get to what goes into an include file in the next section. If `SomeIncludeFile.wxi` was in `C:\Includes`, we could reference it by referencing that folder, as follows:

```
candle Product.wxs -IC:\Includes -trace
```

I have also given the `-trace` flag, which instructs Candle to display any errors during compilation, such as failure to find the `Includes` directory. The included directory may be an absolute or relative path.

-nologo

Candle prints its version number and copyright at the top of its output. However, if you supply the `-nologo` flag this will be suppressed.

-o

The `-o` or `-out` argument tells Candle where to place the new `.wixobj` file after compiling the WiX source code and, if compiling a single source file, what the name of that file will be.

-p

An intermediate step performed by Candle is to process your `.wxs` file into a well-formed XML document. You can see this intermediate XML document by adding the `-p` flag.

-pedantic

The `-pedantic` flag tells the compiler to show messages that you wouldn't normally see. The examples include, not explicitly setting a keypath for a component.

-sfdvital

Ordinarily, all `File` elements in WiX are marked as "Vital". This means that if, during an installation, a file cannot be copied to the end user's system, the installer won't be able to proceed. Setting the `-sfdvital` flag switches this default behavior off.

-ss

As Candle compiles your project, it validates it against the WiX schema found in `wix.xsd`. You can turn this validation off by adding the `-ss` flag.

-sw

If you don't care much about compiler warnings (maybe you only care about errors), you can suppress them with the -sw flag. Without any argument, all warnings will be suppressed. To exclude only a specific warning, reference its ID, such as -sw1009. You can find a full list of errors and their message IDs by downloading the WiX source files, and then opening the *Wix* solution and looking at messages.xml.

-trace

If you get a compile-time error, such as when an include file cannot be found, you may consider turning on trace logging.

-v

The -v flag, which stands for "verbose", tells the compiler to display the *Information* level messages during processing.

-wx

To treat all compile-time warnings as errors, add the -wx flag. You can also supply a specific message ID (from messages.xml in the WiX source files) to elevate only that particular warning to error status.

Compile-time variables

WiX lets you specify variables that are evaluated at compile time. You might use this to get environmental variables from the build machine, get the directory where your source files are, or access custom variables you've set up in a separate WiX **include file** (.wxi).

WiX has three classifications for compile-time (otherwise known as preprocessor) variables: **Custom**, **Environment**, and **System**. We'll discuss each in the following sections.

Custom compiler variables

To set your own compile-time variables, also known as preprocessor variables, use the <?define ?> directive in your WiX markup:

```
<?define myVar = "myvalue" ?>
```

Although you can do this in any of your `.wxs` files, it's common to do it in a separate **include file** (`.wxi`) file, for which there is a Visual Studio template. The include files allow you to gather your preprocessor statements into a single place. At compile time, your variables will be inserted into your source files wherever you've referenced them. Here's an example `.wxi` file called `MyVariables.wxi`:

```
<?xml version="1.0" encoding="utf-8"?>
<Include>
<?define Config = "Debug" ?>
<?define ProductId = "{89CC4C03-1059-4523-8670-50DEA04B9892}" ?>
<?define UpgradeCode = "{49D09A05-12D9-461E-8DEE-9DD5615AF9FE}" ?>
<?define Version = "1.0.0.0" ?>
</Include>
```

As I mentioned, we define compile-time variables with the `<?define ?>` directive. Begin and end the file with an `Include` element. This file can then be referenced in your `.wxs` files using an `<?include ?>` directive. Variables are inserted using the `$(var.VariableName)` syntax, such as:

```
<?include MyVariables.wxi ?>

<Product Id="$(var.ProductId)"
         Name="Amazing Software"
         Language="1033"
         Version="$(var.Version)"
         Manufacturer="Amazing Software Inc."
         UpgradeCode="$(var.UpgradeCode)">
```

You can also define variables from the command line by using the `-d` flag. They will be referenced in the same way:

candle.exe Product.wxs -dVersion="1.0.0.0"

There are other preprocessor statements at your disposal, such as `if` and `foreach`. We'll cover those soon, but for now let's discuss the two other types of compile-time variables: *Environment* and *System*.

Environment variables

Environment variables are set in the environment where the build process is running, usually from the command prompt. The following statement sets an environment variable called `myVar` to the value `myvalue`. This uses the basic Windows command, `set`.

set myVar=myvalue

To pass this to your WiX project, build your `.wxs` files from the same command window using Candle. Now access the environment variable in your markup by using a dollar sign and parentheses, prefixing the variable name with `env`. The following is an example:

```
<Property Id="property1" Value="$(env.myVar)" />
```

System variables

System variables are a lot like environment variables. They have a similar syntax (in this case you'll prefix the variable name with `sys`), but there are a finite number of them, and they're defined for you. The following system variables, which are always uppercase, are available:

- `CURRENTDIR`: The current directory where the build process is running
- `SOURCEFILEDIR`: The directory containing the file being processed
- `SOURCEFILEPATH`: The full path to the file being processed
- `PLATFORM`: The platform (Intel, x64, Intel64) this package is compiled for (set by the –arch flag)

The first two, which contain directory paths, always end in a backslash. So, you can use them in the following way:

```
$(sys.SOURCEFILEDIR)myFile.wxs
```

Conditional statements and iterations

In this section, we'll take a look at the conditional and looping statements that are available at compile time.

if...elseif...else

The **if** statement checks whether a preprocessor variable is set to a certain value. If it is, the markup between the opening `if` statement and the closing `endif` will be compiled. Optionally, it can be followed by an `elseif` or `else` statement, allowing you to compile other code if the initial condition is false. The entire block must end with `endif`. The following snippet is an example that only compiles a `Property` element if the preprocessor variable `myVar` is equal to 10:

```
<?if $(var.myVar) = 10 ?>
<Property Id="newProperty" Value="5" />
<?endif?>
```

Here's a more complex example that utilizes the `elseif` and `else` statements:

```
<?if $(var.myVar) = 10 ?>
<Property Id="newProperty" Value="5" />
<?elseif $(var.myVar) > 10?>
<Property Id="newProperty" Value="6" />
<?else?>
<Property Id="newProperty" Value="7" />
<?endif?>
```

Other conditional operators are available, including not equal to (`!=`), greater than (`>`), greater than or equal to (`>=`), less than (`<`), and less than or equal to (`<=`). In addition, you can use the `Or` and `And` keywords to combine conditions. Use the `Not` keyword to negate a conditional statement:

```
<?if Not $(var.myVar) = 10 And Not $(var.myVar) = 11 ?>
<Property Id="newProperty" Value="5" />
<?endif?>
```

ifdef

The `ifdef` statement is used to check whether a preprocessor variable is defined. If it is, the WiX markup that follows will be compiled. The variable should be the name only, not the `$(var.myVariable)` syntax. Here is an example that checks if `myVar` is defined:

```
<?ifdef myVar ?>
<Property Id="newProperty" Value="1" />
<?endif?>
```

ifndef

The `ifndef` statement is similar to the `ifdef` statement, except that it checks if a variable is *not* defined. Here's an example:

```
<?ifndef myVar ?>
<Property Id="newProperty" Value="1" />
<?endif?>
```

Iterations

WiX has a preprocessor statement, **foreach,** that you can use to repeat a block of code a number of times. For example, you might loop through a list of directory names and create a new `Directory` element for each one; maybe to create a directory for each language your software supports.

First, you'll need to define a list to iterate through in the form of a string containing several values, each separated by a semicolon. To keep things clear, you could define a preprocessor variable to hold it, as in the following example:

```
<?define myLanguages=en_us;de_de;it_it?>
```

Next, define a top-level folder to hold all of your new directories. Here, we'll call it `languages` and place it inside our `INSTALLLOCATION` directory:

```
<DirectoryRef Id="INSTALLLOCATION">
   <Directory Id="languagesFolder" Name="languages" />
</DirectoryRef>
```

Now you can use a `foreach` statement to loop through each value in the `myLanguages` string. For each iteration, the current value is stored in a temporary variable called `tempVar`.

```
<?foreach tempVar in $(var.myLanguages)?>

<DirectoryRef Id="languagesFolder">
   <Directory Id="$(var.tempVar)" Name="$(var.tempVar)">
      <Component Id="MyComponent.$(var.tempVar)" Guid="*">
         <File Id="$(var.tempVar)File"
               Source="..\$(var.tempVar).xml"
               KeyPath="yes" />
      </Component>
   </Directory>
</DirectoryRef>

<?endforeach?>
```

For each language, a new `Directory` element is created under the `languagesFolder` directory. We set the directory's `Id` and `Name` attributes to the `tempVar` variable's value. We also use it to set the ID of the `Component` element. By using an asterisk (*) as `Guid`, WiX will auto-generate a new one for each component. Then, we use the temporary variable again for the `Id` and `Source` attributes of the language-specific XML file. Be sure that the files `en_us.xml`, `de_de.xml`, and `it_it.xml` really exist! Otherwise, you'll get a compile-time error. The entire structure ends with an `endforeach` statement.

The last thing to do is to add all of our new components to a feature. Here, we can use another `foreach`:

```
<Feature Id="MainFeature" Title="Main Feature" Level="1">
    <?foreach tempVar in $(var.myLanguages)?>
    <ComponentRef Id="MyComponent.$(var.tempVar)"/>
    <?endforeach?>
</Feature>
```

If you were to install this MSI package, you'd get a `languages` folder containing an `en_us`, `de_de`, and `it_it` folder. Each would hold a single XML file corresponding to that locality.

Errors and warnings

Another thing that WiX gives you is the ability to trigger compile-time errors and warnings. For this, use the `<?error error-message ?>` and `<?warning warning-message?>` syntax. An error stops the compilation and shows the error in the build log. A warning, on the other hand, will show up in the log, but won't stop the build. Here's an example that triggers an error if the preprocessor variable `myVariable` isn't defined:

```
<?ifndef myVariable ?>
    <?error myVariable must be defined ?>
<?endif?>
```

Adding warnings and errors like this allows you to keep a closer eye on things, making sure that critical variables are defined like they should be. The example that we just saw used an error, which stops the build if hit. A warning works the same way, but won't stop the build. Here's an example:

```
<?ifndef myVariable ?>
    <?warning myVariable should be defined ?>
<?endif?>
```

Preprocessor extensions

You can create your own variable prefixes (remember `var`, `env`, and `sys`?) and even call C# methods at compile time by writing a **preprocessor extension**. You'll need to make a new C# class library. We'll walk through each step and then look at the complete code afterwards.

Understand that a preprocessor extension is only executed during compilation to insert data into your WiX markup. So, the end user of your installer will never see it. Also, a preprocessor extension is different than extensions such as WixUIExtension, which are technically *compiler extensions*. We'll get to make a compiler extension later in the book.

First, in your new class library, add a reference to Wix.dll from the WiX bin directory, and add a using statement for Microsoft.Tools.WindowsInstallerXml. Next, add a class that extends the WixExtension class. Here, we've called it MyWixExtension:

```
using Microsoft.Tools.WindowsInstallerXml;

namespace MyPreprocessorExtension
{
    public class MyWixExtension : WixExtension
    {
        //our extension code will go here
    }
}
```

The purpose of this class is to override the PreprocessorExtension property from the WixExtension class so that instead of returning null, it returns an instance of the next class we'll be creating—which we'll call MyPreprocessorExtension. We'll define that class in a moment. Add this property to the MyWixExtension class:

```
private PreprocessorExtension preprocessorExtension;

public override PreprocessorExtension PreprocessorExtension
{
    get
    {
        if (this.preprocessorExtension == null)
        {
            this.preprocessorExtension = new
                MyPreprocessorExtension();
        }

        return this.preprocessorExtension;
    }
}
```

The next step is to define the `MyPreprocessorExtension` class. It must extend the `PreprocessorExtension` base class and set up the prefixes you want to use for your new compile-time variables. Here's where we do that:

```
public class MyPreprocessorExtension : PreprocessorExtension
{
    private static string[] prefixes = { "AmazingCo" };

    public override string[] Prefixes
    {
        get { return prefixes; }
    }
```

This sets our prefix to be `AmazingCo`, although you'll likely use the actual name of your company or something else more inspired. As you can see, the `prefixes` variable is an array of strings so if you wanted to, you could create multiple new prefixes here.

The next step is to override the `GetVariableValue` method, which sets up a switch statement that returns a value for the preprocessor variable you'll have passed in from your WiX markup. In other words, we can't set the values of these variables dynamically, they are all hardcoded here.

```
public override string GetVariableValue(
    string prefix, string name)
{
    string result = null;

    switch (prefix)
    {
        case "AmazingCo":
            switch (name)
            {
                // define all the variables under
                // this prefix here...
                case "myvar":
                    result = "myvalue";
                    break;
            }
            break;
    }

    return result;
}
```

For this example, there's only one variable defined under the `AmazingCo` prefix: `myVar`, which has a value of `myvalue`. In your WiX markup, you could access this using the dollar sign and parentheses syntax:

```
<Property Id="myVar" Value="$(AmazingCo.myvar)" />
```

If you want to get fancy, you can add code that calls a preprocessor method. For this, you must override `EvaluateFunction`:

```
public override string EvaluateFunction(
  string prefix, string function, string[] args)
{
    string result = null;

    switch (prefix)
    {
      case "AmazingCo":
        switch (function)
        {
          // add any functions that you can
          // call with your prefix...
          case "sayHelloWorld":
            result = "Hello, World!";
            break;
        }
        break;
    }

    return result;
}
```

In this example, we've added a function called `sayHelloWorld` to our `AmazingCo` prefix. When called in WiX, it will return the string "Hello, World!". In real-world scenarios, it might return a version number of some other string that you'd like to perform some calculation to get.

In WiX, we can now call this function as follows:

```
<Property Id="checkVar"
          Value="$(AmazingCo.sayHelloWorld())" />
```

If you'd like to pass arguments to this method, alter `EvaluateFunction` so that it uses its `args` parameter. Here's a simple example that turns the first parameter that was passed in to uppercase and then returns it:

```
case "sayHelloWorld":
   if(args.Length > 0)
   {
      result = args[0].ToUpper();
   }
   else
   {
      result = String.Empty;
   }
   break;
}
return result;
```

Before your new extension will work, you'll need to do one more thing: add the following `using` statement and attribute to the `AssemblyInfo.cs` file of the class library:

```
using Microsoft.Tools.WindowsInstallerXml;

[assembly: AssemblyDefaultWixExtension(typeof(
   MyPreprocessorExtension.MyWixExtension))]
```

Of course, you'll want to replace `MyPreprocessorExtension.MyWixExtension` with whatever names you gave to your class and its namespace. Then, compile the project to create a new `.dll` file. The final step is to add a reference to it in your WiX project. Be careful not to include the project, if it's in the same solution as your WiX project. You must reference the built `.dll` file.

This is the complete code for the preprocessor extension:

```
using Microsoft.Tools.WindowsInstallerXml;

namespace MyPreprocessorExtension
{
   public class MyWixExtension : WixExtension
   {
      private MyPreprocessorExtension preprocessorExtension;

      public override PreprocessorExtension
         PreprocessorExtension
      {
         get
```

```
        {
            if (this.preprocessorExtension == null)
            {
                this.preprocessorExtension =
                    new MyPreprocessorExtension();
            }

            return this.preprocessorExtension;
        }
    }
}

public class MyPreprocessorExtension :
    PreprocessorExtension
{
    private static string[] prefixes = { "AmazingCo" };

    public override string[] Prefixes
    {
        get
        {
            return prefixes;
        }
    }

    public override string GetVariableValue(
        string prefix, string name)
    {
        string result = null;

        switch (prefix)
        {
            case "AmazingCo":
                switch (name)
                {
                    // define all the variables under
                    // this prefix here...
                    case "myvar":
                        result = "myvalue";
                        break;
                }
                break;
        }
```

```
            return result;
        }

    public override string EvaluateFunction(
        string prefix, string function, string[] args)
    {
        string result = null;

        switch (prefix)
        {
            case "AmazingCo":
                switch (function)
                {
                    // add any functions that you can
                    // call with your prefix...
                    case "sayHelloWorld":
                        result = "Hello, World!";
                        break;
                }
                break;
        }
        return result;
    }
  }
}
```

Light.exe

Light is the WiX linker and binder. Its job is to first resolve all of the references to files, directories, and so on that are stored in the `.wixobj` files (the `linking` phase) and then to stream all of that data into the MSI file, compressing it along the way (the `binding` phase). To see information about its usage type `light -?` at the command prompt; the following is what you should see:

```
light.exe [-?] [-b bindPath] [-nologo]
[-out outputFile] objectFile [objectFile ...] [@responseFile]
```

You'll use the `-out` flag to give a name to the resulting MSI package. You must then reference all of the `.wixobj` files, either individually or with an asterisk (*). For example, this creates an MSI file out of three `.wixobj` files that are in the current directory:

```
light.exe -out myInstaller.msi Product.wixobj Fragment1.wixobj Fragment2.
wixobj
```

We can also use an asterisk:

```
light.exe -out myInstaller.msi *.wixobj
```

If you've created any `.wixlib` files, you can reference them in the same way:

```
light.exe -out myInstaller.msi *.wixobj LibraryOne.wixlib LibraryTwo.
wixlib
```

If you're using any WiX extensions, reference them using the `-ext` flag:

```
light.exe -out myInstaller.msi *.wixobj -ext WixUIExtension
```

In the following sections, we'll cover the rest of the arguments that you can pass to Light. Although some affect linking and others binding, you'll specify both during the same call to Light.

Command-line arguments (linking)

In this section, we will explore the arguments that you can pass to Light that affect linking. **Linking** is the process whereby the symbols in the `.wixobj` files created by Candle are validated to make sure that they will resolve correctly. At this point, elements such as components and features are hooked together and if an undefined symbol is found, an exception will be thrown.

-b

The `-b` flag, which can be set to a directory path, tells Light where to look for the `.wixobj` files. You can add more than one directory by adding more `-b` flags.

-bf

The `-bf` flag is always used with the `-xo` flag, which tells Light to output a `.wixout` file instead of an MSI file. The `.wixout` format is XML as opposed to binary. However, by adding the `-bf` flag, the binary data that would be stored in the MSI file is included with the XML.

-binder

You can define a custom binder in a WiX extension DLL. Use the `-binder` flag to identify the class that represents your custom binder that will be used to replace the default `Microsoft.Tools.WindowsInstallerXml.Binder` class. This is an advanced topic and won't be covered in this book.

-cultures

The -cultures flag tells WiX which .wxl files to load for localization. It accepts a culture string, such as en-us. Only one culture, and in turn one language, can be specified here. This is because an MSI file can only be localized for a single language.

-d

Use the -d flag to define a linker variable. Linker variables can be referenced with the !(wix.VariableName) syntax. Unlike compile-time preprocessor variables, linker variables are evaluated and resolved at link time. They're often used to reference files late in the build process. We'll discuss these in detail later in the chapter.

-dut

The WiX compiler and linker use extra tables, peculiar to WiX, to store metadata about how elements get grouped together. These extra tables don't exist in the MSI specification, and they're not used in the final MSI file. So, they're called **unreal** tables. You can drop these tables from the .wixout or .wixpdb files by adding the -dut flag.

-ext

Use the -ext flag to link in WiX extensions, such as the WixUIExtension.dll file. This loads all of the C# code and .wxs files found in that extension.

```
-ext "%WIX%bin\WixUIExtension.dll"
```

-loc

When you've created .wxl files that contain localized strings for your MSI file, you'll link them in (specify their paths and filenames) with -loc flags. Those with a culture that matches the -cultures flag will be used.

-nologo

Light prints a message at the top of the console window when you use it showing its version and copyright information. You can stop this by adding the -nologo flag.

-notidy

Light produces some temporary files during the course of its processing. It ordinarily cleans up after itself, deleting these files once it's finished. However, by adding the -notidy flag, these files will not be deleted. You'll need to add the -v flag to see where the temporary files are being stored. Look for an entry in the verbose log that says something like **temporary directory located at**....

-o[ut]

Use the -o or -out flag to tell Light the name of the resulting MSI or .wixout file.

-pedantic

To see extra linking information, usually of low importance, add the -pedantic flag.

-sadmin

Often, you won't use the AdminExecuteSequence or AdminUISequence tables during your install. To prevent those tables from being created in the MSI database, add the -sadmin flag.

-sadv

The AdvtExecuteSequence table is used for advertised installations. If you don't need it, you can suppress its creation by adding the -sadv flag.

-sloc

To prevent Light from processing localized variables in your .wxs files, add the -sloc flag. Then, output a file with the .wixout extension via the -o flag. It will contain the variables, such as !(loc.myVariable), instead of the literal value that it would have been expanded to. However, if you specify the -loc or -cultures flag, -sloc will be ignored. You must also specify the -xo flag when you want the output with the .wixout format.

-sma

You can tell your installer to load a file into the Global Assembly Cache by setting the Assembly attribute on that file's File element. This will add two new tables to your MSI: MsiAssembly and MsiAssemblyName. It will also add a new action to InstallExecuteSequence called MsiPublishAssemblies. To suppress this action and these tables from being processed, add the -sma flag.

-ss

Light performs schema validation, using the XML schema found in `outputs.xsd`, to check that the syntax of the `.wixout` or `.wxipdb` file is correct. You can suppress this validation by adding the `-ss` flag.

-sts

Light uses GUIDs to identify row elements in `.wixout` and `.wixpdb` files. You can stop Light from showing these GUIDs in these files by adding the `-sts` flag.

-sui

You can choose to suppress the UI phase of the install by adding the `-sui` flag. This will remove the `InstallUISequence` and `AdminUISequence` tables from the MSI database. You might do this to simplify an MSI database that has no user interface.

-sv

The output from Light can be represented in the XML format in either a `.wixout` or `.wixpdb` file. These files represent an intermediate state of the data before it's turned into an MSI file by Light's binding process. They always contain an element called `wixOutput` that has a `version` attribute. When Light reads these intermediate XML files and transforms them into a finished MSI file, it checks that the `version` attribute in the file matches the version of Light that's installed. That way, it can be sure that the data can be processed correctly.

Imagine, however, that you've stored `.wixout` files that you plan on creating an MSI out of sometime in the future. After all, it's possible to build an MSI file from a `.wixout` file at a later time and your version of Light may have changed. You can suppress this validation by adding the `-sv` flag.

-sw[N]

Light produces several warnings and errors if files can't be found or things can't be linked properly. To turn off all warnings, add the `-sw` flag. You can also specify a particular warning to suppress by setting `-sw` to that warning's number. These numbers can be found in `messages.xml` in the WiX source code.

-usf <output.xml>

Use the -usf flag with the name of an XML file, such as -usf unrefSymbols.xml
to log the symbols from Light's output that were not referenced. For example, adding
the WixUIExtension but not using any of its dialogs will cause some
symbols to be orphaned.

-v

In order to see what's going on behind the scenes with Light, you'll need to add the
-v flag. This displays Light's logging messages such as ICE validation, file copying,
and CAB file creation.

-wx[N]

Ordinarily, warnings from Light don't stop the linking process. However, by
adding the -wx flag, warnings will be treated as errors, which do stop the process.
You can also specify a specific warning message to treat as an error by adding its
message number.

-xo

When you add the -xo flag to Light, it outputs XML in the .wixout format. So, you'll
need to also specify a .wixout filename with the -out flag. You may also want to
add the -bf flag to append binary data for the installer to the .wixout file.

Command-line arguments (binding)

In this section, we will explore the arguments that affect Light's binding phase.
Binding is the process whereby the binary data from your source files that were
resolved during the linking phase are compressed into CAB files that are potentially
stored in the MSI.

-bcgg

When creating a Component element in WiX, you'll usually specify a GUID to
uniquely identify it. However, you can specify an asterisk (*) instead, in which case
Light will choose the GUID for you. The default algorithm Light uses to create a
GUID involves the SHA1 hash. However, by adding the -bcgg flag, you're telling it
to use the older MD5 hash. This is a more backwards compatible algorithm, but is
rarely needed.

-cc <path>

The binding process creates a .cab file, a type of file that holds compressed data, to store the files that the MSI will install. If you plan on calling Light several times, you can save some time by caching the .cab file and reusing it. To cache it, specify the -cc flag and the path to cache it to. Later on, you can add the -reusecab flag to tell Light to look for the .cab file in the path you've specified. For example, you could specify that the .cab file be cached to a directory called cabcache like this: -cc ".\cabcache".

-ct <N>

You can change the number of threads Light uses when creating .cab files. The default is to use the number stored in the %NUMBER_OF_PROCESSORS% environment variable. You can change it by setting the -ct flag to a number.

-cub <file.cub>

Windows Installer uses files with the .cub extension to store ICE validation checks. There are two files it uses routinely: darice.cub (for MSIs) and mergemod.cub (for MSMs). To add your own .cub file with new ICE tests, specify the path to it with the -cub flag. We won't cover how to create custom ICE checks in this book.

-dcl:level

By default, Light uses MSZIP to compress .cab files. You can change the compression by adding the -dcl flag and setting it to one of the following: low, medium, high, none, or mszip.

-eav

Light uses a workaround to prevent Windows Installer from complaining if the version stored in the MsiAssemblyName table doesn't fit the fileVersion column created by the -fv flag. By specifying -eav, you're telling Light to not use this workaround.

-fv

If you add the -fv flag, Light will add a column called fileVersion to the MsiAssemblyName table. This is a table used to install assemblies to the GAC. The recommended way to update an assembly in the GAC is to install the new version with a new strong name. You'd use -fv when you want to ignore this recommendation and update an assembly in the GAC without changing its strong name.

-ice <ICE>

If you've created your own ICE checks and referenced their containing file with the -cub flag, you'll need to specify which to use with the -ice flag. For example, to add a test called ICE9999, and add the following: -ice:ICE9999. Specify the number of the test after a semicolon. Refer to the MSDN documentation for more information about creating your own ICE checks: http://msdn.microsoft.com/en-us/library/aa372423%28VS.85%29.aspx.

-pdbout <output.wixpdb>

Light ordinarily creates a .wixpdb file that has the same name as the MSI that you're creating. However, you can change the name of the .wixpdb file by specifying it with the -pdbout flag.

-reusecab

If you've used the -cc flag to cache the .cab files that Light creates, you can tell Light to re-use those cabinets by adding the -reusecab flag. You'll need to specify the -cc flag again, which tells Light where the .cab files have been cached. If Light can't find the .cab files there, it will resort to creating them again.

-sa

When storing an assembly in the GAC, Light finds the file information on the .dll file for you (culture, name, architecture, public key token, and version) and stores it in a table called MsiAssemblyName. You can suppress this by adding the -sa flag.

Light can't use reflection on .NET assemblies that use a newer version of the **Common Language Runtime (CLR)** than was available when Light was built. You can see the supported runtimes by opening light.exe.config, found in the WiX bin folder, in a text editor and searching for the supportedRuntime element.

In such a situation, you may be better off using -sa and adding the assembly information to the *MsiAssemblyName* table yourself. That is, unless there's a newer version of Light available for download.

-sacl

During Light's binding phase, it copies the finished MSI file to your output folder. If the file can't be copied because its permissions (its ACLs) are too restrictive (adopted from the permissions of the source directory), then Light changes the file's permissions to be *Full Control* for the current user.

Once it has copied the file to the output folder, it sets things right again by giving the MSI file the permissions of the output folder. If you add the -sacl flag, Light will skip this step and the MSI file will be left with the unrestricted permissions. You might do this if the permissions of the output folder are also too restrictive. For example, if you're sending the output to a network share, but you don't want the MSI file to adopt the permissions of that share.

-sf

The -sf flag has the same behavior as the -sa and -sh flags added together.

-sh

If you add the -sh flag, Light will not add the MsiFileHash table to the final MSI. This table is used to eliminate the unnecessary copying of a file if the end user's computer already has a file that's scheduled to be installed.

-sice: <ICE>

You can suppress a specific ICE validation check by adding its number after the -sice flag. You should specify a new -sice flag for each check that you want to suppress. For example, to suppress ICE20, add the following: -sice:ICE20.

-sl

By adding the -sl flag, you're telling Light to not embed the CAB file in the MSI package. Once the MSI is built, you can check the Media table and see that the Cabinet column's value does *not* start with a pound sign (#), showing that the CAB file is not embedded.

-spdb

The -spdb flag tells WiX to not create a .wixpdb file.

-sval

To prevent Light from running any of the ICE validation checks, add the -sval flag.

Link-time variables

Like Candle, Light allows you to specify variables that will be interpreted when your project is built. Here, however, the variables are processed at link time. There are three types of link-time variables: **localization**, **binder**, and **custom**. We will take a look at each in the following sections.

Localization variables

WiX gives you something unique in the MSI-building world — a way to re-use one set of .wxs files for many different languages. The way to do it is to use a variable anywhere that you'd normally place text, such as on dialog controls, feature labels, directory names, and so on. At link time, these localization variables will be swapped with the text specific to the language you're building.

Use the !(loc.*VariableName*) syntax in your WiX markup, as follows:

```
<Directory Id="TARGETDIR" Name="SourceDir">
<Directory Id="ProgramFilesFolder">
<Directory Id="INSTALLLOCATION"
          Name="!(loc.InstallDirName)" />
</Directory>
</Directory>
```

Here, we're not setting the name of our install directory in stone. We're using a variable instead and will swap it out with real text at link time. You can then create a .wxl file to store the language-specific value of your variable. One .wxl file for each language. We'll talk more about this later in the book when we discuss localization. For now, it's enough to know that these variables are expanded at link time.

Binder variables

There are a number of binder variables that are predefined for you and that become available just before Light creates the final output. You'll use the !(bind.*VariableName*.*FileID*) syntax to access them.

The following list shows the variables that are available. You'll replace `FileID` with the ID of the `File` element you're trying to get information about. The first two are available to all of the files that you add with the `File` element. The remainder is only available to those that specified the `Assembly` attribute and set it to either `.net` or `win32`.

Variable name	Example
`bind.fileLanguage.FileID`	`!(bind.fileLanguage.MyFile)`
`bind.fileVersion.FileID`	`!(bind.fileVersion.MyFile)`
`bind.assemblyCulture.FileID`	`!(bind.assemblyCulture.MyAssembly)`
`bind.assemblyFileVersion.FileID`	`!(bind.assemblyFileVersion.MyAssembly)`
`bind.assemblyFullName.FileID`	`!(bind.assemblyFullName.MyAssembly)`
`bind.assemblyName.FileID`	`!(bind.assemblyName.MyAssembly)`
`bind.assemblyProcessorArchitecture.FileID`	`!(bind.assemblyProcessorArchitecture.MyAssembly)`
`bind.assemblyPublicKeyToken.FileID`	`! (bind.assemblyPublicKeyToken.MyAssembly)`
`bind.assemblyType.FileID`	`!(bind.assemblyType.MyAssembly)`
`bind.assemblyVersion.FileID`	`!(bind.assemblyVersion.MyAssembly)`

Grabbing information off of incoming files as they're bound into the MSI could be valuable in a number of ways. One potential use is to reference the file version of your software's EXE to set the version of the MSI. So, assuming you have defined a `File` element with an `Id` attribute of `MyApplicationEXE`, given as follows:

```
<Component Id="CMP_MyApplicationEXE"
          Guid="28FC0A8D-3E8A-4414-9413-E12B98DE668E">
    <File Id="MyApplicationEXE" Source="MyApplication.exe" />
</Component>
```

You could use that file's version in the `Product` element's `Version` attribute:

```
<Product Id="*"
         Name="PracticeWix"
         Language="1033"
         Version="!(bind.fileVersion.MyApplicationEXE)"
         Manufacturer="Awesome Company"
         UpgradeCode="3c1789e3-5b3d-4cb5-9c73-a03f2cc09c26">
```

Now the version of the MSI is tied to the version of your software.

Custom linker variables

If you were to look back to *Chapter 6, Adding a User Interface*, where we covered the standard WiX user interfaces, you'd see that we set linker variables to pull in a custom RTF license agreement or to change the images that are shown. These link-time variables are perfect for pulling in a file dynamically, rather than setting it in stone. It is possible to set your own linker variables as well.

There are two ways to define a custom variable: via the command line with the `-d` flag or in your WiX markup with the `WixVariable` element. When using the `-d` flag, you can specify the variable name and its value, separated by an equals sign:

-dmyVariable="some value"

When using the `WixVariable` element, you'll use its `Id` attribute to define its name and its `Value` attribute to define its value:

```
<WixVariable Id="myVariable" Value="my value" />
```

Either way, the variable can be referenced elsewhere in your markup by using the `!(wix.VariableName)` syntax. The following example inserts the value of a variable as the name of a file that's scheduled to be installed.

```
<Component Id="cmp_myFile"
           Guid="8E74ECD6-782F-45e7-9432-6F4FB4E08CED">
   <File Id="file_myFile"
         Source="!(wix.myVariable)"
         KeyPath="yes" />
</Component>
```

You can only set a custom variable in one place. So, you can't set it with both a `WixVariable` element and on the command line. Doing so will cause a link-time error.

Building an installer without Visual Studio

Now that you've been shown Candle and Light, it may help to see a complete example of compiling and linking a WiX project to get an MSI. First off, create a new directory for your project and call it PracticeWix. Next, add a text file to it called InstallMe.txt. This will give us something to install. Then, create a file with the .wxs extension and call it PracticeWix.wxs, as shown in the following screenshot:

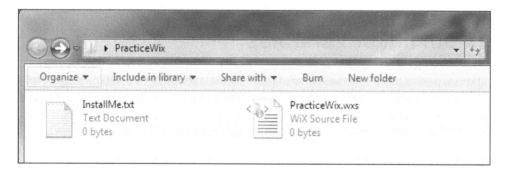

Open PracticeWix.wxs with a text editor such as Notepad and add the following markup. It will install the text file to a directory called PracticeWix. We'll add one of the built-in WiX dialogs too.

```xml
<?xml version="1.0"?>
<Wix xmlns="http://schemas.microsoft.com/wix/2006/wi">
    <Product
        Id="*"
        Name="PracticeWix"
        Language="1033"
        Version="1.0.0.0"
        Manufacturer="Awesome Company"
        UpgradeCode="B9B82C37-34EC-4F50-9D0E-0DF8F06F1F64">

        <Package Compressed="yes" InstallScope="perMachine" />
        <MediaTemplate  EmbedCab="yes" />

        <Directory Id="TARGETDIR" Name="SourceDir">
          <Directory Id="ProgramFilesFolder">
            <Directory Id="INSTALLFOLDER"
                      Name="PracticeWix" />
          </Directory>
```

```
        </Directory>

        <ComponentGroup Id="MainComponents"
                        Directory="INSTALLFOLDER">
            <Component
                Id="CMP_InstallMeTXT"
                Guid="825F0C9A-AACC-4E37-B8A2-30A452EB58F9">

                <File Id="FILE_InstallMeTXT"
                        Source="InstallMe.txt"
                        KeyPath="yes" />
            </Component>
        </ComponentGroup>

        <Feature Id="PracticeWix" Title="PracticeWix" Level="1">
            <ComponentGroupRef Id="MainComponents" />
        </Feature>

        <UIRef Id="WixUI_Minimal" />
    </Product>
</Wix>
```

Now, to compile it, open a command prompt window and navigate to the `PracticeWix` folder. Assuming you've added the WiX `bin` directory to your `PATH` environment variable, the following command will call Candle to build our one `.wxs` file:

candle.exe -v -ext WixUIExtension -out PracticeWix.wixobj PracticeWix.wxs

This will create a new file in the `PracticeWix` folder called `PracticeWix.wixobj`. Next, use Light to turn that into an MSI:

light.exe -v -ext WixUIExtension -out PracticeWix.msi PracticeWix.wixobj

You should see a fairly long output of the linking process, including the ICE validation checks. In the end, this should create the MSI file. Go ahead and double-click on it to launch the installer.

Summary

In this chapter, we discussed the command line tools Candle, the WiX compiler, and Light, the linker/binder. Although Visual Studio uses them for you, you can call them from the command prompt without using Visual Studio at all.

In the next chapter, we'll switch gears and cover something completely different: how to read and write to the Windows Registry at install time.

10

Accessing the Windows Registry

Where to store software configuration settings in Windows has been a moving target for a long time. Although using the registry for this purpose has fallen out of favor, developers lean more towards using XML configuration files in the application's directory or storing them in %APPDATA%, %PROGRAMDATA%, or in Isolated Storage, it's still useful to know the ins and outs of reading and writing to the registry.

Several of the WiX extensions query the registry for an array of data, such as finding the installed version of .NET, and you're bound to run into Windows settings that can only be found in the registry. You might also find it useful to store small amounts of installer-specific data, such as the application's install path.

In this chapter, we'll discuss the following topics:

- Reading data stored in the registry
- Writing to the registry
- Performing miscellaneous tasks in the registry such as setting user permissions for registry keys

Reading from the registry

To read data stored in the registry, you'll use the **RegistrySearch** element. If the value you're looking for exists, it will be saved into a property you'll have placed as a parent element to `RegistrySearch`. Here's an example that looks for the `myValue` value stored in **HKEY_CURRENT_USER\Software\MyCompany** and stores it in a property called `REGISTRY_RESULT`. Whichever property you decide to use, make sure that it is public (uppercase). An example is as follows:

```
<Property Id="REGISTRY_RESULT">
    <RegistrySearch Id="MyRegistrySearch"
                    Root="HKCU"
                    Key="Software\MyCompany"
                    Name="myValue"
                    Type="raw" />
</Property>
```

By placing the `RegistrySearch` element inside of a `Property` element we're saying that we want the registry value to be stored in that property. The attributes on the `RegistrySearch` element mostly tell Windows Installer where to look for the value. The `Id` attribute gives the search a unique identity in the MSI database and can be set to whatever you like.

The `Root` attribute sets which top-level node, or *hive*, in the registry to look under. Your options are described in the following table:

Set Root to	Stands for	Description
HKLM	**HKEY_LOCAL_MACHINE**	Contains data used to support the operating system and settings for installed software that is accessible by all users
HKCR	**HKEY_CLASSES_ROOT**	Provides information regarding registered COM objects, mostly for backwards compatibility with 16-bit systems
HCKU	**HKEY_CURRENT_USER**	Gives a view of the currently logged-on user's profile settings as well as software configuration specific to that user
HKU	**HKEY_USERS**	Stores profile and software settings for all active users

The **Key** attribute sets what registry key to look for and **Name** sets the value to read inside that key. So, in the last example, we want to read the myValue value in the MyCompany key. The **Type** attribute tells the installer what sort of data is stored in myValue. Most of the time, you'll set this to raw.

Setting Type to raw, as opposed to file or directory, which we'll discuss next, means that the data you get back will contain extra characters to help you distinguish what kind of data it is. If you've worked with the registry before, you know that there are several types of data you can store: DWORD, REG_BINARY, REG_SZ, and so on. The following is a table that explains the special characters that are added to the value once you've retrieved it:

Type of data	Characters added to value
DWORD	A # sign is added to the beginning, which may be followed by a + or -.
REG_BINARY	A #x is added to the beginning and each hexadecimal digit is shown as an ASCII character prefixed with another #x.
REG_EXPAND_SZ	A #% is added to the beginning.
REG_MULTI_SZ	A [~] is added to the beginning.
REG_SZ	No extra characters are added. Any # signs in the value, however, will be escaped by turning them into two # signs.

Setting Type to either file or directory is used when what is stored in the value is the path to a file or directory on the local machine. Use this when you want to check if that file or directory actually exists. For example, this would check if the file path stored in pathToFile really exists:

```
<Property Id="MY_PROPERTY">
    <RegistrySearch Id="myRegSearch"
                    Root="HKLM"
                    Key="Software\WIXTEST"
                    Name="PathToFile"
                    Type="file">

        <FileSearch Id="myFileSearch" Name="[MY_PROPERTY]" />
    </RegistrySearch>
</Property>
```

If the path doesn't exist, the property won't be set. Notice that we have to add a `FileSearch` element to do the checking. Simply set its `Name` attribute to the `Id` attribute of your property surrounded by brackets. You can also check if a directory exists, as in the next example, by setting `Type` to `directory` and adding a `DirectorySearch` element:

```
<Property Id="MY_PROPERTY">
    <RegistrySearch Id="myRegSearch"
                    Root="HKLM"
                    Key="Software\WIXTEST"
                    Name="PathToDirectory"
                    Type="directory">

        <DirectorySearch Id="myDirSearch"
                         Path="[MY_PROPERTY]" />
    </RegistrySearch>
</Property>
```

Here, if the directory can't be found the property MY_PROPERTY won't be set.

Another attribute that you can add to the `RegistrySearch` element is `Win64`. When set to `yes`, your installer will read from the 64-bit portion of the registry on a 64-bit system. Most of the time, WiX handles this for you, setting this flag if you've built your project to target a 64-bit platform. Setting it manually allows you to explicitly choose where to search. For example, you may set it to `no` to search the 32-bit portion on a 64-bit system. The 32-bit registry is located in the **Wow6432Node** found at **HKEY_LOCAL_MACHINE\SOFTWARE\Wow6432Node** and **HKEY_CURRENT_USER\Software\Wow6432Node**.

Writing to the registry

To write to the registry, you'll use the `RegistryValue` element by itself or paired with a `RegistryKey` element. By itself, `RegistryValue` can perform simple writes. Writing multiple things to the same place is easier when you use `RegistryKey`. We'll discuss both of these in the next sections. Writing occurs during the deferred stage of the Execute sequence during an action called `WriteRegistryValues`.

Writing a single value

Writing to the registry is sort of like installing something on the end user's computer. So, you'll have to place your RegistryValue element inside a Component element. This is actually a good thing as it gives you the opportunity to set component-level conditions to enable or disable the writing. You could use this to only record to the registry if a certain condition is met. Refer back to *Chapter 4, Improving Control with Launch Conditions and Installed States*, for a discussion on component-level conditions.

Just like when you're installing a file, you must mark something inside the component as the KeyPath item. In this case, we can mark RegistryValue itself. Here's an example that writes to a value called myValue in the **HKLM\Software\ WixTest\Test** key:

```
<ComponentGroup Id="RegistryComponents"
                Directory="INSTALLLOCATION">

    <Component Id="CMP_WriteToRegistry"
               Guid="DA01C245-8633-4147-92F0-C063003DB493">

        <RegistryValue Id="myRegistryValue"
                    KeyPath="yes"
                    Action="write"
                    Root="HKLM"
                    Key="Software\WixTest\Test"
                    Name="myValue"
                    Value="my value"
                    Type="string" />
    </Component>
</ComponentGroup>
```

Because the element is packaged inside a Component element, it will be removed for us during an uninstall, freeing us from that responsibility. The RegistryValue element's Id attribute simply serves to uniquely identify it in the MSI database. We use the KeyPath attribute to mark it as the keypath for the component.

The Action attribute can take one of three values: append, prepend, or write. You'd use append or prepend when the type of data you're storing is REG_MULTI_SZ and you aren't creating a new value, but rather updating an existing one. REG_MULTI_SZ is a type that contains multiple items of data in a single value. If you use either of these and there isn't an existing value, one will be created. Setting Action to write tells the installer to overwrite any existing value or to otherwise create a new one.

The `Root`, `Key`, and `Name` attributes set the path in the registry to write to. `Root` can be set to any of the values available to `RegistrySearch` with one addition—`HKMU`. This is a registry hive that's only related to installs. It means that if this is a per-user install, the value will be written under `HKEY_CURRENT_USER`. If it's a per-machine install it will be written under `HKEY_LOCAL_MACHINE`.

Set the `Value` attribute to the data to store in the specified registry value. You'll establish what type of data it is with the `Type` attribute, which can be one of the following:

- `string`: This means a `REG_SZ` type
- `integer`: This means a `REG_DWORD` type
- `binary`: This means a `REG_BINARY` type
- `expandable`: This means a `REG_EXPAND_SZ` type
- `multiString`: This means a `REG_MULTI_SZ` type

When writing more than one value to the same registry key, it's easier to use the `RegistryKey` element, which we'll cover in the next section.

Writing multiple values

With the `RegistryKey` element, you can set the key you want to write to once, and then nest several `RegistryValue` elements inside. Use its `Root` and `Key` attributes to set the key, as in this example:

```
<Component ...>
   <RegistryKey Root="HKCU"
                Key="Software\MyCompany">
      <RegistryValue Name="myValue"
                     Action="write"
                     Value="myValue"
                     Type="string"
                     KeyPath="yes" />

      <!--Other RegistryValues under the same key-->
   </RegistryKey>
</Component>
```

Here, we've set the `RegistryKey` element to write to the `HKCU\Software\MyCompany` key. The child `RegistryValue` element specifies what to set the `myValue` value to. Now, to write to more values in the same key simply add more `RegistryValue` elements. Notice that we've set the `RegistryValue` element in the previous example as the `KeyPath` item. If you add more values, you should set their `KeyPath` attributes to `no`. Also notice that neither element requires an `Id` attribute.

The `RegistryKey` element has two other optional attributes: `ForceDeleteOnUninstall` and `ForceCreateOnInstall`. By setting `ForceDeleteOnUninstall` to `yes`, during an uninstall not only will the values you've written *during* the install be removed—which is the behavior you get just for having your `RegistryKey` inside a `Component` element—but also all other sub keys that are children to that key. This is probably not the desired behavior in most cases, but might come in handy under special circumstances, such as when your software has added keys that you'd like to remove at uninstall time. The following is an example:

```
<Component ...>
   <RegistryKey Root="HKCU"
                Key="Software\MyCompany"
                ForceDeleteOnUninstall="yes">
      <RegistryValue Name="myValue"
                     Action="write"
                     Value="myValue"
                     Type="string"
                     KeyPath="yes" />
   </RegistryKey>
</Component>
```

The `ForceCreateOnInstall` attribute allows you to create an empty key without any values. Without it, the installer won't create the key. It can be a little tricky getting this to work if you're targeting the `HKCU` hive. This is because of the ICE38 validation test that checks that you've marked a registry value as the keypath. In our case, we don't want to create any values. One solution is to nest the key under another key that does have a `RegistryValue` marked as the keypath, as in the following example:

```
<ComponentGroup Id="RegistryComponents"
                Directory="PersonalFolder">

   <Component Id="CMP_RegistryWrite"
              Guid="3BF28DC8-4AFC-43E8-B605-AA6456B06921">
      <RegistryKey Root="HKCU"
                   Key="Software\MyCompany">
         <RegistryValue Type="string"
                        Action="write"
```

```
                                 Name="myValue"
                                 Value="123"
                                 KeyPath="yes" />


            <RegistryKey Key="Subkey1"
                              ForceCreateOnInstall="yes" />
         </RegistryKey>

      </Component>
   </ComponentGroup>
```

Another use for `RegistryKey` is to set a REG_MULTI_SZ value. Remember that this type of value can hold multiple items of data. This technique looks just like the last example except that the `Name` attribute of each `RegistryValue` element stays the same to signify that they're writing data to the same place. Here's an example that writes two values to `myValue`:

```
<Component ... >
   <RegistryKey Root="HKLM"
                   Key="SOFTWARE\MyCompany">

      <RegistryValue Id="myRegistryValue"
                    Name="myValue"
                    Value="first value"
                    Type="multiString"
                    KeyPath="yes" />

      <RegistryValue Id="myRegistryValue2"
                    Name="myValue"
                    Action="append"
                    Value="second value"
                    Type="multiString"
                    KeyPath="no" />
   </RegistryKey>
</Component>
```

In this example, both `RegistryValue` elements have their `Type` attributes set to `multiString` to show that they are writing to a REG_MULTI_SZ value. Notice that the second one has an `Action` attribute of `append`. You could set this on both the elements, but for the first it isn't necessary. You can also use `prepend` to add a string to the beginning of the value.

Setting NeverOverwrite

When writing to the registry, you have the option of specifying that you only want to create the key or value if it doesn't already exist. For this, you'll add the `NeverOverwrite` attribute to the parent `Component` element. The next example only adds the registry value `myValue` if it doesn't exist:

```
<Component Id="CMP_regvalue"
           Guid="7088AC98-898E-4FB4-98A6-6549AD3495E8"
           NeverOverwrite="yes">

    <RegistryValue Root="HKLM"
                   Key="Software\MyCompany"
                   Name="myValue"
                   Value="a new value"
                   Type="string"
                   Action="write"
                   KeyPath="yes"/>
</Component>
```

Removing registry values

When it comes to uninstalling your product, you don't need to worry too much about the registry keys you've created. Windows Installer will make sure that all components, including registry keys, are cleaned up. However, in case you want to remove items from the registry that you didn't create—perhaps they were created by one of your other products—WiX provides a way to do it.

Two elements are used to remove data from the registry: `RemoveRegistryKey` and `RemoveRegistryValue`. We'll cover both in the following sections.

Remove all keys recursively

You'll use the `RemoveRegistryKey` element when you want to remove a key from the registry and all of its sub keys. It must be placed inside a `Component` element, as in this example:

```
<ComponentGroup Id="RegistryComponents"
                Directory="INSTALLLOCATION">

    <Component Id="CMP_RemoveRegistryKey"
               Guid="3B0C6FD9-D73A-4CE9-8053-BBBB2BE8716B"
               KeyPath="yes">
        <RemoveRegistryKey Id="MyRemoveRegistryKey"
```

```
                              Root="HKLM"
                              Key="Software\WixTest\myKey"
                              Action="removeOnInstall" />

        </Component>
    </ComponentGroup>
```

Here, the `Component` element is marked as the keypath since you cannot do this with the `RemoveRegistryKey` element. The `RemoveRegistryKey` element's `Id` attribute sets the unique key for this entry in the MSI database. `Root` specifies the hive where the key we're removing is located and `Key` lists the path to it. You can, via the `Action` attribute, specify when to remove this key. It can be set to either `removeOnInstall` or `removeOnUninstall`.

Removing a single value

Whereas `RemoveRegistryKey` removes a key and all of its sub keys, the `RemoveRegistryValue` element is more targeted. It allows you to remove a specific value inside a particular key. It should be placed inside a `Component` element, as in the following code snippet:

```
<ComponentGroup Id="RegistryComponents"
                Directory="INSTALLLOCATION">

    <Component Id="CMP_RemoveRegistryValue"
               Guid="A07AEF74-C9A9-4D61-8852-A4EC3F9E13F9"
               KeyPath="yes">
        <RemoveRegistryValue Id="MyRemoveRegistryValue"
                             Root="HKLM"
                             Key="Software\WixTest\MyKey"
                             Name="myValue" />
    </Component>
</ComponentGroup>
```

The syntax of `RemoveRegistryValue` is very similar to `RemoveRegistryKey` except that it adds a `Name` attribute to specify the value to remove from the key. Notice that there's no `Action` attribute because you don't have the option of removing a value during an uninstall.

Copying registry values

WiX doesn't provide a specific element for copying data from one registry value
to another. However, you can accomplish this task by pairing a `RegistrySearch`
element with `RegistryValue`. First, you'll store the value in a property by using a
`RegistrySearch` element. Then, you'll reference that property in the `Value` attribute
of the `RegistryValue` element. Here's an example:

```
<Property Id="MY_REG_VALUE">
    <RegistrySearch Id="MyRegistrySearch"
                    Root="HKLM"
                    Key="Software\MyCompany\MyKey"
                    Name="MyDWORDValue"
                    Type="raw" />
</Property>

<ComponentGroup Id="RegistryComponents"
                Directory="INSTALLLOCATION">

    <Component Id="CMP_CopyRegValue"
               Guid="747965AA-90F4-4262-BE55-3C1F4F7F65B4">
        <RegistryValue Id="MyRegistryValue"
                       KeyPath="yes"
                       Root="HKLM"
                       Key="Software\MyCompany\MyKey"
                       Name="MyCopiedValue"
                       Value="[MY_REG_VALUE]"
                       Action="write"
                       Type="string" />
    </Component>
</ComponentGroup>
```

The first thing we did was use a `RegistrySearch` element to look up `MyDWORDValue`
stored in the `HKLM\Software\MyCompany\MyKey` key. Its value is then stored in a
property called `MY_REG_VALUE`.

Next, we create a new component and add a `RegistryValue` element to it. It
specifies that it will create a new registry value under the same key as the original,
but called `MyCopiedValue`. We set its value with the `Value` attribute, which
references the `MY_REG_VALUE` property in square brackets.

Notice that we can set the `Type` to `string` here even though the value we're copying is actually of type `DWORD`. Because the value stored in the property is retrieved using the `raw` type, it will contain special characters to denote its data type. When we copy it to our new value, Windows will infer the data type by this. So, in essence, it doesn't matter what you put for the `RegistryValue` element's `Type` attribute. Windows can figure out on its own what type it should be.

Registry permissions

Every key in the registry has a set of permissions saved to it that affects which users can read or write to it. You can see this in the Registry Editor by going to **Run | regedit**, right-clicking on a key, and selecting **Permissions**. WiX allows you to change these permissions with its `PermissionEx` element.

`PermissionEx` isn't in the default WiX namespace, but rather in `WixUtilExtension`. So, you'll need to add a reference in your project to `WixUtilExtension`, found in the WiX `bin` directory, and add the `UtilExtension` namespace to your `Wix` element. Here's the updated `Wix` element:

```
<Wixxmlns="http://schemas.microsoft.com/wix/2006/wi"
xmlns:util="http://schemas.microsoft.com/wix/UtilExtension">
```

We've assigned the `UtilExtension` namespace to the prefix `util`. Now, when we create a registry key with a `RegistryKey` element, we'll nest a `PermissionEx` element inside it to set its permissions. The next example sets the permissions of a key called `MyKey` so that a user named `nickramirez` has all permissions to it:

```
<DirectoryRef Id="INSTALLLOCATION">
    <Component Id="CMP_WriteToRegistry"
               Guid="DA01C245-8633-4147-92F0-C063003DB493">

        <RegistryKey Id="MyRegistryKey"
                     Root="HKLM"
                     Key="Software\MyCompany\MyKey">

            <RegistryValue ... />

            <util:PermissionEx User="nickramirez"
                               GenericAll="yes" />
        </RegistryKey>
    </Component>
</DirectoryRef>
```

Use the `User` attribute to set the name of the Windows user account to apply permissions to the account. We've given them the `GenericAll` permission. The following table lists all of your options:

Attribute	As seen on the key	What it does
GenericAll	Full Control	Gives user all permissions.
GenericRead	Read	Grants `QueryValue`, `EnumerateSubkeys`, `Notify`, and `ReadControl`. Must have at least one other permission specified.
GenericExecute	n/a	Same privileges as `GenericRead`, but it can be specified alone.
GenericWrite	n/a	Grants `SetValue`, `CreateSubkey`, and `ReadControl`.
ChangePermission	Write DAC	Allows the user to read the discretionary access control list for the key.
CreateLink	Create Link	Allows the user to create symbolic links to the key.
CreateSubkeys	Create Sub key	Allows the user to create new sub keys inside the key.
Delete	Delete	Allows the user to delete the key.
EnumerateSubkeys	Enumerate Sub keys	Allows the user to identify all of the sub keys in the key.
Notify	Notify	Allows the user to receive an audit message about the key.
Read	Query Value	Allows the user to read the values in the registry key.
ReadPermission	Read Control	Allows the user to read the information in the key's **access control list** (ACL).
Synchronize	n/a	Sets whether to wait to access the key until another thread has finished accessing it.
TakeOwnership	Write Owner	Makes the user the owner of the key.
Write	Set Value	Allows the user to set the values of the registry key.

You can nest several `PermissionEx` elements inside a single `RegistryKey` element to set access levels for various users. Be sure not to be so restrictive that no user has enough rights to remove the key. That would cause problems during an uninstall. You can also nest a `PermissionEx` element inside a `RegistryValue` element to apply rights to that value's parent key.

Summary

In this chapter, we discussed how to read from and write to the Windows Registry at install time. Reading stores a value from the registry in a Windows Installer property that you can then use elsewhere in your markup. Writing is done with the `RegistryKey` and `RegistryValue` elements. The former is used for writing multiple values and the latter for writing a single value. You have the option of setting permissions on these values and specifying whether or not to remove existing keys that weren't included in your MSI.

In the next chapter, we'll cover how to interact with Windows services. WiX gives you the capability to create, start, stop, and remove services. We'll also see how to configure a service's user account and recovery options.

11
Controlling Windows Services

A Windows service is an application that runs continuously in the background and doesn't interact with the user of the computer. They typically start up when the computer is booted. You can see a list of installed services in Windows 7 by navigating in your Start menu to **Control Panel | Administrative Tools | Services**, or by selecting **Run** from your Start menu and entering `services.msc`.

During an installation, your MSI package may need to interact with services that already exist on the end user's computer or even install and configure its own. In this chapter, we'll cover the WiX elements that allow you to do this. Specifically, we'll cover the following topics:

- Creating a simple Windows service
- Registering and configuring services with the `sc.exe` utility
- Installing a service with the `ServiceInstall` element
- Using `ServiceControl` to start, stop, and remove a service
- Setting a user account, dependencies, and recovery options

Creating a simple Windows service

A Windows service always maps back to an executable file that's stored on the local hard drive. Although that executable could host a sophisticated program such as a Windows Communication Foundation service, here we'll create one that's much simpler. Our service will simply write to a log file periodically.

Visual Studio provides a project template for creating a Windows service. Go to **File | New | Project | Windows | Windows Service**.

Once you've created this new project, right-click on the Service1.cs file in the **SolutionExplorer** and select **ViewCode**. The C# code that you'll see displays a class, here named Service1, that is derived from System.ServiceProcess.ServiceBase. It overrides the OnStart and OnStop methods.

These are the methods that every Windows service must implement so that they can be started and stopped by the **Service Control Manager (SCM)**. The SCM is a process that tracks which services are installed and monitors their individual status. Later on, we'll cover how to issue some basic commands to the SCM from the command line.

The following code in Service1.cs adds the functionality necessary to write to a log file every five seconds:

```
namespace WindowsService1
{
    using System;
    using System.IO;
    using System.ServiceProcess;
```

```csharp
using System.Threading;

public partial class Service1 : ServiceBase
{
    private Thread thread;
    private bool threadActive;

    public Service1()
    {
        InitializeComponent();
    }

    protected override void OnStart(string[] args)
    {
        this.threadActive = true;
        ThreadStart job = new ThreadStart(this.WriteToLog);
        this.thread = new Thread(job);
        this.thread.Start();
    }

    protected override void OnStop()
    {
        this.threadActive = false;
        this.thread.Join();
    }

    protected void WriteToLog()
    {
        string appDataDir = Environment.GetFolderPath(
            Environment.SpecialFolder.CommonApplicationData);

        string logDir = Path.Combine(appDataDir,
            "TestInstallerLogs");

        string logFile = Path.Combine(logDir,
            "serviceLog.txt");

        while (this.threadActive)
            {
            if (!Directory.Exists(logDir))
            {
                Directory.CreateDirectory(logDir);
```

```
            }

            using (var sw = new StreamWriter(logFile, true))
            {
                sw.WriteLine("Log entry at {0}", DateTime.Now);
            }

            Thread.Sleep(5000);
        }
      }
    }
}
```

As you can see, we spin up a new thread in the OnStart method. This begins the writing to a file called serviceLog.txt under the C:\ProgramData\ TestInstallerLogs directory. An easy way to get to that directory in the Windows file explorer is to enter the %PROGRAMDATA% environment variable into the explorer's address bar. The OnStop method sets a Boolean value to wind down the worker thread, and then joins it to the main thread. A private method called WriteToLog handles the actual logic. We separate the job into its own thread so that the service can start in a timely manner without getting hung up.

Compile the project to get the executable file for our service. Next, we'll see how to use the SCM to register and configure it.

Using sc.exe

To communicate with the Service Control Manager, you can use a command-line tool called **sc.exe**. Note that you ought to be logged in as an administrator before running this utility. To register our executable as a service, we'll use its create command. Every service gets a behind-the-scenes short name such as testsvc. Specify the new name as the first parameter to create. The binPath parameter sets the path to the executable. Be sure that the equal sign has no spaces before it and one after it. Follow this convention with all sc.exe parameters that use an equal sign.

```
sc create testsvc binPath= "C:\WindowsService1.exe"
```

 On Windows 8, this requirement of having a space after the equals sign has been removed.

After running this command, you'll see the new service in the services management console (`services.msc`) among the other installed services. Yours will show up as `testsvc`. It won't be started yet for you. You'll have to start it manually, either through the services management console or with the `sc.exe` tool's `start` command.

```
sc start testsvc
```

You'll always have to start your service the first time. However, you can change how it starts from then on. For example, you could have it start up each time the computer is turned on. To do that, add the `start` argument to the `create` command, as shown in the following code snippet:

```
sc create testsvc binPath= "C:\WindowsService1.exe" start= auto
```

The following table lists the possible values for the start argument:

Start value	Meaning
demand	This is the default argument. Service must be started manually.
auto	Starts the service each time the computer is restarted.
boot	Mostly used for device drivers. Starts the service at boot time.
system	Mostly used for device drivers. Starts the service at kernel initialization.
disabled	The service cannot be started.

Something more that the `create` command can do is set a more user-friendly name to be displayed in the services management console. So, if you'd rather have users see "Test Service" instead of `testsvc`, you can add the `DisplayName` argument to the `create` command.

```
sc create testsvc binPath= "C:\WindowsService1.exe" start= auto
DisplayName= "Test Service"
```

If you need to stop the service, you can use the `stop` command. Here is an example:

```
sc stop testsvc
```

To delete the service, use the `delete` command:

```
sc delete testsvc
```

Notice that even if you've assigned the service a display name, you still have to reference the `testsvc` name when issuing commands. You can find the service name of any installed service by right-clicking on it in the services management console and selecting **Properties**. You can also find it with `sc.exe`'s `GetKeyName` command which takes the `DisplayName` as a value and returns the service name, among other information. The following example looks up the service name for the `Test Service` service, returning the result `testsvc`.

```
sc GetKeyName "Test Service"
```

Something else to look at is how to set dependencies for your services. You'd use this if your service required other services to be running before it could be started. As an example, suppose `testsvc` couldn't start unless `dependencySvc` was already running. You could specify that by adding the `depend` argument:

```
sc create testsvc binPath= "C:\WindowsService1.exe" depend= dependencySvc
```

You can specify more than one dependency by separating each name with a forward slash (/). Windows will make sure that each service is started up in the correct order if it depends upon another.

One final thing to look at is setting the error logging level of your service. By default, this is set to `normal`, meaning that when the computer is powered on, if there is an error while trying to start the service, it will be logged and a message box will be displayed to the user. You may decide to change this to either `ignore`, in which case the error is logged but the user doesn't see a message box, or `critical`, meaning that if the service can't be started, the computer will try to restart with the last known good configuration. This is set with the `create` command's `error` argument.

```
sc create testsvc binPath= "C:\WindowsService1.exe" error= ignore
```

Using WiX to install a service

Now that you know how to install a service from the command line, let's look at how to do it with an installer. WiX has an element called **ServiceInstall** that you can use to add a new service to the services management console. This assumes that you've already created the executable file that will become the end point for your service, as discussed earlier.

First of all, we'll use the familiar `Component` and `File` elements to install the `.exe` to the `install` directory on the target machine. Add the following code to your WiX project:

```
<DirectoryRef Id="INSTALLFOLDER">
   <Component
       Id="CMP_WindowsService1"
       Guid="3D3DE5C1-7154-4c61-9816-248A85F6DEBF">

       <File
           Id="WindowsService1.exe"
           Name="WindowsService1.exe"
           KeyPath="yes"
           Source=".\WindowsService1.exe" />
   </Component>
</DirectoryRef>
```

Next, add a `ServiceInstall` element to the same component to register the `WindowsService1.exe` file as a service. Notice that a lot of the functionality from `sc.exe` is present here, such as setting `DisplayName`, the startup type, and error logging level. Each of the attributes shown is required except for `DisplayName`:

```
<DirectoryRef Id="INSTALLFOLDER">
   <Component
       Id="CMP_WindowsService1"
       Guid="3D3DE5C1-7154-4c61-9816-248A85F6DEBF">

       <File
           Id="WindowsService1.exe"
           Name="WindowsService1.exe"
           KeyPath="yes"
           Source=".\WindowsService1.exe" />

       <ServiceInstall
           Id="InstallWindowsService1"
           Name="testsvc"
           DisplayName="Test Service"
           Start="auto"
           ErrorControl="normal"
           Type="ownProcess" />
   </Component>
</DirectoryRef>
```

When `Type` is set to `ownProcess`, it means that the service will execute in its own Windows process. When set to `shareProcess`, it can be grouped into the same process as other services running in the same executable. If you choose `shareProcess`, then if even one of the services in the process fails, all of the services in that process will fail. It is safer to separate services into their own processes, if possible. Of course, that may be up to the team writing the service.

There are several other optional attributes available, some of which we'll discuss in more detail later in the chapter. They are as follows:

Attribute name	Description
Arguments	Specify any command-line arguments required to run the service.
Account	The account under which to start the service, valid only when `ServiceType` is `ownProcess`.
Password	The password for the account, valid only when the account has a password.
Description	The text that will be under the `Description` label for your service in the services management console.
Vital	Either `yes` or `no`, the overall installation should fail if this service can't be installed.
LoadOrderGroup	A group of services that your service can join (or create) to be started when the computer starts up.

Be aware that the `ServiceInstall` element behaves a bit differently than other WiX elements in that it won't automatically remove your Windows service during an uninstall. That task, along with sending start and stop messages, is handled by the `ServiceControl` element, which we'll discuss in the following section.

Starting, stopping, and uninstalling a service

The `ServiceInstall` element works well for installing a service, but doesn't provide a way to start, stop, or uninstall one. For that, you'll use the `ServiceControl` element. It can be added to the same component as the `ServiceInstall` element thereby sending signals to the `testsvc` test service you're installing.

The following example starts the service during install and stops and removes it during uninstall. These actions happen during the deferred stage of the Execute sequence:

```
<DirectoryRef Id="INSTALLFOLDER">
    <Component ... >

        <File ... />

        <ServiceInstall ... />

        <ServiceControl
            Id="sc_WindowsService1"
            Name="testsvc"
            Start="install"
            Stop="both"
            Remove="uninstall"
            Wait="yes" />
    </Component>
</DirectoryRef>
```

The Name attribute specifies the service that you want to control. Start, Stop, and Remove can each be set to one of the following values: install, uninstall, or both. In this example, we've set Stop to both so that if our service is already installed (from a previous install), we'll stop it before installing the new version and starting it up again. It is essential that you set the Remove attribute or else the service won't be removed during an uninstall.

WiX schedules these actions during the Execute sequence in the following order:

- StopServices
- DeleteServices
- RemoveFiles
- InstallFiles
- InstallServices
- StartServices

Notice that other actions that deal with installing and removing files are performed after services have been stopped and deleted, and before services are installed and started. That way, those processes are freed up before the underlying executable files are modified.

Getting back to the previous example, the Wait attribute tells the installer whether it should pause and wait for each action to complete before moving on. If the rest of your install depends on your service being in a certain state, then you should set Wait to yes. Setting Wait to yes will also cause the installer to show a message box to the user asking whether they'd like or retry to cancel if the service can't be started:

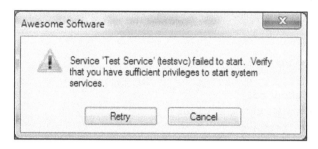

The ServiceControl element isn't limited to sending signals to services you're installing. It can do the same for any service that's installed on the end user's computer. All you have to do is change the Name attribute. For example, if we wanted to stop the DHCP Client service (named Dhcp) before installing files and start it up again afterwards, we could do so by adding a ServiceControl element with a Name attribute of Dhcp:

```
<Directory ... >
    <Component ... >
        <File ... />

        <ServiceControl
            Id="startAndStopDhcp"
            Name="Dhcp"
            Start="both"
            Stop="both"
            Wait="yes" />
    </Component>
</Directory>
```

Notice that we don't have to include a ServiceInstall element to use ServiceControl. Also, ServiceControl here doesn't use the Remove attribute, which tells the installer when to uninstall the service. We should leave the DHCP Client service after our application has been uninstalled.

Setting the service's user account

Ordinarily, when you install a service, it runs under the **LocalSystem** account. You can see this by opening the services management console, right-clicking on a service, selecting **Properties**, and choosing **Log On** tab. LocalSystem is a special account used by the SCM that gives wide-ranging privileges to interact with the computer. If you'd like to give your service more limited access, you can assign it to another user account.

Two accounts that you might consider are **LocalService** and **NetworkService**. These accounts have fewer privileges than LocalSystem, but are still built-in and ready to use. To set a new user account for your service, add the Account and Password attributes to ServiceInstall. If the account doesn't have a password, which is the case with LocalService and NetworkService, you can omit the Password attribute. Here's an example:

```
<DirectoryRef Id="INSTALLFOLDER">
    <Component
        Id="CMP_WindowsService1"
        Guid="3D3DE5C1-7154-4c61-9816-248A85F6DEBF">

        <File
            Id="WindowsService1.exe"
            Name="WindowsService1.exe"
            KeyPath="yes"
            Source=".\WindowsService1.exe" />

        <ServiceInstall
            Id="InstallWindowsService1"
            Name="testsvc"
            DisplayName="Test Service"
            Description="Test service for WiX"
            Start="auto"
            ErrorControl="normal"
            Type="ownProcess"
            Account="NT AUTHORITY\LocalService" />

        <ServiceControl
            Id="sc_WindowsService1"
            Name="testsvc"
            Start="install"
            Stop="both"
            Remove="uninstall"
            Wait="yes" />
    </Component>
</DirectoryRef>
```

We've added the `Account` attribute to the `ServiceInstall` element and set it to `NT AUTHORITY\LocalService`. You'll be able to see this after installing the MSI by opening the services management console, right-clicking on the new service, selecting **Properties**, and clicking on the **Log On** tab, as shown in the following screenshot:

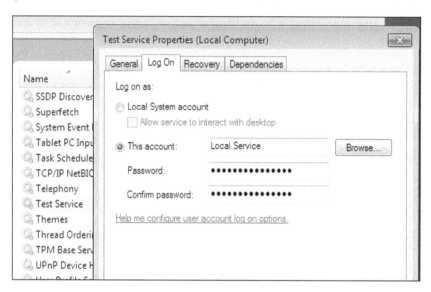

Hardcoding `NT AUTHORITY\LocalService` or `NT AUTHORITY\NetworkService` won't work on non-English operating systems, as the names won't translate. So, you should instead use WiX properties that will be translated into the proper user account names at install time. `WixUtilExtension` offers these properties. You can find a list at `http://wix.sourceforge.net/manual-wix3/osinfo.htm`.

Here's an example that uses the `WIX_ACCOUNT_LOCALSERVICE` property in place of `NT AUTHORITY\LocalService`. You must first add a `PropertyRef` element to reference the property in your project:

```
<PropertyRef Id="WIX_ACCOUNT_LOCALSERVICE"/>

<DirectoryRef Id="INSTALLFOLDER">
    <Component ...>
        <File ... />

        <ServiceInstall
            Id="InstallWindowsService1"
            Name="testsvc"
            DisplayName="Test Service"
            Description="Test service for WiX"
```

```
                Start="auto"
                ErrorControl="normal"
                Type="ownProcess"
                Account="[WIX_ACCOUNT_LOCALSERVICE]" />

        <ServiceControl ... />
    </Component>
</DirectoryRef>
```

You can also set the account to a local user or domain user. Be sure to always include the domain name or computer name, such as `DomainName\UserName`. For the next example, we'll create a new user during the course of the install and then assign that account to the service.

To create a new local user, use the `User` element from `WixUtilExtension`. After adding a reference in your project to `WixUtilExtension.dll`, add the following namespace to your `Wix` element:

```
<Wix xmlns="http://schemas.microsoft.com/wix/2006/wi"
    xmlns:util="http://schemas.microsoft.com/wix/UtilExtension"
  >
```

Now, you can use the `User` element in your markup. This new component will add `JoeUser` as a local user account:

```
<Property Id="MY_PASSWORD" Hidden="yes" Value="password" />

<DirectoryRef Id="INSTALLFOLDER">
    <Component
        Id="CMP_NewUser"
        Guid="29019429-AA87-401C-AF87-5BA4798EE6F1"
        KeyPath="yes">

        <util:User
            Id="addNewUser"
            LogonAsService="yes"
            CreateUser="yes"
            Name="JoeUser"
            UpdateIfExists="yes"
            Password="[MY_PASSWORD]"
            PasswordNeverExpires="yes"
            RemoveOnUninstall="yes" />
    </Component>
</DirectoryRef>
```

In order to create a Windows service that starts automatically, the assigned user account must have the *Logon as a Service* right from the computer's local security policy. You can give the new account this by setting the `User` element's `LogonAsService` attribute to `yes`. Without this, the system won't be able to log in as the account and an error will occur. You can check permission-related errors in the Windows event log.

The `CreateUser` attribute tells the installer to create this user account if it doesn't exist. `Name` sets the account's name. `UpdateIfExists` tells the installer to only update the account's settings if it *does* already exist. For example, if the account exists but does not have the *Logon as a Service* permission, it will be updated to have it. `Password` sets the password for the account. Here, we're using a hardcoded property, but in practice you'd probably gets its value from the user. The `PasswordNeverExpires` attribute prevents the password from ever expiring and `RemoveOnUninstall` ensures that the account will be deleted when the product is uninstalled.

Now, we can use this account in the `ServiceInstall` element:

```
<DirectoryRef Id="INSTALLFOLDER">
    <Component
        Id="CMP_WindowsService1"
        Guid="3D3DE5C1-7154-4c61-9816-248A85F6DEBF">

        <File
            Id="WindowsService1.exe"
            Name="WindowsService1.exe"
            KeyPath="yes"
            Source=".\WindowsService1.exe" />

        <ServiceInstall
            Id="InstallWindowsService1"
            Name="testsvc"
            DisplayName="Test Service"
            Description="Test service for WiX"
            Start="auto"
            ErrorControl="normal"
            Type="ownProcess"
            Account=".\JoeUser"
            Password=[MY_PASSWORD] />

        <ServiceControl
            Id="sc_WindowsService1"
            Name="testsvc"
            Start="install"
```

```
            Stop="both"
            Remove="uninstall"
            Wait="yes" />
    </Component>
</DirectoryRef>
```

You can use `.\` before the account name to reference the local computer name, if you don't know it. You can also specify a domain account here by prefixing the name with the domain name. You should also know that a local user account can only start a service if the `ServiceInstall` element has an `Interactive` attribute set to `no`, which is the default, and a `Type` set to `ownProcess`.

Adding service dependencies

If your service requires that other services be started before it can function properly, you can use the `ServiceDependency` element to add those services as dependencies. You'll place it inside the `ServiceInstall` element. Here's an example that states that the DNS Client service, named `Dnscache`, must be started before starting our Test Service:

```
<ServiceInstall
    Id="InstallWindowsService1"
    Name="testsvc"
    DisplayName="Test Service"
    Description="Test service for WiX"
    Start="auto"
    ErrorControl="normal"
    Type="ownProcess">

    <ServiceDependency Id="Dnscache" />
</ServiceInstall>
```

The `ServiceDependency` element's `Id` attribute sets the name of the service to depend on. Now, Windows will make sure that the DNS Client service is started before the Test Service. You can add more `ServiceDependency` elements for additional dependencies.

You can also set Id to the Name attribute of another ServiceInstall element. That way, if you're installing two services, you can specify that one should be started before the other. Here's an example:

```
<DirectoryRef Id="INSTALLFOLDER">
    <Component ... >
        <File ... />

        <ServiceInstall
            Id="InstallWindowsService1"
            Name="testsvc1"
            DisplayName="Test Service 1"
            Start="auto"
            ErrorControl="normal"
            Type="ownProcess" />

        <ServiceControl ... />
    </Component>

    <Component ... >
        <File ... />

        <ServiceInstall
            Id="InstallWindowsService2"
            Name="testsvc2"
            DisplayName="Test Service 2"
            Start="auto"
            ErrorControl="normal"
            Type="ownProcess">

            <ServiceDependency Id="testsvc1" />
        </ServiceInstall>

        <ServiceControl ... />
    </Component>
</DirectoryRef>
```

Here, the service called TestService2 will be started after TestService1 has been started.

Another thing you can do is add one of your services to a **load order group** and then start that entire group before starting one of your other services. A load order group is simply a category under which several services are grouped. You can use the `ServiceInstall` element's `LoadOrderGroup` attribute to join an existing group. If that group name doesn't exist, it will be created for you. The next example joins the `TestService1` service to the `TestGroup` group:

```
<ServiceInstall
    Id="InstallWindowsService1"
    Name="testsvc1"
    DisplayName="Test Service 1"
    Start="auto"
    ErrorControl="normal"
    Type="ownProcess"
    LoadOrderGroup="TestGroup" />
```

If we then had another service, we could specify, via the `ServiceDependency` element, that all services in `TestGroup` should be started first. You'd add the `Group` attribute, set to `yes`, to signify that the `Id` attribute in the `ServiceDependency` element refers to a group name:

```
<ServiceInstall
    Id="InstallWindowsService2"
    Name="testsvc2"
    DisplayName="Test Service 2"
    Start="auto"
    ErrorControl="normal"
    Type="ownProcess">

    <ServiceDependency Id="TestGroup" Group="yes" />
</ServiceInstall>
```

When you set a dependency for a service, be aware that if the dependency can't be started, an error will occur. If this happens during the install, then the user will be given the option to retry or cancel. In the next section, we'll tackle what should happen if the service fails during the normal course of its life. You can tell Windows what to do when this happens with the `ServiceConfig` element.

Service recovery with Util:ServiceConfig

Windows allows you to set actions to be taken if your service fails at some point while it's running. Note that at this point, we're handling errors that crash the service during its lifetime and not errors during the installation. Your three options are: try to restart the service, run an executable file or script, or reboot the machine. You can see these settings in the services management console by viewing **Properties** of your service and clicking on the **Recovery** tab.

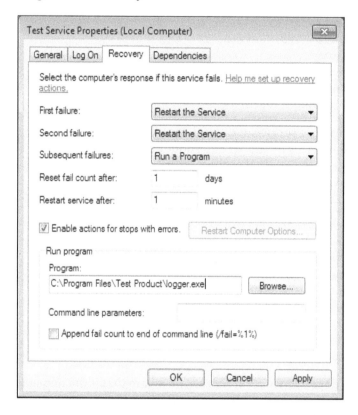

First, let's alter the original Windows service that we created by changing the WriteToLog function so that it throws an error the third time it prints a message. As this error is uncaught, it will cause the service to stop running. This will give the failure recovery actions a chance to kick in. The following is the new code for WriteToLog:

```
protected void WriteToLog()
{
    int count = 0;

    string appDataDir = Environment.GetFolderPath(
```

```
        Environment.SpecialFolder.CommonApplicationData);

    string logDir = Path.Combine(appDataDir,
        "TestInstallerLogs");

    string logFile = Path.Combine(logDir, "serviceLog.txt");

    while (this.threadActive)
    {
        count++;

        if (count >= 3)
        {
            throw new Exception("Service failed.");
        }

        if (!Directory.Exists(logDir))
        {
            Directory.CreateDirectory(logDir);
        }

        using (var sw = new StreamWriter(logFile, true))
        {
            sw.WriteLine("Log entry at {0}", DateTime.Now);
        }

        Thread.Sleep(5000);
    }
}
```

Now the service will fail after writing to the log twice. Going back to our WiX project, let's add a project reference to WixUtilExtension, if it's not already there. Be sure to add the util namespace:

```
<Wix xmlns="http://schemas.microsoft.com/wix/2006/wi"
    xmlns:util="http://schemas.microsoft.com/wix/UtilExtension"
  >
```

This allows us to use the `ServiceConfig` element through which we can set the failure recovery options. If you want to set the options for a service that's already installed, place the `ServiceConfig` element inside its own `Component` element. If, however, you want to set the options of a new service you're installing, place it inside that `ServiceInstall` element, as in the following example:

```
<ServiceInstall
    Id="InstallWindowsService1"
    Name="testsvc"
    DisplayName="Test Service"
    Description="Test service for WiX"
    Start="auto"
    ErrorControl="normal"
    Type="ownProcess">

    <util:ServiceConfig
        ServiceName="testsvc"
        FirstFailureActionType="restart"
        SecondFailureActionType="restart"
        ThirdFailureActionType="runCommand"
        RestartServiceDelayInSeconds="5"
        ProgramCommandLine=
            "C:\Program Files\Test Product\logger.exe"
        ResetPeriodInDays="1" />
</ServiceInstall>
```

Here, we've set recovery actions for the `testsvc` service. The first time it fails, the action specified by the `FirstFailureActionType` attribute will be performed. The second time, it will be the action in `SecondFailureActionType` and then `ThirdFailureActionType` the third time. Each should be set to one of three values: `restart`, `runCommand`, or `reboot`.

Specifying `restart` means that Windows will attempt to restart the service after a delay time of seconds specified by the `RestartServiceDelayInSeconds` attribute. Here, we've set it up so that the service will restart five seconds after it fails.

Notice that we've set both the first and second action types to `restart`, meaning that the service will try to restart itself twice before running the command specified by the `ProgramCommandLine` attribute. You may also use a property to set the path to the program to execute:

```
<util:ServiceConfig
    ServiceName="testsvc"
    FirstFailureActionType="restart"
    SecondFailureActionType="restart"
```

```
ThirdFailureActionType="runCommand"
RestartServiceDelayInSeconds="5"
ProgramCommandLine=
    "&quot;[INSTALLFOLDER]logger.exe&quot;"
ResetPeriodInDays="1" />
```

Notice that we must place the XML entity `&quot;` around the value so that the spaces in the path are preserved. Another option is to set a property with a custom action, perhaps with the `SetProperty` element, and then reference that property in the `ProgramCommandLine` attribute. The following is an example where we create the property with a custom action:

```
<SetProperty Id="SERVICE_RECOVERY_CMD"
        Value="&quot;[INSTALLFOLDER]logger.exe&quot;"
        After="InstallInitialize"
        Sequence="execute" />
```

You can also set an action to `reboot` in which case the computer will reboot. You can add the `RebootMessage` attribute, set to a string, to show a custom message to the user telling them that the system will restart. Or, you can omit it to keep the default. Often, however, this message isn't shown. It's all up to the operating system.

We've set the `ResetPeriodInDays` attribute to 1, meaning that it will be one full day before the error count is reset to zero. This, unfortunately, doesn't give you the fine-grained control that you get with `sc.exe`, which lets you specify the value in seconds. If the error count goes higher than three, it just keeps executing the action specified by the `ThirdFailureActionType` attribute. Resetting the count brings you back to the `FirstFailureActionType` attribute.

Summary

In this chapter, we discussed Windows Services both from the standpoint of working with them via the command line with the `sc.exe` utility and with WiX. WiX lets you add a new service to the services management console and configure its startup, error logging level, and user account. Services can also be configured so that they depend on other services and have failure recovery. Having all of this functionality built-in can really simplify things.

In the next chapter, we will discuss how to localize an install package for different languages. WiX simplifies this process by allowing you to use variables in place of text that can be swapped out for each language and culture. With the arrival of WiX 3.6, this experience has even been improved with the new ability to tailor the sizing and positioning of user interface elements.

12

Localizing Your Installer

Localization is the process of making a piece of software, or in this case an installer, suitable for the culture and region where it will be used. This can include changing the language of displayed text, making sure that images and colors are culturally appropriate, and resizing UI elements to fit longer or shorter words.

In this chapter, we'll cover the following aspects of localization:

- Setting the language and code page attributes of your `Product` and `Package` elements
- Adding WiX localization files
- How to use Light.exe to localize an MSI
- Translating built-in error messages and the end-user license agreement
- Creating a single multi-language installer

WiX localization files

Suppose, to create an MSI for each language, you had to maintain a separate Visual Studio project for each one. That would become a hassle pretty quickly. With WiX **localization files** (`.wxl`), you can re-use the same WiX markup, but swap out the text for each language you build. Light, the WiX linker, lets you specify a `.wxl` file to use.

A `.wxl` file contains strings for a particular language. These can be swapped with placeholders (localization variables) when Light runs, creating an MSI with language-specific text. To create a new `.wxl` file, right-click on your WiX project in Visual Studio's **Solution Explorer** and select **Add | New Item | WiX Localization File**.

The convention is to name each .wxl file using an IETF language tag—such as en-us.wxl—corresponding to the language it contains. Allow me to give a little more background on this naming scheme. The first half is a two-letter abbreviation of the language such as "en" for English, "fr" for French, or "es" for Spanish. The second half is a region such as "us" for United States to specify a regional dialect of the language. You can also have a neutral-language tag by omitting the region portion, such as simply en.wxl to mean English spoken anywhere.

The following is an example .wxl file that contains several strings localized for English; the file will be named as en-us.wxl:

```
<?xml version="1.0" encoding="utf-8"?>
<WixLocalization
    Culture="en-us"
    Codepage="1252"
    xmlns= «http://schemas.microsoft.com/wix/2006/localization»>

    <String Id=»ProductName»>Awesome Software</String>
    <String Id=»Comments»>(c) All rights reserved</String>
    <String Id=»InstallButtonText»>Install</String>
</WixLocalization>
```

The root element is called WixLocalization and references a specialized namespace: http://schemas.microsoft.com/wix/2006/localization. This element's Culture attribute accepts a language tag, such as "en-us", to label the strings within the file. If your strings contain characters that aren't included in the ASCII character set, add the Codepage attribute to specify a numeric code page that includes them. It overrides the code page on the Product element if you've set one. We'll cover that later on.

Inside the WixLocalization element are String elements that define the text you want to localize. Each will become a variable that you can then use in your WiX markup. For example, the first String element, which has an Id attribute of ProductName and a value of Awesome Software, can be used to give localized names to our targeted install folder:

```
<Directory Id="TARGETDIR" Name="SourceDir">
    <Directory Id="ProgramFilesFolder">
        <Directory Id="INSTALLFOLDER"
                   Name="!(loc.ProductName)" />
    </Directory>
</Directory>
```

Of course, you could use this variable in multiple places in your markup. The syntax for using a localization variable is !(loc.*PropertyName*). Everywhere that you would use normal text you can use a localization variable: labels on UI controls, feature titles and feature descriptions, directory names, and so on. Then, simply by switching the .wxl file you reference, the values of those variables change.

The String element has two optional attributes: **Localizable** and **Overridable**. Localizable is purely for documentation purposes. It tells the person translating the text into another language that this string doesn't need to be localized. You might set it to no on String elements that don't contain actual words, but rather non-words such as code page numbers that you're storing in the .wxl file. For example, you may store a different code page for each version of the installer, as follows:

```
<String Id="Codepage" Localizable="no">1252</String>
```

You could then set the Package element's SummaryCodepage attribute like so:

```
<Package InstallerVersion="200"
         Compressed="yes"
         InstallScope="perMachine"
         SummaryCodepage="!(loc.Codepage)" />
```

Setting Overridable to yes lets you set two String elements with the same Id attribute. Ordinarily, doing so would cause an error. However, if one of the String elements is Overridable, then it will be overwritten by the other. For example, suppose you have two .wxl files that specify the same culture and each defines a String element with an Id attribute of MyString. If one has the Overridable attribute set to yes and the other doesn't, the element that doesn't will be used. The UI dialogs that come with the WiX toolset define .wxl files for many languages, and they set the Overridable attribute on all of their strings. This allows you to replace the default strings with your own by adding your own .wxl files.

The standard dialogs from WixUIExtension use localization variables extensively. Here's some of the markup they use for the WelcomeDlg dialog. You can see several localization variables at work:

```
<Dialog Id="WelcomeDlg"
        Width="370"
        Height="270"
        Title="!(loc.WelcomeDlg_Title)">

    <Control Id="Next"
             Type="PushButton"
             X="236"
             Y="243"
             Width="56"
```

```
                    Height="17"
                    Default="yes"
                    Text="!(loc.WixUINext)" />

        <Control Id="Cancel"
                    Type="PushButton"
                    X="304"
                    Y="243"
                    Width="56"
                    Height="17"
                    Cancel="yes"
                    Text="!(loc.WixUICancel)">
            <Publish Event="SpawnDialog"
                    Value="CancelDlg">1</Publish>
        </Control>

        <Control Id="Bitmap"
                    Type="Bitmap"
                    X="0"
                    Y="0"
                    Width="370"
                    Height="234"
                    TabSkip="no"
                    Text="!(loc.WelcomeDlgBitmap)" />
```

The WiX source code that's compiled into `WixUIExtension` contains the `.wxl` files that define these variables. Here's a sample from the Spanish version:

```
<String Id="WelcomeDlgTitle"
        Overridable="yes">
          {\WixUI_Font_Bigger}
          Le damos la bienvenida a la Instalación de
          [ProductName].
</String>

<String Id="WixUINext"
        Overridable="yes">&amp;Siguiente</String>

<String Id="WixUICancel"
        Overridable="yes">Cancelar</String>

<String Id="WelcomeDlgBitmap"
        Overridable="yes">WixUI_Bmp_Dialog</String>
```

I've added whitespace to make the file easier to read, but in practice you should remove all beginning and trailing whitespace from your strings. Otherwise, it will be included in the final value. `WixUIExtension` comes with `.wxl` files for more than thirty languages including Spanish, German, French, Hungarian, Polish, Japanese, and Russian. Remember, you can override these strings by creating your own `.wxl` files and adding `String` elements with `Id` attributes that match those defined by WiX. You can also make your own UI and localize it with completely new strings.

The role of Light.exe

If you've added a `.wxl` file to your WiX project in Visual Studio, or maybe several `.wxl` files—perhaps `en-us.wxl` for English and `es-es.wxl` for Spanish—building the project will create an installer for each one. They'll be stored in the `bin` folder under separate subfolders. This is without declaring which languages you want to build for. By default, Visual Studio detects all of the languages you've added and creates an MSI for each one.

The commands used to build the MSIs are the same that you learned about in *Chapter 9, Working from the Command Line*. First, Visual Studio calls Candle to compile the `.wxs` source code files into `.wixobj` object files. Then, it makes a distinct call to Light for each `.wxl` file, passing the `-loc` and `-cultures` flags. The following is the build process, truncated and formatted for readability:

```
Candle.exe -out obj\Debug\ -arch x86 Product.wxs


Light.exe -out "bin\Debug\en-us\MyInstaller.msi"
    -cultures:en-us
    -loc en-us.wxl
    -loc es-es.wxl
    obj\Debug\Product.wixobj


Light.exe -out "bin\Debug\es-es\MyInstaller.msi"
    -cultures:es-es
    -loc en-us.wxl
    -loc es-es.wxl
    obj\Debug\Product.wixobj
```

Each time that Light is called, *all* of the detected `.wxl` files are provided via the `-loc` flags. However, recall that each `.wxl` contains a `WixLocalization` element. Only those with a `Culture` attribute on their `WixLocalization` element that matches the language tag set by the `-cultures` flag will be used. In this example, the first call to Light builds an installer with the "en-us" strings. The second uses the "es-es" strings.

You can also limit the languages to build in the project's **Properties**. Visual Studio has a **Cultures to build** text field on the **Build** page. You can set one or more language tags here. Visual Studio will build a separate installer for each language you specify. It does this by calling Light multiple times.

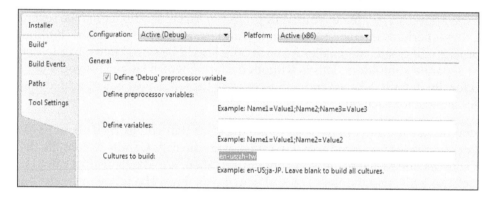

You can set more than one language by separating them with semicolons. If you leave this field blank, Visual Studio will build an MSI for every `.wxl` file you have in the project.

Now, let's inspect the syntax of the `-loc` and `-cultures` flags a little more. Candle doesn't do any processing on `.wxl` files. It leaves that up to Light. So, any localization variables that you've inserted into your markup will remain unresolved in the `.wixobj` files until Light is called.

Light looks for `-loc` and `-cultures` flags given to it on the command line. You can specify more than one `-loc` flag, each pointing to a `.wxl` file. The `-cultures` flag tells WiX *which* `.wxl` file(s) to use. Any that have a matching `Cultures` attribute on their `WixLocalization` element will be used. Here's an example that might be run directly from the command line (formatted for readability):

```
Light.exe -out myInstaller.msi
    -cultures:en-us
    -loc en-us.wxl
    -loc en-us2.wxl
    -loc de-de.wxl
    "*.wixobj"
```

Here we've specified that we want to build our MSI using the `en-us` culture. Assuming that `en-us.wxl` and `en-us2.wxl` both have that culture, both will be used. The `de-de.wxl` file will be ignored. You can specify more than one culture by separating each with a semi-colon, as in the following example:

```
Light.exe -out myInstaller.msi
    -cultures:de-de;en-us
    -loc en-us.wxl
    -loc de-de.wxl
    "*.wixobj"
```

The effect is different than when setting multiple cultures in Visual Studio's **Cultures to build** text field. In this context, it will set the first culture as the primary one to use and those that follow it as the fallback in case a particular string isn't defined in the first. The next example builds the installer using German strings ("de-de"), but falls back to English strings if a localization variable isn't defined in German. If neither defines it, then you'll get a build-time error.

Setting language and code page attributes

When you localize your MSI package, you'll need to alter your `Product` and `Package` elements to suit. To do so, you'll leverage code pages and locale identifiers (LCIDs). So the first thing to do is define what we mean by these terms.

A **locale identifier** is an ID used to classify a particular language and the region where it's spoken. It serves the same purpose as an IETF language tag, such as "en-us", but is formatted as a number. For example, "1033" means *English as spoken in the United States*. A full chart of LCIDs can be found at Microsoft's MSDN web site by searching for *locale ID*. The URL is:

`http://msdn.microsoft.com/en-us/goglobal/bb964664.aspx`

Although that page also provides LCIDs in hexadecimal form, you should always use the decimal form in WiX.

A **code page** is an add-on of extra printable characters that aren't covered in the basic set of 128 ASCII characters. I might as well break the news that WiX does not use Unicode. It has to do with the fact that Windows Installer itself doesn't have strong support for Unicode. For most tasks, this shouldn't present much of a problem. ASCII covers all of the English alphabet and common punctuation marks. You can see a chart displaying ASCII at:

```
http://msdn.microsoft.com/en-us/library/60ecse8t%28VS.80%29.aspx
```

However, it doesn't cover non-Latin characters (such as Chinese) or characters with accents over them such as those found in French and Spanish. So, to print the accents marks over Spanish letters, you'll need a code page. Without it, your installer won't know how to render the characters you want. A full list of code pages can be found at Microsoft's MSDN website:

```
http://msdn.microsoft.com/en-us/library/dd317756
```

As an example, you could specify a code page of "950" to make Traditional Chinese characters available. In the following sections, we'll see how the `Product` and `Package` elements make use of LCIDs and code pages.

The Package element

First, let's look at the `Package` element. Its job is to sum up details about the installer such as who the author is and what platform it supports. Another important piece of information it publishes is the language that's supported. An MSI package only lists one supported language and it does so by setting the `Package` element's `Languages` attribute. The attribute name is plural because the `Package` element is also used in merge modules and they can list multiple supported languages. Here's an example that sets the supported language to `1033` (English - United States):

```
<Package Compressed="yes"
         InstallerVersion="301"
         Manufacturer="Awesome Company"
         Description="Installs Awesome Software"
         Languages="1033" />
```

When the end user launches the installer, their computer looks to the `Package` element to find out what the supported language is. If that language isn't installed locally, an error will be displayed telling the user so.

Here's a message I got when I tried to install an MSI package that specified an LCID of `1085`, *Yiddish*, as the supported language:

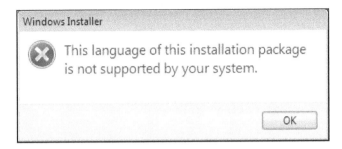

Also, if your own development computer doesn't have that language installed, an exception will be thrown when you try to build the WiX project, as shown in the following screenshot:

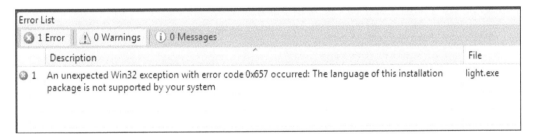

Windows Installer stores the supported language in something called the **Template Summary** property. You can find more information about it at the following website:

`http://msdn.microsoft.com/en-us/library/Aa372070`

Open your MSI with Orca and select **View | Summary Information** to see it. It will be listed as the **Platform** and **Languages** fields.

Getting back to the `Languages` attribute on the `Package` element, you have the option of using a localization variable instead of a hardcoded value, as in the following example:

```
<Package Compressed="yes"
        InstallerVersion="301"
        Manufacturer="Awesome Company"
        Description="Installs Awesome Software"
        Languages="!(loc.LocaleId)" />
```

Here, we've specified the variable `!(loc.LocaleId)` for the `Languages` attribute. The value for this variable will be filled in by a WiX localization file (`.wxl`). Here's a sample `.wxl` file that defines this variable for Spanish localization:

```
<?xml version="1.0" encoding="utf-8"?>
<WixLocalization Culture="es-es" Codepage="1252"
xmlns="http://schemas.microsoft.com/wix/2006/localization">
    <String Id="LocaleId">1034</String>

    <!--Other strings defined here-->
</WixLocalization>
```

The `Package` element has another attribute called `SummaryCodepage` that's used to set the code page for the summary properties. Summary properties are the details shown when you right-click on an MSI file and view its **Properties**. If any of these use characters outside of the ASCII set, they'll need a code page to display them.

You could set a hardcoded value, as in this example:

```
<Package Compressed="yes"
         InstallerVersion="301"
         Manufacturer="Awesome Company"
         Description="Installs Awesome Software"
         Languages="!(loc.LocaleId)"
         SummaryCodepage="1252" />
```

Here we've specified that the code page to use is `1252`, which is the code page containing additional Latin character such as the copyright symbol and characters with accents. If you don't specify the `SummaryCodepage` attribute it defaults to `1252`. You might explicitly set this attribute if you use extended characters such as those for Chinese. If we had used Chinese characters in, for example, the `Description` attribute, we would have had to specify a code page such as `950`.

You can also use a localization variable like this:

```
<Package Compressed="yes"
         InstallerVersion="301"
         Platform="x86"
         Manufacturer="Awesome Company"
         Description="Installs Awesome Software"
         Languages="!(loc.LocaleId)"
         SummaryCodepage="!(loc.SummaryCodepage)" />
```

The Product element

While the `Package` element publishes the summary properties that describe the MSI, the `Product` element contains the MSI's actual content. As such, setting *its* language and code page properties affects the characters stored in any of the tables in the installer and any error messages shown to the end user.

The `Product` element has an attribute called **Language** that defines the language *used* by the installer. Note the difference between it and the `Languages` attribute on the `Package` element which defines the *supported* language for the installer. Unlike the `Package` element's `Languages` attribute, which is optional, you must always set the `Product` element's `Language` attribute. Here's an example that sets `Language` to `1033`:

```
<Product Id="3E786878-358D-43AD-82D1-1435ADF9F6EA"
         Name="Awesome Software"
         Language="1033"
         Version="1.0.0.0"
         Manufacturer="Awesome Company"
         UpgradeCode="B414C827-8D81-4B4A-B3B6-338C06DE3A11">
```

To make life easy when localizing your package for more than one language, use a localization variable that can then be defined in `.wxl` files:

```
<Product Id="3E786878-358D-43AD-82D1-1435ADF9F6EA"
         Name="Awesome Software"
         Language="!(loc.LocaleId)"
         Version="1.0.0.0"
         Manufacturer="Awesome Company"
         UpgradeCode="B414C827-8D81-4B4A-B3B6-338C06DE3A11">
```

The `Product` element is also responsible for setting the code page for the characters used throughout the MSI database. You can set its `Codepage` attribute, as in this example:

```
<Product Id="3E786878-358D-43AD-82D1-1435ADF9F6EA"
         Name="Awesome Software"
         Language="!(loc.LocaleId)"
         Codepage="1252"
         Version="1.0.0.0"
         Manufacturer="Awesome Company"
         UpgradeCode="B414C827-8D81-4B4A-B3B6-338C06DE3A11">
```

This attribute cannot take a localization variable. However, setting the `Codepage` attribute on the `WixLocalization` element in your `.wxl` file will override the value. To see this for yourself, change the code page using the `WixLocalization` element's `Codepage` attribute and then inspect your MSI with Orca. Navigate to **Tools | Code Page** to verify that it has been set.

One last thing to note: There are a number of experts who agree that you should change the `Product` element's `Id` attribute for each different language. Luckily, that attribute can accept a localization variable. That's probably the best way to go if you want to keep strict control over your product codes. However, you may also put an asterisk (*) to request that WiX create a new GUID for you each time you build.

Localizing the UI

As you've seen, you can use localization files and variables to handle most of the text in your installer, whether that be labels on controls, the names of directories, or the titles and descriptions of your features. So what's left? In the next few sections we'll expand our scope to include the error messages that are baked into Windows Installer, the status messages that are shown over a progress bar, the end-user license agreement, and the size of user interface controls.

Error messages

Windows Installer responds to certain errors by displaying a message box with text about what went wrong. You can see a list of these errors at:

`http://msdn.microsoft.com/en-us/library/aa372835(VS.85).aspx`

Unfortunately, they're always in English. You can see an example of this by triggering the **Source not found** error. Follow these steps:

1. Create a simple `.wxs` file, but set the `EmbedCab` attribute on the `MediaTemplate` element to `no`. This means that the installer won't embed the CAB file in the MSI. Windows Installer will expect to find it in the same directory as the installer during installation. The `MediaTemplate` element will look like this:

   ```
   <MediaTemplate EmbedCab="no" />
   ```

2. Add a project reference to `WixUIExtension` and add one of the standard dialog sets, such as `WixUI_Minimal`:

   ```
   <UIRef Id="WixUI_Minimal" />
   ```

3. On the **Build** page of the project's **Properties**, set **Cultures to build** to **es-es**. WixUI_Minimal has a `.wxl` file for Spanish already baked in.

4. Compile the `.wxs` file into an MSI and then remove the CAB file from the output directory.

5. Launch the installer, accept the license agreement, and click **Instalar**.

You'll see a message like in the following screenshot:

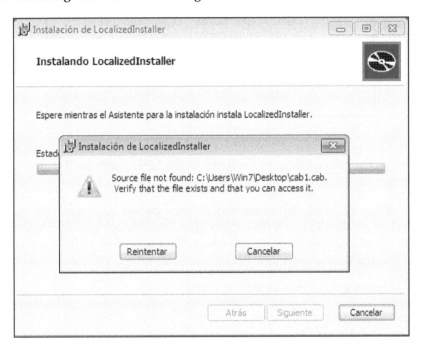

By setting **Cultures to build** to **es-es**, we've said that we want to use the Spanish `.wxl` files from `WixUIExtension`. This means that most of the text in the UI will be translated for us. However, the error message, which comes from the underlying Windows Installer, isn't.

To correct this problem, we'll have to replace the default error message with a localized one. Each message is identified by a number. For **Source not found**, it's **1311**. To override the message, add an `Error` element inside a `UI` element in your `.wxs` file. Set its `Id` attribute to the error number and the inner text to the localized message. Here's an example:

```
<UI>
  <Error Id="1311">Archivo no encontrado: [2].Compruebe que el archivo
  existe y que puedes acceder a él.</Error>
</UI>
```

Trusting that Google Translate knows its stuff (lean towards having a professional translator if you can), this should be the Spanish translation of the original message. Rebuild the MSI, delete the CAB file, and try to install. You should see the new message, as shown in the following screenshot:

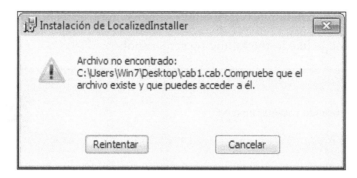

Notice that we used [2] as a placeholder for the missing file's path. Windows Installer fills in the information for us. Refer to the MSDN site for the template to use for each error.

There's one thing left to do. We've hardcoded the Spanish translation for the message. What we should really do is place that into a Spanish .wxl file and use a localization variable inside the Error element. That way, we can have translations for all of the languages we support. Follow this example:

```
<?xml version="1.0" encoding="utf-8"?>
<WixLocalization Culture="es-es"          xmlns="http://schemas.
microsoft.com/wix/2006/localization">

  <String Id="Error_1311">Archivo no encontrado: [2]. Compruebe que el
archivo existe y que puedes acceder a él.</String>
</WixLocalization>
```

Now we can use a localization variable:

```
<UI>
  <Error Id="1311">!(loc.Error_1311)</Error>
</UI>
```

This variable can be replaced for each different language.

Now the good news is that `WixUIExtension` has translated these error messages for you. By adding a reference to the extension and then adding a `UIRef` to `WixUI_ErrorProgressText`, you'll let WiX do the heavy lifting for you. Add the following markup to your main WiX source file:

```
<?xml version="1.0" encoding="UTF-8"?>
<Wix xmlns="http://schemas.microsoft.com/wix/2006/wi">
    <Product ...>
      <Package ... />


      <UIRef Id="WixUI_ErrorProgressText"/>
      <UIRef Id="WixUI_Minimal"/>
```

This technique will work when using one of the dialog sets that comes with WiX, as we've done here, or when using a custom UI. You can also override these error messages if you like. Add localized strings that match those set in `WixUIExtension`. They look like the following code snippet:

```
<String Id="Error0" Overridable="yes">{{Error irrecuperable: }}</
String>
<String Id="Error1" Overridable="yes">{{Error [1]. }}</String>
<String Id="Error2" Overridable="yes">Advertencia [1]. </String>
<String Id="Error4" Overridable="yes">Información [1]. </String>
```

Progress bar messages

For the upcoming examples, create a WiX project and add a reference to `WixUIExtension`. Then, add one of the dialog sets, such as `WixUI_Minimal`:

```
<UIRef Id="WixUI_Minimal"/>
```

Add a component to install, such as a text file:

```
<ComponentGroup Id="ProductComponents"
                Directory="INSTALLFOLDER">
   <Component Id="cmpInstallMeTXT"
           Guid="9B29875D-7311-4E64-933F-A54D316777C0">
     <File Source="InstallMe.txt" />
   </Component>
</ComponentGroup>
```

Open the project's **Properties** page and specify that you want to build the **es-es** culture using the **Build** tab's **Cultures to build** text field. Build the project and launch the resulting Spanish installer. As you watch the progress bar, you may notice that the text over it is in English, despite the rest of the window being in Spanish, as shown in the following screenshot:

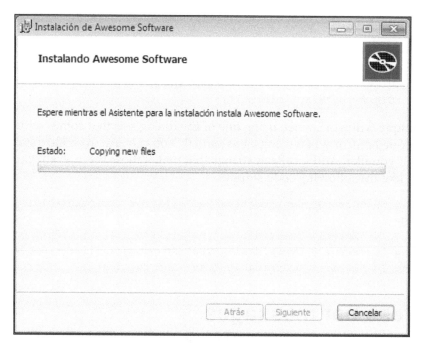

Custom progress messages are defined by a table in the MSI called `ActionText`. However, by default this table isn't included. Without it, the messages, as you've seen, are the stock English versions.

To add the `ActionText` table with strings for your progress messages, add a `ProgressText` element inside a UI element for each standard action found in the Execute sequence. For example, to add a localized message for the `InstallFiles` action, add the following markup to one of your `.wxs` files:

```
<UI>
    <ProgressText Action="InstallFiles"
                  Template="!(loc.InstallFilesTemplate)">
        !(loc.InstallFiles)
    </ProgressText>
</UI>
```

The `Action` attribute identifies the action to associate the message with. The `Template` attribute sets the format for the part of the message that Windows Installer will fill in the blanks for. To see the format to use for each action, consult the MSI SDK documentation that was installed with WiX. It's also available online at:

```
http://msdn.microsoft.com/en-us/library/windows/desktop/
aa372023(v=vs.85).aspx
```

The inner text of the `ProgressText` element sets the so-called `Description` for the action and will be displayed over the progress bar along with the `Template` message. In the next snippet, we'll set the localization variables that we used in the last example to display a custom message for the `InstallFiles` action.

```xml
<?xml version="1.0" encoding="utf-8"?>
<WixLocalization Culture="en-us" xmlns="http://schemas.microsoft.com/
wix/2006/localization">

  <String Id="InstallFiles">Tractor beam files!</String>
  <String Id="InstallFilesTemplate">File: [1], Size: [6], Directory:
[9]</String>
</WixLocalization>
```

Here's the result:

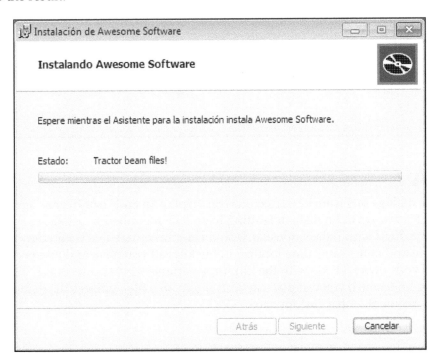

Now that you understand the concept of the `ProgressText` element, you should also know that `WixUIExtension` defines all of them for you, in many different languages. Simply add a `UIRef` element to your `Product.wxs` file that points to `WixUI_ErrorProgressText`:

```
<UIRef Id="WixUI_ErrorProgressText"/>
```

Rebuild the project, launch the Spanish installer, and you'll see that the progress messages are now translated.

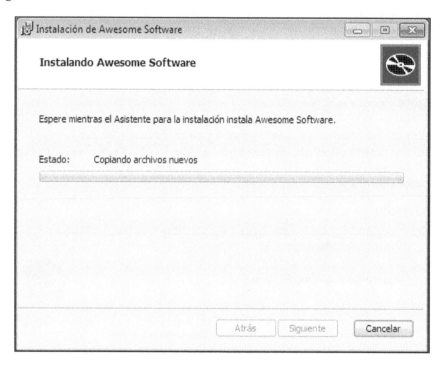

EULA

All of the dialogs sets from `WixUIExtension` display an **end-user license agreement (EULA)**. It's always in English, defaulting to an RTF file called `License.rtf` that's embedded within the extension. You'll want to replace this with your own agreement and at the same time localize it. Luckily, all you have to do is specify a path to your own RTF file with the link-time variable `WixUILicenseRtf`. The following line, which you can place in your main `.wxs` file, replaces the default license agreement with a custom one:

```
<WixVariable Id="WixUILicenseRtf"
             Value="CustomAgreement.rtf" />
```

You can also set this value from the command line when calling Light via the -d flag:

```
Light.exe -dWixUILicenseRtf=CustomAgreement.rtf -loc es_es.wxl
  -cultures:es-es -ext WixUIExtension.dll
  -out "es-es\AwesomeSoftware.msi" .\*.wixobj
```

Another option is to set it from within Visual Studio. Right-click on the project, select **Properties**, and add the variable in the text field labeled **Define variables**, as shown in the following screenshot:

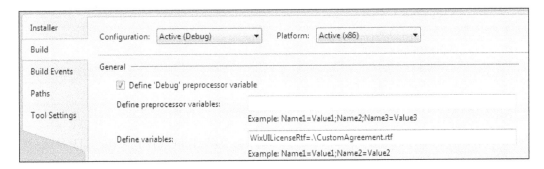

Once you've pointed this variable to the new file, you'll see your RTF text for the license agreement, as shown in the following screenshot:

You can use this technique to create a language-specific EULA for each localized MSI. Another way of localizing the EULA is to create a custom dialog that displays the license agreement and then use a localization variable for the license content. That way, you can store your RTF text in a `.wxl` file. This gives you more control than using `WixVariable`. Here's an example of a `ScrollableText` control that uses a localization variable to display a localized license agreement:

```
<Control Id="LicenseText"
         Type="ScrollableText"
         X="20"
         Y="60"
         Width="330"
         Height="140"
         Sunken="yes"
         TabSkip="no">
  <Text>!(loc.LicenseText)</Text>
</Control>
```

Now you can create a `String` element in your `.wxl` file that contains the RTF text, as shown:

```
<String Id="LicenseText">
<![CDATA[
  {\rtf1\ansi\ansicpg1252\deff0\deflang1033
    {\fonttbl{\f0\fswiss\fcharset0 Arial;}}
  {\*\generator Msftedit 5.41.21.2500;}
  \viewkind4\uc1\pard\f0\fs20 Custom License Agreement\par}]]>
</String>
```

Resizing controls

Something that we've gained in WiX 3.6 is the ability to resize user interface controls with localization variables. This is a great addition because words in, say, German can be much longer than those in English. Take the English word "Install". In German we get "Installieren". If we were to use a one-size fits all button for both, we might be left with a label that crowds or overflows the space available. Here's the markup that sets a hardcoded value for a `PushButton` control's `Width` attribute:

```
<Control Id="Install"
  Type="PushButton"
  Text="Install"
  Height="17"
  Width="56"
  X="50"
  Y="50"
```

```
    Default="yes">
    <Publish Event="EndDialog" Value="Return" />
</Control>
```

The English version MSI looks ok:

However, the German version looks a little cramped:

Let's replace the hardcoded `Width` with a localization variable, as follows:

```
<Control Id="Install"
  Type="PushButton"
  Text="!(loc.Install)"
  Height="17"
  Width="!(loc.InstallButtonWidth)"
  X="50"
  Y="50"
  Default="yes">
  <Publish Event="EndDialog" Value="Return" />
</Control>
```

We'll then add an `en-us.wxl` file with the following markup:

```
<?xml version="1.0" encoding="utf-8"?>
<WixLocalization Culture="en-us" xmlns="http://schemas.microsoft.com/
wix/2006/localization">
  <String Id="Install">Install</String>
  <String Id="InstallButtonWidth">56</String>
</WixLocalization>
```

Add a `de-de.wxl` file as well:

```xml
<?xml version="1.0" encoding="utf-8"?>
<WixLocalization Culture="de-de" Codepage="1252" xmlns="http://
schemas.microsoft.com/wix/2006/localization">
  <String Id="Install">Installieren</String>
  <String Id="InstallButtonWidth">66</String>
</WixLocalization>
```

Now the button in German is a little bit wider:

Width isn't the only attribute you can localize. You may also change a control's `Height` attribute or move it with the `X` and `Y` attributes.

Creating a multi-language MSI

In addition to being able to create multiple separate MSIs for each language, it's also possible to create a single MSI that shows a different language depending on the end user's language settings. The process is automatic for the user. They don't need to choose the language.

 Note that the procedure you'll learn here isn't supported by Microsoft, but is widely used.

To get started, build separate MSIs for each language. For a simple example, add a project reference to `WixUIExtension`. Then add a `UIRef` element to your markup to reference one of the standard dialog sets and set **Cultures to Build** in Visual Studio to **es-es;en-us;de-de**. This will build Spanish, English, and German installers using the `.wxl` files that are embedded in `WixUIExtension`. This is depicted in the following screenshot:

Cultures to build: es-es;en-us;de-de

Example: en-US;ja-JP. Leave blank to build all cultures.

Build the project. Visual Studio, by default, sends the output of each localized MSI to its own folder.

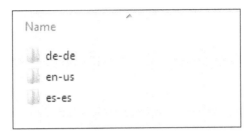

Each folder contains an MSI for a different language. To merge these installers into one, you'll need to verify that your project's `Product.wxs` file has the following:

- The `Product` element has a `Language` attribute set to a localized variable. We will call it `!(loc.ProductLanguage)`.

- Add `.wxl` files to your project for each language: `en-us.wxl`, `es-es.wxl`, and `de-de.wxl`. Next, add a `String` element to each one with an `Id` attribute of `ProductLanguage`, setting it to the LCID that matches that language: `1033` for en-us, `1034` for es-es, and `1031` for de-de.

Rebuild if necessary. Now, we're ready to merge the various MSIs into one. We'll embed each language-specific MSI inside a single installer. Basically, we're going to create **transform files** that will enable us to alter the language of our installer at the time the user runs it. A transform file (`.mst`) contains a comparison between two MSIs. Often they're used when building patches. However, they work for our needs too.

We'll compare each language-specific MSI against the English version (our **base**) to produce a transform file that contains the differences between the two languages. We'll then bundle all of the transform files inside the English MSI and when the end user launches it, it will dynamically choose which transform file to apply. The transform will alter the MSI (sort of like a patch) then and there *at install time* so that the language of the transform replaces all of the current strings.

To make the comparison between English and each other language and make our transform files, we'll use a tool that ships with WiX called **Torch**. Torch takes an input file, an `updatedInput` file to compare it to, and an output file as parameters. Here is the general syntax:

```
torch.exe [-?] [options] targetInput updatedInput -out outputFile
[@responseFile]
```

Here's an example that compares the English and Spanish versions and creates a transform file called `es-es.mst`:

```
torch.exe -t language "en-us\MyInstaller.msi"

"es-es\MyInstaller.msi" -out "transforms\es-es.mst"
```

It's a good idea to name your `.mst` files so that it's obvious which language they contain. Include the `-t` flag, set to `language`. The `-t` stands for `template` and without it you won't be able to compare MSIs that have different code pages. In this example, we're storing the output in a folder called `transforms`. Make sure that this folder exists before you call Torch.

The next step is to embed all of the transforms inside the English MSI. WiX doesn't have a tool to do this, so we'll have to look elsewhere. The Windows SDK comes with several VBScript files that perform various MSI-related tasks. You may need to download the SDK from the MSDN website. The scripts are included in the **Win32** samples. You can find more information at:

```
http://msdn.microsoft.com/en-us/library/aa372865%28VS.85%29.aspx
```

The VBScript file we're interested in is called `WiSubStg.vbs` and can usually be found in the `Samples` directory of the Windows SDK. On my computer, it's located at `C:\Program Files\Microsoft SDKs\Windows\v7.0\Samples\sysmgmt\msi\scripts`. Once you've found it, copy it to your project's directory and execute the following command:

```
WiSubStg.vbs "en-us\TestInstaller.msi" "transforms\es-es.mst" 1034
```

The first argument is the path to the English version MSI. The second is the path to one of the transform files. You'll need to repeat this call for each one. The third parameter gives a name to the transform for when it's embedded inside the MSI. The convention is to name it the LCID of the language, such as `1034` for Spanish. This process embeds each transform file inside the English MSI.

The next step is to set the value of the `Languages` attribute on the `Package` element so that it publishes all of the languages that the MSI now supports. We don't have to alter the MSI directly. We can use another tool from the Windows SDK called `WiLangId.vbs`. Copy `WiLangId.vbs` to your project's directory. The following command will set the `Languages` attribute to the three languages we've embedded inside the MSI: 1033 (English), 1034 (Spanish), and 1031 (German).

```
WiLangId.vbs "en-us\TestInstaller.msi" Package 1033,1034,1031
```

That's it. The MSI is now a multi-language MSI. To test it out, change the language settings of your user profile to Spanish. Go to **Control Panel | Region and Language**, select the **Formats** tab, and select **Spanish (Spain)** as your language, as shown in the following screenshot:

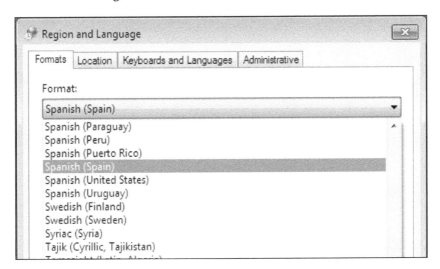

Launch the MSI and it should be the Spanish version. If you change your language back to English, the MSI should then display itself in English. If the user's preferred language is not one of the languages supported by your MSI, it will default to showing English since that was the base MSI without any transforms applied to it. The downside, however, is that **Summary Properties** will always be in English since the transform is applied when the MSI is launched. Right-clicking on the installer and viewing its properties won't activate the transform.

Summary

In this chapter, we discussed how to localize a WiX installer. Localization files make this task much simpler and faster, saving you from having to maintain a separate project for each language. Localization may encompass many aspects including changing the text shown in the user interface, altering the sizing and position of controls, and publishing the language that the installer supports. WiX handles all of these tasks with style.

In the next chapter, we'll cover how to plan for and perform software upgrades using WiX markup. There are a number of different types of upgrades and it pays to get to know your options early on. The good news is that WiX 3.6 has simplified the XML element you need to get the job done.

13
Upgrading and Patching

In this chapter, we'll discuss planning for and authoring updates for your software. Windows Installer offers an impressive set of functionality in this area and it pays to learn your options early on, before the first version of your software is released into the wild. As you'll learn, building your initial MSI with updates in mind will make your job much easier when it finally comes to sending out changes.

We'll cover the following topics:

- Planning for updates, including choosing the type of update to perform
- Authoring a major upgrade
- Deploying a minor upgrade or small update with a patch

Planning for updates

In the Windows Installer world, people tend to categorize updates into three groups: **major upgrades**, **minor upgrades**, and **small updates**. The primary distinction between these groups is the size of the update, or in other words, the number of changes that will take place. Speaking at a high level, a major upgrade completely replaces the existing software with a new set of files, registry keys, and so on. By contrast, minor upgrades and small updates only replace some of the files and leave the rest as they are.

In this section, we'll discuss how to plan for an update. It's beneficial to do this from the start before you actually need to author an update. In some cases, if you haven't authored your original installer in a way that supports updates, you'll find the task much harder later on.

Choosing an update type

A **major upgrade** is the simplest type of update to set up. It's really a complete MSI, just like any other you've created previously, with all of the components of your software included just like the original install. The difference is that if it detects an older version, it removes it.

You should use a major upgrade if any of the following are true:

- Enough of the product has changed to warrant completely replacing it.

- You've removed a feature from the install or moved it in the feature hierarchy—for example, made it a child to another feature.

- You've moved a component from one feature to another or deleted one.

- You simply want to keep things simple. Major upgrades are easier to implement than any other option.

A major upgrade changes the installer's `ProductCode` property (the `Product` element's ID) to indicate that this is a completely new product. However, as it's still the same type of product—as in, you're replacing one calculator with another calculator—you'll keep the installer's `UpgradeCode` attribute the same. For the lifetime of a product, through all of its incarnations, the `UpgradeCode` attribute should *never* change. You'll also increment the `Product` element's `Version` attribute.

A **minor upgrade** updates existing files without uninstalling the original product. It can be used to fix bugs or add features and components. Instead of changing the `ProductCode` property, you'll only increment the product's version number. That way, you're saying that this is still the same product, but with changes. It can be distributed as a patch file (`.msp`) or, like a major upgrade, as an MSI. Although you can add new features and components with a minor upgrade, you should not re-organize the feature-component tree.

A **small update** is distributed as a patch. It's smaller in scope than a minor upgrade, typically only changing a few files. It has so few changes that you won't even need to bother changing the version number.

The following table sums up when you'll need to change the `Product` element's `Version` and `Id` attributes:

Update type	Change product version?	Change product ID?
Major upgrade	Yes	Yes
Minor upgrade	Yes	No
Small update	No	No

Per-user or per-machine

When your update is going to remove a previous version of your software, such as during a major upgrade, Windows searches the registry to find information about the previous product such as its `ProductCode` property, and the location of its features and components. If your original install was installed as *per-machine*, meaning not for a specific user, then your update will have to do the same. Otherwise, the installer may look in the wrong section of the registry, the part belonging to the current user, and not find the product. To keep things consistent, you should always set this scope, even in your original installer.

You can set the `ALLUSERS` property as follows:

```
<Property Id="ALLUSERS" Value="1" />
```

When set to 1, the install is *per-machine*. When set to an empty string, it uses the *per-user* context. If set to a 2, the context will be *per-machine* if the user has administrative rights, otherwise it will be *per-user*. However, this isn't a hard-and-fast rule and changes depending on the operating system. View the MSI documentation for more information.

You can also use the `Package` element's `InstallScope` attribute to the same effect. Behind the scenes it will set the `ALLUSERS` property for you. You can set it to `perMachine` or `perUser`. If you go this route, be sure to remove any markup that sets `ALLUSERS` directly:

```
<Package InstallerVersion="301"
         Compressed="yes"
         InstallScope="perMachine" />
```

Preparing a major upgrade

A major upgrade is a full installation package that removes any older versions of the same product. To create one, you'll need to do the following:

- Change the `Product` element's `Id` attribute to a new GUID
- Increment the `Product` element's `Version` attribute
- Add and configure a `MajorUpgrade` element

We'll go over each step. Before we get to that, let's make an MSI that will install the *old* software — the software to update. You can use the following markup in a new WiX project called `OldInstaller`.

You may recall that you can use an asterisk (*) for Id in the `Product` element, and WiX will choose a new GUID for you each time you compile the project. You can do that here, if you choose to. However, we will use a hardcoded GUID to draw attention to that we are definitely changing it during a major upgrade. As you'll see, we will not be changing it when making a minor upgrade or small update:

```xml
<?xml version="1.0" encoding="UTF-8"?>
<Wix xmlns="http://schemas.microsoft.com/wix/2006/wi">

    <Product
        Id="3E786878-358D-43AD-82D1-1435ADF9F6EA"
        Name="Awesome Software"
        Language="1033"
        Version="1.0.0.0"
        Manufacturer="Awesome Company"
        UpgradeCode="B414C827-8D81-4B4A-B3B6-338C06DE3A11">

        <Package InstallerVersion="301"
                 Compressed="yes"
                 InstallScope="perMachine" />

        <MediaTemplate EmbedCab="yes" />

        <Directory Id="TARGETDIR" Name="SourceDir">
           <Directory Id="ProgramFilesFolder">
              <Directory Id="INSTALLFOLDER"
         Name="Awesome Software" />
           </Directory>
        </Directory>

        <ComponentGroup Id="ProductComponents"
                        Directory="INSTALLFOLDER">
           <Component
              Id="CMP_InstallMeTXT"
              Guid="E8A58B7B-F031-4548-9BDD-7A6796C8460D">
              <File Id="FILE_InstallMeTXT"
                    Source="InstallMe.txt"
                    KeyPath="yes" />
           </Component>
        </ComponentGroup>

        <Feature Id="ProductFeature"
                 Title="Main Product"
                 Level="1">
           <ComponentGroupRef Id="ProductComponents" />
        </Feature>

    </Product>
</Wix>
```

Notice that the `Product` element's `Version` attribute is `1.0.0.0`. We'll be incrementing that number in the upgrade. This MSI installs a text file called `InstallMe.txt`, so be sure to add one to your project. To show that this is the old version, you could write some text in `InstallMe.txt` such as `This file comes from the old version`. During the upgrade, we'll replace this file with a new one.

Build this example and install it. Later on, when we have the upgraded version, we'll have this older version to replace. Next, create a new WiX project and call it `NewInstaller`. You can re-use the entire markup from the previous example except for the `Product` element's `Id` and `Version` attributes which need to be changed.

```
<Product
        Id="B55596A8-93E3-47EB-84C4-D7FE07D0CAF4"
        Name="Awesome Software"
        Language="1033"
        Version="2.0.0.0"
        Manufacturer="Awesome Company"
        UpgradeCode="B414C827-8D81-4B4A-B3B6-338C06DE3A11">
```

By changing the `Id` attribute, we're setting up a major upgrade. We'll be replacing the old product with a new one. We've also changed the `Version` attribute to `2.0.0.0` to show that this is the newer product. Windows Installer ignores the fourth digit when detecting other versions of your software, so you should only rely on the first three.

Next, change the text inside the `InstallMe.txt` file to say something like `This file comes from the new version`. The component's GUID should stay the same. If you wanted to, you could add or remove components, but in this example we're replacing an existing one.

At this point, if we installed both the old and the new package, the old would not be removed. You'd be able to see both in **Programs and Features**.

Uninstall or change a program

To uninstall a program, select it from the list and then click Uninstall, Change, or Repair.

Organize ▼

Name	Publisher	Installed On	Size	Version
Awesome Software	Awesome Company	8/26/2012	36.0 KB	1.0.0.0
Awesome Software	Awesome Company	8/26/2012	36.0 KB	2.0.0.0

We can remove the older version before installing the new one by adding a `MajorUpgrade` element to the `NewInstaller` project as a child to the `Product` element.

 It doesn't hurt to have a `MajorUpgrade` element in all of your installers, even in our so-called `OldInstaller`.

Here's an example that shows adding a `MajorUpgrade` element to the `NewInstaller` project's `Product.wxs` file:

```xml
<?xml version="1.0" encoding="UTF-8"?>
<Wix xmlns="http://schemas.microsoft.com/wix/2006/wi">

<Product
        Id="B55596A8-93E3-47EB-84C4-D7FE07D0CAF4"
        Name="Awesome Software"
        Language="1033"
        Version="2.0.0.0"
        Manufacturer="Awesome Company"
        UpgradeCode="B414C827-8D81-4B4A-B3B6-338C06DE3A11">

    ...


    <MajorUpgrade DowngradeErrorMessage="A newer version of [ProductName]
    is already installed."/>
```

By adding the `DowngradeErrorMessage` attribute, we're dealing with the question, "What happens if the user tries to install an older version than the one that they've already got installed?" By default, the `MajorUpgrade` element prevents this from happening and displays the text from the `DowngradeErrorMessage` attribute to them instead. The following is what the user would see when trying to downgrade:

If you want to allow the user to downgrade their software to an older version, remove this attribute and set the `AllowDowngrades` attribute to `yes`.

The inverse of this scenario is prohibiting the user from upgrading to a newer version. In the next example, we allow downgrades but not upgrades:

```
<MajorUpgrade
    AllowDowngrades="yes"
    Disallow="yes"
    DisallowUpgradeErrorMessage="You cannot upgrade this product." />
```

The `Disallow` attribute prevents upgrades and `DisallowUpgradeErrorMessage` is the message to show to the user. The following screenshot is the result when trying to run the `NewInstaller` MSI:

When allowing upgrades, you have several options of how the old package is removed. The removal happens during a standard action in the Execute sequence called `RemoveExistingProducts`. The following table explains how scheduling this action to run at different times will give you different results, especially if an error happens during the installation:

Scheduled when	Effect
After `InstallInitialize`	Installer removes the old version completely before installing the new one. If the install fails, a rollback will cause the old version to be brought back. This should not be used if you're installing files to the GAC or the `WinSxS` folder, as there is a bug: `http://support.microsoft.com/kb/905238`.
Before `InstallInitialize`	Installer removes the old version completely before installing the new one. If the install of the new version fails, the old version will not be brought back.
Before `InstallFinalize`	The new version is installed and then the old version is removed. If the install fails, a rollback will bring the old version back (it may not have even been removed at that point). This is more efficient because files that haven't changed don't need to be replaced. To use this sequence, you must also schedule `InstallExecute` before `RemoveExistingProducts`.

Scheduled when	Effect
After `InstallFinalize`	The new version is installed and then the old version is removed. If the uninstall of the old version fails, the new version remains and the old version is also kept. On the other hand, if the install of the new version fails, only the old version will remain.

By default, the `MajorUpgrade` element schedules the removal before `InstallInitialize` (specifically by scheduling it after the `InstallValidate` action). You can change this by setting the `Schedule` attribute to one of the following values:

- `afterInstallValidate` (default): This schedules the removal before `InstallInitialize`.

- `afterInstallInitialize`: This schedules the removal after `InstallInitialize`.

- `afterInstallExecute`: This schedules the removal before `InstallFinalize`. It handles scheduling `InstallExecute` for you.

- `afterInstallFinalize`: This schedules the removal after `InstallFinalize`.

- `afterInstallExecuteAgain`: This schedules the removal after `InstallExecuteAgain`. It works the same as `afterInstallExecute`.

The following is an example that schedules the upgrade before `InstallFinalize`, which is arguably the most efficient way to do it:

```
<MajorUpgrade
    . . .
    Schedule="afterInstallExecute" />
```

If you'd like to ignore a failed attempt to remove the existing software then set the `IgnoreRemoveFailure` attribute to `yes`. In other words, a rollback won't be triggered if it otherwise would have been.

Two other interesting attributes are `MigrateFeatures` and `RemoveFeatures`. Setting `MigrateFeatures` to `yes`, which is the default, enables only those features that were installed last time. Setting it to `no` means that the currently installed features will have no effect on what gets enabled this time around. The `RemoveFeatures` attribute can be set to a comma-delimited list of features to remove before beginning the upgrade. By omitting it, all features are removed. The benefit of utilizing this is that if some features and their components have not changed, it could be more efficient to leave them in place and only replace what needs replacing.

Now you're ready to build the `NewInstaller` project and install it. It should remove the older version. You'll notice that there are no dialogs that tell the user that the old version is being removed. From their perspective, it's a seamless process.

The following is the full markup for our new installer:

```xml
<?xml version="1.0" encoding="UTF-8"?>
<Wix xmlns="http://schemas.microsoft.com/wix/2006/wi">

    <Product
        Id="B55596A8-93E3-47EB-84C4-D7FE07D0CAF4"
        Name="Awesome Software"
        Language="1033"
        Version="2.0.0.0"
        Manufacturer="Awesome Company"
        UpgradeCode="B414C827-8D81-4B4A-B3B6-338C06DE3A11">

        <Package InstallerVersion="301"
                 Compressed="yes"
                 InstallScope="perMachine" />

        <MediaTemplate EmbedCab="yes" />

        <Directory Id="TARGETDIR" Name="SourceDir">
           <Directory Id="ProgramFilesFolder">
              <Directory Id="INSTALLFOLDER"
               Name="Awesome Software" />
           </Directory>
        </Directory>

        <ComponentGroup Id="ProductComponents"
                        Directory="INSTALLFOLDER">
           <Component
               Id="CMP_InstallMeTXT"
               Guid="E8A58B7B-F031-4548-9BDD-7A6796C8460D">
              <File Id="FILE_InstallMeTXT"
                    Source="InstallMe.txt"
                    KeyPath="yes" />
           </Component>
        </ComponentGroup>

        <Feature Id="ProductFeature"
                 Title="Main Product"
              Level="1">
           <ComponentGroupRef Id="ProductComponents" />
```

```
        </Feature>

        <MajorUpgrade Schedule="afterInstallExecute"
                      DowngradeErrorMessage="A newer version of
 [ProductName] is already installed." />

    </Product>
</Wix>
```

The minor upgrade

Although a minor upgrade, like a major upgrade, can be distributed as a full MSI, in this chapter we'll focus on the more efficient methods of distributing it as a **patch file** (.msp). In this case, a minor upgrade doesn't uninstall the previous version. It only replaces some of the existing files or adds new ones. I'll show you two ways to make a patch, the first using .wixpdb files and the second using .wixout files.

Before we get to that, let's discuss the WiX source file that defines your patch. A .wixmsp defines the characteristics of your patch, setting fields such as Description and Comments that will appear in the patch file's properties. This file also sets up the sequencing of all of the patches for a particular product so that, say, patch 1.0.2.0 will be applied after 1.0.1.0. In this way, even if a user installs a patch out of order, it won't overwrite a newer patch that's already been applied. This file also defines the CAB files to embed in the patch and which product it applies to.

Authoring a .wixmsp file

To create a patch file, we need to make a new WiX source file that will define the patch's characteristics. Create a new .wxs file and call it Patch.wxs. Don't add it to your MSI project. It should exist on its own outside of your installer. The following is the markup to add to it:

```
<?xml version="1.0" encoding="UTF-8"?>
<Wix xmlns="http://schemas.microsoft.com/wix/2006/wi">
    <Patch
        AllowRemoval="yes"
        Classification="Update"
        Comments="Patch for Awesome Software v. 1.0.0.0"
        Description="Updates Awesome Software to v. 1.0.1.0"
        DisplayName="Awesome Software Patch 2012-09-01"
        Manufacturer="Awesome Company"
        MoreInfoURL="http://www.mysite.com/patchinfo.html"
```

```
            TargetProductName="Awesome Software">

            <Media Id="1000" Cabinet="MyPatch.cab">
               <PatchBaseline Id="MyPatch" />
            </Media>

            <PatchFamily
               Id="MyPatchFamily"
               Version="1.0.1.0"
               ProductCode="44139BED-5F1A-4C1E-BE12-C7148BE11189"
               Supersede="yes" />
         </Patch>
      </Wix>
```

The **Patch** element is the root element in this file. Its **AllowRemoval** attribute configures the patch so that it can be removed after it's been applied without having to uninstall the entire product. So you know, you can uninstall a patch file from the command line by setting the MSIPATCHREMOVE property to the path of the patch file. You use msiexec as follows:

msiexec /i MyInstaller.msi MSIPATCHREMOVE=C:\MyPatch.msp

You can also go to **Programs and Features** and click on the **View Installed Updates** link to see a list of patch updates that have been installed. The resultant screenshot is given as follows:

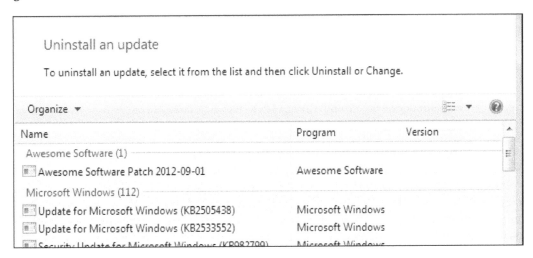

Classification contains the category for the patch. It's up to you what to set this to, but your options are: *Critical Update*, *Hotfix*, *Security Rollup*, *Security Update*, *Service Pack*, *Update*, and *Update Rollup*.

The **Comments** and **Description** attributes let you add additional information about the patch and will be displayed in the file's **Properties** page. DisplayName also appears in **Properties** and should be set to a user-friendly name for the file. Manufacturer should be set to the name of your company.

You can use the MoreInfoURL attribute, which is also displayed in the file's **Properties** page, to provide a website address where customers can get more information about the patch. The TargetProductName attribute can be set to the name of the software that this patch applies to. If this .wxs file contains characters that rely on a code page, you can set the optional CodePage attribute.

Next, inside the Patch element, add a Media element with a child PatchBaseline element.

```
<Media Id="1000" Cabinet="MyPatch.cab">
   <PatchBaseline Id="MyPatch" />
</Media>
```

The Media element's Id attribute should be higher than any Media record used in the MSI package you want to update. So, it's safer to use a high number such as 1000. You can give the CAB file any name you like using the Cabinet attribute.

The PatchBaseline element is used to define a name that we can reference later as we're building the patch file. I've given it the same name as the CAB file.

The last thing to do in this file is add a PatchFamily element. This will define the product that this patch applies to and whether or not earlier patches should be overwritten.

```
<PatchFamily
      Id="MyPatchFamily"
      Version="1.0.1.0"
      ProductCode="44139BED-5F1A-4C1E-BE12-C7148BE11189"
      Supersede="yes" />
```

A PatchFamily contains the updates of your patch. The Id attribute gives your new PatchFamily a name. The Version attribute is used to sequence your changes in relation to other patches and could be set to the version number of your Product element. However, the Version attribute here has no relation to the target product's ProductVersion. So, you could come up with an unrelated numbering scheme, such as 0.0.0.100, 0.0.0.200, 0.0.0.300, and so on. Behind the scenes, patches are ordered first by the Product element's Version number and then by the PatchFamily element's Version. This allows you, as you'll see, to provide an order for small update patches that don't change the Product element's Version attribute at all.

You can use the `ProductCode` attribute to target a specific product to patch. It should match the `Id` attribute of the `Product` element in your MSI project. If you don't set it, the patch can be applied to any targeted product, as identified by the `Patch` element's `TargetProductName` attribute. `Supersede`, when set to `yes`, signals that this patch should override other earlier patches.

You have the option of nesting `ComponentRef` elements inside the `PatchFamily` element to pull in only specific files that you want to update. Otherwise, omit the `ComponentRefs` as we've done here and the patch will find all of the files that have changed. Note that, like when working with the `Fragment` elements in other areas, pulling in one component will pull in all neighboring components from the same `Fragment` or `Product` element.

We're now ready to build our patch, which we'll have to do from the command line. We'll discuss this in the next section.

Creating a patch from .wixpdb files

When you compile your WiX source files with Candle and then link them together with Light, you get an MSI file and a `.wixpdb` file. The `.wixpdb` file contains the paths to your source files, but not the data that's in them. In other words, the files are not bound into the `.wixpdb` file like they are into the MSI. So, when building a patch with `.wixpdb` files, you must have the original source files.

For the next example, create a folder called `MinorUpgrade` and then create three subfolders named `Old`, `New`, and `Patch`. Add a file called `Product.wxs` to the `Old` directory and fill in the following markup:

```xml
<?xml version="1.0" encoding="UTF-8"?>
<Wix xmlns="http://schemas.microsoft.com/wix/2006/wi">
    <Product
        Id="44139BED-5F1A-4C1E-BE12-C7148BE11189"
        Name="Awesome Software"
        Language="1033"
        Version="1.0.0.0"
        Manufacturer="Awesome Company"
        UpgradeCode="3de16078-12fd-472d-8b3d-eb857b75d467">

        <Package InstallerVersion="200"
                Compressed="yes"
                InstallScope="perMachine" />
```

```
        <MajorUpgrade DowngradeErrorMessage="A newer version of
[ProductName] is already installed." />

        <MediaTemplate EmbedCab="yes" />

    <Feature Id="ProductFeature"
            Title="Main Product" Level="1">
        <ComponentGroupRef Id="ProductComponents" />
    </Feature>
</Product>

<Fragment>
    <Directory Id="TARGETDIR" Name="SourceDir">
        <Directory Id="ProgramFilesFolder">
            <Directory Id="INSTALLFOLDER"
                        Name="OldInstaller" />
        </Directory>
    </Directory>
</Fragment>

<Fragment>
    <ComponentGroup Id="ProductComponents"
                    Directory="INSTALLFOLDER">
        <Component
            Id="CMP_InstallMeTXT"
            Guid="5EE3620A-0C41-470D-9B48-434885EBA6AD">
            <File Id="FILE_InstallMeTXT"
                    Source="InstallMe.txt"
                    KeyPath="yes" />
        </Component>
    </ComponentGroup>
</Fragment>
</Wix>
```

This is a simple installer that will serve as the original package that we want to patch.
It installs a text file called `InstallMe.txt`. Next, add a text file to the same directory
and name it `InstallMe.txt`. Write something in it such as `This comes from the`
`old installer`.

The next step is to create a second pair of MSI and `.wixpdb` files that we'll compare the original against. Copy both files from the `Old` directory into the `New` directory but change the `Version` attribute of the `Product` element to `1.0.1.0` and change the text in the text file to `This comes from the patch`. The following is a snippet from the new `Product.wxs` file:

```
<Product Id="44139BED-5F1A-4C1E-BE12-C7148BE11189"
         Name="Awesome Software"
         Language="1033"
         Version="1.0.1.0"
         Manufacturer="Awesome Company"
         UpgradeCode="3de16078-12fd-472d-8b3d-eb857b75d467">
```

Next, add a `Patch.wxs` file like we discussed earlier to the `Patch` directory. Your directory structure should look like this:

```
MinorUpgrade\
    Old\
        Product.wxs
        InstallMe.txt

    New\
        Product.wxs
        InstallMe.txt

    Patch\
        Patch.wxs
```

Now we're ready to open a command prompt, navigate to the `MinorUpgrade` directory and start compiling our files. First, use Candle and Light against the `Old` and `New` WiX source files to create MSI and `.wixpdb` files. We can send the output to a folder called `Output`. This assumes that you've added `%WIX%bin` to your `PATH` environment variable. See *Chapter 9, Working from the Command Line*, for details.

```
candle Old\Product.wxs -out Old\
light Old\Product.wixobj -out Output\Old.msi
```

```
candle New\Product.wxs -out New\
light New\Product.wixobj -out Output\New.msi
```

You can do the same for the `Patch.wxs` file to create a `.wixmsp` file:

```
candle Patch\Patch.wxs -out Patch\
light Patch\Patch.wixobj -out Output\Patch.wixmsp
```

The next step is to record the differences between the two `.wixpdb` files and store them in a transform file. Our transform file here will be in XML format, a `.wixmst` file. Use `torch.exe`, which comes with the WiX toolset:

```
torch -p -xi Output\Old.wixpdb Output\New.wixpdb
-out Output\Differences.wixmst
```

The last step is to join the transform file with the `.wixmsp` file to create a patch (`.msp`). We'll use another tool from the WiX toolset called **pyro.exe**.

```
pyro Output\Patch.wixmsp -t MyPatch Output\Differences.wixmst
-out Output\Patch.msp
```

The `-t` argument accepts the `Id` attribute we gave to the `PatchBaseline` element in our `Patch.wxs` file. This is followed by the name of the `.wixmst` file created by Torch. The `-out` argument allows us to name the resulting `.msp` file.

In the end, our `Output` folder has quite a few files in it, but the important ones are the `Old.msi` file, which is our original product, and `Patch.msp`, which is the patch shown in the following screenshot:

`Patch.msp` is a file that looks like an MSI, can be read with Orca, and that the end user can double-click to install. It's smaller than an MSI though. Running the patch applies the changes. This is our *minor upgrade*. It can also be run from the command line:

```
msiexec /p Patch.msp
```

Creating a patch from .wixout files

There's a downside to using `.wixpdb` files: the binary data from your software isn't bundled up into them. These files only contain the paths to your files. That means that you need to keep copies of your sources files (both old and new) when making a patch. Also, it can be cumbersome to get Pyro to resolve the paths correctly if the `.wixmst` and `.wixmsp` files aren't in the correct directory relative to the source files.

An alternative is to use .wixout files. These *do* bundle up the binary data of your software, allowing them to be moved around or backed up for later. They're just like MSI files, but in an XML format that makes them easy to make a patch out of. Instead of making an MSI out of your WiX source files, you output .wixout files.

When compiling your old and new Product.wxs files, you can use the markup from our .wixpdb example, provide the -bf, -xo, and -out flags to Light. You can add these flags to Light either in your Visual Studio project's **Tool Settings** properties or directly on the command line.

```
candle Old\Product.wxs -out Old\
light Old\Product.wixobj -bf -xo -out Output\Old.wixout


candle New\Product.wxs -out New\
light New\Product.wixobj-bf-xo -out Output\New.wixout
```

Once you've created a .wixout file for your old and new software, run Torch on them:

```
torch -p -xi Output\Old.wixout Output\New.wixout
-out Output\Differences.wixmst
```

Followed by Pyro, using the .wixmsp file created from the Patch.wxs file, like before:

```
candle Patch\Patch.wxs -out Patch\
light Patch\Patch.wixobj -out Output\Patch.wixmsp


pyro Output\Patch.wixmsp -t MyPatch Output\Differences.wixmst
-out Output\Patch.msp
```

You'll end up with an .msp file, just like when using .wixpdb files. The difference is that you can move the intermediate .wixout files around or back them up for later without worrying that the paths to your software's files will fail to resolve when you want to make a patch.

The small update

A `small update` is like a minor upgrade except that it's usually smaller in scope. You might use it when only a few files have changed and you don't intend to change the `Product` element's version number.

The steps to create it are the same as when creating a minor upgrade patch with the exception of not changing the `Product` element's `Version`. They are as follows:

1. Using Candle and Light, compile and link your original installer into a `.wixout` file.

2. Make changes to your software's files and then create a second `.wixout` file. Do not change the `Product` element's `Id` or `Version` attribute.

3. Make a `Patch.wxs` file and, using Candle and Light, compile and link it to create a `.wixmsp` file. Set the `PatchFamily` element's `Version` attribute so that this patch will be sequenced correctly related to other patches.

4. Use Torch to create a `.wixmst` file that contains the differences between your two `.wixout` files.

5. Use Pyro to combine the `.wixmsp` and `.wixmst` files into a final `.msp` patch file.

This gives you a patch file that when used will update files, but won't change the software's `ProductCode` or `Version` values.

Summary

In this chapter, we talked about the three types of updates. *Major upgrades* are the easiest to do, but are the least efficient for small sets of changes. They perform a complete uninstall of any older versions of your software. *Minor upgrades* and *small updates* are typically delivered as patch files and are smaller in scope. They only replace some of the existing files and add new features, but don't take any away. These can be an ideal method for keeping customers up-to-date on bug fixes.

In the next chapter, we'll see how to add new functionality to WiX by building our own WiX extension. It will be of the same variety as `WixUIExtension` or `WixUtilExtension`. You'll see that once you've associated your custom WiX elements with custom actions, the sky is the limit.

14
Extending WiX

WiX facilitates plenty of use cases out of the box. However, there are tasks that just don't come built into Windows Installer by default. Thankfully, the WiX team and others have extended WiX to cover a range of extra functionality such as installing websites, creating users, and editing XML files. In this chapter, we will cover how you can join in the fun by building your own extensions. This allows you to craft custom WiX elements that bind to custom actions to perform complex tasks, but stay consistent with the WiX declarative, XML style.

We will explore the following topics:

- Hooking into the WiX extension model using classes from the `Microsoft.Tools.WindowsInstallerXml` namespace
- Defining an XML schema for new WiX elements
- Parsing those elements when they're used in a WiX project and storing the result in the MSI database
- Associating the elements with custom actions to be run at install time

Building a custom WiX extension

You've been exposed to several of the WiX extensions already. `WixUIExtension` adds a premade user interface. `WixNetFxExtension` gives you information about the version of .NET that's installed. `WixUtilExtension` provides a number of elements for jobs such as adding users, editing XML files, and setting Internet shortcuts.

There are also other extensions that we haven't covered, including `WixSqlExtension` that can set up an MSSQL database, `WixIIsExtension` for adding websites, app pools and virtual directories to IIS, and `WixDifxAppExtension` for installing Windows drivers. For more information about these extensions, check out the WiX documentation at `http://wix.sourceforge.net/manual-wix3/schema_index.htm`. In this chapter, you will learn to make your own extension and bend WiX to your will for fortune and glory.

To get started, let's define what an extension is and what it would take to make one.

Setting the stage

A **WiX extension** is a .NET assembly that, when added to a WiX Setup project, provides new XML elements for additional functionality. As such we will need to create a new C# class library project and reference `wix.dll` from the WiX `bin` directory. For the example in this chapter I will name the project `AwesomeExtension`.

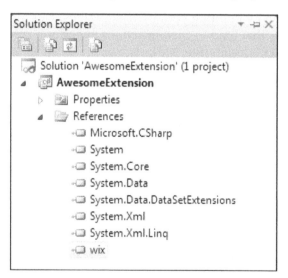

Extending the CompilerExtension class

The first thing we'll do is add a new class to our project and call it `AwesomeCompiler`. This class should extend the `CompilerExtension` class. Be sure to add a `using` statement targeting the `Microsoft.Tools.WindowsInstallerXml` namespace. We will immediately override a property called `Schema` that returns an instance of `XmlSchema`:

```
namespace AwesomeExtension
{
```

```
using System.Reflection;
using System.Xml;
using System.Xml.Schema;
using Microsoft.Tools.WindowsInstallerXml;

public class AwesomeCompiler : CompilerExtension
{
    private XmlSchema schema;

    public AwesomeCompiler()
    {
        this.schema =
            CompilerExtension.LoadXmlSchemaHelper(
                Assembly.GetExecutingAssembly(),
                "AwesomeExtension.AwesomeSchema.xsd");
    }

    public override XmlSchema Schema
    {
        get
        {
            return this.schema;
        }
    }
}
```

The Schema property returns an object of type XmlSchema, which is an in-memory representation of an XSD file. The XSD file, which we'll add to our project soon, will define the syntax for our custom XML elements such as the names of the elements, the attributes they can have, and where they can be placed in an XML document relative to other elements.

We are setting this property in the class's constructor using a static method called LoadXmlSchemaHelper from the base class. The first parameter to this method is the currently executing assembly and the second is the name of the XSD file. We will be embedding the XSD file in the class library so to reference it you should prefix the file's name with the project's default namespace, such as AwesomeExtension. AwesomeSchema.xsd. This is assuming you place the XSD in the root folder of the project. If you decide to place it in a subfolder, include the name of that folder in the string. For example, if you place it in a folder called Schemas, you would reference AwesomeExtension.Schemas.AwesomeSchema.xsd. You can know for sure what to use by compiling your project and opening the outputted assembly with ILDASM, the .NET disassembler. There you can see the names of all embedded resources by looking inside the manifest.

In the next section, we'll see how to make an XML schema and embed it in our assembly.

Adding an XML schema

Visual Studio comes with a template for adding an XSD file to your project. Right-click on your project and select **Add | New Item | Data | XML Schema**. In this example, I'll be adding it to the root folder of the project and calling it AwesomeSchema.xsd.

Once you have it, right-click on the file in **Solution Explorer** and select **Properties**. Change **Build Action** to **Embedded Resource**. Next, right click on the file again and choose **View Code**. You should see a schema element with various XML namespaces defined. I would modify it to use the XmlSchemaExtension namespace for defining parent-child relationships of elements. Also, change the domain name to use something other than tempuri.org.

```
<?xml version="1.0" encoding="utf-8"?>
<xs:schema
    elementFormDefault="qualified"
    targetNamespace="http://www.mydomain.com/AwesomeSchema"
```

```
    xmlns="http://www.mydomain.com/AwesomeSchema"
    xmlns:xs="http://www.w3.org/2001/XMLSchema"
    xmlns:xse=
"http://schemas.microsoft.com/wix/2005/XmlSchemaExtension"
>
</xs:schema>
```

The next step is to define our custom WiX elements. These will go inside the `schema` element. Add the following markup:

```
<?xml version="1.0" encoding="utf-8"?>
<xs:schema ...>

  <xs:annotation>
    <xs:documentation>
      The schema for the Awesome WiX Extension
    </xs:documentation>
  </xs:annotation>

  <xs:element name="SuperElement">
    <xs:annotation>
      <xs:appinfo>
        <xse:parent namespace="http://schemas.microsoft.com/wix/2006/
wi" ref="Product" />
        <xse:parent namespace="http://schemas.microsoft.com/wix/2006/
wi" ref="Fragment" />
      </xs:appinfo>
      <xs:documentation>
        A custom element for declaring level of awesomeness.
      </xs:documentation>
    </xs:annotation>

    <xs:complexType>
      <xs:attribute name="Id"
                    use="required"
                    type="xs:string">
        <xs:annotation>
          <xs:documentation>The ID for the element.</xs:documentation>
        </xs:annotation>
      </xs:attribute>

      <xs:attribute name="Type" use="required">
        <xs:annotation>
          <xs:documentation>The type of awesomeness: Super,
TotallySuper or RockStar.</xs:documentation>
```

```
        </xs:annotation>
        <xs:simpleType>
          <xs:restriction base="xs:string">
            <xs:enumeration value="Super" />
            <xs:enumeration value="TotallySuper" />
            <xs:enumeration value="RockStar" />
          </xs:restriction>
        </xs:simpleType>
      </xs:attribute>
    </xs:complexType>
  </xs:element>

</xs:schema>
```

Use the `annotation` and `documentation` elements to give helpful descriptions
to your elements and attributes. We use them in various places in this example
including at the top of the document to convey the purpose of the schema.

```
<xs:annotation>
    <xs:documentation>
      The schema for the Awesome WiX Extension
    </xs:documentation>
  </xs:annotation>
```

Use the `appinfo` and `parent` elements to define the WiX elements yours should be
placed within. For example, a *SuperElement* should only be placed within a `Product`
or `Fragment` element, as shown:

```
<xs:appinfo>
    <xse:parent namespace="http://schemas.microsoft.com/wix/2006/wi"
ref="Product" />

    <xse:parent namespace="http://schemas.microsoft.com/wix/2006/wi"
ref="Fragment" />
</xs:appinfo>
```

When defining attributes for your elements you can stick to the simple data types
such as strings, shown here for the `Id` attribute:

```
<xs:attribute name="Id"
              use="required"
              type="xs:string"/>
```

Alternatively, you can also build complex types such as enumerated values. In the example shown, we are defining an attribute called `Type` that can be set to `Super`, `TotallySuper`, or `RockStar`:

```
<xs:attribute name="Type" use="required">
   <xs:simpleType>
      <xs:restriction base="xs:string">
         <xs:enumeration value="Super" />
         <xs:enumeration value="TotallySuper" />
         <xs:enumeration value="RockStar" />
      </xs:restriction>
   </xs:simpleType>
</xs:attribute>
```

Now that we have our schema, let's jump back to our `AwesomeCompiler` class and add a method for parsing our `SuperElement` element when someone uses it in a WiX project.

Parsing custom elements

Next, we need to add logic to our `AwesomeCompiler` class to parse our new element when it's used. Override the `ParseElement` method from the base class:

```
public override void ParseElement(
    SourceLineNumberCollection sourceLineNumbers,
    XmlElement parentElement,
    XmlElement element,
    params string[] contextValues)
{
    switch (parentElement.LocalName)
    {
        case "Product":
        case "Fragment":
            switch (element.LocalName)
            {
                case "SuperElement":
                    this.ParseSuperElement(element);
                    break;
                default:
                    this.Core.UnexpectedElement(
                        parentElement,
                        element);
                    break;
            }
            break;
```

```
        default:
            this.Core.UnexpectedElement(
                parentElement,
                element);
            break;
    }
}
```

When someone uses our extension in their WiX project and then compiles it, Candle will call the ParseElement method. Our *override* parses only SuperElements that are children to Product or Fragment elements. In your own extension, feel free to add more case statements for all of the elements you've defined in your schema. We'll be calling a method called ParseSuperElement to handle the specific parsing logic. You should call the UnexpectedElement method if the element passed in isn't recognized so that Candle will throw an error.

The ParseSuperElement method takes an XmlNode object—our SuperElement. The following is the code to add:

```
private void ParseSuperElement(XmlNode node)
{
    SourceLineNumberCollection sourceLineNumber =
        Preprocessor.GetSourceLineNumbers(node);

    string superElementId = null;
    string superElementType = null;

    foreach (XmlAttribute attribute in node.Attributes)
    {
        if (attribute.NamespaceURI.Length == 0 ||
            attribute.NamespaceURI == this.schema.TargetNamespace)
        {
            switch (attribute.LocalName)
            {
                case "Id":
                    superElementId = this.Core.GetAttributeIdentifierValue(
                        sourceLineNumber,
                        attribute);
                    break;
                case "Type":
                    superElementType =
                        this.Core.GetAttributeValue(
                            sourceLineNumber,
                            attribute);
```

```
                    break;
                default:
                    this.Core.UnexpectedAttribute(
                        sourceLineNumber,
                        attribute);
                    break;
            }
        }
        else
        {
            this.Core.UnsupportedExtensionAttribute(
                sourceLineNumber,
                attribute);
        }
    }

    if (string.IsNullOrEmpty(superElementId))
    {
        this.Core.OnMessage(
            WixErrors.ExpectedAttribute(
                sourceLineNumber,
                node.Name,
                "Id"));
    }

    if (string.IsNullOrEmpty(superElementType))
    {
        this.Core.OnMessage(
            WixErrors.ExpectedAttribute(
                sourceLineNumber,
                node.Name,
                "Type"));
    }

    if (!this.Core.EncounteredError)
    {
        Row superElementRow =
            this.Core.CreateRow(
                sourceLineNumber,
                "SuperElementTable");

        superElementRow[0] = superElementId;
        superElementRow[1] = superElementType;
    }
}
```

All parsing methods follow a similar structure. First, use the `Preprocessor.GetSourceLineNumbers` method to get a `SourceLineNumberCollection` object. This will be used in various places throughout the rest of the function.

```
private void ParseSuperElement(XmlNode node)
{
    SourceLineNumberCollection sourceLineNumber =
        Preprocessor.GetSourceLineNumbers(node);
}
```

Next, loop through each item in the `node` object's `Attributes` collection to get each attribute that was set on our `SuperElement`. There are quite a few specialized functions for retrieving the value of different types of attributes, but the simplest is `GetAttributeValue`, which returns the value as a string. I'm also using `GetAttributeIdentifierValue`, which does some additional validation checks to make sure the `Id` attribute contains valid characters for an ID.

Call the `UnexpectedAttribute` method as a fallback in case an unrecognized attribute is used on our `SuperElement`. You should also call the `UnsupportedExtensionAttribute` method if an attribute is prefixed with a namespace that isn't our schema's target namespace.

```
foreach (XmlAttribute attribute in node.Attributes)
{
    if (attribute.NamespaceURI.Length == 0 ||
      attribute.NamespaceURI == this.schema.TargetNamespace)
    {
        switch (attribute.LocalName)
        {
            case "Id":
                superElementId =
                 this.Core.GetAttributeIdentifierValue(
                   sourceLineNumber,
                   attribute);
                break;
            case "Type":
                superElementType =
                    this.Core.GetAttributeValue(
                        sourceLineNumber,
                        attribute);
                break;
            default:
                this.Core.UnexpectedAttribute(
                    sourceLineNumber,
                    attribute);
```

```
                    break;

            }
        }
        else
        {
            this.Core.UnsupportedExtensionAttribute(
                sourceLineNumber,
                attribute);
        }
    }
```

After extracting each attribute's value, we will do some validation to make sure all required attributes have been set. You can use the OnMessage method to have Candle display an error if the mandatory attribute is missing, as shown in the following code:

```
if (string.IsNullOrEmpty(superElementId))
{
    this.Core.OnMessage(
        WixErrors.ExpectedAttribute(
            sourceLineNumber,
            node.Name,
            "Id"));
}

if (string.IsNullOrEmpty(superElementType))
{
    this.Core.OnMessage(
        WixErrors.ExpectedAttribute(
            sourceLineNumber,
            node.Name,
            "Type"));
}
```

Finally, use the CreateRow method to add the data from the element to the MSI database. Given the name of the table you want to create and the source line number where the element was parsed, you'll get a Row object that you can treat as an array. Each index in the array is associated with column in the row. In this example, we're creating a row in a table called SuperElementTable and setting the first column to the element's Id attribute and the second to its Type attribute, given as follows:

```
if (!this.Core.EncounteredError)
{
    Row superElementRow =
```

```
      this.Core.CreateRow(
         sourceLineNumber,
         "SuperElementTable");

   superElementRow[0] = superElementId;
   superElementRow[1] = superElementType;
}
```

Next, let's dig into how to declare the structure of this table.

Creating a new MSI table

Assuming the WiX compiler can successfully parse our element, we need to define how that data is going to be stored in the MSI. This part is actually pretty simple. We just need to add an XML file that establishes the structure of a table in the MSI called `SuperElementTable`. Each `SuperElement` that's used will be added as a row in this table.

Add an XML file to your class library project and call it `TableDefinitions.xml`. As we did for the XSD, set the **Build Action** option of this file to **Embedded Resource**. The root element will be called `tableDefinitions` and should reference the XML namespace `http://schemas.microsoft.com/wix/2006/tables`. Add the following markup:

```xml
<?xml version="1.0" encoding="utf-8" ?>
<tableDefinitions
   xmlns="http://schemas.microsoft.com/wix/2006/tables">

   <tableDefinition
      name="SuperElementTable"
      createSymbols="yes">

   </tableDefinition>

</tableDefinitions>
```

Inside the `tableDefinitions` element, we've added a `tableDefinition` element with a `name` attribute set to `SuperElementTable`. That's what we're calling the new table in the MSI. The `createSymbols` attribute should be set to `yes`.

Next, add a `columnDefinition` element for each attribute defined by `SuperElement`. These will define the columns in the table. They are shown as follows:

```
<?xml version="1.0" encoding="utf-8" ?>
<tableDefinitions
    xmlns="http://schemas.microsoft.com/wix/2006/tables">

  <tableDefinition
     name="SuperElementTable"
     createSymbols="yes">

    <columnDefinition
        name="Id"
        type="string"
        length="72"
        primaryKey="yes"
        category="identifier"
        description="Primary key for this element" />

    <columnDefinition
        name="Type"
        length="72"
        type="string"
        category="formatted"
        nullable="no"
        description="Type of SuperElement" />

  </tableDefinition>

</tableDefinitions>
```

Here we are adding columns for the `Id` and `Type` attributes. Marking the `Id` attribute as a `primaryKey` means that it can't be duplicated by another row and that it will serve as the primary key on the table.

You can also mark a column as a foreign key by setting the `keyTable` attribute to the name of another table and `keyColumn` attribute to the number, counting from left to right, of the column on that table to reference. The WiX linker will do some validation on the foreign keys including checking that the referenced column exists and that the foreign key isn't also a primary key. If you run into an error about modularization types, just make sure that your `columnDefintion` element sets an attribute called `modularize` to the same as it is on the referenced column. The error message will tell you what it has to be.

The type attribute can be set to one of the values described in the following table:

Column Type	Meaning
string	Column is a string.
localized	Column is a localizable string.
number	Column is a number.
object	Column is a binary stream.
preserved	Column is a string that is preserved in transforms.

The category attribute can be set to a valid column data type. You can find a list in the section titled *Column Data Types (Windows)* in the MSI SDK documentation that came with WiX. A list can also be found at:

```
http://msdn.microsoft.com/en-us/library/windows/desktop/
aa367869(v=vs.85).aspx
```

In our example, Id has a Category attribute of identifier, meaning that it can only contain ASCII characters, underscores, and periods. Type has a Category attribute of formatted, meaning that it can accept a WiX property value as well as a string. One last useful attribute: if you want to allow nulls in a column, set the nullable attribute to yes.

You can get a good idea about the syntax to use in your table definitions by looking at those defined by WiX. Download the source code and check out the src\wix\ Data\tables.xml file.

Extending the WixExtension class

The next step is to add a class that extends the WixExtension class. The purpose of this class is to return an instance of our AwesomeCompiler and also our table definitions. Add a new class to your project and call it AwesomeWixExtension. It should override the CompilerExtension property to return an instance of our AwesomeCompiler class:

```
namespace AwesomeExtension
{
    Using System.Reflection;
    using Microsoft.Tools.WindowsInstallerXml;

    public class AwesomeWixExtension : WixExtension
    {
```

```
            private CompilerExtension compilerExtension;

            public override CompilerExtension CompilerExtension
            {
                get
                {
                    if (this.compilerExtension == null)
                    {
                        this.compilerExtension =
                            new AwesomeCompiler();
                    }

                    return this.compilerExtension;
                }
            }

        }
    }
```

Next, override the `TableDefinitions` property and use the
`LoadTableDefinitionHelper` method to get the table definitions from our XML file:

```
    private TableDefinitionCollection tableDefinitions;

    public override TableDefinitionCollection TableDefinitions
    {
        get
        {
            if (this.tableDefinitions == null)
            {
                this.tableDefinitions =
                    WixExtension.LoadTableDefinitionHelper(
                        Assembly.GetExecutingAssembly(),
                        "AwesomeExtension.TableDefinitions.xml");
            }

            return this.tableDefinitions;
        }
    }
```

One last thing to do: open your project's `AssemblyInfo.cs` file and add the
following attribute:

```
[assembly: AssemblyDefaultWixExtension(typeof(
    AwesomeExtension.AwesomeWixExtension))]
```

This will mark our new `AwesomeWixExtension` class as the default WiX extension in the assembly.

Using the extension in a WiX project

At this point, you could use your extension in a WiX project to get a feel for what it will do. So far, we've added code to parse `SuperElement` and store it in the MSI. Later on we will tie a custom action to `SuperElement` so that when someone uses it the action will be run during the installation. To use the extension, follow these steps:

1. Copy the extension assembly and its dependencies to a WiX project.
2. Add the extension as a project reference.
3. Use the custom XML namespace in the WiX project's `Wix` element.
4. Add `SuperElement` to the markup and compile.

Step 1 is to copy the output from our `AwesomeExtension` to a folder in a WiX project. I'll assume you've created a simple WiX project. A common strategy is to add a `lib` folder to the WiX project and copy the output files there:

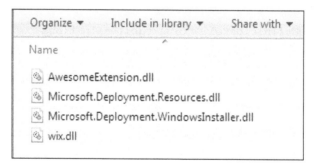

Then, add `AwesomeExtension.dll` as a project reference:

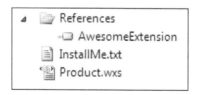

You can accomplish the same thing from the command line by passing the -ext flag to Candle and Light, followed by the path to the assembly.

Now that we have a reference to the extension we can include our custom XML namespace. Change the `Wix` element in your main WiX source file so that it contains `http://www.mydomain.com/AwesomeSchema`.

```
<Wix xmlns="http://schemas.microsoft.com/wix/2006/wi"
xmlns:awesome="http://www.mydomain.com/AwesomeSchema">
```

You're then able to use `SuperElement`, like so:

```
<awesome:SuperElement Id="super1" Type="Super" />
```

This element can be placed within the `Product` element or a `Fragment` element. Compile the WiX project and use `Orca.exe` to see that the custom table has been added:

Tables	Id	Type
AdminExecuteSequence	super1	Super
AdminUISequence		
AdvtExecuteSequence		
Component		
Directory		
Feature		
FeatureComponents		
File		
InstallExecuteSequence		
InstallUISequence		
LaunchCondition		
Media		
MsiFileHash		
Property		
SuperElementTable		

You should see a row in the table containing the data from `SuperElement`. If you'd like to see Visual Studio IntelliSense when typing the custom element, copy the `AwesomeSchema.xsd` file we created into Visual Studio's `Xml/Schemas` folder. If using Visual Studio 2010, it can be found at `C:\Program Files (x86)\Microsoft Visual Studio 10.0\Xml\Schemas`. Close and re-open Visual Studio and you should see the parameter information pop up as you type:

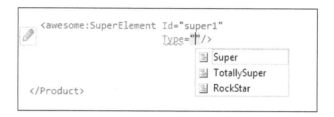

Tying a custom action to the custom element

Having a table full of rows in the MSI gets us halfway. The other half is defining a custom action that reads from that table and does something useful with the data at install time. The extensions that come with WiX already do all sorts of handy things, such as create SQL databases and tables, edit XML files, add users and set permissions, add websites to IIS, and so on. Your extension will add to this list, allowing an installer to do new, uncharted things! However, in this example we'll keep it simple and only display a message box for each row in the `SuperElementTable` table.

This is going to be a three-step process. First, we'll define the custom action in C#. Then, we'll embed the custom action DLL inside a WiX library (`.wixlib`). Finally, we'll embed that library inside our extension. In the same Visual Studio solution where we defined our extension, add a new project using the **C# Custom Action Project** template. Call it `SuperElementActions`.

Now, if we were going to perform our custom action during the immediate phase of the UI or Execute sequence, things would be pretty simple. Let's assume, however, that we are making an action that changes the end users' computer and so should only be run during the deferred stage of the Execute sequence. This gives us an extra challenge: we can't read the MSI database during the deferred stage.

The trick is to read the database during the immediate phase, store the results in a property, and then read that property during the deferred phase. In short, we need *two* custom actions. The first will read the database and looks like the following code snippet:

```
namespace SuperElementActions
{
    using System;
    using System.Collections.Generic;
    using Microsoft.Deployment.WindowsInstaller;

    public class CustomActions
    {
        [CustomAction]
        public static ActionResult ShowMessageImmediate(Session session)
        {
            Database db = session.Database;

            try
            {
                View view = db.OpenView("SELECT `Id`, `Type` FROM
`SuperElementTable`");
                view.Execute();

                CustomActionData data = new CustomActionData();

                foreach (Record row in view)
                {
                    data[row["Id"].ToString()] = row["Type"].ToString();
                }

                session["ShowMessageDeferred"] = data.ToString();

                return ActionResult.Success;
            }
            catch (Exception ex)
            {
                session.Log(ex.Message);
                return ActionResult.Failure;
            }
            finally
            {
                db.Close();
            }
        }
    }
}
```

In the `ShowMessageImmediate` method, we're reading from the currently executing MSI database by accessing `session.Database`, calling `OpenView` on it to select the rows from our custom table, and then `Execute` on the view that's returned. We then iterate over each row in the table by using a `foreach` statement on the view.

The data is stored in a new `CustomActionData` object. This class can be used like a hash table, so I'm using each `SuperElement` element's `Id` attribute as the key and the `Type` attribute as the value. After we've set all of the key-value pairs in the hash table, we serialize it out to a new session property called `ShowMessageDeferred`. By naming the property that, a custom action with the same name can have access to the data. It's a way of passing data from the immediate phase to the deferred phase.

The next step is to define the deferred custom action. Add a new method to the same class and call it `ShowMessageDeferred`. The following is the code:

```
[CustomAction]
public static ActionResult ShowMessageDeferred(Session session)
{
    try
    {
        CustomActionData data = session.CustomActionData;

        foreach (KeyValuePair<string, string> datum in data)
        {
            DisplayWarningMessage(
                session,
                string.Format("{0} => {1}", datum.Key, datum.Value));
        }

        return ActionResult.Success;
    }
    catch (Exception ex)
    {
        session.Log(ex.Message);
        return ActionResult.Failure;
    }
}

private static void DisplayWarningMessage(Session session, string
message)
{
    Record record = new Record(0);
    record[0] = message;
    session.Message(InstallMessage.Warning, record);
}
```

Here we're reading from the `CustomActionData` property on the `Session` object to get the `SuperElement` data that was set by the other custom action. We use another `foreach` statement to iterate over each item and display it in a message box, using a small helper function called `DisplayWarningMessage`.

Now we can move on to storing these custom actions in a WiX library. The reason is so that we can schedule the custom actions using WiX markup. Add a new **Setup Library Project** template to your solution and call it `AwesomeLibrary`, as shown in the following screenshot:

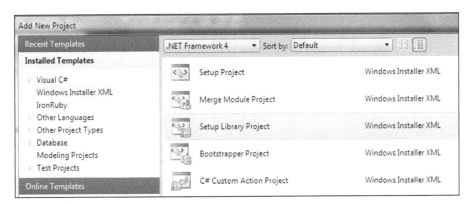

The setup library will contain a file called `Library.wxs`. We can modify it to point to our C# custom actions:

```xml
<?xml version="1.0" encoding="UTF-8"?>
<Wix xmlns="http://schemas.microsoft.com/wix/2006/wi">
  <Fragment>
    <Binary Id="CA_DLL"
            SourceFile="SuperElementActions.CA.dll" />

    <CustomAction Id="ShowMessageImmediate"
                  BinaryKey="CA_DLL"
                  DllEntry="ShowMessageImmediate"
                  Execute="immediate"
                  Return="check" />

    <CustomAction Id="ShowMessageDeferred"
                  BinaryKey="CA_DLL"
                  DllEntry="ShowMessageDeferred"
                  Execute="deferred"
                  Return="check" />

    <InstallExecuteSequence>
```

```
        <Custom Action="ShowMessageImmediate"
                Before="ShowMessageDeferred">
            NOT Installed</Custom>

        <Custom Action="ShowMessageDeferred"
                After="InstallInitialize">
            NOT Installed</Custom>
      </InstallExecuteSequence>
    </Fragment>
  </Wix>
```

Note that the `Binary` element references a DLL called `SuperElementActions.CA.dll`. The easiest way to make that true is to add the custom actions project as a reference in the `AwesomeLibrary` project. Then, use preprocessor variables to reference the DLL from that project's output folder. Update the `Binary` element in the following manner:

```
<Binary Id="CA_DLL"
        SourceFile=
"$(var.SuperElementActions.TargetDir)SuperElementActions.CA.dll" />
```

The two custom actions are both scheduled to run during `InstallExecuteSequence`, but the first will run during the immediate phase and the other during the deferred phase. I've added a condition to each `Custom` element so that these actions will only run during an install and not during an uninstall or repair.

Because we don't want to have to deploy our custom actions' DLL separately from our extension, we should embed it inside the WIXLIB. To do so you can add the **-bf** flag to the **Librarian** settings of the project's properties, as shown in the following screenshot:

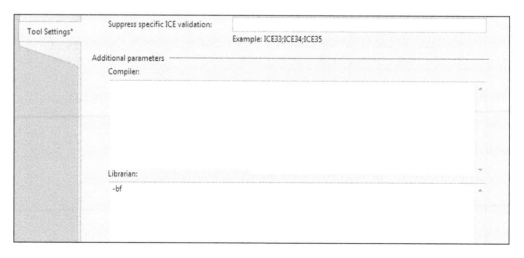

Alternatively, check the box labelled **Bind files into the library file** on the properties'
Build page:

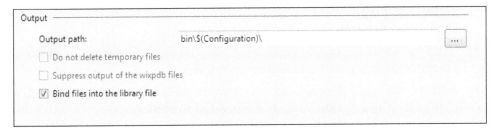

Copy the output from this `.wixlib` project to the `AwesomeExtension` project's folder.
You'll probably want to use a post-build step in Visual Studio to do this. Add the
`AwesomeLibrary.wixlib` file to the `AwesomeExtension` project using the **Solution
Explorer** window and change its **Build Action** value to **Embedded Resource**.
You should now have three projects: **AwesomeExtension**, **AwesomeLibrary**, and
SuperElementActions, as shown in the following screenshot:

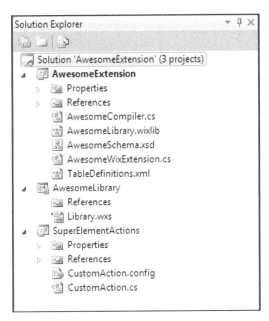

I'll summarize the steps we take to link them together:

- Use a project reference to `SuperElementActions` in the `AwesomeLibrary` project and preprocessor variables to include `SuperElementActions.CA.dll` in a `Binary` variable.

- Copy `AwesomeLibrary.wixlib` to the `AwesomeExtension` project's folder. Consider using a post-build action to do this.

- Add the `AwesomeLibrary.wixlib` file to the `AwesomeExtension` project, and change its **Build Action** value to **Embedded Resource**.

We'll need to add another method to the `AwesomeWixExtension.cs` file called `GetLibrary`. This will retrieve the WiX library from the extension. The following is the code to add:

```
private Library library;

public override Library GetLibrary(
    TableDefinitionCollection tableDefinitions)
{
    if (this.library == null)
    {
        this.library =
            WixExtension.LoadLibraryHelper(
                Assembly.GetExecutingAssembly(),
                "AwesomeExtension.AwesomeLibrary.wixlib",
                 tableDefinitions);
    }

    return this.library;
}
```

The `LoadLibraryHelper` method takes the currently executing assembly, the name of the embedded WIXLIB, and the table definitions collection that was passed into the method and returns the library.

Next, add a call to `CreateWixSimpleReferenceRow` to the end of the `ParseSuperElement` method. This will create a relationship between our WIXLIB and the MSI, sort of like pulling a `Fragment` element into a project, by referencing one of the elements in the library. I'm referencing the `ShowMessageImmediate` action from the `CustomAction` table here to make this link:

```
this.Core.CreateWixSimpleReferenceRow(
    sourceLineNumber,
    "CustomAction",
    "ShowMessageImmediate");
```

Now when you use `SuperElement` in a WiX project, the `ShowMessageImmediate` and `ShowMessageDeferred` custom actions will be added to the `CustomAction` table in the MSI. All other elements in the WIXLIB will also be pulled in.

When you install the MSI you will see a message displayed for each `SuperElement`, as shown in the following screenshot:

Summary

In this chapter, we discussed how to extend WiX to perform custom operations at install time. Our extension provided new WiX elements that tie to custom actions. All of this is bundled up into a .NET assembly so that others can use it too. With this knowledge, you've opened the door to advanced WiX functionality for yourself and possibly the WiX community at large.

In the next chapter, we will have a look at the new Burn engine that was introduced in WiX 3.6. Burn provides bootstrapping capabilities that allow us to bundle our software and its dependencies into a single setup executable. The potential uses for this are many and we'll dig into what you need to know to get started.

15

Bootstrapping Prerequisites with Burn

If you're like most of us, your software relies on some framework, third-party component, database, or process. Maybe it's the .NET Framework, the Java runtime, or SQL Server. Up until now, we would use a launch condition to show the user a friendly error message if the required prerequisite wasn't found, swiftly ending our installation. What we needed is a **bootstrapper** — a mechanism for getting those prerequisites installed prior to installing our own software. With the arrival of WiX 3.6, we have one.

Burn is a new tool in the WiX arsenal that fills the bootstrapper gap, but its feature set extends well beyond that of a simple bootstrapper. In this chapter, we'll cover the following topics:

- The ins and outs of getting your prerequisites installed using the new **Bootstrapper Project** template available in Visual Studio
- Displaying a single progress bar while installing multiple installation packages
- Downloading installers from the Internet at runtime
- Bundling patches together with your MSI to get your software up-to-date from the start

Using the Bootstrapper Project template

Create a new project in Visual Studio using the **Bootstrapper Project** template that's installed with the WiX toolset. Go to **New Project | Windows Installer XML | Bootstrapper Project**.

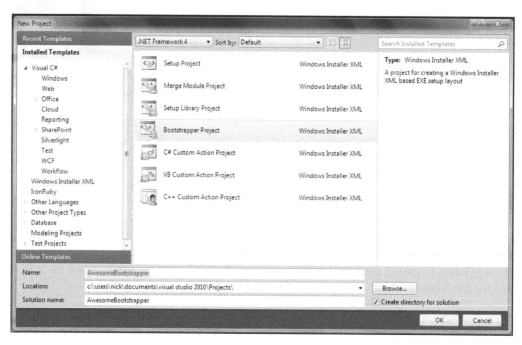

It will contain a file called `Bundle.wxs` with the following markup:

```xml
<?xml version="1.0" encoding="UTF-8"?>
<Wix xmlns="http://schemas.microsoft.com/wix/2006/wi">
<Bundle Name="Awesome Software"
        Version="1.0.0.0"
        Manufacturer="Awesome Company"
        UpgradeCode="c352f5c7-1dbe-416c-820d-685b058270d5">

    <BootstrapperApplicationRef
        Id="WixStandardBootstrapperApplication.RtfLicense" />

    <Chain>
        <!--TODO: Define the list of chained packages.-->
    </Chain>
</Bundle>
</Wix>
```

The root element is called **Bundle**. The name reflects a major aspect of Burn in that it *bundles* your installer with its prerequisites into a single, tidy executable. Double-clicking on that executable will install each installation package in turn. The **Chain** element sets up which packages are embedded and the order in which they're installed.

In the following sections we will discuss the `Bundle` and `Chain` elements in more detail.

Describing the Bundle element

The `Bundle` element has several attributes at its disposal for describing what eventually gets shown in **Programs and Features**. When the end user installs a Burn bundle, it will be added as an entry in the programs list. This presents a single point at which a piece of software and all of its dependencies can be uninstalled or repaired. The advantage of this design is that it simplifies these tasks for the user.

The following snippet sets these attributes:

```
<Bundle Name="Awesome Software"
        Version="1.0.0.0"
        Manufacturer="Awesome Company"
        HelpTelephone="123-456-7890"
        HelpUrl="http://www.mydomain.com/help"
        UpdateUrl="http://www.mydomain.com/update"
        AboutUrl="http://www.mydomain.com/about"
        ... >
```

You may also use localization variables. Localization works the same as it does for an MSI. The following is an example:

```
<Bundle Name="!(loc.BundleName)"
        Version="1.0.0.0"
        Manufacturer="!(loc.Manufacturer)"
        HelpTelephone="!(loc.HelpPhone)"
        HelpUrl="!(loc.HelpUrl)"
        UpdateUrl="!(loc.UpdateUrl)"
        AboutUrl="!(loc.AboutUrl)"
        ... >
```

Then, add a `.wxl` file to your bootstrapper project:

```xml
<?xml version="1.0" encoding="utf-8"?>
<WixLocalization Culture="en-us"
   xmlns="http://schemas.microsoft.com/wix/2006/localization">

   <String Id="Manufacturer">Awesome Software Company</String>
   <String Id="BundleName">Awesome Software Bundle</String>
   <String Id="HelpPhone">123-456-7890</String>
   <String Id="HelpUrl">www.mysite.com/help</String>
   <String Id="UpdateUrl">www.mysite.com/update</String>
   <String Id="AboutUrl">www.mysite.com/about</String>
</WixLocalization>
```

A few of these attributes deserve more explanation. The **Name** attribute will be the name of the software in the programs list. **Version** is comprised of four integers, each between 0 and 65534, separated by dots. In addition to being displayed in **Programs and Features**, it comes into play when detecting previously installed versions of the same bundle. We'll touch on that more shortly. The rest of the attributes shown give additional contact information or links to online resources. Different operating systems show these attributes in their own particular way. You may see some or all of them.

Ordinarily, **Programs and Features** gives you the option to uninstall, modify, or repair your software. You can disable each with the `DisableRemove`, `DisableModify`, and `DisableRepair` attributes. Each takes a `yes` value to remove that particular option. Additionally, if you set `DisableModify` to `button` then you'll get a single **Uninstall/Change** button instead of two separate buttons.

Other attributes are also available, not related to **Programs and Features**. The `Copyright` attribute can be set to your copyright text to be displayed in the executable file's properties. Setting `Compressed` to `no` will prevent the packages, such as your MSI and its dependencies, from being compressed inside the bundle. Instead, they will be copied to the output folder along with the executable. The `IconSourceFile` attribute can be set to the path to an ICO file. The icon will be displayed on the executable file itself and in **Programs and Features**.

Restricting the install by the operating system

A final attribute to consider is `Condition`. You'll set this to a conditional statement that, should it evaluate to false, the system will display an error dialog and abort the installation. The dialog's text is unchangeable and looks like the following screenshot:

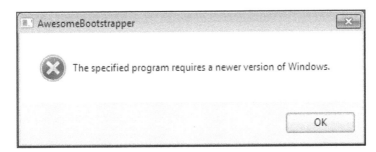

Because the condition is evaluated early on, you can only use built-in variables listed at the following URL:

`http://wix.sourceforge.net/manual-wix3/bundle_built_in_variables.htm`

However, because you can't change the error message, and the error message always says that the program requires a newer version of Windows, you should really only be checking the operating system version. A variable fit for this purpose is `VersionNT`. Compare it to an OS version number, formatted as a decimal preceded by v. For example, Windows 7 is Version 6.1. The following example checks that the operating system is Windows 7:

```
<Bundle Name="Awesome Software"
        Condition="VersionNT = v6.1"
        ... >
```

Note that the format for the `VersionNT` Burn variable is different than the `VersionNT` property used in a WiX setup project, where the values are whole numbers that aren't preceded by v. You can view a list of operating system version numbers at the following site:

`http://msdn.microsoft.com/en-us/library/windows/desktop/ms724832(v=vs.85).aspx`

Although the `Condition` attribute's error message can't be changed, you may use a child element called `Condition` that allows custom text. This element comes as a part of `BalExtension`. The `BalExtension` element provides hooks into the Burn engine for customizing the bootstrapper's UI and logic. First, add the `BalExtension` namespace to the `Wix` element and then nest the new `Condition` element inside `Bundle`, as shown in the following code snippet:

```
<Wixxmlns="http://schemas.microsoft.com/wix/2006/wi"
    xmlns:bal="http://schemas.microsoft.com/wix/BalExtension">

<Bundle Name="Awesome Software"
        Version="1.0.1.0"
        Manufacturer="Awesome Company"
        Copyright="(c) All rights reserved."
        UpgradeCode="3601032C-A8C9-4323-88E0-1967A9C2145E">

    <bal:Condition Message="This software can only be installed on
Windows Vista.">
        <![CDATA[VersionNT = v6.0]]>
    </bal:Condition>
```

In this case, if the operating system isn't Windows Vista, you'll get an error like the one shown in the following screenshot:

As with the `Condition` attribute, you can only use the built-in Burn variables mentioned before.

UpgradeCode and detecting related bundles

In this section we will find out how to detect and update older versions of your bundle.

Updating existing bundles

Each time that you compile your bootstrapper project in Visual Studio, it is assigned a new identity—a GUID called `BundleId` that you cannot change. In this respect, every bundle that you create is unique. The `UpgradeCode` attribute allows us to link two bootstrappers, making them *related bundles*. This relationship allows one bundle to detect and upgrade the installed packages of the other.

The `UpgradeCode` attribute is set on the `Bundle` element, as shown:

```
<Bundle Name="Awesome Software Bundle"
        Version="1.0.0.0"
        Manufacturer="Awesome Company"
        Copyright="(c) All rights reserved."
        UpgradeCode="3601032C-A8C9-4323-88E0-1967A9C2145E">
```

Now, having two bundle executables with the same `UpgradeCode` attribute does not mean that one will automatically replace the other. Their versions have a big part to play. Two bundles with the same `UpgradeCode` attribute *and* the same version will simply be installed side-by-side. You could try this out for yourself by installing a bundle, recompiling the project, installing again, and then checking **Programs and Features**. You'll see both bundles listed. For one to replace the other, its `Bundle` element's `Version` attribute must be higher.

After you've incremented the bundle's `Version`, during installation the bootstrapper will search for any previously installed bundles that have the same `UpgradeCode` attribute. If it finds one, it will check if the MSI packages installed by that bundle are older (by version) than the one it is installing. If they are older, it replaces them. If not, it leaves them as they are. No need to replace a package that's already up-to-date, after all.

Let's try this out. Create two new WiX setup projects. These will compile into two MSIs that we'll install with our bootstrapper. This goes to show that Burn can install more than just prerequisites. It can also install a group of software applications, as in a suite. I will call my MSIs `Awesome1` and `Awesome2`. The following is the markup for `Awesome1`. Note that it is installing a single text file:

```
<?xml version="1.0" encoding="UTF-8"?>
<Wix xmlns="http://schemas.microsoft.com/wix/2006/wi">
```

```xml
<Product
    Id="*"
    Name="Awesome1"
    Language="1033"
    Version="1.0.0.0"
    Manufacturer="Awesome Company"
    UpgradeCode="9b380bd4-cb7c-40a2-9c15-fb38c862a7e7">

    <Package InstallerVersion="200"
             Compressed="yes"
             InstallScope="perMachine" />

    <MajorUpgrade DowngradeErrorMessage="A newer version of
[ProductName] is already installed." />

    <MediaTemplate EmbedCab="yes" />

    <Feature Id="ProductFeature"
             Title="Awesome1"
             Level="1">
    <ComponentGroupRef Id="ProductComponents" />
    </Feature>
  </Product>

  <Fragment>
    <Directory Id="TARGETDIR" Name="SourceDir">
      <Directory Id="ProgramFilesFolder">
        <Directory Id="INSTALLFOLDER" Name="Awesome1" />
      </Directory>
    </Directory>
  </Fragment>


  <Fragment>
    <ComponentGroup Id="ProductComponents"
                    Directory="INSTALLFOLDER">
      <Component
        Id="CMP_InstallMeTXT"
        Guid="F643B5B5-59A8-428E-8E7A-FB4BDC024F83">

        <File Id="FILE_InstallMeTXT"
              Source="InstallMe.txt"
              KeyPath="yes" />
      </Component>
```

```
        </ComponentGroup>
    </Fragment>
</Wix>
```

You can imagine that Awesome2 is the same except that it will have a different UpgradeCode and ProductId. It should also install a different text file with a different component GUID.

To the same Visual Studio solution, add **Bootstrapper Project** and call it AwesomeBootstrapper. The Bundle element should make sense to you now. The Chain element, which we'll discuss in more detail later on, adds the two MSIs to our bootstrapper:

```
<?xml version="1.0" encoding="UTF-8"?>
<Wixxmlns="http://schemas.microsoft.com/wix/2006/wi"
    xmlns:bal="http://schemas.microsoft.com/wix/BalExtension">

    <Bundle Name="Awesome Software"
            Version="1.0.0.0"
            Manufacturer="Awesome Company"
            Copyright="(c) All rights reserved."
            UpgradeCode="3601032C-A8C9-4323-88E0-1967A9C2145E">

        <BootstrapperApplicationRef
            Id="WixStandardBootstrapperApplication.RtfLicense" />

        <Chain>
            <MsiPackageSourceFile="Awesome1.msi" />
            <MsiPackageSourceFile="Awesome2.msi" />
        </Chain>
    </Bundle>
</Wix>
```

This markup assumes that the MSIs have been copied to the bootstrapper project's folder. You could also add the setup projects as references in the bootstrapper project. Then, use preprocessor variables to access their output:

```
<Chain>
    <MsiPackageSourceFile=
        "$(var.Awesome1.TargetDir)Awesome1.msi" />
    <MsiPackageSourceFile=
        "$(var.Awesome2.TargetDir)Awesome2.msi" />
</Chain>
```

In any case, your solution ought to look like the following screenshot:

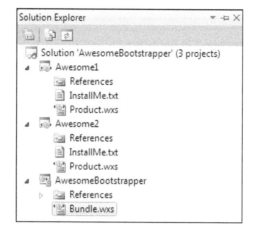

When you build the solution, the bootstrapper project will compress the two MSIs into its output executable, as shown in the following screenshot:

Launch this executable (I prefer to do this on a virtual machine, in case something goes wrong and I'm not able to uninstall) and you'll see the default user interface, as shown in the following screenshot:

Complete the install and you'll find that the text files of the two MSI packages were installed under **Program Files**. You'll also notice, if you look in **Programs and Features**, that there is only a single entry. This is depicted in the following screenshot:

Uninstall or change a program

To uninstall a program, select it from the list and then click Uninstall, Change, or Repair.

Organize ▼

Name	Publisher	Installed On	Size	Version
Awesome Software	Awesome Company	9/29/2012	64.0 KB	1.0.0.0

Now, let's create a second bootstrapper that upgrades our files. To make things interesting, we'll only change the text file—perhaps alter its text to say Installed by the new version!—and the version of our Awesome1 installer. The second MSI, Awesome2, we'll keep the same. Here is the updated Product element for Awesome1 where we update the Version to 1.0.1.0:

```
<Product Id="*"
         Name="Awesome1"
         Language="1033"
         Version="1.0.1.0"
         Manufacturer="Awesome Company"
         UpgradeCode="9b380bd4-cb7c-40a2-9c15-fb38c862a7e7">
```

Update the bootstrapper bundle version too. If we don't, the new bundle will be installed side-by-side with the existing one:

```
<Bundle Name="Awesome Software"
        Version="1.0.1.0"
        Manufacturer="Awesome Company"
        Copyright="(c) All rights reserved."
        UpgradeCode="3601032C-A8C9-4323-88E0-1967A9C2145E">
```

You may recall that Windows Installer ignores the fourth digit of the Product element's Version attribute when detecting previously installed packages. However, the Bundle element does not have this behavior. Its fourth digit is significant.

Build the solution again and install to the same machine where you installed the last bundle. This time, the process is going to take a little longer. That's because the bootstrapper is detecting and replacing the outdated Awesome1 MSI with the new version. It will find that the version of Awesome2 hasn't changed and will skip it.

Installation logs for Burn can be found in the `%TEMP%` directory. Here's what you'll find in the file that logged the new bundle being installed:

```
Detect 2 packages

Detected related bundle: {c1526489-bd4c-4732-835f-0b3819bfea17},
type: Upgrade, scope: PerMachine, version: 1.0.1.0, operation: None

Detected related package: {94625113-C05E-4FED-97BE-21B49F32CB48},
scope: PerMachine, version: 1.0.1.0, language: 0 operation: Downgrade

Detected package: Awesome1.msi, state: Obsolete, cached: Complete

Detected package: Awesome2.msi, state: Present, cached: Complete

Detect complete, result: 0x0

Plan 2 packages, action: Uninstall

Will not uninstall package: Awesome2.msi, found dependents: 1
```

Notice that it labels `Awesome1.msi` as obsolete, but `Awesome2.msi` is present and up-to-date. It then decides that `Awesome2` does not need to be uninstalled.

> Burn stores logs in the `%TEMP%` folder, incorporating the name of the bundle into the log file's name, such as `Awesome_Software_Bundle_20121105154610.log`. You'll also find logs for the MSIs that you're installing, such as `Awesome Software Bundle_20121105154610_0_Awesome1.msi`.

Finding other related bundles

So you have now seen that having two bundles with the same `UpgradeCode` attribute creates a relationship between the two. If one has a higher version than the other, it can upgrade the previously installed files. You can also relate two bundles that have different upgrade codes by using the `RelatedBundle` element. The following is an example that forms a relationship with another bundle that has an `UpgradeCode` of `8A5496B3-0BFA-4C2B-8129-7C8A7E3F51D9`:

```
<Bundle Name="Awesome Software"
        Version="1.0.0.0"
        Manufacturer="Awesome Company"
        Copyright="(c) All rights reserved."
        UpgradeCode="3601032C-A8C9-4323-88E0-1967A9C2145E">

    <RelatedBundle Id="8A5496B3-0BFA-4C2B-8129-7C8A7E3F51D9"
                   Action="Upgrade" />
```

The RelatedBundle element's Id matches the UpgradeCode attribute of the other bundle. The Action attribute, when set to Upgrade, informs the bootstrapper that it should upgrade the previously installed bundle if it finds it. When you set UpgradeCode on the Bundle element, behind the scenes Burn is really just creating a RelatedBundle element on your behalf.

Where the packages are cached

Another interesting thing to watch is the so-called **Package Cache**. Look for the Package Cache folder under the %ProgramData% or %AppData% directory, depending on whether the installed MSI was perMachine or perUser. After we installed the bundle the first time, Burn cached the two MSIs there. This allows for easier repair of the software's files without having to prompt for source, or in other words requesting the original installation media. The second time we installed the bundle, it replaced the obsolete, cached MSI with the newer one.

If you tried out the last example, you should see that Awesome2, the MSI that did not have its version changed, is still at Version 1.0.0.0. In other words, it was left as it is. Awesome1 and the bootstrapper executable were replaced in the cache. This is further proof that Burn optimizes the upgrade process to only replace what needs to be replaced.

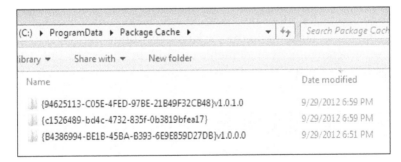

You can elect to turn off package caching on a per-package basis by setting the Cache attribute to no. We'll cover the various types of packages in detail later in the chapter.

Chaining packages

You briefly saw that we use the `Chain` element to identify the MSI packages we'd like to install with our bootstrapper. However, MSIs aren't the only thing that can be referenced. The list may also contain patch files (MSPs), executables, and Microsoft updates (MSUs). Before getting to the specifics, let's take a look at the `Chain` element itself.

The Chain element

The `Chain` element enumerates the packages that you want to install together. This may include a suite of products that you'd like to install in one go, a single MSI with its prerequisites, or a group of patches, just to name a few possibilities. The packages are installed in the same order as they're listed in the markup. For example, here, `Awesome1` is installed before `Awesome2`:

```
<Bundle ... >

    <Chain>
        <MsiPackage SourceFile="Awesome1.msi" />
        <MsiPackage SourceFile="Awesome2.msi" />
    </Chain>
```

You can change that order either by changing which element comes before the other or by adding the `After` attribute to the package. The following is an example where we keep the same arrangement of elements but add an `After` attribute to control the installation order:

```
<Chain>
    <MsiPackage Id="Awesome1"
                SourceFile="Awesome1.msi"
                After="Awesome2" />

    <MsiPackage Id="Awesome2"
                SourceFile="Awesome2.msi" />
</Chain>
```

The `Chain` element has three optional attributes: `DisableRollback`, `DisableSystemRestore`, and `ParallelCache`. If you set `DisableRollback` to yes, should a package fail to install properly only it will be rolled back. The other packages that had been installed up to that point will remain installed. The default, no, signals that if a package fails all previously installed packages should also be rolled back.

Setting `DisableSystemRestore` to `yes` prevents a system restore point from being created when the end user installs, uninstalls, modifies, or repairs your bundle. Ordinarily, each of these actions creates a restore point. You can see this by navigating in your Windows Start menu to **All Programs** | **Accessories** | **System Tools** | **System Restore**. When the utility opens, select the **Choose a different restore point** option to see a list of restore points. The following is what it might look like after a few actions have been performed on our bundle:

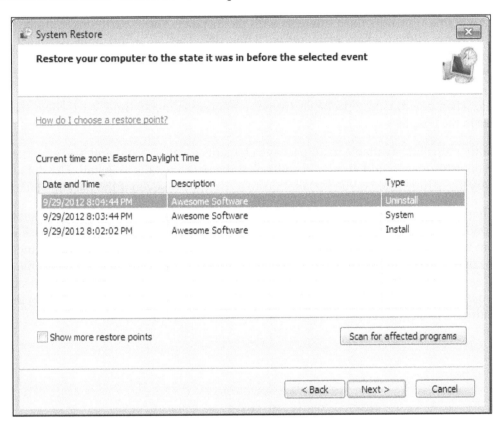

The `DisableSystemRestore` attribute stops these restoration points from being created.

The last attribute, `ParallelCache`, offers a slight optimization to the installation process. When set to `yes`, packages will start to install themselves without waiting for all of the other packages to be added to the package cache. In the following sections, we will explore the different types of packages that can be added to the bootstrapper's chain.

The MsiPackage element

The `MsiPackage` element is used to add an MSI installer to a bundle. Here's an example that includes `Awesome.msi` in the chain:

```
<Chain>
    <MsiPackageSourceFile="Awesome1.msi" />
```

There's a good number of optional attributes, common to all of the package elements, that will fine-tune how Burn interacts with the installer. These attributes could be used on any of the package elements we'll describe. The `Cache` attribute, when set to `no`, will prevent the package from being stored in the Package Cache. Setting `Compressed` to `no` will stop it from being compressed inside the bootstrapper executable. Instead, it will be deployed alongside it. You will also set `Compressed` to `no` when downloading packages from the Internet at install time. We'll cover that later in the chapter.

Another attribute available to all package elements is called **Vital** and sets whether the bootstrapper should abort and rollback if the package fails to install. The default is `yes`. By setting it to `no`, the installation will continue on even if the package fails.

A final interesting attribute I'd like to mention is `InstallCondition`. It can be set to a conditional statement that, should it evaluate to false, stops that particular package from being installed. Additionally, if the bundle is being repaired or modified and the condition is false the package will be uninstalled. That is, unless you've set the `MsiPackage` element's `Permanent` attribute to `yes`. The `Permanent` attribute is used to mark packages that should not be uninstalled. You may use Burn variables in the condition, which can be set directly with the `Variable` element, like so:

```
<Variable Name="MyVar" Value="false"/>

<Chain>
    <MsiPackage SourceFile="Awesome1.msi"
                InstallCondition="MyVar = &quot;true&quot;" />
</Chain>
```

In this example, I've used the `Variable` element to declare a Burn variable called `MyVar` and set it to `false`. The `InstallCondition` attribute checks this variable against a value of `true`. I've used the XML entity `&quot;` in place of double quotes so that the XML parser doesn't get confused. Note that to reference `myVar`, we simply state the name. No other special notation is required.

The `Visible` attribute, which is unique to the `MsiPackage` element, sets whether the MSI should be shown in **Programs and Features**. When set to `yes`, it will be displayed in **Programs and Features** instead of only showing the Burn bundle. Here's an example that sets the `Visible` attribute:

```
<MsiPackage SourceFile="Awesome1.msi" Visible="yes" />
```

The result is that both the bundle and the MSI are listed in **Programs and Features**, as shown in the following screenshot:

This may come in handy if your requirements dictate that each package in the bundle must be displayed, but for most situations showing a single entry in **Programs and Features** is probably preferable.

If you need to set a Windows Installer property on the MSI package, use the `MsiProperty` element. The following example demonstrates setting a property called `MY_PROPERTY` on the `Awesome1.msi` package. To make things interesting, we'll set the property to the value held in the `MyVar` Burn variable. Notice that we must use the square bracket notation to reference the variable, as shown in the following code snippet:

```
<Variable Name="MyVar" Value="abc" />

<Chain>
   <MsiPackage SourceFile="Awesome1.msi">
      <MsiProperty Name="MY_PROPERTY" Value="[MyVar]" />
   </MsiPackage>
</Chain>
```

The ExePackage element

The `ExePackage` element adds an executable package to the bootstrapper's install chain. As an example, let's say we wanted to install the **Java Runtime Environment (JRE)**. It can be downloaded from Oracle's site as an executable file. The URL is `http://www.oracle.com/technetwork/java/javase/downloads/index.html`.

The following example installs the JRE:

```
<Chain>
   <ExePackage SourceFile="jre-7u7-windows-x64.exe" />
</Chain>
```

There are two version of the JRE installer—one for 64-bit systems and another for 32-bit systems. We can compress both installers into our bootstrapper but use install conditions to install only the appropriate one, like so:

```
<ExePackage SourceFile="jre-7u7-windows-x64.exe"
            InstallCondition="VersionNT64" />

<ExePackage SourceFile="jre-7u7-windows-i586.exe"
            InstallCondition="NOT VersionNT64" />
```

Here we're checking for the `VersionNT64` variable. Since it is only set on 64-bit systems, we use it to prevent the 32-bit JRE from being installed on machines with that architecture. The Burn UI is nice enough to display a progress bar for us:

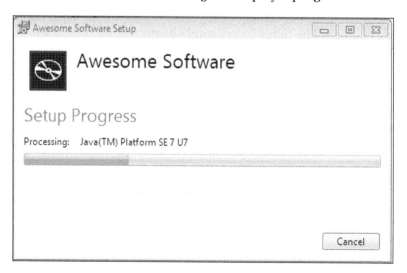

However, we did not pass any flags to the JRE installer and its default behavior is to display its own UI over the top of our own:

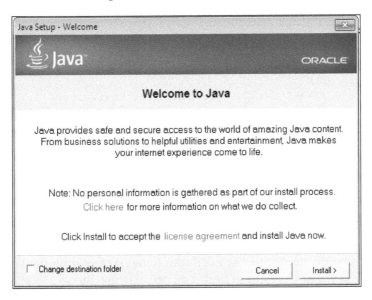

We can suppress this by passing the appropriate flags to the executable via the `InstallCommand` attribute. In this case, for a silent install, we would pass the `/s` flag, as shown in the following snippet:

```
<ExePackage SourceFile="jre-7u7-windows-x64.exe"
            InstallCondition="VersionNT64"
            InstallCommand="/s" />
```

Our next step is to handle uninstallation. When the user decides to uninstall the bundle we'll need to tell Burn how to detect if the JRE has been installed. We can do this by searching the Windows Registry for keys installed by the JRE. `WixUtilExtension` provides new search elements that can be used in your Burn markup. We'll use the new `RegistrySearch` element to search for a key located at `HKEY_LOCAL_MACHINE\SOFTWARE\JavaSoft\Java Runtime Environment\1.7`. If it is found, we will know that JRE 1.7 is currently installed.

Start by adding a reference in your project to `WixUtilExtension` and adding the `util` namespace to the `Wix` element, as shown in the following snippet:

```
<Wixxmlns="http://schemas.microsoft.com/wix/2006/wi"
xmlns:util="http://schemas.microsoft.com/wix/UtilExtension">
```

Next, add `RegistrySearch` elements to check if the JRE has been installed. The results will be stored in Burn variables called `JavaInstalled_x64` and `JavaInstalled_x86`.

```
<Bundle ...>

  <util:RegistrySearch
     Root="HKLM"
     Key="SOFTWARE\JavaSoft\Java Runtime Environment\1.7"
     Result="exists"
     Variable="JavaInstalled_x64"
     Win64="yes"/>

  <util:RegistrySearch
     Root="HKLM"
     Key="SOFTWARE\JavaSoft\Java Runtime Environment\1.7"
     Result="exists"
     Variable="JavaInstalled_x86" />
```

Here we are using the `Root` and `Key` attributes to navigate within the Windows Registry to the key that we want to find. You can also use the `Value` attribute to check for a specific value within the key. The result will be stored in the variable identified by the `Variable` attribute. I have set the `Result` attribute to `exists` to indicate that I want the variable to be set to 1 or 0, depending on if the key exists.

Finally, by setting `Win64` to `yes`, the search will check the 64-bit portion of the registry for the keys set by the 64-bit installer. You may recall from our discussion about the registry in *Chapter 10, Accessing the Windows Registry,* that Windows stores keys for 32-bit software under the **HKEY_LOCAL_MACHINE\SOFTWARE\Wow6432Node** and **HKEY_CURRENT_USER\Software\Wow6432Node** keys on a 64-bit system.

We could then set the `DetectCondition` attribute on the `ExePackage` elements using these variables. Burn uses `DetectCondition` to determine if the EXE package is installed. That way, it can make sensible decisions regarding whether the package is eligible for install or uninstall. The following is an example that sets the `DetectCondition` attribute using the two variables we defined earlier:

```
<ExePackage SourceFile="jre-7u7-windows-x64.exe"
            InstallCommand="/s"
            InstallCondition="VersionNT64"
            DetectCondition="JavaInstalled_x64" />

<ExePackage SourceFile="jre-7u7-windows-i586.exe"
            InstallCommand="/s"
            InstallCondition="NOT VersionNT64"
            DetectCondition="JavaInstalled_x86" />
```

When I uninstall the bundle, the log file affirms that the JRE has been detected:

Setting numeric variable 'JavaInstalled_x64' to value 1

Condition 'JavaInstalled_x64' evaluates to true.

Detected package: jre_7u7_windows_x64.exe, state: Present, cached: Complete

The last step would ordinarily be to add the `UninstallCommand` attribute to be run during uninstallation. Burn will pass any flags specified to the original executable, which would have been cached on the user's machine. The JRE installer doesn't provide any uninstall flags, so we're at a bit of a loss when it comes to uninstalling it. An alternative might be to extract the MSI from the EXE package, and use `MsiPackage` instead. Burn is able to uninstall MSIs without a problem. However, let's imagine that the JRE *did* provide an `/uninstall` flag. The markup would have looked like the following code:

```
<ExePackage SourceFile="jre-7u7-windows-x64.exe"
            InstallCommand="/s"
            UninstallCommand="/s /uninstall"
            InstallCondition="VersionNT64"
            DetectCondition="JavaInstalled_x64" />
```

As we've seen, the JRE does not support a command-line uninstall. However, you might be thinking to yourself that you wouldn't want to uninstall the JRE anyway. You would want to be able to uninstall your own software while leaving the JRE intact. The good news is that Burn provides a way to do *package ref counting* so that if another bundle has also installed the JRE, it won't be removed until all bundles that rely on it have been removed. We will see how later in the chapter. Of course, if you want to prevent your bundle from even attempting to uninstall the JRE, simply add the `Permanent` attribute, set to `yes`, to the `ExePackage` element.

Before moving on, note that there is also a `RepairCommand` attribute for passing command-line flags to the executable when a repair is triggered.

The MspPackage element

As you may recall, an MSP file is a patch file. Burn lets you deploy patches in a streamlined way, grouping related patches for example, or deploying patches with the original software they're meant to update. The latter scenario is known as **patch slipstreaming** and comes with some specialized support in Burn. The idea is to install your software and then immediately apply a patch or set of patches to it.

The next example adds an MSI package to the installation chain, followed by two patch files that immediately update it:

```
<Chain>
   <MsiPackage SourceFile="OriginalProduct.msi" />
   <MspPackage SourceFile="Patch1.msp" Slipstream="yes" />
   <MspPackage SourceFile="Patch2.msp" Slipstream="yes"/>
</Chain>
```

The `MspPackage` element's `SourceFile` attribute points to the patch file to add to the chain. The `Slipstream` attribute is needed or else the patch won't be applied to the `OriginalProduct.msi`. The nice thing here is that we don't have to specify that `Patch1` and `Patch2` apply to `OriginalProduct`. By using the `Slipstream` attribute, Burn figures out that you want them to apply to an MSI that's in the same bundle.

An alternate syntax is to nest `SlipstreamMsp` elements inside the `MsiPackage`:

```
<Chain>
   <MsiPackage SourceFile="OriginalProduct.msi">
   <SlipstreamMsp Id="Patch1"/>
   <SlipstreamMsp Id="Patch2"/>
   </MsiPackage>

      <MspPackage Id="Patch1" SourceFile="Patch1.msp" />
      <MspPackage Id="Patch2" SourceFile="Patch2.msp" />
</Chain>
```

Patches in the chain are also allowed to update software that has already been installed. In that case, you would not slipstream them. Also, because patches contain the information they need to detect and update the software that they apply to, it is not necessary to specify that information on the `MspPackage` element.

The MsuPackage element

An MSU file is a Microsoft Update standalone installer. These types of files can be installed on Windows Vista or later, and typically contain some sort of update to the Windows operating system or tools. Should you need to install one as a part of your bootstrapper chain, you can use the `MsuPackage` element. The following is an example that installs an MSU file:

```
<Chain>
   <MsuPackage SourceFile="Windows6.1-KB2656373-v2-x64.msu"
            KB="KB2656373" />
</Chain>
```

The MSU file in this case is a security update for .NET 3.5 on Windows 7 SP1. We specify the MSU with the `SourceFile` attribute. The **KB** attribute allows the file to be uninstalled later and identifies the knowledge base article (KB) that documents the problems that the update is meant to resolve.

Downloading packages

If you can find an installer, which could be any of the package types we've seen (MSI, EXE, MSP, or MSU), that can be easily downloaded from the Internet or a local network, you may choose to download it at the time of installation. That way, the bootstrapper executable that you give to your users will be smaller in size. So, instead of compressing the prerequisite into your bundle you'll provide a link to where it can be downloaded and Burn will get it for you at install time.

You will still need to download the package locally while you do your development. Burn needs to reference it during compilation. However, you'll set the `Compressed` attribute to `no`, and provide a `DownloadUrl` value where the package can be found. Here is an example that downloads and installs SQL Server 2012 Express:

```
<ExePackage  Id="SQLSERVER"
            DownloadUrl="$(var.SqlDownloadUrl)"
            Name="SQLEXPR_x64_ENU.exe"
            Compressed="no"
            DetectCondition="SqlInstanceFound"
            InstallCommand="$(var.SqlInstallCommand)"
            UninstallCommand="$(var.SqlUninstallCommand)"
            RepairCommand="$(var.SqlRepairCommand)">

    <RemotePayload
        Description="Microsoft SQL Server 2012 Express Edition"
        ProductName="Microsoft SQL Server 2012 Express Edition"
        Version="11.0.2100.60"
        Size="138412032"
        Hash="e4561d5caa761a5d1daa0d305f4fecedc6a0d39c" />
</ExePackage>
```

Notice that instead of using a `SourceFile` parameter to point to the package, we're using `Name`. It must also point to a local file, but when paired with `DownloadUrl`, just acts as a placeholder for the file while in development. For readability, I am using preprocessor variables for the attributes that can get pretty long. The following is how I would define them for a basic install:

```
<?define SqlServerInstance=TEST ?>

<?define
SqlDownloadUrl=http://download.microsoft.com/download/8/D/D/8DD7BDBA-
CEF7-4D8E-8C16-D9F69527F909/ENU/x64/SQLEXPR_x64_ENU.exe ?>

<?define SqlInstallCommand=/ACTION=Install /Q /
IACCEPTSQLSERVERLICENSETERMS /FEATURES=SQLEngine /INSTANCENAME=$(var.
SqlServerInstance) /SQLSYSADMINACCOUNTS=BUILTIN\Administrators /
SECURITYMODE=SQL /SAPWD=password1 ?>

<?define SqlUninstallCommand=/ACTION=Uninstall /Q /FEATURES=SQLEngine
/INSTANCENAME=$(var.SqlServerInstance) ?>

<?define SqlRepairCommand=/ACTION=Repair /Q /FEATURES=SQLEngine /
INSTANCENAME=$(var.SqlServerInstance) /FEATURES=SQLENGINE ?>
```

These preprocessor directives can go at the top of your Burn file, above the `Bundle` element. The `ExePackage` element is also using a `DetectCondition` attribute to check if SQL Server has already been installed. I define the search with a `RegistrySearch` element from `WixUtilExtension`, as shown in the following code snippet:

```
<util:RegistrySearch
    Id="SqlInstanceFound"
    Root="HKLM"
    Key=
"SOFTWARE\Microsoft\Microsoft SQL Server\Instance Names\SQL"
    Value="$(var.SqlServerInstance)"
    Result="exists"
    Variable="SqlInstanceFound" />
```

If an instance is found, the `SqlInstanceFound` variable will be set to 1.

SQL Server 2012 Express requires Service Pack 1 and .NET 3.5 or later on a Windows 7 64-bit system. You may want to add a `Condition` element to check that the target system has this installed or include them as packages in your bootstrapper.

Inside `ExePackage`, we've added a `RemotePayload` element:

```
<RemotePayload
   Description="Microsoft SQL Server 2012 Express Edition"
   ProductName="Microsoft SQL Server 2012 Express Edition"
   Version="11.0.2100.60"
   Size="138412032"
   Hash="e4561d5caa761a5d1daa0d305f4fecedc6a0d39c" />
```

This serves as a validation check on the package that is to be downloaded, as specified by the `ExePackage` element's `DownloadUrl` attribute. `Description`, `ProductName`, `Version`, and `Size` (in bytes) can often be found on the executable itself. To get a hash of the file, you may want to use a tool such as Microsoft File Checksum Integrity Verifier, which can be downloaded at:

http://www.microsoft.com/en-us/download/details.aspx?id=11533.

It's a command-line utility that can create a SHA1 hash for an executable file.

Downloading `MsiPackage` benefits from a simpler syntax because Burn can extract more attributes on its own from an MSI package than it can from an EXE package. The following is an example that downloads the Python installer and runs it:

```
<MsiPackage
   Id="PYTHON"
   SourceFile="python-2.7.3.msi"
   DownloadUrl=
      "http://www.python.org/ftp/python/2.7.3/python-2.7.3.msi"
   Compressed="no" />
```

The `DownloadUrl` attribute serves the same purpose as when used on `ExePackage`. It sets the location where the package can be downloaded from. Otherwise, we only need to specify the `SourceFile` and `Compressed` attributes. `SourceFile` will point to a local copy of the MSI. `Compressed` should be set to `no`, so that the MSI is not embedded inside the bootstrapper.

If you author your bootstrapper to download packages, what happens if the end user doesn't have an Internet connection? One option is to pass the `/layout` flag to your bundle when an Internet connection *is* available. Burn adds in this functionality automatically. The `/layout` flag downloads the packages and copies them to a local directory. The end user can then take these files to the computer that doesn't have an Internet connection and install them. As an example, if this command were run when a connection was available, it would create a new bootstrapper that could be run without a connection:

AwesomeBootstrapper.exe /layout "Local Bootstrapper"

This will copy the bootstrapper to a folder called `Local Bootstrapper` along with all packages downloaded and extracted. This is shown in the following screenshot:

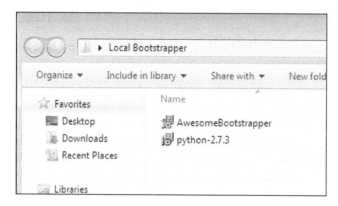

Counting package references

Some of the dependencies you install, such as SQL Server, may be used by several different software bundles. For example, you might have an application that stores customer records in the database. Later on, another piece of software is installed that stores log information in that same SQL Server instance. You may not want to remove it until all interested parties have been uninstalled. For example, uninstalling the logging piece shouldn't remove the SQL instance because the customer records software is still using it.

To solve these sorts of dependency issues, Burn provides an element for package reference counting as part of its **DependencyExtension**. To use it, first add a reference in your Burn project to `DependenyExtension`. Then, update the `Wix` element to contain the new namespace, as shown:

```
<Wix xmlns="http://schemas.microsoft.com/wix/2006/wi" xmlns:dep=
    "http://schemas.microsoft.com/wix/DependencyExtension">
```

Next, add a `Provides` element inside the `ExePackage` element—in this case a SQL Server Express package—that your bundles will share a reference to.

> Note that the `MsiPackage` element does not need to use this functionality because it already has reference counting built-in.

```
<ExePackage Id="SQLSERVER"
        SourceFile="SQLEXPR_x64_ENU.exe"
        DetectCondition="SqlInstanceFound"
        InstallCommand="$(var.SqlInstallCommand)"
```

```
          UninstallCommand="$(var.SqlUninstallCommand)"
          RepairCommand="$(var.SqlRepairCommand)">


  <dep:Provides Key="SqlServerExpress_TEST"
                Version="11.0.2100.60" />

</ExePackage>
```

When you install the bundle—let's say in addition to having the SQL Server package, it also contains an `MsiPackage` element for the customer records software—a new entry will be created in the Windows Registry. Look under the **HKCR\Installer\ Dependencies** key to see the SQL Server package and its dependencies.

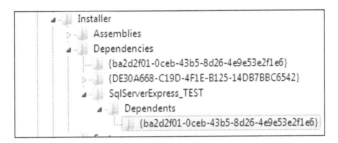

Here you can see that we've added the bundle as a dependency to the SQL Server instance. If you were then to install a different bootstrapper, containing different `Name` and `UpgradeCode` elements—let's say this is our logging software—and add the same SQL Server `ExePackage` with the `Provides` element, you would notice (in the following screenshot) that the entry in the registry gets another dependency:

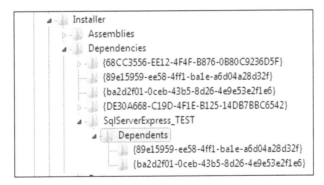

Now the SQL Server package has two bundles, the customer records software and logging software, that are dependent upon it. We can see their bundle IDs listed below the **Dependents** node within the **SqlServerExpress_TEST** key in the registry.

Uninstalling one of the bundles would not remove the SQL Server instance. It will only be removed when all software that is dependent on it is uninstalled. Each time that a dependent bundle is removed, the registry is updated.

It's likely that you will always want to nest a `Provides` element inside of an `ExePackage` element. Otherwise, when you upgrade the bundle, and the old bundle is removed, you may find that the dependency, such as the SQL Server instance, is removed unexpectedly. Maintaining a reference count protects you against this during bundle upgrades.

Rollback boundaries

Let's say you've included three MSIs in your install chain. The user launches the bootstrapper, the first two MSIs install successfully but the third fails. You may decide to keep the first two but roll back only the third. By default, all three will roll back. Use `RollbackBoundary` elements to create checkpoints past which the install won't roll back. The following is an example:

```
<Chain>
    <MsiPackage... />
    <MsiPackage ... />
    <RollbackBoundary />
    <MsiPackage... />
</Chain>
```

If the third MSI package fails, only *it* will be rolled back. The first two packages will remain installed. Another scenario is to roll back a failed install and then skip past it to the next rollback boundary. In the next example, if the second MSI fails, it will skip forward to the next `RollbackBoundary` and continue. The key is to add the `Vital` attribute on a `RollbackBoundary` element, set to `no`, that precedes the `MsiPackage` element:

```
<Chain>
    <MsiPackage ... />
    <RollbackBoundary Vital="no" />
    <MsiPackage ... />
    <RollbackBoundary />
    <MsiPackage ... />
</Chain>
```

Here, if the second MSI fails, it will roll back to the boundary that preceded it. Because we've marked it as not vital, it will then skip forward to the next boundary and continue installing. This is almost equivalent to marking the `MsiPackage` element itself as not vital:

```
<Chain>
   <MsiPackage ... />
   <MsiPackage Vital="no" ... />
   <MsiPackage ... />
</Chain>
```

The difference is that marking the package as not vital means that if it fails, the bootstrapper simply continues on. If the MSI rolls itself back that's all fine and good. However, when a `RollbackBoundary` element is marked as not vital, Burn explicitly tries to uninstall the failed packages before skipping ahead to the next boundary.

PackageGroups

To split your package definitions up for more modularity, place them within `PackageGroup` elements. You can then reference the group within your `Chain` element with `PackageGroupRef`. The following is an example where we separate the detection (via `RegistrySearch`) and installation of SQL Server into its own fragment:

```
<Bundle Name="Awesome Software Bundle"
        Version="1.0.0.0"
        Manufacturer="Awesome Company"
        Copyright="(c) All rights reserved."
        UpgradeCode="3601032C-A8C9-4323-88E0-1967A9C2145E">

    <BootstrapperApplicationRef
        Id="WixStandardBootstrapperApplication.RtfLicense" />

    <Chain>
        <PackageGroupRef Id="SQL_SERVER_2012_EXPRESS"/>
    </Chain>
</Bundle>

<Fragment>
    <util:RegistrySearch
        Id="SqlInstanceFound"
        Root="HKLM"
        Key="SOFTWARE\Microsoft\Microsoft SQL Server\Instance Names\SQL"
        Value="$(var.SqlServerInstance)"
        Result="exists"
```

```
            Variable="SqlInstanceFound" />


    <PackageGroup Id="SQL_SERVER_2012_EXPRESS">
        <ExePackage
            Id="SQLSERVER"
            DownloadUrl="$(var.SqlDownloadUrl)"
            Name="SQLEXPR_x64_ENU.exe"
            Compressed="no"
            DetectCondition="SqlInstanceFound"
            InstallCommand="$(var.SqlInstallCommand)"
            UninstallCommand="$(var.SqlUninstallCommand)"
            RepairCommand="$(var.SqlRepairCommand)">

            <RemotePayload
                Description=
                    "Microsoft SQL Server 2012 Express Edition"
                ProductName=
                    "Microsoft SQL Server 2012 Express Edition"
                Version="11.0.2100.60"
                Size="138412032"
                Hash="e4561d5caa761a5d1daa0d305f4fecedc6a0d39c" />
        </ExePackage>
    </PackageGroup>
</Fragment>
```

The `PackageGroup` element, which I've included in a separate `Fragment` element, contains the `ExePackage` element that installs SQL Server. We can then reference this package group within our `Chain` element using the `PackageGroupRef` element. Its `Id` attribute should match the `Id` attribute on the `PackageGroup` element.

`WixNetFxExtension` contains several package groups for installing versions of the .NET Framework. To include .NET 4, you could reference the `NetFx40Web` package group, as shown in the following snippet:

```
<Chain>
    <PackageGroupRef Id="NetFx40Web"/>
</Chain>
```

You can also install the .NET Framework 4.5 using `NetFx45WebPackageGroup`.

The Standard Bootstrapper UI

Burn comes with two built-in user interfaces. The main purpose is to display a single progress bar while the packages within the `Chain` element are being installed.

 If you'd rather show the UI from your MSI package, set the **DisplayInternalUI** attribute on the `MsiPackage` element to "yes".

The first is called **WixStandardBootstrapperApplication.RtfLicense** and the other **WixStandardBootstrapperApplication.HyperlinkLicense**. We will discuss each one in the following sections.

The RtfLicense user interface

Start off by adding the `BootstrapperApplicationRef` element to your Burn markup. The following snippet adds the `RtfLicense` UI to our bootstrapper:

```
<Bundle ... >
    <BootstrapperApplicationRef
        Id="WixStandardBootstrapperApplication.RtfLicense" />
```

This provides you with a dialog containing an end-user license agreement that can be customized with your own RTF text file. To customize the text, reference the `BalExtension` namespace in your `Wix` element and then add a `WixStandardBootstrapperApplication` element inside of your `BootstrapperApplicationRef`. The license is specified with the `LicenseFile` attribute:

```
<Wixxmlns="http://schemas.microsoft.com/wix/2006/wi"
xmlns:bal="http://schemas.microsoft.com/wix/BalExtension">

<Bundle ... >
<BootstrapperApplicationRef
    Id="WixStandardBootstrapperApplication.RtfLicense">

    <bal:WixStandardBootstrapperApplication
        LicenseFile="customEula.rtf" />
</BootstrapperApplicationRef>
```

While we're at it, we might as well change the logo that's shown on the dialog. The default image is a PNG 63 x 63 pixels in size. Use the `LogoFile` attribute to point to a new image, as shown in the following snippet:

```
<BootstrapperApplicationRef
    Id="WixStandardBootstrapperApplication.RtfLicense">

    <bal:WixStandardBootstrapperApplication
        LicenseFile="customEula.rtf"
        LogoFile="customLogo.png" />
</BootstrapperApplicationRef>
```

Here is the result:

The **Options** button lets the end user change the targeted install directory. You can hide this button by setting the `SuppressOptionsUI` attribute on the `WixStandardBootstrapperApplication` element to `yes`.

The HyperlinkLicense user interface

The `HyperlinkLicense` UI is similar to `RtfLicense` except that instead of referencing a local RTF file for the license agreement and displaying it in a textbox, it provides a link to it. Set the `LicenseUrl` attribute to a URL where your license agreement is hosted. The following is an example:

```
<BootstrapperApplicationRef
    Id="WixStandardBootstrapperApplication.HyperlinkLicense">

    <bal:WixStandardBootstrapperApplication
```

```
            LicenseUrl="http://www.mydomain.com/CustomEula.rtf"
            LogoFile="customLogo.png" />
    </BootstrapperApplicationRef>
```

This produces the following result:

It's possible to customize the look of these themes by adding a new THM file to your project and referencing it with the `WixStandardBootstrapperApplication` element's **ThemeFile** attribute. At the time of this writing there's no way to add, as an example, a textbox to the UI and set a variable with its value. Burn does provide a textbox control, called `Editbox`, but there isn't a way to set a variable with what the user types into it. To do so, you'd need to alter and recompile `BalExtension` to accept the new input. You can, however, make cosmetic changes to the theme.

If you'd like to go down this route, download the WiX source code and copy either the `RtfTheme.xml` or `HyperlinkTheme.xml` from the `src\ext\BalExtension\wixstdba\Resources` folder to your project. Set the `ThemeFile` attribute on the `WixStandardBootstrapperApplication` element to point to this new file.

 Theme files can have either the `.thm` or `.xml` extension. You could use the **ThmViewer** utility found in the WiX `bin` folder to view theme files. Beware that if there is an error in the theme file's markup or if one of its dependencies cannot be found, such as a `.wxl` file, logo image, or RTF file, then `ThmViewer` will not display the theme.

You may then change the attributes of the dialogs such as the size of the window, background color, or fonts. Refer to the XML schema `src\dutil\xsd\thmutil.xsd` for more information about the format of the elements found in the theme file. You'll find that each window in the theme is defined by a `Page` element that contains the UI controls displayed. The following is the markup for the initial *Install* window found in `RtfLicense`:

```
<Page Name="Install">
<Richedit Name="EulaRichedit" X="11" Y="80" Width="-11" Height="-70"
TabStop="yes" FontId="0" HexStyle="0x800000" />

<Checkbox Name="EulaAcceptCheckbox" X="-11" Y="-41" Width="260"
Height="17" TabStop="yes" FontId="3" HideWhenDisabled="yes">#(loc.
InstallAcceptCheckbox)</Checkbox>

<Button Name="OptionsButton" X="-171" Y="-11" Width="75"
Height="23" TabStop="yes" FontId="0" HideWhenDisabled="yes">#(loc.
InstallOptionsButton)</Button>

<Button Name="InstallButton" X="-91" Y="-11" Width="75" Height="23"
TabStop="yes" FontId="0">#(loc.InstallInstallButton)</Button>

<Button Name="WelcomeCancelButton" X="-11" Y="-11" Width="75"
Height="23" TabStop="yes" FontId="0">#(loc.InstallCloseButton)</
Button>
</Page>
```

As you can see, a `Richedit` control is used to show the EULA and a `Checkbox` control allows the user to accept the license terms. You might change the size of these elements or their position on the dialog.

Summary

In this chapter, we discussed the structure of the bootstrapper bundle and how to chain different types of installers into it. We touched on how to download packages from the Internet, slipstream patches, and control rollback behavior and command-line flags passed to the installers.

In the next chapter, we will discover how to fully customize the Burn install wizard via a custom WPF user interface. This will allow you to collect new user input and add dialogs.

16
Customizing the Burn UI

In the last chapter, we learned that for many bootstrapping tasks the standard user interfaces, RtfLicense and HyperlinkLicense, will be more than adequate. However, we are limited on how much we can customize the design and workflow of these dialogs. We're also limited in that the standard UIs do not allow us to collect information from the end user and store them in Burn variables.

In this chapter, we will build our own user interface using **Windows Presentation Foundation (WPF)** and C#. We will cover the following topics:

- The extension points offered by Burn and how to hook into them
- How to organize our code using the MVVM pattern
- Events to handle when communicating with the Burn engine
- Collecting user input and storing it in Burn variables

Burn extension points

When you install the WiX toolset, you are given an assembly called BootstrapperCore.dll. You'll find it in the WiX SDK directory, which, on my computer, is located at C:\Program Files (x86)\WiX Toolset v3.6\SDK. This library is all we need to plug a new user interface into the Burn engine. It contains base classes for us to override in our own code, events to hook into, and methods that allow us to control the bootstrapper.

In this chapter, we will build a UI using WPF and C#. WPF uses an XML markup called **XAML** for designing its interface. This allows designers to work on the layout of the window while developers work on the C# business logic separately. WPF has a number of other benefits including strong support for data binding, reusable styles, and a variety of containers for organizing UI controls. That's not to say this is our only option. We could use Windows Forms or unmanaged code if we chose to. However, WiX's own installer is written with WPF and offers a good example for how to proceed. If you want more examples, I highly recommend downloading the WiX source code and looking at the WiX setup. It can be found in the `src\Setup\ WixBA` folder.

The UI we will build won't be fancy. Nor will it be as sophisticated as the WiX installer. As a basic example, it will simply be able to install the packages that are in our bundle's chain, uninstall those packages, and cancel either of those two operations. In the end, here's what it will look like:

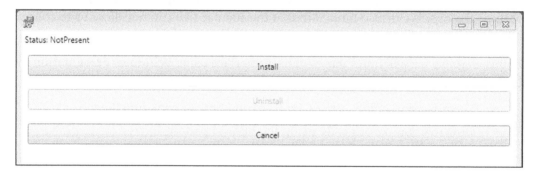

Creating the class library

So how do we begin to extend the Burn UI? In short, we will build a C# class library (`.dll`) that references `BootstrapperCore.dll`. Our class library will then be referenced within our bootstrapper markup. When the bootstrapper starts up, it will have been configured to use this assembly. Our assembly will have WPF code inside of it, ready to show a window as it simultaneously drives forward the Burn engine. Clicking a button on our UI will call methods provided by `BootstrapperCore`. Simple, right? Let's dive into it.

Create a new C# **Class Library** project in Visual Studio and name it `CustomBA`. Once you have it, add a reference to `BootstrapperCore.dll`, which can be found in the WiX SDK directory. To use WPF, we'll also need to reference the following .NET assemblies:

- `PresentationCore`
- `PresentationFramework`

- System.Xaml
- WindowsBase

We'll be using the **Model-View-ViewModel (MVVM)** pattern to organize the code. This will allow us to keep our UI and backend layers decoupled, and usually results in cleaner markup and code. MVVM is a design pattern for decoupling the presentation and business logic of a Windows application that has become popular with the WPF crowd. In a large part, this has to do with WPF being so well-suited for it.

When it comes to implementing the MVVM pattern, there are several libraries available that make it easy. I like to use **Prism** because it adds several convenient classes such as **DelegateCommand**, a class that allows you to bind events such as mouse clicks to handler functions that aren't in the code-behind class. You can either download it from `http://compositewpf.codeplex.com` or, easier in my opinion, install it via **NuGet**. NuGet is a package manager for Visual Studio. It comes built into Visual Studio 2012, but can be downloaded from *Codeplex*, `http://nuget.codeplex.com`, for Visual Studio 2010. Once you've got it, the NuGet command for installing Prism is simply:

```
Install-Package Prism
```

The most important assembly you'll need from this library is `Microsoft.Practices.Prism`. This contains the classes, such as `DelegateCommand`, that we will use in this chapter. If you're using NuGet, all necessary references will be added to your project.

Next, to pave the way for a well-organized project, create three subfolders: `Models`, `ViewModels`, and `Views`. This folder structure will help keep us sane as we add additional files. We also need to add the XML configuration file that will tell Burn to use our new assembly. It must be called `BootstrapperCore.config` and you can copy an existing version of it from the `WiX SDK` folder to your project. Be sure to change its properties in Visual Studio so that the **Copy to Output Directory** setting is set to **Copy if newer**. Open it and replace the `host` element's `assemblyName` attribute with the name of our assembly, `CustomBA`. The following is what it should look like:

```
<configuration>
    <configSections>
        <sectionGroup name="wix.bootstrapper" type="Microsoft.
Tools.WindowsInstallerXml.Bootstrapper.BootstrapperSectionGroup,
BootstrapperCore">
            <section name="host" type="Microsoft.Tools.
WindowsInstallerXml.Bootstrapper.HostSection, BootstrapperCore" />
        </sectionGroup>
    </configSections>
    <startup useLegacyV2RuntimeActivationPolicy="true">
```

```
            <supportedRuntime version="v4.0" />
            <supportedRuntime version="v2.0.50727" />
        </startup>
        <wix.bootstrapper>
            <host assemblyName="CustomBA" />
        </wix.bootstrapper>
    </configuration>
```

Our `CustomBA.dll`, `BootstrapperCore.config`, and `Microsoft.Practices.Prism.dll` class libraries will eventually need to be copied to our bootstrapper project so that they can be referenced and embedded within the executable. We'll cover that in more detail further on in the chapter.

The last part of our setup is to add an attribute called `BootstrapperApplicationAttribute` to the `Properties\AssemblyInfo.cs` file:

```
    using CustomBA;
    using Microsoft.Tools.WindowsInstallerXml.Bootstrapper;

    [assembly: BootstrapperApplication(
        typeof(CustomBootstrapperApplication))]
```

This identifies the class in our assembly that extends the `BootstrapperApplication` class. Burn looks for this class and automatically calls its `Run` method. That will be our jumping-on point into the Burn process. In the next section, we will define this `CustomBootstrapperApplication` class.

Extending the BootstrapperApplication class

The first class we'll add to our project will provide the bridge between our code and the Burn engine. Add a new C# class file and name it `CustomBootstrapperApplication`. It should extend the `BootstrapperApplication` class from the `Microsoft.Tools.WindowsInstallerXml.Bootstrapper` namespace. Add the following code:

```
    using CustomBA.Models;
    using CustomBA.ViewModels;
    using CustomBA.Views;
    using Microsoft.Tools.WindowsInstallerXml.Bootstrapper;
    using System;
    using System.Windows.Threading;

    namespace CustomBA
```

```
{
    public class CustomBootstrapperApplication :
      BootstrapperApplication
    {
        public static Dispatcher Dispatcher { get; set; }

        protected override void Run()
        {
            Dispatcher = Dispatcher.CurrentDispatcher;

            var model = new BootstrapperApplicationModel(this);
            var viewModel = new InstallViewModel(model);
            var view = new InstallView(viewModel);

            model.SetWindowHandle(view);

            this.Engine.Detect();

            view.Show();
            Dispatcher.Run();
            this.Engine.Quit(model.FinalResult);
        }
    }
}
```

We're using a few classes, such as `InstallViewModel`, which will
process commands triggered by the view and pass data to the model, and
`BootstrapperApplicationModel`, which will wrap the calls to the Burn engine, that
we haven't defined yet. Don't worry; we'll get to those soon.

The first thing we do is override the `Run` method. This is our UI's primary entry
point. It will be called by the Burn engine. Within this method, we instantiate a new
`Dispatcher` object and store it in a static property. A `Dispatcher` object provides
a means for sending messages between the UI thread and any backend threads.
It provides a handy `Invoke` method that we can use to update the state of our UI
controls. Without it, the UI thread would ignore our attempts to interact with it from
another thread.

Next we create **model**, **viewmodel**, and **view** objects. The purpose of the model is to
encapsulate some of the calls to the bootstrapper. It's essentially a wrapper, further
separating the UI logic from the bootstrapper logic. The viewmodel gets data from
and calls methods on the model while also responding to events triggered by the
view. It's the workhorse of the three, acting as the middleman. Up last is the view.
It is mostly written in XAML and contains the structure of the visible window
displayed to the user.

The MVVM pattern provides mechanisms such as commands and data binding for handling communication between the layers in a decoupled way. In this chapter, the intended design is for the viewmodel to have knowledge of the model, but not vice versa. Furthermore, the viewmodel should not have any direct knowledge to the view object. Similarly, the view object's only tie to viewmodel will come through data binding. You can see that we've reinforced this design by passing an instance of the model object into the viewmodel object's constructor and then viewmodel into the view object's constructor:

```
var model = new BootstrapperApplicationModel(this);
var viewModel = new InstallViewModel(model);
var view = new InstallView(viewModel);
```

An improved design would use interfaces or abstract classes to further decouple the objects that are being passed around from their implementation. To keep things simple I am using the objects directly.

The next thing we do is pass the view into a helper method we've yet to define called `SetWindowHandle`. This goes against the grain of our MVVM design, but is a necessary evil dictated by the `BootstrapperCore` library. This method will get a handle to the WPF window, which is needed by the Burn engine when performing the install or uninstall.

```
model.SetWindowHandle(view);
```

Next, we start the ball rolling by calling the `Detect` method:

```
this.Engine.Detect();
```

This gives Burn the go-ahead to check if our bundle is already installed. That way, when our window is shown, we'll know whether we need to present an **Install** button or an **Uninstall** button. Note that we are calling this *after* instantiating our view, viewmodel, and model objects. That's because the viewmodel needs to set up some event handlers and if we fire `Detect` too quickly, it will miss the boat. Specifically, it will miss the event handler that fires when `Detect` is complete.

The last thing we do is call `Show` on the view to display the WPF window. Immediately afterward we call `Dispatcher.Run()`, which halts execution of this method at that line until the `Dispatcher` is shut down. In the meantime, the `Dispatcher` object will loop in place, waiting for messages and providing methods for communicating with the UI thread—which is the current thread. Calling `Dispatcher.Run()` prevents our own `Run` method from exiting prematurely, which would terminate our process:

```
view.Show();
Dispatcher.Run();
this.Engine.Quit(model.FinalResult);
```

When we decide to shut down the window, we'll call `InvokeShutdown` on the `Dispatcher` object, causing our `Run` method to continue its execution. At that point, `Engine.Quit` will be called with whatever status code we've collected at that point (be it an error code or a success code) and gracefully wind down the bootstrapping process.

Defining the model

Our model class is going to be fairly small. Its main purpose will be to encapsulate calls to the bootstrapper so as to present a simplified API to the viewmodel. Add a new C# class file to the `Models` folder and name it `BootstrapperApplicationModel`. Update it with the following code:

```
using Microsoft.Tools.WindowsInstallerXml.Bootstrapper;
using System;
using System.Windows;
using System.Windows.Interop;

namespace CustomBA.Models
{
    public class BootstrapperApplicationModel
    {
        private IntPtr hwnd;

        public BootstrapperApplicationModel(
          BootstrapperApplication bootstrapperApplication)
        {
            this.BootstrapperApplication =
              bootstrapperApplication;
            this.hwnd = IntPtr.Zero;
        }

        public BootstrapperApplication BootstrapperApplication { get;
private set; }

        public int FinalResult { get; set; }

        public void SetWindowHandle(Window view)
        {
            this.hwnd = new WindowInteropHelper(view).Handle;
        }

        public void PlanAction(LaunchAction action)
        {
```

```
            this.BootstrapperApplication.Engine.Plan(action);
        }

        public void ApplyAction()
        {
            this.BootstrapperApplication.Engine.Apply(this.hwnd);
        }

        public void LogMessage(string message)
        {
            this.BootstrapperApplication.Engine.Log(
              LogLevel.Standard,
              message);
        }
    }
}
```

The constructor of this class expects a parameter of type BootstrapperApplication. As you saw earlier, we are passing our CustomBootstrapperApplication class in here. Several of the methods in this model, such as PlanAction, ApplyAction, and LogMessage only serve to wrap calls to this object:

```
public BootstrapperApplicationModel(
    BootstrapperApplication bootstrapperApplication)
{
    this.BootstrapperApplication = bootstrapperApplication;
    this.hwnd = IntPtr.Zero;
}
```

Also in the constructor, we are initializing the pointer to our WPF window, which will be needed by the ApplyAction method. The true pointer is set when SetWindowHandle is called by the CustomBootstrapperApplication class in its Run method. For now, we only set it to zero.

Quick descriptions of PlanAction and ApplyAction are that the former is given a task to prepare for, such as installation, uninstallation, repair, or modify, and the latter executes that task.

```
public void PlanAction(LaunchAction action)
{
    this.BootstrapperApplication.Engine.Plan(action);
}

public void ApplyAction()
{
    this.BootstrapperApplication.Engine.Apply(this.hwnd);
}
```

Therefore, the usual workflow is that when a button is clicked on the UI, we call `PlanAction`, passing in the task that we want to execute. Once planning has completed, we invoke `ApplyAction`. `Plan` and `Apply`, along with `Detect`, are among the most important events you'll interact with.

Another method that we're defining is a helper for appending messages to the bootstrapper's log, which can be found in the `%TEMP%` directory.

```
public void LogMessage(string message)
{
    this.BootstrapperApplication.Engine.Log(
        LogLevel.Standard,
        message);
}
```

A final point of interest is the `FinalResult` property. We will use this to store the exit status code that the Burn engine returns after the bootstrapper has finished.

```
public int FinalResult { get; set; }
```

This status code will be passed to the `Engine.Quit(model.FinalResult)` method at the end of the `Run` method in our `CustomBootstrapperApplication` class. As we saw earlier, this will be used to finalize the installation and end the process.

Implementing the viewmodel

Now let's move on to viewmodel. Add a new C# class file to the `ViewModels` folder and name it `InstallViewModel`. Add the following code:

```
using CustomBA.Models;
using Microsoft.Practices.Prism.Commands;
using Microsoft.Practices.Prism.ViewModel;
using Microsoft.Tools.WindowsInstallerXml.Bootstrapper;
using System;
using System.Windows.Input;

namespace CustomBA.ViewModels
{
    public class InstallViewModel : NotificationObject
    {
        public enum InstallState
        {
            Initializing,
            Present,
            NotPresent,
```

```
            Applying,
            Cancelled
        }

        private InstallState state;
        private string message;

        private BootstrapperApplicationModel model;

        public ICommand InstallCommand { get; private set; }

        public ICommand UninstallCommand { get; private set; }

        public ICommand CancelCommand { get; private set; }

        public string Message
        {
            get
            {
                return this.message;
            }
            set
            {
                if (this.message != value)
                {
                    this.message = value;
                    this.RaisePropertyChanged(() => this.Message);
                }
            }
        }

        public InstallState State
        {
            get
            {
                return this.state;
            }
            set
            {
                if (this.state != value)
                {
                    this.state = value;
                    this.Message = this.state.ToString();
                    this.RaisePropertyChanged(() => this.State);
```

```
                this.Refresh();
            }
        }
    }

    public InstallViewModel(
      BootstrapperApplicationModel model)
    {
        this.model = model;
        this.State = InstallState.Initializing;

        this.WireUpEventHandlers();

        this.InstallCommand = new DelegateCommand(() =>
            this.model.PlanAction(LaunchAction.Install),
            () => this.State == InstallState.NotPresent);

        this.UninstallCommand = new DelegateCommand(() =>
            this.model.PlanAction(LaunchAction.Uninstall),
            () => this.State == InstallState.Present);

        this.CancelCommand = new DelegateCommand(() =>
        {
            this.model.LogMessage("Cancelling...");
            if (this.State == InstallState.Applying)
            {
                this.State = InstallState.Cancelled;
            }
            else
            {
                CustomBootstrapperApplication.Dispatcher
                  .InvokeShutdown();
            }
        }, () => this.State != InstallState.Cancelled);
    }

    protected void DetectPackageComplete(
      object sender,
      DetectPackageCompleteEventArgs e)
    {
        if (e.PackageId.Equals(
          "MyInstaller.msi", StringComparison.Ordinal))
        {
            this.State = e.State == PackageState.Present ?
```

```
                      InstallState.Present : InstallState.NotPresent;
      }
    }

    protected void PlanComplete(
      object sender, PlanCompleteEventArgs e)
    {
        if (this.State == InstallState.Cancelled)
        {
            CustomBootstrapperApplication.Dispatcher
              .InvokeShutdown();
            return;
        }

        this.model.ApplyAction();
    }

    protected void ApplyBegin(
      object sender, ApplyBeginEventArgs e)
    {
        this.State = InstallState.Applying;
    }

    protected void ExecutePackageBegin(
      object sender, ExecutePackageBeginEventArgs e)
    {
        if (this.State == InstallState.Cancelled)
        {
            e.Result = Result.Cancel;
        }
    }

    protected void ExecutePackageComplete(
      object sender, ExecutePackageCompleteEventArgs e)
    {
        if (this.State == InstallState.Cancelled)
        {
            e.Result = Result.Cancel;
        }
    }

    protected void ApplyComplete(
      object sender, ApplyCompleteEventArgs e)
    {
```

```
            this.model.FinalResult = e.Status;
            CustomBootstrapperApplication.Dispatcher
                .InvokeShutdown();
        }

        private void Refresh()
        {
            CustomBootstrapperApplication.Dispatcher.Invoke(
                (Action)((() =>
                {
                    ((DelegateCommand)this.InstallCommand)
                        .RaiseCanExecuteChanged();
                    ((DelegateCommand)this.UninstallCommand)
                        .RaiseCanExecuteChanged();
                    ((DelegateCommand)this.CancelCommand)
                        .RaiseCanExecuteChanged();
                }));
        }

        private void WireUpEventHandlers()
        {
            this.model.BootstrapperApplication.DetectPackageComplete
+= this.DetectPackageComplete;
            this.model.BootstrapperApplication.PlanComplete += this.
PlanComplete;
            this.model.BootstrapperApplication.ApplyComplete += this.
ApplyComplete;

            this.model.BootstrapperApplication.ApplyBegin += this.
ApplyBegin;

            this.model.BootstrapperApplication.ExecutePackageBegin +=
this.ExecutePackageBegin;
            this.model.BootstrapperApplication.ExecutePackageComplete
+= this.ExecutePackageComplete;
        }
    }
}
```

There's quite a bit happening here so let's take it one piece at a time. Within the next few sections we will dissect this class into logic parts.

Declaring the properties and fields

The `InstallViewModel` class extends a base class called `NotificationObject`.
This is a helper class from the Prism library that facilitates notifying the view
when a property is updated in the viewmodel. Within the class we define an
enum named `InstallState`.

```
public class InstallViewModel : NotificationObject
{
  public enum InstallState
  {
    Initializing,
    Present,
    NotPresent,
    Applying,
    Cancelled
  }
```

This will track which phase of the bootstrapping process we are in so that we can
enable and disable buttons as appropriate. It will also allow us to track whether the
user has canceled the install. If they have, and we're already installing—otherwise
known as **Applying**—we will know to not immediately shut down the process, but
rather send a flag to the bootstrapper so that it can roll back any installed packages.
If, on the other hand, we have not begun the **Apply** phase, it is safe to shut down the
bootstrapper immediately.

We then define three private fields:

```
private InstallState state;
private string message;
private BootstrapperApplicationModel model;
```

The first, `state`, is used to hold the current status of the installation, utilizing the
enumeration that we just defined. The second is called `message` and stores text that
we want to display on the WPF window. The last one is a reference to our model
class and is simply called `model`.

Next we set up properties of type `ICommand`. The view will bind to these so that
when a button is clicked, one of these commands will be executed. We will define
them later on in this class' constructor.

```
public ICommand InstallCommand { get; private set; }

public ICommand UninstallCommand { get; private set; }

public ICommand CancelCommand { get; private set; }
```

Next we set up two more properties: Message and State. These are the publicly accessible versions of the message and state fields we defined before. We make them public so that the view can bind to them as shown in the following snippet:

```
public string Message
{
   get
   {
      return this.message;
   }
   set
   {
      if (this.message != value)
      {
         this.message = value;
         this.RaisePropertyChanged(() => this.Message);
      }
   }
}

public InstallState State
{
   get
   {
      return this.state;
   }
   set
   {
      if (this.state != value)
      {
         this.state = value;
         this.Message = "Status: " +
                     this.state.ToString();

         this.RaisePropertyChanged(() => this.State);
         this.Refresh();
      }
   }
}
```

Each property checks that it's being set to something different than what it's already set to before performing the update. That way, we save some processing power if the change isn't needed. To notify the view that the property has been changed, we call the RaisePropertyChanged method, passing in a lambda expression that identifies the property.

The State property also calls a private method called Refresh that will enable or disable our UI's buttons depending on InstalledState. We will describe that method later in the chapter. Also note that the State property sets the Message property to a stringified version of itself. I do this just to show something changing on the view as we progress through the phases.

Defining the constructor

Our viewmodel's constructor looks like this:

```
public InstallViewModel(BootstrapperApplicationModel model)
{
    this.model = model;
    this.State = InstallState.Initializing;

    this.WireUpEventHandlers();

    this.InstallCommand = new DelegateCommand(() =>
        this.model.PlanAction(LaunchAction.Install),
        () => this.State == InstallState.NotPresent);

    this.UninstallCommand = new DelegateCommand(() =>
        this.model.PlanAction(LaunchAction.Uninstall),
        () => this.State == InstallState.Present);

    this.CancelCommand = new DelegateCommand(() =>
    {
        this.model.LogMessage("Cancelling...");
        if (this.State == InstallState.Applying)
        {
            this.State = InstallState.Cancelled;
        }
        else
        {
            CustomBootstrapperApplication.Dispatcher
                .InvokeShutdown();
        }
    },
    () => this.State != InstallState.Cancelled);
}
```

Our constructor accepts an instance of `BootstrapperApplicationModel`, our model class, in its list of parameters. We store this in the instance variable `model`. We'll be able to use it to call any of the model's methods.

Next, we set the initial value of the `State` property to `Initializing` and then call a helper method called `WireUpEventHandlers`. As you'll see, this method associates event handlers with the events that are fired by the bootstrapper.

We then move on to initializing our command objects. We are using the `DelegateCommand` class, which comes from the Prism library. The first parameter to `DelegateCommand` is an anonymous method to invoke when the command is executed. The second parameter is another anonymous method that returns a Boolean value that signifies whether the command, and all UI controls that are bound to it, should be enabled. In each case, we are basing this check on the current value of the `State` property.

Taking a closer look, `InstallCommand` and `UninstallCommand` call the model's `PlanAction` method when they are executed. As you'll remember, by passing the type of action we want to perform to `PlanAction`, we initiate the bootstrapper's workflow, to be completed later when `ApplyAction` is called.

When `CancelCommand` is executed, we either shut the UI and bootstrapper down immediately, via the `Dispatcher.InvokeShutdown` method or, if changes are already being applied, we set `State` to `Cancelled` so that other event handlers down the line can gracefully wind down the process.

Setting up the event handlers

Next, we'll examine the event handlers. First up is the `DetectPackageComplete` method. You'll see later on that we wire up these events handlers in a helper method called `WireUpEventHandlers`.

```
protected void DetectPackageComplete(
    object sender,
    DetectPackageCompleteEventArgs e)
{
    if (e.PackageId.Equals(
        "MyInstaller.msi",
        StringComparison.Ordinal))
    {
        this.State = e.State == PackageState.Present ?
            InstallState.Present : InstallState.NotPresent;
    }
}
```

This method is called when the `Detect` method that we called in the `CustomBootstrapperApplication` class' `Run` method completes. We begin by checking the `DetectPackageCompleteEventArgs` object to see if the package that was detected was an installer called `MyInstaller.msi`. You would substitute this with the name of your own software's installer. If it finds a match, we then check whether that package is currently installed on the end user's computer via the `PackageState` enumeration. If it is `Present`, we set the `State` property to `InstallState.Present`, otherwise it is set to `InstallState.NotPresent`.

The `Present/NotPresent` value will be used by the `InstallCommand` and `UninstallComand` properties to enable or disable the UI controls that are bound to them. If it isn't present, we enable the **Install** button. Otherwise, we enable the **Uninstall** button. A quick glance back at those two commands shows this to be the case:

```
this.InstallCommand = new DelegateCommand(() =>
    this.model.PlanAction(LaunchAction.Install),
    () => this.State == InstallState.NotPresent);

this.UninstallCommand = new DelegateCommand(() =>
    this.model.PlanAction(LaunchAction.Uninstall),
    () => this.State == InstallState.Present);
```

Remember that after we've called `PlanAction` to kick off the installation or uninstallation and planning has completed, we then want to trigger `ApplyAction`. This hand off is performed in the `PlanComplete` event handler. Additionally, if the user has canceled the install — and at this stage we haven't applied any changes to the computer — we are free to simply call `InvokeShutdown` on the `Dispatcher` object, essentially stopping before we've even begun:

```
protected void PlanComplete(
    object sender,
    PlanCompleteEventArgs e)
{
    if (this.State == InstallState.Cancelled)
    {
        CustomBootstrapperApplication.Dispatcher
            .InvokeShutdown();
        return;
    }

    this.model.ApplyAction();
}
```

The `ApplyBegin` method is very simple. It sets the `State` property to `Applying` once the `Apply` phase has begun, as illustrated in the following snippet:

```
protected void ApplyBegin(
    object sender,
    ApplyBeginEventArgs e)
{
    this.State = InstallState.Applying;
}
```

The next two methods, `ExecutePackageBegin` and `ExecutePackageComplete`, are triggered before and after each package in the chain is installed or uninstalled. They provide excellent hooks for us to check for the `Cancelled` state:

```
protected void ExecutePackageBegin(
    object sender,
    ExecutePackageBeginEventArgs e)
{
    if (this.State == InstallState.Cancelled)
    {
        e.Result = Result.Cancel;
    }
}

protected void ExecutePackageComplete(
    object sender,
    ExecutePackageCompleteEventArgs e)
{
    if (this.State == InstallState.Cancelled)
    {
        e.Result = Result.Cancel;
    }
}
```

If we find that the bootstrapper has been canceled, we set the `Result` property on `EventArgs` to `Result.Cancel`. This will inform Burn that it should roll back any packages that have been installed up to that point. This is a graceful way of handling a cancelation, rather than shutting down the process outright.

The last event hander is `ApplyComplete`. It's called, as you might have guessed, when the installation is fully complete and the planned action has been applied. At this point, we store the bootstrapper's final status code in the `FinalResult` property and call `InvokeShutdown` on the `Dispatcher` object:

```
protected void ApplyComplete(
    object sender, ApplyCompleteEventArgs e)
```

```
{
    this.model.FinalResult = e.Status;
    CustomBootstrapperApplication.Dispatcher
        .InvokeShutdown();
}
```

Helper methods

The remainder of the `InstallViewModel` class includes `private` helper methods:

```
private void Refresh()
{
    CustomBootstrapperApplication.Dispatcher.Invoke(
        (Action)(() =>
        {
            ((DelegateCommand)this.InstallCommand)
                .RaiseCanExecuteChanged();

            ((DelegateCommand)this.UninstallCommand)
                .RaiseCanExecuteChanged();

            ((DelegateCommand)this.CancelCommand)
                .RaiseCanExecuteChanged();
        }));
}

private void WireUpEventHandlers()
{
    this.model.BootstrapperApplication.DetectPackageComplete +=
        this.DetectPackageComplete;

    this.model.BootstrapperApplication.PlanComplete +=
        this.PlanComplete;

    this.model.BootstrapperApplication.ApplyComplete +=
        this.ApplyComplete;

    this.model.BootstrapperApplication.ApplyBegin +=
        this.ApplyBegin;

    this.model.BootstrapperApplication.ExecutePackageBegin +=
        this.ExecutePackageBegin;

    this.model.BootstrapperApplication.ExecutePackageComplete +=
        this.ExecutePackageComplete;
}
```

The `Refresh` method calls `RaiseCanExecuteChanged` on each of the command properties. This allows the UI to update the enabled/disabled status of buttons that are bound to these commands. Notice that we've nested these calls inside `Dispatcher.Invoke`. We must do this because it's likely that the `Refresh` method will be called by a background thread that won't have access to the UI thread. The `Dispatcher` ferries messages between the two.

The `WireUpEventHandlers` method wires our event handling methods to the events fired by the Burn engine. There are actually quite a few other events that we could respond to, but this bare-bones set will get us most of what we need.

Marking up the view

The last piece of the puzzle is the WPF window itself, which we are calling, in MVVM parlance, the **view**. Add a WPF `User Control` file called `InstallView` to the `Views` folder. We will need to change the file to use the `Window` element instead of the `UserControl` element. Replace the markup in the `InstallView.xaml` file with the following code:

```xml
<Window x:Class="CustomBA.Views.InstallView"
    xmlns=
"http://schemas.microsoft.com/winfx/2006/xaml/presentation"
    xmlns:x="http://schemas.microsoft.com/winfx/2006/xaml"
    xmlns:mc=
"http://schemas.openxmlformats.org/markup-compatibility/2006"
    xmlns:d=
"http://schemas.microsoft.com/expression/blend/2008"
    mc:Ignorable="d"
    d:DesignHeight="300" d:DesignWidth="300">

    <Window.Resources>
        <Style TargetType="{x:Type Button}">
            <Setter Property="Margin" Value="10" />
            <Setter Property="Height" Value="30" />
        </Style>
    </Window.Resources>

    <Grid>
        <StackPanel>
            <Label Content="{Binding Message}" />

            <Button Command="{Binding InstallCommand}">
```

```
          Install</Button>

      <Button Command="{Binding UninstallCommand}">
          Uninstall</Button>

      <Button Command="{Binding CancelCommand}">
          Cancel</Button>
    </StackPanel>
  </Grid>
</Window>
```

In an attempt to keep things simple, we are only using some basic styles in our XAML. This is just a bare-bones implementation, but it should give you a good starting point.

We have added a Label element that is bound to Message. Later, when we set the DataContext object for the view, this will match up with the Message property on our InstallViewModel class. That way, when we update that property's text in the viewmodel logic, it will be redrawn here.

The three buttons are similarly bound to our three command objects. Using Prism's DelegateCommand class is an improvement over the built-in RoutedCommand, which would have forced us to associate each command with an event handling method in the XAML file's code-behind.

Now that we've set up our XAML, let's open the code-behind file, InstallView. xaml.cs, and add the following code:

```
using CustomBA.ViewModels;
using System.Windows;

namespace CustomBA.Views
{
    public partial class InstallView : Window
    {
        public InstallView(InstallViewModel viewModel)
        {
            this.InitializeComponent();
            this.DataContext = viewModel;

            this.Closed += (sender, e) =>
                viewModel.CancelCommand.Execute(this);
        }
    }
}
```

We've changed the class' constructor to inherit from the `Window` class instead of the `UserControl` class. We've also added a parameter of type `InstallViewModel`. We will use the viewmodel that's passed in as the `DataContext` object for our window. That way, the buttons and label in the XAML are bound to a concrete implementation. A refactoring of this code might have the viewmodel implement an interface and then change the view to accept that interface for better decoupling between view and viewmodel.

The last part of the method sets an anonymous method for the window's `Closed` event. This will be called if the user closes the window instead of clicking on the **Cancel** button. Our method guides the code to execute our `CancelCommand`. At this point, we have everything we need to compile our custom user interface and try it out in a Burn bundle. We'll discuss the steps for doing so in the next section.

Referencing the UI in a Burn bundle

When you compile the `CustomBA` project you should see the `CustomBA.dll`, the Prism library assemblies, and the `CoreBootstrapper.config` file copied to the output folder. You could either copy these files to a new bootstrapper project or add `CustomBA` as a project reference. Then you'll be able to use preprocessor variables to reference the files you need in `Bundle.wxs`.

Create a new project in Visual Studio using the **Bootstrapper Project** template and call it `MyBootstrapper`. Add `CustomBA` as a project reference. Next, update the markup in the `Bundle.wxs` file in the bootstrapper project to contain the following code:

```xml
<?xml version="1.0" encoding="UTF-8"?>
<Wix xmlns="http://schemas.microsoft.com/wix/2006/wi">
  <Bundle Name="MyBootstrapper"
          Version="1.0.0.0"
          Manufacturer="WiX Tests"
          UpgradeCode="416b6bbf-2beb-4187-9f83-cdb764db2840">

    <BootstrapperApplicationRef
      Id="ManagedBootstrapperApplicationHost">
      <Payload
        SourceFile="$(var.CustomBA.TargetDir)CustomBA.dll" />
        <Payload SourceFile=
          "$(var.CustomBA.TargetDir)BootstrapperCore.config" />
        <Payload SourceFile=
        "$(var.CustomBA.TargetDir)Microsoft.Practices.Prism.dll" />
    </BootstrapperApplicationRef>

    <WixVariable Id="WixMbaPrereqLicenseUrl" Value=""/>
```

```
        <WixVariable Id="WixMbaPrereqPackageId" Value=""/>

    <Chain>
      <MsiPackage SourceFile="Lib\MyInstaller.msi" />
    </Chain>
  </Bundle>
</Wix>
```

I've added an `MsiPackage` element inside the `Chain` element, simply to have something to install. The important thing about it is that it is named `MyInstaller.msi`. Recall that the `DetectPackageComplete` method in our viewmodel is watching for a package with this name. So, if you change it here, be sure to change it there too. The reason for having the viewmodel check for a specific package is that we need a constant to focus our detection on. The WiX installer does the same thing for its `Wix` package.

The bigger focus here is on the `BootstrapperApplicationRef` element. Setting its `Id` attribute to `ManagedBootstrapperApplicationHost` will pull in prerequisites such as the `BootstrapperCore.dll` library. Our own assemblies should be referenced using `Payload` elements. The `Payload` element will embed assemblies and other types of resources into the bundle. In this example, we are referencing `CustomBA.dll`, `BootstrapperCore.config`, and `Microsoft.Practices.Prism.dll`.

We must also set two `WixVariable` elements: `WixMbaPrereqLicenseUrl` and `WixMbaPrereqPackageId`. The reason we need to do this is that the `ManagedBootstrapperApplicationHost` expects them. However, we aren't using them in our WPF application so it's safe to set them to empty strings. Compile the project and you'll get a bootstrapper executable that, when run, will display our new user interface.

Passing user input to a bundled MSI

One reason for authoring a new user interface is to collect user information that the standard Burn UI doesn't enable us to. For example, suppose we wanted to collect a username? This is actually quite easy. We will use the `StringVariables` property on the `Engine` class. This property is a collection of key-value pairs and can be used to set a Burn variable.

We could start off by adding a new method to our `BootstrapperApplicationModel` class called `SetBurnVariable`. The following is the code:

```
public void SetBurnVariable(string variableName, string value)
{
    this.BootstrapperApplication.Engine
        .StringVariables[variableName] = value;
}
```

This method will now accept the name of the variable that we want to set and the value to set it to. It passes this information to the `StringVariables` property, which passes it to the bootstrapper.

To use this we might add a new `TextBox` control to our view to collect a username. The following is the markup for a `TextBox` control:

```
<WrapPanel>
    <Label VerticalAlignment="Center">Username:</Label>
    <TextBox Text="{Binding Username}"
             Margin="10"
             MinWidth="150" />
</WrapPanel>
```

We will be binding the `TextBox` control to a property called `Username`, which we'll define on the viewmodel in the following manner:

```
private string username;
public string Username
{
    get
    {
        return this.username;
    }
    set
    {
        this.username = value;
        this.model.SetBurnVariable("Username", this.username);
    }
}
```

We see that when the `Username` property is set, we call `SetBurnVariable`. Back in our Burn bundle, we can nest an `MsiProperty` element inside of an `MsiPackage` element, using the `Username` variable to set a WiX property called `USERNAME`, shown as follows:

```
<Chain>
  <MsiPackage SourceFile="Lib\MyInstaller.msi">
    <MsiProperty Name="USERNAME" Value="[Username]"/>
  </MsiPackage>
</Chain>
```

We do not need to declare the `Username` Burn variable in our markup. Setting it through `CustomBA` will do the job.

Displaying progress

If you'd like to show a progress bar during the installation, you can handle two events: `CacheAcquireProgress` and `ExecuteProgress`. The former will give you a percentage completed for caching the packages. The latter will give you a percentage for packages executed. To get a *total* progress percentage, we add them both together and divide by two—if we didn't divide by two we'd end up with a final result of 200 since both events count up to 100.

First, let's add a `Label` control to our view that displays the percentage as text and also a `ProgressBar` control to go with it. Here's the markup to add to our XAML file:

```
<WrapPanel Margin="10" >
  <Label VerticalAlignment="Center">Progress:</Label>

  <Label Content="{Binding Progress}" />

  <ProgressBar Width="200"
               Height="30"
               Value="{Binding Progress}"
               Minimum="0"
               Maximum="100" />
</WrapPanel>
```

Our `Label` and `ProgressBar` controls are bound to a property called `Progress`. We'll define that on our viewmodel in the following manner:

```
private int progress;

public int Progress
{
```

```
get
{
   return this.progress;
}
set
{
   this.progress = value;
   this.RaisePropertyChanged(() => this.Progress);
}
}
```

Next, we'll add event handlers for the CacheAcquireProgress and ExecuteProgress events. Add fields for storing the two types of progress:

```
private int cacheProgress;
private int executeProgress;
```

Add the following code to the viewmodel's constructor:

```
this.model.BootstrapperApplication.CacheAcquireProgress +=
   (sender, args) =>
{
   this.cacheProgress = args.OverallPercentage;
   this.Progress =
      (this.cacheProgress + this.executeProgress) / 2;
};

this.model.BootstrapperApplication.ExecuteProgress +=
   (sender, args) =>
{
   this.executeProgress = args.OverallPercentage;
   this.Progress =
      (this.cacheProgress + this.executeProgress) / 2;
};
```

Our new controls will now update themselves during the installation, as shown in the following screenshot:

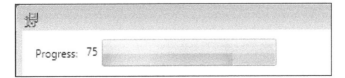

Downloading packages

As we saw in the previous chapter, we can download a package from the Internet or a local network, as in the following example where we use the NetFx40Web package from WixNetFxExtension to download the .NET Framework:

```
<Chain>
    <PackageGroupRef Id="NetFx40Web"/>
    <MsiPackage SourceFile="Lib\MyInstaller.msi" />
</Chain>
```

In order for our custom UI to allow this download to proceed, we must handle the ResolveSource event. The following is an example that uses an anonymous method in our viewmodel's constructor:

```
this.model.BootstrapperApplication.ResolveSource +=
    (sender, args) =>
{
    if (!string.IsNullOrEmpty(args.DownloadSource))
    {
        // Downloadable package found
        args.Result = Result.Download;
    }
    else
    {
        // Not downloadable
        args.Result = Result.Ok;
    }
};
```

We check if the package has a DownloadSource attribute and if it does, we set the Result property to Result.Download. This will allow the download to continue. Otherwise, we set Result to Result.Ok. The WiX Setup takes this a bit further by trying to download a failed package up to three times before calling it a day and moving on, setting Result to Result.Ok. It keeps track of which package has failed, based on ResolveSourceEventArgs.PackageOrContainerId.

Collecting command-line arguments

To accept command-line arguments passed to your UI, use the `Command.GetCommandLineArgs` method, accessible via the `BootstrapperApplication` class. For example, we could add a method to our model class called `GetCommandLine`, like so:

```
public string[] GetCommandLine()
{
    return this.BootstrapperApplication.Command
        .GetCommandLineArgs();
}
```

Internally, this method will call the `GetCommandLineArgs` method, which returns an array of strings. Each index in the array will contain one of the arguments passed to the bootstrapper. If the user were then to pass an argument called "foo" to our executable, such as:

MyBootstrapper.exe /foo

Then `/foo` would be stored in the string array. Note, however, that the Burn engine intercepts some common command-line arguments and stores them in the `Command` object's `Action` property. We would use the `Action` property to access these arguments. For example, if the user passed `/?`, which is commonly known to be a request for a help screen, we could discover it like so:

```
public bool HelpRequested()
{
    return this.BootstrapperApplication.Command.Action ==
        LaunchAction.Help;
}
```

Our viewmodel might call this method and show a message box if it returns true, as shown in the following screenshot:

Flags that are intercepted by Burn include the following—each is set to a
`LaunchAction` value:

Command-line argument	LaunchAction value
`/layout`	Layout
`/help` or `/?`	Help
`/uninstall`	Uninstall
`/install` or no argument sent	Install
`/modify`	Modify
`/repair`	Repair

If you check the `Action` property, it's up to you to take the appropriate steps to make
the action work.

Summary

In this chapter, we explored how to create a customized user interface to plug into
the Burn engine. We went about it by using WPF and C#. We saw that there are a
number of events published by the bootstrapper that we can handle. There are also
a few methods that we must call, such as `Detect`, `Plan` and `Apply`, to drive the
process forward.

By no means have we covered all of the possibilities available when it comes to
customizing Burn. For more examples, I recommend downloading the WiX source
code and digging through the WiX Setup. Also, post your questions on the WiX Users
mailing list at `http://wix.sourceforge.net/mailinglists.html`. Hopefully
you've gained enough knowledge to start building your own unique dialogs.

Index

AppSearch 125
CostFinalize 126
CostInitialize 125
ExecuteAction 126
FileCost 126
FindRelatedProducts 125
LaunchConditions 125
MigrateFeatureStates 126
ValidateProductID 125
Underline attribute 169
UnexpectedAttribute method 368
UnexpectedElement method 366
Uninstall button 424
UninstallCommand attribute 405
UnpublishFeatures action 128
unreal tables 266
UnsupportedExtensionAttribute
method 368
update
per-machine 343
per-user 343
update planning
about 341
major updates 341
minor updates 341
small updates 341
update type, choosing 342
UpgradeCode attribute 391
User 71
UserExit dialog 182
user interface
adding 40, 41
Util:ServiceConfig
service recovery 310-313
util namespace 71

V

ValidateProductID 125
ValidateProductID event 229
Value attribute 284
Version attribute 19, 388
view
about 423
marking up 439-441
viewmodel
about 423

implementing 427
viewmodel implementation
about 427-431
constructor, defining 434, 435
event handlers, setting up 435-437
fields, declaring 432, 434
helper methods 438, 439
properties, declaring 432, 434
Vital attribute 300, 400
VolumeCostList 215, 216
VolumeSelectCombo 216-218
Votive 13

W

Window class 441
WindowsFolder property 24
Windows Installer
about 12
predefined properties 86
Visual Studio package 13
Windows Installer XML. *See* **WiX**
Windows Presentation Foundation. *See*
WPF
WINDOWSSDKCURRENTVERSION
property 110
WireUpEventHandlers method 439
WiX
about 7, 8
features 7, 9
GUIDs 16
latest version 10
localization files 315
new version, installing 12
options 8
project 16
project templates 13
resources 43
standard dialog sets 155
tools 11
using, for service installation 298, 300
Visual Studio package 13-16
WiX extension 360
WixFailWhenDeferred 144
WiX library (.wixlib) 54
WiX localization files
about 315

Thank you for buying
WiX 3.6: A Developer's Guide to Windows Installer XML

About Packt Publishing

Packt, pronounced 'packed', published its first book "*Mastering phpMyAdmin for Effective MySQL Management*" in April 2004 and subsequently continued to specialize in publishing highly focused books on specific technologies and solutions.

Our books and publications share the experiences of your fellow IT professionals in adapting and customizing today's systems, applications, and frameworks. Our solution based books give you the knowledge and power to customize the software and technologies you're using to get the job done. Packt books are more specific and less general than the IT books you have seen in the past. Our unique business model allows us to bring you more focused information, giving you more of what you need to know, and less of what you don't.

Packt is a modern, yet unique publishing company, which focuses on producing quality, cutting-edge books for communities of developers, administrators, and newbies alike. For more information, please visit our website: www.packtpub.com.

About Packt Open Source

In 2010, Packt launched two new brands, Packt Open Source and Packt Enterprise, in order to continue its focus on specialization. This book is part of the Packt Open Source brand, home to books published on software built around Open Source licences, and offering information to anybody from advanced developers to budding web designers. The Open Source brand also runs Packt's Open Source Royalty Scheme, by which Packt gives a royalty to each Open Source project about whose software a book is sold.

Writing for Packt

We welcome all inquiries from people who are interested in authoring. Book proposals should be sent to author@packtpub.com. If your book idea is still at an early stage and you would like to discuss it first before writing a formal book proposal, contact us; one of our commissioning editors will get in touch with you.

We're not just looking for published authors; if you have strong technical skills but no writing experience, our experienced editors can help you develop a writing career, or simply get some additional reward for your expertise.

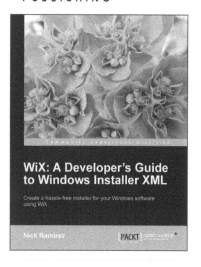

Microsoft Windows Azure
Development Cookbook

ISBN: 978-1-84968-222-0   Paperback: .392 pages

Over 80 advanced recipes for developing scalable
services with the Windows Azure platform

1. Packed with practical, hands-on cookbook
   recipes for building advanced, scalable
   cloud-based services on the Windows
   Azure platform explained in detail to
   maximize your learning

2. Extensive code samples showing how to use
   advanced features of Windows Azure blobs,
   tables and queues.

3. Understand remote management of Azure
   services using the Windows Azure Service
   Management REST API

Learning SQL Server 2008
Reporting Services

ISBN: 978-1-84719-618-7   Paperback: 512 pages

A step-by-step guide to getting the most of Microsoft
SQL Server Reporting Services 2008

1. Everything you need to create and deliver
   data-rich reports with SQL Server 2008
   Reporting Services as quickly as possible

2. Packed with hands-on-examples to learn and
   improve your skills

3. Connect and report from databases,
   spreadsheets, XML Data, and more

4. No experience of SQL Server Reporting
   Services required

Please check **www.PacktPub.com** for information on our titles

Lightning Source UK Ltd.
Milton Keynes UK
UKHW03f0633061018
330083UK00009B/328/P